Lecture Notes in Computer Science

Lecture Notes in Artificial Intelligence 16259

Founding Editor

Jörg Siekmann

The series Lecture Notes in Artificial Intelligence (LNAI) was established in 1988 as a topical subseries of LNCS devoted to artificial intelligence.

The series publishes state-of-the-art research results at a high level. As with the LNCS mother series, the mission of the series is to serve the international R & D community by providing an invaluable service, mainly focused on the publication of conference and workshop proceedings and postproceedings.

Matteo Baldoni · Franziska Klügl · Andrei Olaru ·
Alexandru Sorici · Adina Magda Florea
Editors

Multi-Agent Systems

22nd European Conference, EUMAS 2025
Bucharest, Romania, September 3–5, 2025
Proceedings, Part II

Springer

Editors
Matteo Baldoni
University of Turin
Turin, Italy

Franziska Klügl
Örebro University
Örebro, Sweden

Andrei Olaru
National University of Science
and Technology Politehnica Bucharest
Bucharest, Romania

Alexandru Sorici
National University of Science
and Technology Politehnica Bucharest
Bucharest, Romania

Adina Magda Florea
National University of Science
and Technology Politehnica Bucharest
Bucharest, Romania

ISSN 0302-9743 ISSN 1611-3349 (electronic)
Lecture Notes in Artificial Intelligence
ISBN 978-3-032-22819-2 ISBN 978-3-032-22820-8 (eBook)
https://doi.org/10.1007/978-3-032-22820-8

LNCS Sublibrary: SL7 – Artificial Intelligence

This Springer imprint is published by the registered company Springer Nature Switzerland AG
The registered company address is: Gewerbestrasse 11, 6330 Cham, Switzerland

Preface

These two volumes constitute the proceedings of the 22nd European Conference on Multi-Agent Systems (EUMAS 2025), held from the 3rd to 5th September at the National University of Science and Technology POLITEHNICA Bucharest, Romania.

For several decades, research in Multi-Agent Systems (MAS) has addressed the complex challenges that arise when multiple agents interact, cooperate, or compete. The field has developed mature theoretical and practical frameworks that remain highly relevant for understanding coordination, negotiation, and collective intelligence. In recent times, the growing attention to so-called "agentic AI" and workflow-oriented multi-agent setups has caused exploding interest in these questions – also rediscovering challenges that the MAS community has long explored. The European Multi-Agent Systems Conference series has provided a forum for both advancing core MAS research and connecting it to emerging AI paradigms since 2003. The contributions in this volume reflect this diversity, ranging from more MAS research to novel works that link large language models and agentic AI with established multi-agent principles.

The EUMAS conference series aims to provide the primary forum for academics and practitioners in Europe to discuss current MAS research and applications. EUMAS 2025 followed the tradition of previous editions from Oxford 2003 to Dublin 2024. EUMAS is the flagship annual event of the European Association for Multi-Agent Systems (EURAMAS) and we thank the board for its kind support and encouragement. The conference would not have been possible without the support of the Romanian Association for Artificial Intelligence.

The conference received 60 submissions, of which 56 were evaluated by 44 Program Committee (PC) members who put an emphasis on both quality and relevance to the community. Each submission to EUMAS 2024 was peer reviewed by at least two PC members in a single-blind fashion.

Out of 56 reviewed submissions, 30 papers were accepted as full papers for oral presentation, 3 in a special AgentToolkit track and 3 in a Demo Track. Due to the general high quality of submissions and their predicted value for discussion, it was decided after the reviewing process, to accept 9 additional papers as short papers. These were presented in pitches and discussed in a poster session on the first day.

With the accepted presentations and posters, a three-day conference program was designed. It was special in 2025 as it featured a one-day overlap with the European Agent Systems Summer School, which was organized at the same venue by the EUMAS local organization team on September 1st to 3rd. The first, shared day was planned with many interactive elements such as the poster session, demonstrations, as well as the Agent Toolkit community sessions. The other two days were filled with intensive sessions and discussions during opulent coffee breaks.

The shared day featured an industrial keynote by Andrei Rusu (UIPath, Romania) titled "Transforming Automation: Advancing from RPA to Increasingly Reliable Agentic

Workflows". This very interesting talk was about how UIPath measures and ensures reliability in complex workflows made-up of LLM-based agents. The second keynote, given by Amit K. Chopra (University of Bath, UK) on September 4th, was titled "Interaction-Oriented Foundations for Agentic AI". Amit explicitly discussed among other things the differences between complex Agentic Workflows and Multi-Agent Systems.

Like in 2024, a particular success was the AgentToolkit Community Session. This was a two-hour session freely organized by Katharine Beaumont and Andrei Ciortea. Researchers on site and online discussed research results and practical experiences without the constraints of a formal peer-reviewing process. A summary of their discussions can be also found in these proceedings.

Thank you all for this wonderful conference in Bucharest 2025.

November 2025

Matteo Baldoni
Franziska Klügl
Andrei Olaru
Alexandru Sorici
Adina Magda Florea

Organization

Organizing Committee

Andrei Olaru	POLITEHNICA Bucharest, Romania
Alexandru Sorici	POLITEHNICA Bucharest, Romania
Adina Magda Florea	POLITEHNICA Bucharest, Romania

Program Committee Chairs

Matteo Baldoni	University of Torino, Italy
Franziska Klügl	Örebro University, Sweden

Program Committee

Natasha Alechina	Utrecht University, Netherlands
Matteo Baldoni	Università di Torino, Italy
Cristina Baroglio	Università di Torino, Italy
Nick Bassiliades	Aristotle University of Thessaloniki, Greece
Katharine Beaumont	University College Dublin, Ireland
Francesco Belardinelli	Imperial College London, UK
Frederico Bergenti	Università di Parma, Italy
Olivier Boissier	École des Mines de Saint-Étienne, France
Robert Bredereck	TU Clausthal, Germany
Rafael Cardoso	University of Aberdeen, UK
Amit Chopra	University of Lancaster, UK
Andrei Ciortea	University of St Gallen, Switzerland
Rem Collier	University College Dublin, Ireland
Paul Davidsson	Malmö University, Sweden
Ivana Dusparic	Trinity College Dublin, Ireland
Piotr Faliszewski	AGH University of Science and Technology, Poland
Angelo Ferrando	University of Modena and Reggio Emilia, Italy
Maria Ganzha	Warsaw University of Technology, Poland
Davide Grossi	University of Groningen, Netherlands
Zahia Guessoum	Université de Reims Champagne-Ardenne, France
Feyza Merve Hafızoğlu	Istanbul Ticaret University, Turkey

Timotheus Kampik	Umeå University, Sweden
Franziska Klügl	Örebro University, Sweden
Florin Leon	Gheorghe Asachi University of Iaşi, Romania
Yves Lesperance	York University, Canada
Fabian Lorig	Malmö University, Sweden
Vanina Martinez	IIA-CSIC, Barcelona, Spain
Viviana Mascardi	University of Genoa, Italy
Simon Mayer	University of St Gallen, Switzerland
Stefania Monica	University of Modena and Reggio Emilia, Italy
Conor Muldoon	Manchester Metropolitan University, UK
Sascha Ossowski	Universidad Rey Juan Carlos, Spain
Julian Padget	University of Bath, UK
Georgios Papasotiropoulos	University of Warsaw, Poland
Marcin Paprzycki	Polish Academy of Sciences, Poland
Gauthier Picard	Onera, Toulouse, France
Roxana Rădulescu	Utrecht University, Netherlands
Alessandro Ricci	University of Bologna, Italy
Rosaldo Rossetti	University of Porto, Portugal
Alexandru Sorici	University POLITEHNICA of Bucharest, Romania
Nikolaos Spanoudakis	Technical University of Crete, Greece
Harko Verhagen	Stockholm University, Sweden
Nicolas Verstaevel	University of Toulouse, France
Neil Yorke-Smith	TU Delft, Netherlands

Sponsors

IFAAMAS -- International Foundation for Autonomous Agents and Multiagent Systems https://ifaamas.org

ANNT -- Association for the Advancement of Science and Technology, Bosnia and Herzegovina https://annt.ba

ARIA -- Romanian Association for Artificial Intelligence http://aria-romania.org

Contents

Short Papers

Demonstrators

Formal approaches

Supporting Accountability in Business Processes

Matteo Baldoni, Cristina Baroglio, Elisa Marengo(✉), and Roberto Micalizio

Computer Science Department, University of Turin, Turin, Italy
{matteo.baldoni,cristina.baroglio,elisa.marengo, roberto.micalizio}@unito.it

Abstract. Business processes specify patterns of activities expected to occur in an organization to achieve a business goal. However, actual executions may deviate from the expected ones and not necessarily because of mistakes, but also due to adaptation to circumstances or circumvention of limitations. To cope with this issue, organizations rely on accountability frameworks to get reliable information about deviations to undertake corrective measures for their processes, goals, or organization. However, to be effectively carried out, accountability has to rely on additional structures to be put in place, such as approvals and checking activities, which come at a price. So, these additional structures should be parsimoniously introduced. The paper presents a strategy to identify the activities that are riskier than others, and for which it is reasonable to foresee accountability structures. This evaluation is based on execution logs, analyzing which activities are not executed as expected from the business process.

Keywords: Accountability · Business Processes · Process Alignments

1 Introduction

A Business Process (BP) is defined as "a set of activities performed in coordination in an organizational and technical environment. These activities jointly realize a business goal" [26]. In this paper, we rely on BPs as a specification of the desired coordination in a Multi-agent Organization (MAO) [5] and we leverage the *process alignment* technique to reason about *accountability*.

Business processes are often characterized by complex patterns of activity flows. This poses several challenges as concerns their coordinated execution, since activities are carried out by members playing roles at different levels of the MAO hierarchy. Moreover, their actual execution may deviate from what is expected. It is worth noticing, however, that not all deviations are symptoms of problems; for example, sometimes it is convenient to invert the order of two activities, or to skip some steps altogether to avoid threatening the correct completion of processes [2, 3]. These variants, which are not directly captured by the process model, can

M. Baldoni et al. (Eds.): EUMAS 2025, LNAI 16259, pp. 3–16, 2026.
https://doi.org/10.1007/978-3-032-22820-8_1

bring great value in a phase of business process re-engineering. To this aim, however, the process executors should have the means to provide explanations about their decisions, in particular those that deviate from the model. The reason is that the business process engineers are not aware of the context in which a decision is taken, and hence cannot assess whether a deviation is acceptable, or not. Only having such information, business process re-engineering can take advantage of past experiences.

Accountability [12,15] enables exactly this form of information acquisition. Accountability has been studied from several point of views, including philosophy, social sciences, and tort law. It has also been proposed as a design tool for robust MASs [6,11], and has been applied in business processes [1]. Recently, it has gained attention [18,22,23] as a pillar in the realization of trustworthy AI.

Cabanillas at al. [9] introduce the notion of RACI-Aware Business Process. RACI matrices are well known in organizations and consist in assigning the roles of Responsible, Accountable, Consulted and Informed to the resources that are involved in each of the organization activities [20]. Cabanillas at al. [9] integrate within a BPMN model the distribution of RACI assignments to organizational roles [20]. Roughly speaking, their solution consists of a set of patterns that turn a business process into a RACI-aware process. As far as accountability is concerned, the solution proposes to add a dedicated *Approve* activity after every process activity, whose Responsible and Accountable labels differ in the given RACI matrix. The proposal, though interesting, has the drawback of causing a proliferation of *Approve* activities, which comes at a cost: first of all, each *Approve* activity requires time to be completed because the auditor has to examine what was done. Then, each auditor should keep a record of facts that support the judgment. Process designers may ask for such justifications to perform process re-engineering. It follows that accountability cannot be implemented by adding *Approve* activities naively (e.g., after every process activity), rather, these should be introduced with great care. Moreover, RACI are not universally adopted in organizations and where they are, often they are not updated while the organization changes.

In our view, inspired by [18,23], the notion of *risk* should be used as a guide to assess where in the process accountability is more critical. Risk in business processes has been studied and approached in different ways (see e.g., [19]). In line with Frost et al. [17], we consider risk as uncertain future events whose occurrence could influence the achievement of the organization's objectives.

Generally speaking, risk is characterized by two features: (i) *impact*: the (usually deleterious) consequence of the event occurrence related to the process; and (ii) *probability*: the chance that the event will occur during process execution. As far as we are concerned in this paper, we only consider the probability aspect, since we are interested in intercepting the possible occurrence of risk events, but we do not intend to investigate their (domain-dependent) impact on the process execution. To intercept risk in a business process, we need a risk estimator to be associated with each activity in the process under consideration.

We propose to estimate the risk associated with an activity in terms of deviations observed in real cases w.r.t. The expected behavior captured in a process model. Process alignment techniques can be used to estimate the distance between the actual executions of a process (traced by a log of events), and the model of the same process: the higher the distance, the higher the risk, and hence the need for setting up accountabilities.

The paper is organized as follows. Section 2 introduces the concepts of accountability, RACI matrices and RACI-aware business processes. In Sect. 3 we present the introduction of activities supporting the accountability by means of an example. Section 4 presents our proposal for supporting accountability based on risk. Discussion and conclusion in Sect. 5 end the paper.

2 Accountability in Organizations and Business Processes

Accountability is a fundamental notion of human societies. As noted by Dubnick et al. [12], it "emerges as a primary characteristic of governance where there is a sense of agreement and certainty about the legitimacy of expectations between the community members." The term can convey different nuances of meanings depending on the context in which it is used. In this paper, we adopt the notion put forward by the "Executive Board of the United Nations Development Programme (UNDP) and of the United Nations Population Fund" [15], which promotes functional innovation of organizational processes. Specifically, UNDP's accountability framework describes organization-wide processes for monitoring, analyzing, and improving performance in all aspects of the organization. It is an essential function that allows verifying the achievement of results, and assessing performance, based on actual data. To achieve this goal, an accountability framework must provide the infrastructure that is necessary to a body of (geographically distributed) offices and individuals to collect information, and provide it to those who are competent to interpret it and to those who can take decisions (the former and the latter group do not necessarily coincide). Setting up an accountability framework is therefore a substantial endeavor, that needs to be carefully designed and that requires time and resources to be carried on.

In [6] we have argued the accountability is a fundamental requirement for achieving robust organizations; that is, organizations that are resilient to unexpected, and possibly problematic changes. Specifically, the paper introduces an accountability framework, grounded on the notion of responsibility, where accountabilities are explicitly modeled as relationships of the form $\mathbb{A}(x, y, u, v)$: x and y are roles of the organization, while u and v are workflow expressions (i.e., sub-processes). The idea is that $\mathbb{A}(x, y, u, v)$ encapsulates a mutual agreement between x and y: x is said accountability taker (a-taker), y is the accountability giver (a-giver), and both agree that x has the right to ask y an account about process v when u has occurred; on the other hand, y accepts to provide such an account once asked upon, provided that u has already occurred. The accountability relationship also encapsulates that the a-giver can produce an account since it has (directly or indirectly) reliable information about v. This means that either y is responsible for v (i.e., it performs v directly), or it relies on accounts by other roles about v. In other terms, these relationships represent explicitly the accountability structures that need to be set up within an organization to cope with specific perturbations. Of course, the challenge is to identify the minimal number of such structures since each of them represents also a cost from a practical point of view.

To give just an example, the relation $\mathbb{A}$(*office head*, *clerk*, *sign document*, *archive document*) models an accountability between the *office head* and the *clerk* where the first can ask an account about the *archive task* (i.e., whether it has been completed, or not), but only after that the document has been *signed.* It is worth noting that the a-taker (e.g., the office head) has the permission of asking for an account, but it is not obliged, this in fact is part of its internal decision making.

In [5] we have proposed a conceptual model integrating an accountability framework within multi-agent organizations. In such a framework, the agreement between the agents establishes not only the permission for the a-taker to ask for an account and the obligation for the a-giver to provide the account, but also the format of the account; that is, what information are to be collected and provided upon request. In the rest of the paper we build upon this framework, and assume that the agents (i.e., the business players) exploit an infrastructure adhering to the conceptual model in [5].

RACI Matrices. Business organizations are well-aware of the importance of accountability, and often adopt, since the 1950's, RACI matrices [20] as a simple yet powerful way to trace it. A RACI matrix has one row for each task in a process, and one column for each organizational role. At each intersection between rows and columns one can specify the part that specific organizational role plays in that specific task, if any (Fig. 1 shows an excerpt of a RACI matrix as an example). *Responsible* means that the organizational role is in charge of the execution of the task (many roles can be labeled as responsible for the same task). *Accountable* denotes the role that is answerable for the task; only one role can be accountable for each task. *Consulted* denotes roles that can be consulted during the execution of the task. *Informed* specifies roles that need to be notified about any relevant information about the task. RACI matrices, thus, provide a minimal structure of control over the execution of a business process. However, they lack the workflow dimension, which instead is captured by formalisms such as BPMN and Petri nets.

BPMN and RACI are built up on the notion of activity, so it is natural to have a RACI matrix for each business process, where each activity mentioned in the matrix also occurs in the process, and vice versa. However, as already noted by Cabanillas et al. [9], BPMN and RACI, which are complementary models from the perspective of information content, are usually kept disjoint, and this is a potential source of inconsistencies. Considering only one of them results in a partial representation of the process. For instance, a BPMN captures the execution flow, but lacks information about who accounts for what and who can legitimately be involved in the completion of an activity.

To overcome this issue, Cabanillas et al. proposes a methodology for building RACI-aware BPMN models by ensuring that a BPMN process adheres to specific patterns for each role in a *RASCI* matrix (a variant of RACI that also includes *Support* to denote a role that may assist in completing the corresponding activity). For instance, when an organizational role is responsible for an activity in the RASCI matrix, that activity is placed in a lane corresponding to that role in the BPMN. At the same time, when an organizational role is accountable for an activity in the RASCI matrix, an *Approve* activity is added in the lane corresponding to that role in the BPMN. As noted above, however, accountability demands resources and it should be introduced parsimoniously to avoid bottlenecks and inefficiencies.

As a last remarks it is important to observe that, even though RACI matrices are an important tool in the hands of project managers, they are not universally adopted. It is, indeed, often the case that RACI matrices are not formalized and in some cases they are not even considered useful. This is, for instance, the case of small, stable teams where people more or less share the same competence. We discuss these issues and their consequences in the following sections.

3 The Conference Travel Management Example

We begin with considering the *Conference Travel Management Process* to exemplify the enrichment of a business process with accountability structures that capture the accountability specifications in a RACI matrix. We, first, describe the process, which is an adaptation of the one introduced in [9], together with a RACI matrix defining the involved responsibility and accountability roles. We, then, describe how the process can be modified to be RACI-aware according to [9], and we discuss the implications.

The process (see Fig. 1) specifies steps to request the authorization for and organize the travel to a conference for presenting a paper. The roles that are involved are *Work Package Leader* (WP Leader) and *Project Coordinator*. First, the WP Leader is expected to submit the camera ready of the paper and, then, to *Fill* in the *Travel Authorization* document, containing the details of the travel. Once the document is ready the Project Coordinator *Signs the Travel Authorization* which can, then, be sent by the WP Leader to the Travel Office. The Travel Office, by following an own process, checks the document and returns an answer to the WP Leader. Depending on it, *Problems* may have to be fixed. In this case, the Project Coordinator role is involved as the role appointed to fix problems. If the problems cannot be fixed (e.g., insufficient funds for traveling) the process ends. Otherwise, the request is fixed and the process progresses with the WP Leader registering at the conference and, then, making reservations both for journey and accommodation.

Table 1 reports a part of the RACI matrix of the process. Only the Responsible and Accountable roles are reported, since in this paper we just focus on these figures. WP Leader is responsible for most of the activities, while Project Coordinator is responsible only for the activities *Sign Travel Authorization* and *Fix Problems*.

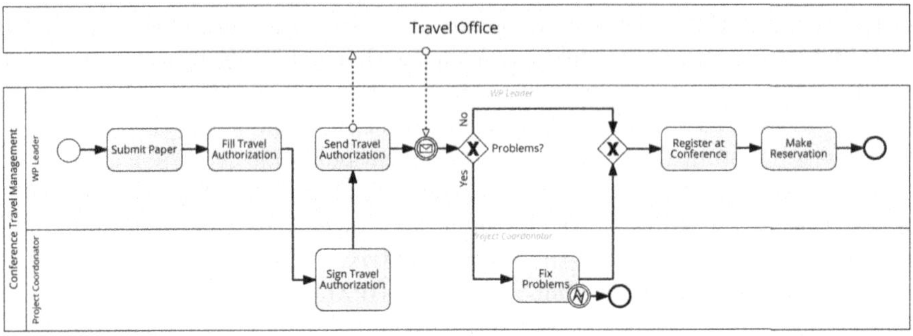

Fig. 1. Conference Travel Management Process.

In line with [9], in a BPMN process we capture that a role is responsible for an activity by assigning the activity to the line of such role, (see Fig. 1).

Concerning being Accountable for an activity, we see in the table that Project Coordinator is Accountable for most of the activities (as project funds administrator). However, the representation in Fig. 1 does not include such information and does not allow to infer it. The proposal in [9] is to add an approval (complex) activity after each activity where the Responsible and Accountable roles do not coincide. This additional activity is placed in the line of the Accountable role, allowing the latter to obtain information about the performed activity. If Responsible and Accountable coincide, instead, the additional activity is not necessary because all the information that is needed is already available.

Table 1. Excerpt of the RACI matrix. Only Responsible and Accountable are shown.

	WP Leader	Project Coordinator
Submit Paper	R	A
Fill Travel Authorization	R, A	
Sign Travel Authorization		R, A
Send Travel Authorization	R, A	
Fix Problems		R, A
Register at Conference	R	A
Make Reservation	R	A

The extended Conference Travel Management Process, including the accountability pattern, is depicted in Fig. 2. For the sake of clarity, the added activities are colored in light blue. Detailing further the complex activities is out of the scope of this paper, but we imagine that the subprocesses allow the accountable person to check, approve and get all the relevant information that is required to solve the obligation of being accountable. A possible implementation is proposed in [9]. The resulting business process consists of the following additional approving activities: *Approve Submit Paper*, *Approve Conference Registration*, and *Approve Reservation*.

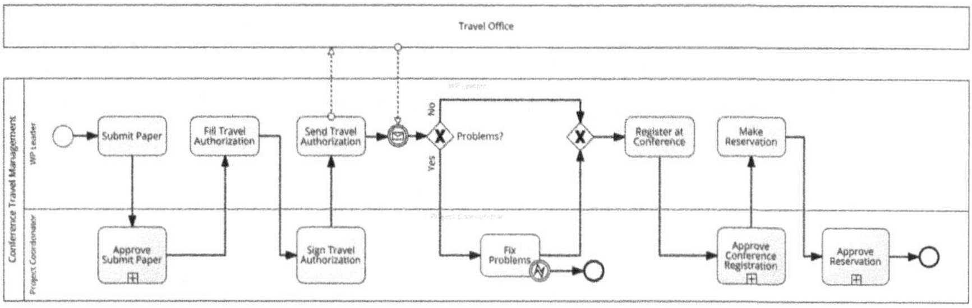

Fig. 2. Conference Travel Management Process extended with approval activities.

The problem with RACI-aware processes stands in the number of *Approve* activities they add because each of them introduces some costs, among which:*i)* changes to the implementation of the process in the organizational information system, including authorization and security updates; *ii)* new resources may be needed, or the existing ones may be required to use part of their time to execute accountability related activities: new documentation will be requested to the responsible roles, additional monitoring and checking activities will be required to the accountable roles; *iii)* resources that are busy with accountability related activities have less time for standard activities, thus, facilitating bottlenecks in process execution. *iv)* the introduction of new activities may impact on the business process as a whole, that may require to re-engineer it, e.g., to meet global constraints, and business goals. As shown in the Conference Travel Management Example, adding accountability structures in the process may result in almost double the number of activities to be performed. Additionally, the new activities may be as complex as those proposed in [9], requiring checks to be performed until the needed information is obtained or until all problems are fixed. In fact, these activities need to be added only for those tasks in a RACI matrix where the role Responsible and Accountable do not coincide.

Our proposal, instead, adds accountability structures by ranking activities from the most to the least risky, as described in the following.

4 Risk Evaluation Based on Event Logs

The European Union Agency ENISA [13] defines *risk management* as a process "*aimed at an efficient balance between realizing opportunities for gains and minimizing vulnerabilities and losses*". The approach to risk assessment they explain comprises: *i)* the identification, *ii)* the analysis, *iii)* the evaluation of the risk. What is worth noticing is that risks are evaluated based on the likelihood of their occurrence, by analyzing empirical and/or statistical values drawn from the experience. For instance, in information security the risk is based on known attacks and incidents of the past.

The approach that we propose is similar in spirit, and consists of evaluating the risk of performing a process differently than what is prescribed in a model. Our proposal is to leverage *conformance checking* techniques from process mining, and in particular to rely on the *process alignment* techniques [10]. These approaches compare a real execution (from an event log) with a sequence of activities from a process model by scanning both stepwise, and trying to match as many activities as possible. In classical process alignment approaches, all mismatches have the same weight, and an optimal alignment is the one that minimizes them. More recent works, instead, propose to consider additional contextual information to weight the impact of a mismatch. Intuitively, not all mismatches have the same weight.

As an example, consider the process in Fig. 1 and consider a real execution where the sequence of activities performed is: ⟨*Fill Travel Authorization (FA), Sign Travel Authorization (SiA), Send Travel Authorization (SeA), Make Reservation (MR), Register at Conference (RC)*⟩. There is no execution in the process model matching this execution for two reasons: *i)* activity *Submit Paper (SP)* is missing (i.e., has been skipped); *ii)* activities *Register for Conference* and *Make Reservation* have been swapped (i.e., they should have been performed in opposite order). By applying process alignment it is possible to identify where the skips occur, obtaining as a solution:

$\gg$	*FA*	*SiA*	*SeA*	$\gg$	*MR*	*RC*
SP	*FA*	*SiA*	*SeA*	*RC*	*MR*	$\gg$

(here the symbol $\gg$ is used in correspondence of a mismatch).

By applying the same approach to all traces in a log, it is possible to identify the process model activities which are skipped most often in the log. If, for instance, the activity *Submit Paper (SP)* results to be skipped more frequently than *Register for Conference (RC)* and *Make Reservation (MR)*, then it would be more convenient to implement accountability structures for the former than for the latter activities.

This approach allows one to evaluate risky activities based on the likelihood that a skip of the activity occurs. As mentioned previously, the risk associated to an event is also evaluated considering the (negative) impact of its occurrence on the system. In this paper, however, we are not interested in modeling this aspect, which is usually domain-dependent. We limit our attention to estimate the probability of a risk event on the basis of existing process logs. The fact of being based on real execution data represents both a prerequisite and an advantage for the approach. Being a prerequisite means that it can only be applied to scenarios where actual processes run for a while and the corresponding event logs are stored. It is an advantage because real executions allow one to measure how likely a situation is to occur. This evaluation of the risk can be complemented with existing approaches to risk analysis considering the importance each activity has for the business at hand.

4.1 Implementation and Case Study

The approach described in Sect. 4 was implemented in Python, relying on the PM4Py [7] library for computing the alignments[1]. We exemplify the proposal by means of a qualitative analysis of the result of the approach performed on the well known Traffic Fine Management Case Study [21].

The dataset consists of an event log of 150370 traces corresponding to 231 variants. As a reference process model we consider the one depicted in Fig. 3. With respect to this model, the event log has a precision (fraction of behavior allowed by the model that was actually observed [25]) of 0.99. The percentage of fitting traces (fraction of observed behavior that is allowed by the model [25]) is 37.27%, with an average trace fitness value of 0.87. This basically means that only few traces are fully compliant with the model. The others match for most of the execution but deviate in some (small) portions. This motivates an in depth analysis of what points in the process deserve more attention than others since are subject to frequent deviations.

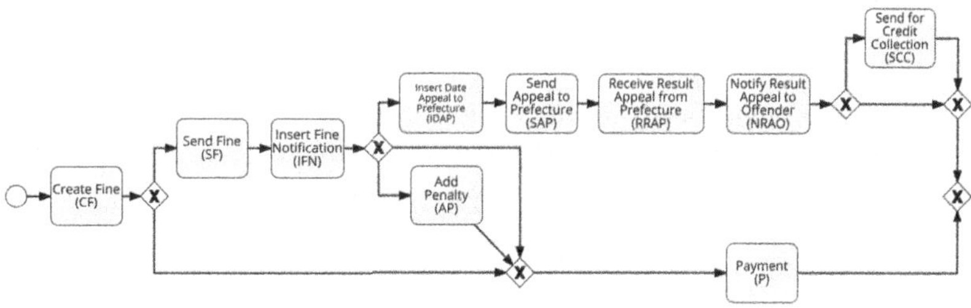

Fig. 3. Process Model of the Traffic Fine Management Process.

The model at our disposal, in Fig. 3, lacks both of the identification of the roles performing the activities, and of the RACI matrix associated with them. This is, unfortunately, often the case in real cases; in fact, as we have already noted, either RACI matrices and BPMN are kept disjointed or RACI matrices are not formally represented. It follows that the approach by Cabanillas et al. [9] could not be properly applied. Indeed, if we assume that for all activities the responsibile and the accountable roles do not coincide, all the ten activities in the model need an accountability structure, hence doubling the number of activities in the RACI-aware process. This is, for instance, the case in which all the activities are carried out by some clerks who report their job to a office head towards which all clerks are accountable.

Looking at the fitness metric gives us the intuition that the executions *mostly* comply with the process model, thus suggesting that the introduction of accountability structures is more critical only for those non-compliant parts. By looking at each activity separately, we can see that the number of skips is as follows:

[1] The implementation can be found at https://di.unito.it/eumas2025.

Payment	88359
Send for Credit Collection	58728
Insert Fine Notification	23752
Send Appeal to Prefecture	3138
Insert Date Appeal to Prefecture	3104
Add penalty	1512
Appeal to Judge	546
Send Fine	375
Notify Result Appeal to Offender	236
Receive Result Appeal from Prefecture	173

For some reasons, there is a big difference between the first three activities in the list *Payment, Send for Credit Collection*, and *Insert Fine Notification*, and the others. The causes for this situation are not directly inferrable from the data. Accountability serves right this purpose: it allows one to investigate why these three activities were skipped so frequently. This information potentially enables the re-engineering of the process either by ensuring their execution, or by adapting the process so as to take advantage of more efficient executions identified by the workers while performing their job.

In the example, our approach suggests to adopt accountability structures for the three activities mentioned above, while would be less convenient to apply them for *Receive Result Appeal from Prefecture*, for instance, or for *Notify Result Appeal to Offender*.

Let us now consider two scenarios showing how accountability supports process re-engineering. In particular, let us assume that we have introduced the approval for the three activities identified above, and have implemented the new process. That is, we have now the possibility to get information about the three critical activities.

Scenario 1. - Insert Fine Notification. Considering the activity *Insert Fine Notification* (IFN), this is expected to be performed after the activity *Send Fine* (SF), but also in the new version of the process we discover that it is often skipped. By analyzing the information recorded thanks to the accountability structure, the process engineer is able to infer that, when the number of fines to be handled is high (e.g., at the beginning of the week), IFN is postponed, and this practice is approved by the office head (accountable for IFN). The office head justifies this decision by the fact that IFN is a time-consuming activity slowing down the entire process. This information suggests that the resources working in the Fine Office Management are not sufficient, at least for some days of the week, and it may lead to a revision of the assignment of personnel to the various activities.

More formally, the following accountability relationship is added to the process: $\mathbb{A}(\textit{office head}, \textit{clerk}, SF, IFN)$ This enables the office head to ask an account for IFN, and hence to get an explanation about the fact that such an activity is actually skipped. To comply with the RACI matrix, we also add the following accountability $\mathbb{A}(\textit{auditor}, \textit{office head}, SF, IFN)$ where the office head becomes a-giver towards an auditor of the organization. This is exactly the structure that allows a process engineer, who is not involved in the process execution, to understand what happened during the execution and consider the possibility of changing the process itself. In this case, for instance, the office head can provide an account about IFN by relying on the account it gets from the clerk. In fact, the RACI matrix underlines that the accountable role is the one that has to justify towards a third-party the job done by the responsible roles. This is naturally captured in our framework by a chain of accountability relationships.

Scenario 2. - Payment. Also the *Payment* activity is particularly critical. The accountability relationship $\mathbb{A}(\mathit{office\ head}, \mathit{clerk}, \mathit{CF}, P \vee \mathit{IDAP})$ allows the office head to verify whether a fine has been payed or appealed to a judge. Indeed, when terms for lodging the appeal expire, the office head is capable to determine that the payment is missing, and possibly may decide to close the procedure signaling the anomaly. As before, this accountability structure allows a process engineer to understand that one of the possible causes of deviations from the expected model is outside the process itself. In fact, the account from the office head suggests that the credit collection process (which is not traced in this model) should be revised.

Remark. Our approach is quite different from Cabanilla's et al. [9] First of all, in their case accountability is achieved via a set of "approve" activities that are added systematically just on the basis of the RACI matrix. On the one hand, this guarantees a fine-grained coverage of the process. On the other hand, however, all these approve actions introduce a significant cost both in terms of time and information that need to be processed. Moreover, such an approach treats all the activities at the same level, but as we have seen, in general some activities are more critical than others. In our case, instead, we specify accountability relationships driven by the likelihood that the execution of the activities could deviate from the expected model. Thus, we just focus on those activities that actually deserve our attention and for which the accountability cost is justified. In addition, by formally specifying the accountability relationships we are able to reason about the robustness of the process as a whole. For instance, in [6] the explicit representation of accountability relationships allows us to enforce robustness against a given perturbation as a design property.

5 Related Work and Conclusions

In this paper, we have presented an approach that supports the identification of the points in a business process where accountability structures should be introduced. The approach is driven by an analysis of risk of deviation of actual executions from the process model.

Risk management and accountability have been widely addressed in the literature from different perspectives, including business organizations and process management. In particular, [19] adapts the well-known risk management framework COSO [24], and focuses on risk analysis at operational level, that is, at the level of each activity, to estimate a measure of risk for the whole process. The authors highlight three main elements to be considered during risk analysis: (*i*) *cost analysis*: how much impact on cost and budget an activity-level risk can generate; (*ii*) *time analysis*: how much impact on time/schedule a risk has on a single activity, and hence on the whole process; (*iii*) *performance/quality analysis*: to what extent quality and performance indicators are affected by risk factors associated with a given activity. In this paper, we also have considered risk at activity level, although we have not fully addressed the risk analysis over these three elements. Rather, we have approximated them by considering as a risk factor the possibility that some process activities are skipped. Our framework can be refined by considering cost and time aspects associated with each activity, and this is a possible extension to the present work.

An interesting framework that considers risk in business organizations, and more generally for their governance, is ReMMo (Responsibility MetaModel) [16]. The author starts from the observation that the notion of responsibility is not clearly modeled in business contexts, especially in relation to the notion of role: "at the business layer, employees are assigned to business roles where the corresponding responsibilities are roughly defined, are incompletely expressed, or do not exist at all." As a consequence, the notion of role may be wrongly interpreted and this may expose the organization to various kinds of risk factors. To cope with this issue, ReMMo is proposed as a metamodel for "modelling a rich concept of responsibility, the accountabilities that are part of it and its links with the employees, the business roles, the tasks, and the rights and capabilities."

ReMMo has the merit of bringing together, for the first time in a single model, the notions of norms and governance rules, responsibility, and accountability. In short, responsibilities stem from governance rules, and responsibilities may be subject to many accountabilities. However, it captures business tasks just in structural terms (i.e., a task can be decomposed into several subtasks), and does not capture the procedural flow of business processes. Moreover, it focuses primarily on the notion or responsibility and does not sufficiently characterize accountability to set up a proper accountability framework.

Since the advent of the GDPR, accountability is emerging as a critical property of many applications in the IT sector, and more recently, with the AI Act, accountability is seen as a pillar to approach risk mitigation [14]. As noted by Novelli et al. [22], four main goals can be ascribed to accountability: *compliance*, *report*, *oversight*, and *enforcement*. For compliance, accountability binds the agent to align with ethical and legal standards; thus, according to Bovens accountability "is used as a normative concept" [8]. The goal of reporting, instead "ensures that the agent's conduct is properly recorded to explain and justify it to the forum (or the principal). The reporting of relevant information enables the forum (or the principal) to challenge and disapprove the agent's conduct." In [4], we have introduced MOCA: an information model for accountability that describes what pieces of data need to be traced so that an accountable subject is able to provide an account of her actions, that is, an objective documentation of facts that support her conduct. Oversight is, in turn, related with the goal of getting evidence and evaluating the agent's conduct. In general terms, this goal aims at assessing whether the explanations given by an agent are consistent with the rules that govern the context at hand. This goal is often bound to the last one, enforcement, which focuses on what consequences the agent must bear (e.g., sanctions, authorization, or prohibitions). From our point of view, oversight could become the prerequisite for a very different goal, rather than sanction, we are more interested in *adaptation and improvement*. In fact, acquiring knowledge about a fact of interest, even an error or a deviation, could be useful for trying to "learn a general lesson", so to avoid similar problems in the future. This is the rationale of our use of accountability in business processes, and in their reengineering.

Acknowledgments. This work is part of the projects NODES, which has received funding from the MUR-M4C2 1.5 of PNRR funded by the European Union - NextGenerationEU (Grant agreement no. ECS00000036).

References

1. Baldoni, M., Baroglio, C., Boissier, O., Micalizio, R., Tedeschi, S.: Accountability and responsibility in multiagent organizations for engineering business processes. In: Engineering Multi-Agent Systems - 7th International Workshop, EMAS 2019, Revised Selected Papers. LNCS, vol. 12058, pp. 3–24. Springer (2019)
2. Baldoni, M., Baroglio, C., Marengo, E., Micalizio, R.: A Responsibility framework for computing optimal process alignments. In: Proceeding of 7th International Workshop on Artificial Intelligence for Business Process Management (AI4BPM). LNBIP, vol. 492, pp. 5 – 17 (2023)
3. Baldoni, M., Baroglio, C., Marengo, E., Micalizio, R.: Reasoning on responsibilities for optimal process alignment computation. Data Knowl. Eng. **154**, 102353 (2024)
4. Baldoni, M., Baroglio, C., May, K.M., Micalizio, R., Tedeschi, S.: MOCA: an ORM model for computational accountability. J. Intelligenza Artificiale **13**(1), 5–20 (2019)
5. Baldoni, M., Baroglio, C., Micalizio, R., Tedeschi, S.: Reimagining robust distributed systems through accountable mas. IEEE Internet Comput. **25**(6), 7–14 (2021a). https://doi.org/10.1109/MIC.2021.3115450
6. Baldoni, M., Baroglio, C., Micalizio, R., Tedeschi, S.: Robustness based on accountability in multiagent organizations. In: Proceedings of the Autonomous Agents and MultiAgent Systems (AAMAS 2021), pp. 142–150. IFAAMAS (2021)
7. Berti, A., van Zelst, S., Schuster, D.: PM4Py: a process mining library for Python. Software Impacts **17**, 100556 (2023)
8. Bovens, M.: Two concepts of accountability: accountability as a virtue and as a mechanism. West Eur. Polit. **33**(5), 946–967 (2010)
9. Cabanillas, C., Resinas, M., Ruiz-Cortés, A.: Mixing RASCI matrices and BPMN Together for responsibility management. In: Conference: VII Jornadas en Ciencia e Ingeniería de Servicios (JCIS'2011) (2011)

10. Carmona, J., van Dongen, B.F., Solti, A., Weidlich, M.: Conformance Checking - Relating Processes and Models. Springer (2018)
11. Cranefield, S., Oren, N., Vasconcelos, W.W.: Accountability for practical reasoning agents. In: Agreement Technologies, International Conference. Lecture Notes in Computer Science, vol. 11327, pp. 33–48. Springer (2018)
12. Dubnick, M.J., Justice, J.B.: Accounting for accountability (2004). Annual Meeting of the American Political Science Association
13. Technical department of ENISA, S.R.M.: Risk Management - Principles and Inventories for Risk Management / Risk Assessment methods and tools (2006)
14. Commission, E.: Artificial Intelligence Act. European Parliamentary Research Service, European Parliament (2021)
15. Executive Board of the United Nations Development Programme and of the United Nations Population Fund: the UNDP Accountability System, Accountability Framework and Oversight Policy. Technical report DP/2008/16/Rev.1, United Nations (2008)
16. Feltus, C.: Aligning Access Rights to Governance Needs with the Responsability MetaModel (ReMMo) in the Frame of Enterprise Architecture. Ph.D. thesis, University of Namur (2014)
17. Frost, C., Allen, D., Porter, J., Bloodworth, P.: Operational Risk and Resilience. Elsevier (2001)
18. Institute for Ethics in AI: establishing a practical organizational framework for AI accountability. White Paper (likely 2022)
19. Jallow, A., Majeed, B., Vergidis, K., Tiwari, A., Roy, R.: Operational risk analysis in business processes. BT Technol. J. **25**(1), 168–177 (2007)
20. Jeston, J., Nelis, J.: Business Process Management: Practical Guidelines to Successful Implementations. Butterworth-Heinemann (2006)
21. de Leoni, M., Mannhardt, F.: Road Traffic Fine Management Process (2015)
22. Novelli, C., Taddeo, M., Floridi, L.: Accountability in artificial intelligence: what it is and how it works. AI Soc. (2023)
23. OECD: Advancing accountability in AI (349) (2023). https://doi.org/10.1787/2448f04b-en
24. Prewett, K., Terry, A.: Coso's updated enterprise risk management framework–a quest for depth and clarity. J. Corp. Account. Fin. **29**(3), 16–23 (2018)
25. Syring, A.F., Tax, N., van der Aalst, W.M.P.: Evaluating conformance measures in process mining using conformance propositions. Trans. Petri Nets Other Model. Concurr. **14**, 192–221 (2019)
26. Weske, M.: Business Process Management: Concepts, Languages. Architectures, Springer Nature (2024)

Equilibrium Synthesis for Generalised Dining Philosophers Games

Johan Pieter van Rooyen[(✉)] and Nils Timm

Department of Computer Science, University of Pretoria, Pretoria, South Africa
johan.vanrooyen@tuks.co.za, ntimm@cs.up.ac.za

Abstract. Generalised Dining Philosophers Games (GDPG) model agents that compete or cooperate for shared resource units, forming multi-agent systems with both qualitative objectives (e.g., fairness, liveness) and quantitative objectives (e.g., maximising goal satisfaction). We represent GDPG as a concurrent game with agent goals expressed in the quantitative, temporal logic, $LTL[\mathcal{F}]$. We extend the $LTL[\mathcal{F}]$ model checking procedure to synthesise strategy profiles that both meet the shared qualitative goals and ensure a Nash equilibrium for the individual quantitative ones.

1 Introduction

Multi-agent systems (MAS) [27] consist of agents operating in an environment that evolves in response to their actions. Each agent pursues predefined objectives, and the system evolves in discrete time steps as agents select actions forming a joint action (action profile) that deterministically updates the state (configuration). A strategy specifies the action an agent should take in each configuration, and a strategy profile maps each agent to a strategy. Strategy synthesis [19] aims to determine such profiles that guarantee satisfaction of specified properties, including individual objectives.

To reason about potential system behaviours, MASs are often modelled as games [24]. Games may be zero-sum, where agents have strictly opposing goals, or non-zero-sum, where agents' objectives may align, allowing cooperation. Agent objectives are typically categorised as qualitative conditions that are either satisfied or not—or quantitative payoffs that agents aim to maximise or minimise.

Rational agents are defined as those that act to achieve their own objectives [19]. This work focuses on the automated synthesis of strategy profiles that are collectively acceptable, i.e., they satisfy a set of qualitative objectives for the entire group while maintaining equilibrium with respect to individual, quantitative objectives.

Qualitative objectives are expressed using temporal logic formulas over sequences of sets of atomic propositions, whereas quantitative objectives are expressed using a quantitative variant of linear temporal logic. A labelling function maps states to the propositions that hold in those states. Strategy synthesis

M. Baldoni et al. (Eds.): EUMAS 2025, LNAI 16259, pp. 17–33, 2026.
https://doi.org/10.1007/978-3-032-22820-8_2

involves determining, for each state, the actions that induce a play that satisfy the collective and individual objectives.

A strategy profile constitutes a Nash equilibrium [24] if no agent can improve its payoff by unilaterally deviating. A collectively acceptable profile is one that both satisfies collective qualitative objectives and constitutes a Nash equilibrium.

The classical Dining Philosophers problem [16] serves as a canonical example of distributed resource allocation. Philosophers, positioned around a table, must share forks to eat and strategies must avoid deadlock and starvation. The Generalised Dining Philosophers Game (GDPG) [15] extends this model to arbitrary numbers of agents and resources, and introduces more complex rules for accessing resources and demand levels. The terminology is generalised: philosophers become agents, forks become resource units, and eating corresponds to objective satisfaction. Similarly to the classical setting, agents can take up resource units, release one or all resource units, or idle. The game is infinite and progresses in discrete steps, and each state captures a current allocation of resources.

Each agent has a demand level which is the number of resource units it needs to collect and they have the objective to collect sufficient resource units to meet that demand level as often as possible and with minimal waiting time. The maximum waiting time for reaching the demand level is quantified and a payoff is assigned to the agent based on this.

GDPG provides a test bed for exploring MAS behaviours in resource-constrained, distributed settings. Finding collectively acceptable strategies in this context is a non-trivial task. Strategies may be constrained by uniformity (pure strategies) and memory limitations. Pure strategies prescribe deterministic actions for each state, while positional strategies depend solely on the current state. This work focuses on synthesis in the pure, positional setting.

Nash equilibria ensure predictable, stable agent behaviour, giving designers confidence that no agent has an incentive to deviate.

This paper outlines a sound, yet incomplete, procedure for synthesising collectively acceptable strategy profiles for generalised dining philosophers games. The agents of a game all have the goal of satisfying their demand for resource units and the same individual objective – which is to minimise their maximum waiting time before reaching their demand level. The strategy profile should thus be a Nash Equilibrium with respect to these individual objectives. Additionally, there is a collective objective – the strategy profile must result in outcomes that are fair to all agents.

Several technicalities are addressed. Firstly, the temporal logic $LTL[\mathcal{F}]$ [3] is explained and the objectives of fairness, as well as agents' individual objective to minimise maximum waiting time for reaching the demand level, are expressed in this logic. $LTL[\mathcal{F}]$ is chosen because it can express qualitative and quantitative, as well as collective and individual objectives and avoids some of the complexity of more expressive logics such as Strategy Logic $SL[\mathcal{F}]$.

The synthesis procedure starts with a translation of the given GDPG into an automaton that represents the state space of the game, thereafter the $LTL[\mathcal{F}]$ model checking procedure is adapted to derive strategy profiles which result in given payoffs to each agent. Thereafter, we can derive unilateral profitable deviations for each strategy profile and consequently, construct Nash equilibrium strategy profiles.

Section 2 establishes terminology and provides definitions of key terms and concepts. Section 3 describes a method for expressing fairness as a quantitative objective. Section 4 explains the complete synthesis procedure. Section 5 discusses related work and Sect. 6 summarises the key findings of this paper.

The *main contributions* of this paper are: further development of GDPG – specifically vis-à-vis equilibrium synthesis; applications of $LTL[\mathcal{F}]$ and its model checking procedure to equilibrium synthesis; quantification of starvation and fairness evaluation functions by means of $LTL[\mathcal{F}]$ formulas.

2 Preliminaries

This section presents existing work on which this paper depends. The subjects defined include the Generalised Dining Philosophers Game and its related concepts; formal models which are used; the temporal logic $LTL[\mathcal{F}]$; and concepts which describe the strategic behaviour of agents and Nash equilibrium.

Definition 1 (Generalised dining philosophers game (GDPG)). *A GDPG, $\mathcal{G}$ is a tuple $\langle Agt, Acc, Bags, d\rangle$ where:*

- $Agt = \{a_1, \ldots, a_n\}$ *is a non-empty set of* agents.
- $Acc : \mathcal{P}(Agt) \setminus \emptyset \rightarrow \mathbb{N}$ *is the* accessibility function, *which maps non-empty subsets of agents to natural numbers.*
- $Acc(A)$ *is the number of resource units that are shared exclusively by the agents in A.*
- $Bags = \{\beta \in \mathcal{P}(Agt) : Acc(A) \neq 0\}$. *A bag is referred to by the set of agents which share exclusive access to the resource units in that bag.*
- $d : Agt \rightarrow \mathbb{N}$ *is a* demand function *defining the number of resource units that each agent needs to carry out its tasks*

Each subset of agents has a shared bag of resource units which are available only to agents in the subset. These bags can be empty. Each agent has access to various bags, each of which is shared with some other group of agents.

Figure 1 shows the state space of a simple GDPG with two agents, a_0, a_1 and one resource bag β. The game starts at the configuration labelled $(a_0 \rightarrow 0, a_1 \rightarrow 0)$ where both agents are holding 0 resource units. If an agent takes, then it fulfils its demand level and releases on the next time step.

Unlike the definition in [15], which models resources as discrete units linked to agents via an accessibility graph, Definition 1 uses resource bags associated with agent subsets. Each bag is accessible only to its corresponding subset, effectively treating resource units as indistinguishable when shared by the same agents. As agents act and redistribute resource units, the game transitions through configurations of resource allocations at a given time. For instance, a configuration may show agent a_i holding x units from a resource bag.

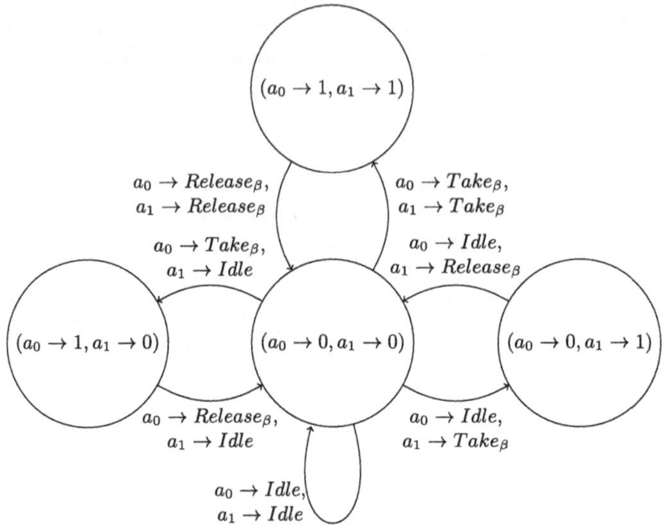

Fig. 1. State space of simple GDPG with 2 agents and 2 resource units.

Definition 2 (GDPG configuration). *Given a GDPG $\mathcal{G}$, a configuration is a function c, which maps a pair of $a \in Agt \cup \{null\}$ and a resource bag to a value in $\mathbb{N}$. $c: ((Agt \cup \{null\}) \times Bags) \to \mathbb{N}$. The inclusion of null allows for a "dummy" agent to represent resource units not allocated to any real agent. Conf is the set of all configurations of the GDPG. $card(a, c)$ is the number of resource units allocated to agent a at configuration c.*

Definition 3 (Actions). *Agents have four types of actions. Given agent a and resource bag β, $Take^a_\beta$ describes agent a taking a free resource unit from bag β; $Release^a_\beta$ describes agent a putting a resource unit back into bag β; $Release^a_{all}$ describes agent a putting all their resource units back in their respective bags; and, $Idle^a$ describes agent a doing nothing. The set of all possible actions is: $Act = \{Take^a_\beta : a \in \beta\} \cup \{Release^a_\beta : a \in \beta\} \cup \{Release^a_{all}\} \cup \{Idle^a\}$ An* action profile *is a tuple of actions – one for each agent*

Definition 4 (Strategies). *A* strategy, *σ is a mapping of configurations to actions, $\sigma : Conf \to Act$ and, a* strategy profile *is a mapping of agents to strategies. It is also sometimes intuitive to think of a strategy profile mapping configurations to action profiles.*

The *play induced by a strategy profile* is an infinite word $c_0ap_0c_1ap_1\dots$ and has a corresponding *path induced by a strategy profile*, $c_0c_1\dots$ which is the same word but with the action profiles removed.

The logic $LTL[\mathcal{F}]$ is used to express quantitative objectives. It replaces the Boolean operators of LTL [26] with arbitrary functions over $[0, 1]$. A detailed treatment of the syntax and semantics of $LTL[\mathcal{F}]$, as well as a description of the model checking procedure for $LTL[\mathcal{F}]$ can be found in [3]. *Satisfaction values* are the possible values which a $LTL[\mathcal{F}]$ formula can evaluate to. For an $LTL[\mathcal{F}]$ formula, φ, the satisfaction values of φ are $V(\varphi) \subseteq [0,1]$ Two mathematical formalisms are used to represent games through the synthesis process. First is the *concurrent game model (CGM)* as defined in [6]. Second is the *non-deterministic, generalised Büchi automaton (NGBA)*, defined in [3,28]. Büchi automata are used for model checking [17], and the model checking procedure for $LTL[\mathcal{F}]$ is the basis for the synthesis algorithm introduced in this paper.

The play generated by the execution of a strategy profile, *sp*, is denoted as π_{sp}. Conversely, the set of strategy profiles which generate the play π is denoted as sp_π. A strategy profile induces a play, which is then evaluated according to $LTL[\mathcal{F}]$ formulas. Given an $LTL[\mathcal{F}]$ formula, there is an implicit ordering of the relative value of each strategy profile – some are "better" than others – based on the evaluation of the $LTL[\mathcal{F}]$ formula over the play induced by the strategy profiles. Since the objective of each agent has an associated $LTL[\mathcal{F}]$ formula, we can think of this ordering as describing the "preferences" of individual agents.

Definition 5 (Profitable deviation). *A profitable deviation is when an agent can change its strategy to achieve a greater payoff. Given strategy profiles, sp and sp′, and an agent a_i with $LTL[\mathcal{F}]$ objective, φ_i, $sp >^{a_i} sp'$ if and only if $[\![\pi_{sp}, \varphi_i]\!] > [\![\pi_{sp'}, \varphi_i]\!]$. That is, the satisfaction value of φ_i along play π_{sp} is greater than its satisfaction value on play $\pi_{sp'}$. Since the $>^{a_i}$ relation is irreflexive, antisymmetric and transitive, it is a* strict total ordering *on the set of all strategy profiles.*

A unilateral deviation is a change from one strategy profile to another by altering the strategy of only a single agent.

Definition 6 (Unilateral deviation). *Given strategy profiles, sp and sp′, and a set of agents $Agt = \{a_1, \ldots, a_n\}$, sp is a unilateral deviation of sp′ for agent a_i if and only if, for all configurations, c, if $sp(c) \neq sp'(c)$, then for all agents, $a_k \in Agt \backslash \{a_i\}$, $sp(c)(a_k) = sp'(c)(a_k)$. That is, the assignments of configurations to actions are the same for all agents except a_i. Unilateral deviation by agent a_i is denoted as $sp \curlyvee^{a_i} sp'$ and is symmetric. Since unilateral deviation is reflexive, symmetric and transitive, it is an* equivalence relation *and thus for each agent, constitutes a partitioning of the set of all strategy profiles.*

A strategy profile is a Nash equilibrium if there does not exist a profitable unilateral deviation for any agent.

Definition 7 (Nash equilibrium). *Given a GDPG with n agents, each with a corresponding $LTL[\mathcal{F}]$ objective φ_i, a strategy profile sp is a Nash Equilibrium if there does not exist some other strategy profile sp′ such that for an agent a_i:*

- $sp' \curlyvee^{a_i} sp$;
- $sp' >^{\varphi_i} sp$.

That is, there does not exist an alternative strategy profile for which there is an agent that can unilaterally deviate to that strategy profile and *the strategy profile provides an improved evaluation to that agent in terms of its individual objective.*

3 Quantifying Agent Objectives

This paper deals with quantitative, individual objectives and qualitative, collective objectives. Agents seek to optimise quantitative objectives, thus in a collectively acceptable strategy, no agents should have any incentive to deviate (i.e., a Nash equilibrium). Collective objectives are qualitative objectives for the agents, these constitute the "law" of the system, and they must be satisfied. In this paper, we use the objective of minimising maximum waiting time for meeting demand levels as the individual objective and a collective objective to ensure overall fairness is within acceptable levels.

3.1 Quantitative Starvation

In qualitative settings, starvation occurs when an agent is never able to reach its goal. Intuitively, this is insufficient because, in actual scenarios, the timeliness of each satisfaction event is important. If an agent can only access a needed resource unit once every 100 years, this would be unacceptable. The logic $LTL[\mathcal{F}]$ is used to express these objectives. Only one quantitative operator is required for expressing quantitative starvation - the *scaling operator* ∇_λ. Let $x \in [0,1]$ be a satisfaction value of an $LTL[\mathcal{F}]$ formula, and $\lambda \in [0,1]$ be a scaling parameter, then $[\![\pi, \nabla_\lambda x]\!] = \lambda \times [\![\pi, x]\!]$. This has the effect of multiplying the satisfaction value of x by some fixed value $\lambda \in [0,1]$. We borrow exponentiation syntax for use in LTL[$\mathcal{F}$] (where p is an atomic proposition and X is the *Next* operator):

$$X^n p = \overbrace{X \cdots X}^{n \text{ times}} p$$

We define the operator, $\tau_n p$ to express delayed satisfaction of the logical formula p. $\tau_n p = X^n p \wedge \bigwedge_{i=0}^{n-1} \neg X^i p$ which is 1 when p is satisfied after waiting for exactly n turns. These are combined to form the *discounted future value operator*, the satisfaction value of which decreases monotonically as the amount of time taken for the satisfaction of a logical formula increases. It is defined as $\mathcal{D}_m p = \nabla_1 p \vee \bigvee_{i=1}^{m} \nabla_{\frac{m-i}{m}} \tau_i p$, where p is a $LTL[\mathcal{F}]$ formula, and $m \in \mathbb{N}$ is the threshold value. The usage of $\bigvee_{i=1}^{m} \nabla_{\frac{m-i}{m}}$ is a specific discounting function. In general, this approach will work with any monotonically decreasing function over $[0,1]$. $\mathcal{D}_m$ is a family of operators, parameterised by the threshold value m. The satisfaction value of $\mathcal{D}_m$ is 1 if p is satisfied immediately along a play and $\frac{m-i}{m}$ if p is satisfied by the suffix π^i - that is if there is a waiting time of i turns. If the agent must wait more than m (the threshold value) turns, the satisfaction value of $\mathcal{D}_m$ is 0. In the context of $LTL[\mathcal{F}]$ the operator G corresponds to *minimum*. Thus, if the atomic proposition p holds when the agent has collected enough resource units to meet its demand level and n is the maximum waiting time in between occasions when the demand level is met, then if $m > n$, $G\mathcal{D}_m p = \frac{m-n}{m}$, otherwise $G\mathcal{D}_m p = 0$. The play π that maximises the satisfaction value of the formula $[\![\pi, G\mathcal{D}_m p]\!]$, will minimise the maximum waiting time for the agent concerned with proposition p.

3.2 Quali-Quantitative Fairness

In a qualitative setting, fairness may refer to plays where all agents reach their goals infinitely often, however, it does not consider the relative amount of times that agents can reach their goals. If one agent satisfies its goal every 5 turns, but another must wait for 500 turns, this is intuitively not fair. Quantitative fairness facilitates this kind of reasoning by using a function to evaluate how fair a play is, and a predicate to decide if this play is fair enough. Each agent will receive a satisfaction value for their objective which is in $[0, 1]$. To adjudicate the fairness of the outcomes, we define a fairness function $f : [0, 1]^k \to [0, 1]$, where k is the number of agents. A fairness function maps a vector of the agents' satisfaction values to an overall fairness score. Note that the functions $\mathcal{F}$ which parameterise $LTL[\mathcal{F}]$ logic are defined as $\mathcal{F} \subseteq \{f : [0, 1]^k \to [0, 1] | k \in \mathbb{N}\}$ [3]. Any function which maps a vector of values in $[0, 1]$ to a value in $[0, 1]$, can be included in $\mathcal{F}$. Thus, the fairness function can be included in the functions of the $LTL[\mathcal{F}]$ used. For example, consider the *range* function. $range(X) = max(X) - min(X)$ where $X \in [0, 1]^k$. If $range(X)$ is higher, then there is a bigger difference between the best and worst payoff, and the outcome might be described as being less fair. Functions of this type are collectively referred to as *dispersion functions*, where high levels of dispersion are considered less fair, and vice versa.

Two further aspects must still be addressed. Firstly, we want to deal with fairness as a collective, qualitative objective but the dispersion function is a real valued function. To resolve this, we define a *fairness interval*, $F = [x, y]$ where $x, y \in [0, 1]$ and $x < y$. If $\varphi \in F$, then φ is considered an adequately fair outcome. Checking if a dispersion value lies within the fairness interval reduces the real-valued dispersion to a Boolean value. The combination of a dispersion function and fairness interval is denoted as $(disp, F)$. Secondly, it is noted that fairness cannot be evaluated in isolation and depends upon the agents' individual objectives. For a set of n agents with objectives φ_i, the evaluation dispersion function $disp$ along play π is $[\![\pi, disp]\!] = disp([\![\pi, \varphi_1]\!], \ldots, [\![\pi, \varphi_n]\!])$. And $\pi \models (disp, F)$ if $[\![\pi, disp]\!] \in F$.

4 Synthesis Procedure

A procedure for synthesising collectively acceptable strategy profiles is presented. Given a GDPG with n agents, individual quantitative objectives and collective fairness objective, we can check strategy profiles which meet the collective fairness objective to see if they are also Nash equilibria. We begin with a conversion procedure for representing the GPDP as a CGM. Next, we introduce payoff profiles and show how $LTL[\mathcal{F}]$ model checking is adapted to synthesise strategy profiles which yield specific payoff profiles. These strategy profiles can then be checked for satisfaction of the fairness objective and, if necessary, checked for Nash equilibrium. This entails constructing the set of profitable unilateral deviations from a given strategy profile – if this set is empty, the strategy profile is a Nash equilibrium. The GPDG will be translated into an equivalent CGM by the following procedure, and thereafter the state space of the CGM can be represented with an NGBA necessary for $LTL[\mathcal{F}]$ model checking.

Definition 8 (Translation of GDPG to CGM). *Let $\mathcal{G} = \langle Agt, Bags, d, Acc\rangle$ be a GDPG with $Conf$ as the set of all configurations in $\mathcal{G}$. Then $\mathcal{G}$ can be translated into a CGM $\mathcal{M} = \langle \mathcal{A}, St, Act, av, out, Prop, L\rangle$ where:*

- $\mathcal{A} := Agt$
- $St := \{c : c \in Conf\}$
- $Act = \{Take^a_\beta : a \in \beta \wedge \beta \in Bags\} \cup \{Release^a_\beta : a \in \beta \wedge \beta \in Bags\} \cup \{Release^a_{all} : a \in Agt\} \cup \{Idle^a : a \in Agt\}$
- *For all pairs of $c \in St$ and $a \in \mathcal{A}$:*

$$\begin{aligned} av(c,a) = &\{Take^a_\beta : a \in \beta \wedge \beta \in Bags \wedge c(\beta)(null) > 0 \wedge card(c,a) < d(a)\} \\ &\cup \{Release^a_\beta : a \in \beta \wedge \beta \in Bags \wedge c(\beta)(a) > 0 \wedge card(c,a) < d(a)\} \\ &\cup \{Release^a_{all} : card(c,a) = d(a)\} \\ &\cup \{Idle^a : card(c,a) \neq d(a)\} \end{aligned}$$

- *Given a configuration c, and an action profile ap, the successor c' is the new configuration which arises when the agents follow ap while in c. Let $out(c, ap) = c'$, then for all resource bags, β:*
  - $c'(\beta)(null) = c(\beta)(null) - |\{a \in Agt : ap(a) = Take^a_\beta \wedge |\{a' \in Agt : ap(a') = Take^{a'}_\beta\}| < c(\beta)(null)\}| + |\{a \in Agt : ap(a) = Release^a_\beta\}| + \sum_{a \in Agt: ap(a) = Release^a_{all}} c(\beta)(a)$
  - *And, for all $a \in Agt$:*

$$c'(\beta)(a) = \begin{cases} c(\beta)(a) + 1 & \textit{iff } Take^a_\beta = ap(a) \wedge \\ & |\{a' \in Agt : ap(a') = Take^{a'}_\beta\}| < c(\beta)(null) \\ c(\beta)(a) - 1 & \textit{iff } Release^a_\beta = ap(a) \\ & \textit{iff } Release^a_{all} = ap(a) \end{cases}$$

  Each resource bag allocation to null is incremented for all Release and $Release_{all}$ actions and decremented for all successful Take actions. Each resource bag allocation to an agent is decremented for all Release and $Release_{all}$ actions by that agent and incremented for all successful Take actions.
- *$Prop := \{p_a : a \in \mathcal{A}\}$, where each p_a is a new atomic proposition introduced for the CGM;*
- *For all $c \in St$, $L(c) := \{p_a : a \in \mathcal{A}, card(a, c) = d(a)\}$. That is, there is an atomic proposition p which holds when the corresponding agent has met its demand level.*

4.1 Payoff Profiles

Conventional model checking involves a Boolean decision procedure where a property is either satisfied or not. For a quantitative logic like $LTL[\mathcal{F}]$, the case is similar. However, the satisfaction values of a $LTL[\mathcal{F}]$ formula are not Boolean. To address this, a predicate which specifies which satisfaction values are accepted must also be provided. Consider for example an agent, with associated atomic proposition p, and the objective $\varphi = G\mathcal{D}_m p$ for a threshold $m \in \mathbb{N}$. If there is a play π where the maximum waiting time is t, then $[\![\pi, \varphi]\!] = \frac{m-t}{m}$. This is a real-valued satisfaction value. To determine if this value is acceptable, let $P \in [0, 1]$, then the satisfaction value of φ on π is acceptable iff $[\![\pi, \varphi]\!] \in P$.

Definition 9 (Payoff profile). *Given a GDPG with agents Agt and possible satisfaction values for their objectives, $V(\varphi)$, a payoff profile, PP, is a mapping of agents to satisfaction values $PP : Agt \to V(\varphi)$.*

A set of predicates can be defined to precisely describe a single payoff profile. A benefit of payoff profiles is that for some collective objectives, there is an intuitive way to look at payoff profiles and assess if plays resulting in the payoff profile produce satisfaction values within the predicate. For example, consider the *range* function and predicate $P_f = \{0\}$ – all payoffs must be the same. It is straightforward to assess a payoff profile for conformance with the fairness objective and predicate. The fairness of a payoff profile can be assessed without any consideration of the underlying objectives and plays.

For example, given three agents, the payoff profile $(PP(a_0) = 0.4, PP(a_1) = 0.6, PP(a_2) = 0, 1)$ describes the payoff allocated to each agent. $range(0.4, 0.6, 0.1) = 0.5 \notin P_f$, so the payoff profile is not fair because the evaluation of the function is not an element of the fairness predicate P_f.

We will take advantage of this above fact to guide the search for Nash equilibria. Only strategy profiles which induce a fair payoff profile need to be considered in the search for Nash equilibria.

4.2 LTL[F] Model Checking for Multiple Agents

The $LTL[\mathcal{F}]$ model checking procedure takes as input a model and a specification (both represented as NGBAs) and then produces an output (also an NGBA) which only accepts a play if it is a valid play of the model and it satisfies the specification. We may wish to ask the questions, "Do all plays satisfy the specification?", or "Does there exist a play which satisfies the specification?". Strategy profile synthesis differs in that it asks the question, "What is the strategic behaviour required to produce a play which satisfies the specification?".

In the classic case of $LTL[\mathcal{F}]$ model checking, a model and an $LTL[\mathcal{F}]$ formula are provided and converted into corresponding NGBAs and only one satisfaction value predicate is provided. A necessary modification of the $LTL[\mathcal{F}]$ model checking procedure, for the procedure presented in this paper, is to have several $LTL[\mathcal{F}]$ objectives, each associated with a distinct predicate $P \in [0, 1]$. The output will then be an NGBA which only accepts plays for which the satisfaction values of each $LTL[\mathcal{F}]$ objective are within the respective predicate. Thus, a set of predicates can be constructed for each possible payoff profile. More details of the $LTL[\mathcal{F}]$ model checking procedure can be found in [4].

After $LTL[\mathcal{F}]$ model checking has completed been for each pair of objective and predicate, the product of the resulting NGBAs can be taken which only accepts a play if the satisfaction value of all objectives, evaluated along that play, results in the desired payoff profile.

Definition 10 (NGBA corresponding to a payoff profile). *Consider a game, $\mathcal{G}$, with n agents, each with a corresponding individual $LTL[\mathcal{F}]$ objective, φ_i and a payoff profile PP. The game is represented as a CGM, $\mathcal{M}$, and the NGBA corresponding to the CGM is $\mathcal{N}_{\mathcal{M}}$. For each agent's individual objective we construct the NGBA $\mathcal{N}_{\varphi_i}^{P_i} = \langle \Lambda, Q', \delta', Q_0', \alpha' \rangle$ where the singleton set, $P_i = \{PP(a_i)\}$, is the predicate. A satisfaction value is only in P_i if it is exactly the value assigned to the agent by the payoff profile. Hence, the NGBA corresponding to $\mathcal{G}$ resulting in the payoff profile PP is $\mathcal{N}_{\mathcal{G}}^{PP} = \mathcal{N}_{\mathcal{M}} \times \mathcal{N}_{\varphi_1}^{P_1} \times \cdots \times \mathcal{N}_{\varphi_n}^{P_n}$. Each word of the language of the automaton is an assignment of satisfaction values to the $LTL[\mathcal{F}]$ objectives of each agent.*

4.3 Strategy Automata

Each play resulting from a strategy profile will result in some payoff profile. Thus, for each payoff profile, we can enumerate the plays which result in that payoff profile, and consequently, we can construct the set of all strategy profiles which result in a given payoff profile. The first step is to modify the NGBA corresponding to a payoff profile resulting from the adapted model checking procedure such that it will become an acceptor of plays. Such an automaton is denoted as a *strategy automaton* which is first defined and then a translation procedure for the NGBA corresponding to a payoff profile to its respective strategy automaton is provided. The procedure for deriving the set of possible strategy profiles from a play is straightforward and thus omitted. A strategy automaton is an acceptor of plays that are possible within the game $\mathcal{G}$, which result in payoff profile PP. Thus, its language is the set of plays induced by the game $\mathcal{G}$.

Definition 11 (Strategy automaton). *Given a GDPG with set of configurations Conf, the model checking automaton, $\mathcal{N}_{\mathcal{G}}^{PP} = \langle 2^{AP}, Q, \delta, Q_0, \alpha \rangle$, can be translated into a strategy automaton $\mathcal{S}_{\mathcal{G}}^{PP} = \langle \Lambda, Q', \delta', Q_0', \alpha' \rangle$, where:*

- *$\Lambda = Conf \times ACT$, the set of all pairs of configurations and action profiles;*
- *$Q' = Q$, the set of states;*
- *$\delta' = \bigcup_{d \in \delta} \{(q, a, q') : (q, r, q') = d \wedge a = imp(d) \wedge r \in 2^{AP}\}$ is the transition function;*
- *$Q_0' = Q_0$ is the set of initial states;*
- *$\alpha' = \alpha$ is the set of accepting sets.*

and $imp(q, r, q')$ is the action profile needed to get from q to q'

From a play induced by the strategy automaton, we can derive strategy profiles which result in specified payoff profiles, but our ultimate goal is to synthesise Nash equilibrium strategy profiles. Nash equilibrium is concerned with unilateral deviations by agents, so next we show how to construct an automaton that will accept all unilateral deviations for a given agent from a particular play.

4.4 Deviation Automata

In Definitions 5 and 6, deviation is defined as a relation between strategy profiles. Since each strategy profile corresponds to a play, these definitions naturally extend to plays. For an agent a_i with objective φ_i, and plays π, π' induced by strategy profiles sp, sp', respectively, π is a profitable deviation of π' for a_i if $sp >^{\varphi_i} sp'$, and a unilateral deviation if $sp \curlyvee^{a_i} sp'$.

Definition 12 (Deviation automaton). *Given a strategy automaton $\mathcal{S}_{\mathcal{G}}^{PP}$ in GDPG $\mathcal{G}$ corresponding to payoff profile PP, the deviation automaton $\mathcal{S}_{PP}^{\Delta a_i}$ is a strategy automaton which accepts all plays which are generated by a strategy profile which is a unilateral deviation by agent a_i from a strategy profile which corresponds to a play accepted by $\mathcal{S}_{\mathcal{G}}^{PP}$. A play will be accepted by the deviation automaton if* any *of the strategy profiles which generate it are a unilateral deviation for agent a_i.*

By Definition 6, every strategy profile—and thus every play—is a unilateral deviation of itself for all agents. Therefore, in a GDPG $\mathcal{G}$ with agent a_i, for any set of strategy profiles A, the set of unilateral deviations D is the set $\{sp : \exists sp'(sp \curlyvee^{a_i} sp')\}$. Note that $A \subseteq D$.

In the Venn diagram in Fig. 2, we can see three sets, A, D and B. Sets A and D are the sets described in the previous paragraph, while B is some other arbitrary set of strategy profiles. Note that $A \cap B = \emptyset$, but $B \cap D \neq \emptyset$.

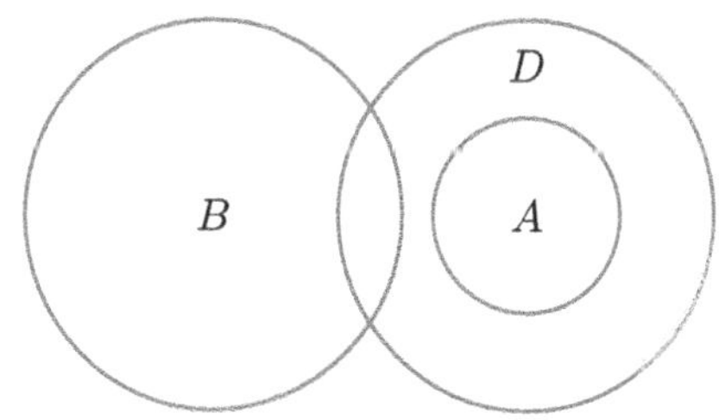

Fig. 2. Venn Diagram showing the languages of 2 strategy automata, one with its associated deviation automaton

Assume two possible payoff profiles, PP_1 and PP_2. Let A denote the set of strategy profiles yielding PP_1, and B those yielding PP_2. The set D then comprises all plays corresponding to strategy profiles sp such that $sp \curlyvee^{a_i} sp'$ for some agent a_i, where sp' induces a play in A. Thus, in any play from D, agent a_i either receives PP_1 or can unilaterally deviate to obtain PP_2.

Consequently, $D \setminus A$ is the set of plays which correspond to a strategy profile which does not result in PP_1, but agent a_i can deviate to achieve PP_1, if it has an incentive to. $(D \setminus A) \cap B$ is the set of all the plays which correspond to strategy profiles which result in payoff profile PP_2, but a_i can unilaterally deviate to achieve the payoff profile PP_1.

Moreover, we can presume the existence of strategy automata $\mathcal{S}_{\mathcal{G}}^{PP1}$ and $\mathcal{S}_{\mathcal{G}}^{PP2}$, such that $\mathcal{L}(\mathcal{S}_{\mathcal{G}}^{PP1}) = A$ and $\mathcal{L}(\mathcal{S}_{\mathcal{G}}^{PP2}) = B$. A deviation automaton $\mathcal{S}_{PP_1}^{\Delta a_i}$ will be defined such that $\mathcal{L}(\mathcal{S}_{PP_1}^{\Delta a_i}) = D$.

Finally, let $PP_1(a_i) > PP_2(a_i)$, that is, agent a_i receives a better payoff from plays in A than in B. We can make the following assertions about the deviation behaviour of an arbitrary play π.

- if $\pi \in A$, then a_i receives a better payoff when following the strategy profile corresponding to π and has no incentive to deviate.
- if $\pi \in (D \backslash A) \cap B$, then a_i is not receiving its best payoff and has an incentive to deviate to A, moreover, it is possible to unilaterally deviate from the strategy profile corresponding to π to a strategy profile that corresponds to a word in A.

Now that the formalities of the sets have been addressed, we can proceed to the construction of the deviation automaton.

Definition 13 (Deviation automaton for an agent corresponding to a strategy automaton). *Given a strategy automaton for a payoff profile,* $\mathcal{S}_{\mathcal{G}}^{PP} = \langle 2^{AP}, Q, \delta, Q_0, \alpha \rangle$, *the deviation automaton for agent* a_i *is a tuple:* $\mathcal{S}_{PP}^{\Delta a_i} = \langle 2^{AP'}, Q', \delta', Q_0', \alpha' \rangle$, *where:* $AP' = AP$; $Q' = Q$; $\delta' = \bigcup_{d \in \delta} dev^{a_i}(\delta)$; $Q_0' = Q_0$; $\alpha' = \alpha$ *and* $dev^{a_i}(c, ap, c') = \{(c, ap', c'') : \forall a_k \in (Agt \setminus \{a_i\}) ap(a_k) = ap'(a_k) \wedge ap' \in av(c, a_i) \wedge out(c, ap') = c''\}$

Thus far, profitable and unilateral deviations have been considered for a single deviating agent and two payoff profiles. To reason about Nash equilibria, these notions must be extended to arbitrary numbers of agents and payoff profiles.

4.5 Nash Automata

To initiate the search for Nash equilibria in a given GDPG $\mathcal{G}$, an arbitrary payoff profile PP_1 is selected. The corresponding strategy automaton $\mathcal{S}_{\mathcal{G}}^{PP_1}$ accepts only those plays that yield PP_1. The procedure involves three key steps: (1) identifying, for each agent, the set of alternative payoff profiles that offer improved outcomes relative to PP_1; (2) using these alternatives to construct the Nash automaton for payoff profile PP_1; and (3) defining the Nash automaton for the game, which accepts only those plays that constitute a Nash equilibrium with respect to the agents' individual objectives. $ALT(a_i, PP_1)$ denotes the payoff profiles which offer improved outcomes for agent a_i.

If $\mathcal{S}_{PP_1}^{\Delta a_i}$ is the deviation automaton for agent a_i from strategy profiles resulting in PP_1, then we can construct the automaton X, such that $\mathcal{L}(X) = \bigcup_{PP \in ALT(a_i, PP_1)} \mathcal{L}(\mathcal{S}_{PP}^{\Delta a_i})$ which accepts all plays which correspond to a strategy profile from which a_i can deviate to *any* of its alternatives which provide a better payoff than PP_1. Next, we can consider all of the agents, and construct the set of all plays which correspond to strategy profiles from which *any* agent can deviate to *any* of its alternatives which provide a better payoff than PP_1.

That is, an automaton Y such that $\mathcal{L}(Y) = \bigcup_{a \in Agt} \bigcup_{PP \in ALT(a,PP_1)} \mathcal{L}(\mathcal{S}_{PP}^{\Delta a})$. Consequently, we can define the Nash automaton for the payoff profile PP_1.

Definition 14 (Nash automaton for payoff profile). *Given a set of agents Agt from a GDPG, $\mathcal{G}$, and a payoff profile PP_1, the Nash automaton for PP_1 is such that $\mathcal{L}(\mathcal{S}_{nash}^{PP_1}) = \mathcal{L}(\mathcal{S}_{\mathcal{G}}^{PP_1}) \setminus \bigcup_{a_i \in Agt} \bigcup_{PP \in ALT(a_i,PP_1)} \mathcal{L}(\mathcal{S}_{PP}^{\Delta a_i})$. This is the set of all plays where no agent can unilaterally and profitably deviate, i.e., plays which are induced by a Nash equilibrium strategy profile. Since the language is constructed using standard operations over other languages, the construction of the automaton is straightforward.*

Next, we combine the Nash automata for all payoff profiles to produce a single automaton.

Definition 15 (Nash automaton). *Given a set of agents Agt from a GDPG, $\mathcal{G}$, and a set of all possible payoff profiles $\mathcal{P}$, the Nash automaton is constructed such that $\mathcal{L}(\mathcal{S}_{nash}) = \bigcup_{PP_i \in \mathcal{P}} \mathcal{L}(\mathcal{S}_{nash}^{PP_i})$.*

The Nash automaton does not identify all Nash equilibria. It might be the case that a play can be induced by two strategy profiles. One of which has a profitable deviation, while the other does not. A play is only accepted if *all* strategy profiles which induce it have no unilateral and profitable deviation. The Nash automaton only provides a sound but incomplete search for Nash equilibria. At this stage, it is unclear if the algorithm herein can be extended for completeness.

The Nash automaton acts as an acceptor of plays which correspond to strategy profiles that are Nash equilibria, but a Nash equilibrium is not sufficient for collectively acceptable strategy profiles. The next section combines $\mathcal{S}_{nash}$ with automata for fairness to construct an automaton which only accepts a play if it corresponds to a collectively acceptable strategy profile. The construction of the Nash automaton is detailed in Algorithm 1.

4.6 Collectively Acceptable Objectives

The overall aim of this paper is to provide an approach to synthesise strategy profiles which are Nash equilibria with respect to individual quantitative objectives and which satisfy collective qualitative objectives.

For a game with n agents, a fairness predicate P_f and dispersion function f, and a set of all payoff profiles $\mathcal{P}$, we can construct the set of all fair payoff profiles. Recall that a play π is fair if $[\![\pi, \Phi]\!] \in P_f$. Thus we define the set $\text{FAIR} = \{PP \in \mathcal{P} : f(PP(a_1), \ldots, PP(a_n)) \in P_f\}$. If $PP \in \text{FAIR}$, then for all plays π which result in PP, we know that $f([\![\pi, \varphi_1,]\!], \ldots, [\![\pi, \varphi_n]\!]) \in P_f$ – the payoffs are fair.

Hence, we can produce $\mathcal{S}_{fair}$ such that $\mathcal{L}(\mathcal{S}_{fair}) = \bigcup_{PP \in \text{FAIR}} \mathcal{L}(\mathcal{S}_G^{PP})$ – a strategy automaton which accepts all plays corresponding to a strategy profile that results in a fair payoff profile. An automaton which only accepts collectively

Algorithm 1. Algorithm for construction of Nash automaton

```
Input: A GDPG 𝒢, a set of all payoff profiles 𝒫, the set of agents from the GDPG, Agt
Output: The Nash automaton for 𝒢
procedure ConstructNashAutomaton(𝒢, 𝒫, Agt)      ▷ Constructs the Nash automaton for a given GDPG
    S_Nash = ∅
    for all PP_k ∈ 𝒫 do
        N_𝒢^{PP_k} := ModelChecking(𝒢, PP_k)                ▷ As per Definition 10
        S_𝒢^{PP_k} := MC2SA(N_𝒢^{PP_k})                      ▷ As per Definition 11
        D := ∅
        for all a_i ∈ Agt do
            D_{a_i} := ∅
            for all PP ∈ ALT(PP_k, a_i) do
                N_𝒢^{PP} := ModelChecking(𝒢, PP)
                S_𝒢^{PP} := MC2SA(N_𝒢^{PP})
                S_{PP}^{Δa_i} := Deviation(S_𝒢^{PP})          ▷ As per Definition 13
                D_{a_i} := D_{a_i} ∪ S_{PP}^{δa_i}
            end for
            D := D ∪ D_{a_i}
        end for
        S_Nash := S_Nash ∪ (S_𝒢^{PP_k} \ D)
    end for
    return S_Nash
end procedure
```

acceptable plays can be expressed simply as $\mathcal{S}$ such that $\mathcal{L}(\mathcal{S}) = \mathcal{L}(\mathcal{S}_{fair}) \cap \mathcal{L}(\mathcal{S}_{nash})$.

5 Related Work

The Generalised Dining Philosophers Game (GDPG) has been studied from a model checking perspective [15], but not for automated synthesis, nor with integrated qualitative and quantitative objectives. Prior synthesis research has separately addressed rational synthesis [19,23], quantitative logics [2,3,5], and Nash equilibrium computation [4,9,10], with some heuristic work on intractable domains such as chess [27]. This paper combines these strands—automated synthesis, quantification, and Nash analysis—within the GDPG.

Rational synthesis treats the environment as rational agents pursuing their objectives [19], modelled using logics such as LTL [25,26], CTL [17], and ATL [6]. Resource Agent Logic (RAL) extends ATL to resource allocation problems [1]. Quantitative extensions of temporal logic include discounting [2] and weighting of formulas [3], which appear in richer logics such as OLTL [9], $LTL[\mathcal{F}]$ [4], $SL[\mathcal{F}]$ [11], and quantitative ATL [18]. We adopt $LTL[\mathcal{F}]$ to represent both qualitative and quantitative objectives.

Alternative quantification methods include mean-payoff games [5], widely studied for Nash equilibria [8,10,12]. Since $LTL[\mathcal{F}]$ cannot fully express mean-payoff, we instead model preferences via minimising maximum waiting time.

Unlike prior work combining qualitative and quantitative goals [21], we assign qualitative objectives to collective goals (fairness, starvation-freedom) and quantitative ones to individual goals (waiting time), assuming agents deviate only when strictly improving outcomes [20,23].

Our approach assumes full observability and no external scheduler [7,13], and does not consider mechanism design [22]. As qualitative LTL rational synthesis is 2EXPTIME-complete [14], adding quantitative objectives and equilibrium reasoning likely increases complexity.

6 Conclusion

The presented procedure addresses the synthesis of strategy profiles in Generalised Dining Philosophers Games by extending the $LTL[\mathcal{F}]$ model checking framework to reason about both quantitative and qualitative objectives. Individual objectives, such as minimising maximum waiting time to prevent starvation, and collective ones, like fairness, are defined using $LTL[\mathcal{F}]$. Strategy profiles induce plays, and we construct automata that accept only those plays yielding specified payoff profiles. For each payoff profile, a strategy automaton and corresponding deviation automata (one per agent) are constructed to identify possible unilateral deviations. A Nash equilibrium is characterised by plays accepted by the strategy automaton but none of the deviation automata, indicating no agent has an incentive to deviate. The union of such plays across all payoff profiles forms the set of Nash equilibria. This automaton-based method leverages existing Büchi automata tools, facilitating implementation, though it is limited to evaluation functions expressible in $LTL[\mathcal{F}]$ and focuses on minimising maximum waiting time for reaching the demand level.

Future work includes a complete construction of the Nash automaton such that all Nash equilibria can be identified, thereafter stochastic and partial observability might be considered. Additionally, rigorous proofs of correctness for the constructions herein and complexity results are planned.

References

1. Alechina, N., Bulling, N., Logan, B., Nguyen, H.N.: The virtues of idleness: a decidable fragment of resource agent logic. Artif. Intell. **245**, 56–85 (2017)
2. Almagor, S., Boker, U., Kupferman, O.: Discounting in ltl. In: International Conference on Tools and Algorithms for the Construction and Analysis of Systems, pp. 424–439. Springer (2014)
3. Almagor, S., Boker, U., Kupferman, O.: Formally reasoning about quality. J. ACM (JACM) **63**(3), 1–56 (2016)
4. Almagor, S., Kupferman, O., Perelli, G.: Synthesis of controllable nash equilibria in quantitative objective game. In: IJCAI, vol. 18, pp. 35–41 (2018)
5. Almagor, S., Kupferman, O., Velner, Y.: Minimizing expected cost under hard boolean constraints, with applications to quantitative synthesis. arXiv preprint arXiv:1604.07064 (2016)

6. Alur, R., Henzinger, T.A., Kupferman, O.: Alternating-time temporal logic. J. ACM **49**(5), 672–713 (2002). https://doi.org/10.1145/585265.585270, https://doi.org/10.1145/585265.585270
7. Avni, G., Henzinger, T.A., Kupferman, O.: Dynamic resource allocation games. Theoretical Computer Science 807, 42–55 (2020). https://doi.org/10.1016/j.tcs.2019.06.031, https://www.sciencedirect.com/science/article/pii/S0304397519304475, in memory of Maurice Nivat, a founding father of Theoretical Computer Science - Part II
8. Bohy, A., Bruyere, V., Filiot, E., Raskin, J.F.: Synthesis from ltl specifications with mean-payoff objectives. In: International Conference on Tools and Algorithms for the Construction and Analysis of Systems, pp. 169–184. Springer (2013)
9. Bouyer, P., Brenguier, R., Markey, N., Ummels, M.: Nash equilibria in concurrent games with büchi objectives. In: IARCS Annual Conference on Foundations of Software Technology and Theoretical Computer Science (FSTTCS 2011). Schloss Dagstuhl-Leibniz-Zentrum fuer Informatik (2011)
10. Bouyer, P., Brenguier, R., Markey, N., Ummels, M.: Concurrent games with ordered objectives. In: Birkedal, L. (ed.) Foundations of Software Science and Computational Structures, pp. 301–315. Springer, Heidelberg (2012)
11. Bouyer, P., Kupferman, O., Markey, N., Maubert, B., Murano, A., Perelli, G.: Reasoning about quality and fuzziness of strategic behaviours. arXiv preprint arXiv:1905.11537 (2019)
12. Bouyer, P., Markey, N., Randour, M., Larsen, K.G., Laursen, S.: Average-energy games (full version) (2016)
13. Bouyer, P., Markey, N., Vester, S.: Nash equilibria in symmetric graph games with partial observation. Inf. Comput. **254**, 238–258 (2017)
14. Condurache, R., Filiot, E., Gentilini, R., Raskin, J.F.: The complexity of rational synthesis. In: 43rd International Colloquium on Automata, Languages, and Programming (ICALP 2016). Schloss Dagstuhl-Leibniz-Zentrum für Informatik (2016)
15. De Masellis, R., Goranko, V., Gruner, S., Timm, N.: Generalising the dining philosophers problem: competitive dynamic resource allocation in multi-agent systems. In: European Conference on Multi-Agent Systems, pp. 30–47. Springer (2018)
16. Dijkstra, E.W.: Operating systems techniques. In: Chapter Hierarchical Ordering of Sequential Processes. Academic Press, New York (1972)
17. Emerson, E.A., Clarke, E.M.: Using branching time temporal logic to synthesize synchronization skeletons. Sci. Comput. Program. **2**(3), 241–266 (1982)
18. Ferrando, A., Luongo, G., Malvone, V., Murano, A.: Theory and practice of quantitative atl. In: International Conference on Principles and Practice of Multi-Agent Systems, pp. 231–247. Springer (2024)
19. Fisman, D., Kupferman, O., Lustig, Y.: Rational synthesis. In: Esparza, J., Majumdar, R. (eds.) Tools and Algorithms for the Construction and Analysis of Systems, pp. 190–204. Springer, Heidelberg (2010)
20. Gutierrez, J., Murano, A., Perelli, G., Rubin, S., Steeples, T., Wooldridge, M.: Equilibria for games with combined qualitative and quantitative objectives. Acta Informatica **58**(6), 585–610 (2021)
21. Gutierrez, J., Murano, A., Perelli, G., Rubin, S., Wooldridge, M.: Nash equilibria in concurrent games with lexicographic preferences (2017)
22. Gutierrez, J., Najib, M., Perelli, G., Wooldridge, M.: Equilibrium design for concurrent games. arXiv preprint arXiv:2106.10192 (2021)
23. Kupferman, O., Perelli, G., Vardi, M.Y.: Synthesis with rational environments. Annal. Math. Artif. Intell. **78**(1), 3–20 (2016)

24. Leyton-Brown, K., Shoham, Y.: Essentials of game theory: a concise multidisciplinary introduction. Synthesis Lectures Artif. Intell. Mach. Learn. **2**(1), 1–88 (2008)
25. Manna, Z., Pnueli, A.: The temporal logic of reactive and concurrent systems: Specification. Springer Science & Business Media, New York (2012)
26. Pnueli, A.: The temporal logic of programs. In: 18th Annual Symposium on Foundations of Computer Science (sfcs 1977), pp. 46–57. IEEE (1977)
27. Russell, S., Norvig, P.: Artificial intelligence: a modern approach (2002)
28. Vardi, M.Y., Wolper, P.: An automata-theoretic approach to automatic program verification. In: 1st Symposium in Logic in Computer Science (LICS). IEEE Computer Society (1986)

Synthesis of Collectively Optimal Strategies for Infinite Runs of Multi-agent Systems via Maximum Satisfiability Solving

Nils Timm(✉) and Steven Jordaan

Department of Computer Science, University of Pretoria, Pretoria, South Africa
ntimm@cs.up.ac.za, u18074848@tuks.co.za

Abstract. Multi-agent systems for resource allocation (MRAs) provide a framework for modelling competitive resource allocation in distributed computing. In an MRA, agents interact over discrete rounds, aiming to satisfy their allocation goals. We present a technique for synthesising collectively optimal strategies for MRAs. A collectively optimal strategy not only guarantees goal satisfaction but also maximises the frequency of goal achievement throughout the system's run. While previous work was limited to synthesising strategies for finite runs that terminate after a fixed number of rounds, our new approach enables the synthesis of optimal strategies for infinite runs, enhancing their practical applicability. Our approach encodes the synthesis problem in propositional logic and solves it using maximum satisfiability (Max-SAT). We encode loops in the state space of an MRA that may arise when agents follow a uniform strategy. The encoding incorporates weighted soft clauses, representing instances in which an agent achieves its goal at a particular state within a loop, given an assumed loop size. Solving Max-SAT yields a truth assignment that maximises the total weight of satisfied soft clauses. In our setting, the assignment characterises a strategy that leads to a loop in which the frequency of goal achievement is collectively optimal. We implemented our approach within the SATMAS tool and conducted experiments demonstrating promising synthesis results.

1 Introduction

Multi-agent systems for resource allocation (MRAs) are a formal model for representing competitive resource allocation problems in distributed computing [14]. An MRA consists of a set of agents and a set of resources, where each agent has access to a subset of the overall resources. Moreover, each agent has a goal in terms of the amount of resources to accumulate. The system evolves in discrete rounds. In each round, every agent selects and simultaneously performs one of several possible actions: requesting an accessible resource, releasing an allocated resource, or idling. Once an agent reaches its goal, it releases all allocated resources and begins the allocation process again in subsequent rounds.

M. Baldoni et al. (Eds.): EUMAS 2025, LNAI 16259, pp. 34–51, 2026.
https://doi.org/10.1007/978-3-032-22820-8_3

Agents may pursue their goals once or repetitively throughout the system's run. Since resources are shared among agents, reaching individual goals is a competitive process. MRAs provide a general and expressive framework for modelling several practically relevant resource allocation scenarios.

A problem associated with MRAs is the synthesis of strategies that ensure agents achieve their goals. An individual strategy of an agent maps each resource allocation state of the system to an action to be performed in that state, whereas a joint strategy is a tuple of individual strategies, one per agent. A strategy is said to be winning if it guarantees that each agent eventually reaches its goal, fulfilling a *qualitative* objective. However, agents may additionally pursue *quantitative* objectives, aiming to achieve their goals as frequently as possible throughout the run of the system. In [23], we introduced the notion of *collectively optimal strategies*, which not only ensure that all agents satisfy their qualitative objectives but also maximise the overall frequency of goal achievement. Such strategies are of higher practical use as they enforce efficiency in the run of an MRA. In [23], we demonstrated that the synthesis of collectively optimal strategies for MRAs can be reduced to the maximum satisfiability problem (Max-SAT). The reduction is based on an encoding of the strategy synthesis problem in propositional logic. From a truth assignment that maximises the number of satisfied clauses in the encoding, a collectively optimal strategy can be directly derived. Thus, strategy synthesis can be performed using Max-SAT solvers such as Open-WBO [20]. The approach presented in [23] is limited to synthesising collectively optimal strategies under the assumption of a *finite* run of the MRA that terminates after a fixed number of rounds. As a result, such strategies only guarantee that each agent achieves its goal at least once, and that the number of rounds in which some agent achieves its goal *before termination* is maximised. This limitation reduces the practical applicability of the approach, as it does not ensure any form of optimality for infinite runs of MRAs.

In this paper, we present an extension of the Max-SAT-based approach that enables the synthesis of collectively optimal strategies for *infinite* runs of MRAs. Our method is based on encoding loops in the state space of an MRA that arise when agents follow a uniform strategy. Under the assumption of uniformity, every infinite run of an MRA will eventually enter a loop, and the size of feasible loops is, in the worst case, bounded by the number of system states. However, the presence of symmetry within an MRA can significantly reduce the number of loop sizes that need to be considered [13]. The loop encoding is extended by constraints that require each agent to achieve its goal at least once within the loop, thereby enforcing the qualitative objective that agents reach their goals infinitely often. Furthermore, for each possible loop size t and for each state where an agent achieves its goal, the encoding includes *soft clauses* weighted by $1/t$. Solving the associated weighted maximum satisfiability problem yields a truth assignment that maximises the total weight of satisfied soft clauses. In our setting, this means that such truth assignment will characterise a strategy that leads to a t-loop in which the frequency of goal achievement is collectively optimal. If the initial state of the MRA—where all resources are unallocated—is not part of the identified loop, then the resulting strategy is only partial. We show that such a partial strategy can be straightforwardly and systematically extended to a complete strategy that produces an infinite run starting from the initial state and eventually reaching the loop.

We developed SATMAS, a tool that implements our strategy synthesis technique for infinite runs of MRAs, built on top of the Max-SAT solver Open-WBO [20]. In an experimental evaluation, we demonstrate that SATMAS is capable of successfully synthesising collectively optimal strategies for a range of MRA instances. SATMAS supports two synthesis modes: a monolithic approach, which uses a single encoding of the entire problem, and an incremental approach, which iterates over possible loop sizes. The incremental approach divides the overall problem into several independent sub problems. Since the sub problems are independent, there is significant potential for performance gains through parallel computation.

2 Related Work

The synthesis of strategies for multi-agent systems has been studied in the context of rational verification [17,18,25]. In rational verification, agents' objectives are qualitative in the sense that each agent has a one-time goal. In contrast, our approach additionally focuses on quantitative objectives: agents aim to achieve their goals as frequently as possible over an infinite run of the system.

Strategies addressing quantitative aspects have been explored in various contexts, including timed automata [2], stochastic systems [22], and systems with specific objectives such as maximising mean pay-off [8] or minimising energy consumption [5]. Several works have proposed solution concepts for the synthesis problem [7,9,11]. Common approaches include quantitative extensions of classical temporal logics and reductions of the synthesis problem to model checking [1,6,12]. In [1], the authors propose the logic LTL[$\mathcal{F}$], which allows the specification of quantitative objectives using temporal logic formulas with real-valued satisfaction values. The logic SL[$\mathcal{F}$] extends LTL[$\mathcal{F}$] to the strategic setting by introducing strategic quantifiers [6]. Another framework for reasoning about agents with both qualitative and quantitative objectives is presented in [12], where the authors augment multi-agent systems with transition pay-offs and introduce a quantitative extension of ATL*. The contributions of the above works are predominantly theoretical, focusing on general complexity results and the algorithmic definition of the synthesis problem. In contrast, our work specifically targets multi-agent systems for resource allocation and includes tool support as well as experimental evaluations.

Our approach reduces the synthesis problem to maximum satisfiability solving (Max-SAT), where qualitative objectives are encoded as hard clauses and quantitative objectives as soft clauses. This is conceptually related to satisfiability-based bounded model checking, where typically only qualitative properties of finite system runs are verified [4,24]. To the best of our knowledge, ours is the first Max-SAT-based approach to synthesising optimal strategies for infinite runs of multi-agent systems. Related applications of Max-SAT include finding optimal coalitions of agents [19], synthesising optimal controllers [15], and model checking of quantitative hyper-properties [16]. Our current focus is on synthesising strategies that enforce all qualitative objectives while ensuring collective optimality. The incorporation of equilibrium concepts, as studied in [1,10], is a direction for future work.

3 Multi-agent Systems for Resource Allocation

In our approach we focus on *multi-agent systems for resource allocation* (MRAs), originally introduced in [14].

Definition 1 (Multi-Agent System for Resource Allocation). *A multi-agent system for resource allocation is a tuple $M = (Agt, Res, d, Acc)$ where*

- $Agt = \{a_1, \ldots, a_n\}$ *is a finite set of agents,*
- $Res = \{r_1, \ldots, r_m\}$ *is a finite set of resources,*
- $d : Agt \to \mathbb{N}$ *is a demand function that defines the number of resources that each agent needs to accumulate in order to achieve its individual goal,*
- $Acc : Agt \to 2^{Res}$ *is an accessibility function that defines the subset of resources that each agent can access.*

Each agent has the goal to gradually accumulate a number of resources such that its demand is finally satisfied. Once this is accomplished the agent releases all resources and starts accumulating them again. The actions that can be performed for this are as follows.

Definition 2 (Actions). *Given an MRA M, the set of actions Act is the union of the following types of actions:*

- *request actions:* $\{req^a_r \mid a \in Agt, r \in Acc(a)\}$
- *release actions:* $\{rel^a_r \mid a \in Agt, r \in Acc(a)\}$
- *release-all actions:* $\{rel^a_{all} \mid a \in Agt\}$
- *idle actions:* $\{idle^a \mid a \in Agt\}$

Hence, an agent can request a particular resource, release a particular resource that it currently holds, release all resources that it currently holds, or just idle. The fact that agents may hold certain resources gives rise to the notion of *states* of an MRA, which we subsequently define. An MRA runs in discrete rounds where in each round each agent chooses its next action. In a round the tuple of chosen actions, one per agent, gets executed simultaneously. The execution of actions leads to an evolution of the system between different states over time.

Definition 3 (States). *A state of an MRA M is a function $s : Res \to Agt^+$ where $Agt^+ = Agt \cup \{a_0\}$ and a_0 is a dummy agent. If $s(r) = a_0$ then resource r is unallocated in state s. If $s(r) = a_i$ and $i > 0$ then r is allocated by agent a_i*

in s. We denote by s_0 *the initial state of* M*, where* $s(r) = a_0$ *for each* $r \in Res$*, i.e., initially all resources are unallocated. We denote by* S *the set of all possible states of* M*. If we want to express that resource* r *is currently allocated by agent* a_i *but the current state is not further specified, then we simply write* $r = a_i$*.*

Hence, states describe the current allocation of resources to agents. An agent may not be able to observe the entire state of the MRA. We assume that agents can only observe the (state of the) resources they have access to.

Definition 4 (State Observations). *Let* M *be an MRA, let* $a_i \in Agt$ *and let* $s \in S$*. Then the observation of agent* a_i *in state* s *is a function* $s_{a_i} : Acc(a_i) \rightarrow Agt^+$ *such that* $s_{a_i}(r) = s(r)$ *for all* $r \in Acc(a_i)$*. We denote by* S_{a_i} *the set of all possible state observations of* a_i*.*

In each state only a subset of actions may be available for execution by an agent, which we define by the protocol:

Definition 5 (Action Availability Protocol). *The action availability protocol is a function* $P : S \times Agt \rightarrow 2^{Act}$ *defined for each* $s \in S$ *and* $a \in Agt$*:*

1. *if* $|s^{-1}(a)| = d(a)$ *then* $P(s, a) = \{rel^a_{all}\}$*;*
2. *otherwise:*
   (a) $rel^a_{all} \notin P(s, a)$*;*
   (b) $req^a_r \in P(s, a)$ *iff* $s(r) = a_0$*;*
   (c) $rel^a_r \in P(s, a)$ *iff* $s(r) = a$*;*
   (d) $idle^a \in P(s, a)$*.*

Thus, if an agent has reached its goal, it has to release all of its allocated resources. Otherwise, an agent can request an accessible resource that is currently unallocated, it can release a resource that it currently holds, and it can idle.

Definition 6 (Action Profiles). *An action profile in an MRA* M *is a mapping* $ap : Agt \rightarrow Act$*.* AP *denotes the set of all action profiles. We say that a profile* ap *is executable in a state* $s \in S$ *if for each* $a \in Agt$ *we have that* $ap(a) \in P(s, a)$*.*

Based on action profiles we can formally define the evolution of an MRA.

Definition 7 (Evolution). *The evolution of an MRA is a relation* $\delta \subseteq S \times AP \times S$ *where* $(s, ap, s') \in \delta$ *iff* ap *is executable in* s *and for each* $r \in Res$*:*

1. *if* $s(r) = a_0$ *then:*
   (a) *if* $\exists a : ap(a) = req^a_r \wedge \forall a' \neq a : ap(a') \neq req^{a'}_r$ *then* $s'(r) = a$*;*
   (b) *otherwise* $s'(r) = a_0$*;*
2. *if* $s(r) = a$ *for some* $a \in Agt$ *then:*
   (a) *if* $ap(a) = rel^a_r \vee rel^a_{all}$ *then* $s'(r) = a_0$*;*
   (b) *otherwise* $s'(r) = a$*.*

If an action profile is executed in a state of an MRA M, this leads to a transition of M into a corresponding successor state, i.e., a change in the allocation of resources according to the actions chosen by the agents. According to the evolution, the request of a resource r by an agent a will only be successful if a is the only agent that requests r in the current round. If multiple agents request the same resource at the same time, then none of the agents will obtain it.

4 Strategies

We are interested in solving strategy synthesis problems with regard to multi-agent systems for resource allocation. A uniform strategy is defined as follows:

Definition 8 (Uniform Strategy). *A strategy of an agent $a \in Agt$ in an MRA is an injective function $\alpha_a : S_a \to Act$. A strategy can also be denoted by a relation $\alpha_a \subseteq S_a \times Act$ where $\alpha_a(s_a, act^a) = true$ iff $\alpha_a(s_a) = act^a$. A joint strategy is a tuple of strategies $\alpha_{Agt} = (\alpha_a)_{a \in Agt}$, one for each $a \in Agt$.*

A strategy determines which action an agent will choose under which observation. A strategy is uniform if the following holds: Each time that an agent makes the same observation, it will perform the same action according to the strategy. The outcome of a strategy α_{Agt} in a state s is an infinite path.

Definition 9 (Outcome of a Strategy). *Let M be an MRA and s a state of M. Moreover, let α_{Agt} be a joint strategy of Agt. Then the outcome of α_{Agt} in state s is a path*

$$\begin{aligned}\pi(s, \alpha_{Agt}) = \; & s_0 s_1 \ldots \mid s_0 = s \;\wedge\; \forall t \in \mathbb{N} : \\ & \Big(s_t, (\alpha_{a_1}((s_t)_{a_1}), \ldots, \alpha_{a_n}((s_t)_{a_n})), s_{t+1}\Big) \in \delta\end{aligned}$$

where $(s_t)_a$ denotes the observation of agent a in state s_t.

We use a temporal strategy logic for specifying strategic goal-achievability properties of agents in MRAs.

Definition 10 (Strategy Logic Syntax). *Let M be an MRA. Then strategy logic formulas $\langle\langle Agt \rangle\rangle \varphi$ over M are defined as follows:*

$$\varphi := a.goal \mid \neg\varphi \mid \varphi \vee \varphi \mid \varphi \wedge \varphi \mid \boldsymbol{G}\varphi \mid \boldsymbol{F}\varphi$$

where $a \in Agt$ and $a.goal$ is an atomic proposition that expresses that agent a has reached its goal, i.e., $s(a.goal) = true$ iff $|s^{-1}(a)| = d(a)$ for $s \in S$.

Here **G** refers to 'globally' and **F** refers to 'finally'. The definition of the strategy logic semantics is as follows:

Definition 11 (Strategy Logic Semantics). *Let M be an MRA and let $s \in S$ be a state of M. Then the evaluation of a strategy logic formula $\langle\langle Agt \rangle\rangle\, \varphi$ on the state s, written $[M, s \models \langle\langle Agt \rangle\rangle\, \varphi]$, is inductively defined as:*

$$\begin{array}{lll} [M, s \models \langle\langle Agt \rangle\rangle\, \varphi] & \equiv & \exists \alpha_{Agt} : [M, \pi(s, \alpha_{Agt}) \models \varphi] \\ [M, \pi \models a.goal] & \equiv & |\pi[0]^{-1}(a)| = d(a) \\ [M, \pi \models \boldsymbol{G}\varphi] & \equiv & \forall t \in \mathbb{N} : [M, \pi[t] \models \varphi] \\ [M, \pi \models \boldsymbol{F}\varphi] & \equiv & \exists t \in \mathbb{N} : [M, \pi[t] \models \varphi] \end{array}$$

where $\pi[t]$ denotes the t-th state of the path π. Moreover, Boolean operators $\neg, \vee, \wedge$ are interpreted with the usual semantics.

The goal-achievability formula that we consider in our approach is

$$\varphi^{\infty} = \bigwedge_{a \in Agt} (\mathbf{GF}a.goal).$$

Hence, each agent shall achieve its goal infinitely often in an infinite run of an MRA. We call a strategy that ensures φ^{∞} a winning strategy.

Definition 12 (Winning Strategy). *Let M be an MRA with initial state s_0 and let φ^{∞} be a goal-achievability formula. Moreover, let α_{Agt} be a joint strategy of Agt. Then α_{Agt} is a* winning strategy *if $[M, \pi(s, \alpha_{Agt}) \models \varphi^{\infty}]$ holds.*

4.1 Collectively Optimal Strategies

The basic goal-achievability formula characterises a purely qualitative objective. In order to also consider optimality in strategy synthesis, we introduce an additional quantitative objective: Goals shall be achieved as frequently as possible. Optimality with regard to this quantitative objective can be measured by means of a pay-off, which we define for states and paths.

Definition 13 (State Pay-Off). *Let M be an MRA and let $a \in Agt$. Then the* pay-off *for agent a in states $s \in S$ of M is a function $\rho_a : S \rightarrow \{0, 1\}$ where*

$$\rho_a(s) \;=\; \begin{cases} 1 & \textit{if } |s^{-1}(a)| = d(a), \\ 0 & \textit{otherwise.} \end{cases}$$

Hence, the pay-off of an agent is 1 in exactly the states where the demand of the agent is satisfied, i.e., the individual resource allocation goal is achieved. Assuming that we want to maximise the frequency of reaching the goal, the pay-off function can be extended to infinite paths. Since the state space of an MRA is finite and the strategies that we consider are uniform, we can assume that infinite paths are of the form $\pi = \pi[0, l-1] \cdot \pi[l, q]^{\omega}$, i.e., they start with a finite prefix $\pi[0, l-1]$ followed by an infinite loop $\pi[l, q]^{\omega}$.

Definition 14 (Path Pay-Off). *Let M be an MRA and let $a \in Agt$ be an agent. Moreover, let $\pi = \pi[0, l-1] \cdot \pi[l, q]^\omega$ be a path of M that starts with the finite prefix $\pi[0, l-1]$ and ends in the infinite loop $\pi[l, q]^\omega$. Then the* path pay-off *for agent a on π is*

$$\rho_a(\pi) = \frac{\sum_{t=l}^{q} \rho_a(\pi[t])}{|\pi[l, q]|}$$

where $\pi[t]$ is the t-th state along π. The collective path pay-off of all agents is

$$\rho_{Agt}(\pi) = \sum_{a \in Agt} \rho_a(\pi).$$

Thus, for infinite paths any pay-off along the finite prefix can be neglected. The individual pay-off of an agent a is its frequency of reaching the goal, i.e., the number of states along the loop in which a's demand is satisfied divided by the length of the loop. The collective pay-off is the sum of the individual pay-offs of all agents. A winning strategy is collectively optimal with regard to frequency if following the strategy results in a path for which the collective pay-off is maximal. We can now formally define collectively optimal strategies:

Definition 15 (Collectively Optimal Strategy). *Let M be an MRA and let φ^∞ be a goal-achievability formula. Moreover, let α_{Agt} be a joint strategy and let $(\rho_a)_{a \in Agt}$ be a tuple of pay-off functions, one for each $a \in Agt$. Then α_{Agt} is a* collectively optimal strategy *with regard to $(\rho_a)_{a \in Agt}$ if the following holds:*

1. $[M, \pi(s_0, \alpha_{Agt}) \models \varphi^\infty]$
2. $\neg\exists \alpha'_{Agt}$ *with* $[M, \pi(s_0, \alpha'_{Agt}) \models \varphi^\infty]$ *and* $\rho_{Agt}(\pi(s_0, \alpha'_{Agt})) > \rho_{Agt}(\pi(s_0, \alpha_{Agt}))$.

Hence, a winning strategy α_{Agt} is collectively optimal if there does not exist an alternative winning strategy α'_{Agt} that results in a greater collective pay-off. We denote the collectively optimal strategy synthesis problem of an MRA M with goal-achievability formula φ^∞ by $[M, s_0 \models \langle\langle Agt \rangle\rangle\, \varphi^\infty]_{Opt}$. A collectively optimal winning strategy ensures that each agent achieves its goal infinitely often (Condition 1), while also maximising the overall pay-off (Condition 2).

5 Max-SAT-Based Strategy Synthesis

In [23], we introduced a strategy synthesis approach restricted to the *once-off* goal-achievability formula $\varphi = \bigwedge_{a \in Agt} (\mathbf{F} a.goal)$ and *finite* path prefixes bounded by some $k \in \mathbb{N}$. We showed that the synthesis problem can be encoded in propositional logic and solved via Max-SAT solving. Here we show how this can be extended to synthesise strategies for *repetitive* goal-achievability $\varphi^\infty = \bigwedge_{a \in Agt} (\mathbf{GF} a.goal)$ that result in *infinite* paths with collectively optimal pay-off. The encoding is a formula in weighted conjunctive normal form:

Definition 16 (Weighted Conjunctive Normal Form (WCNF)). *Let Var be a set of Boolean variables. A propositional logic formula $\mathcal{F}$ over Var in weighted conjunctive normal form is a conjunction of weighted clauses $(\mathcal{C}, w_\mathcal{C})$ where $\mathcal{C}$ is a standard clause and $w_\mathcal{C} \in \mathbb{Q}_\infty$ is its weight. A clause $(\mathcal{C}, w_\mathcal{C})$ with $w_\mathcal{C} \in \mathbb{Q}$ is called a soft clause and a clause $(\mathcal{C}, \infty)$ is called a hard clause.*

We typically just write $\mathcal{C}$ for hard clauses $(\mathcal{C}, \infty)$. WCNF formulas can be written as a conjunction $\mathcal{H} \wedge \mathcal{S}$ where $\mathcal{H}$ are the hard clauses and $\mathcal{S}$ are the soft clauses. For WCNF formulas the following optimisation problem has been defined [3]:

Definition 17 (Maximum Satisfiability Problem). *Let $\mathcal{F} = \mathcal{H} \wedge \mathcal{S}$ over Var be a propositional logic formula in WCNF where $\mathcal{H}$ are the hard clauses and $\mathcal{S}$ are the soft clauses. The maximum satisfiability problem with regard to $\mathcal{F}$ is the problem of finding a truth assignment $\alpha : Var \to \{\mathit{0}, \mathit{1}\}$ that maximises*

$$\sum_{(\mathcal{C}, w_\mathcal{C}) \in \mathcal{S}} \alpha(\mathcal{C}) \cdot w_\mathcal{C}$$

subject to the condition that $\alpha(\mathcal{H}) = \mathit{1}$ holds.

Hence, the solution of Max-SAT with regard to $\mathcal{F}$ is a truth assignment α that *maximises* the sum of weights of the satisfied soft clauses, under the condition that *all* hard clauses are satisfied. If no such assignment exists, then the problem has no solution. For WCNF formulas $\mathcal{F} = \mathcal{H} \wedge \mathcal{S}$ over a set of variables Var and assuming that $\mathcal{A}(Var)$ is the set of all possible truth assignments over Var we define maximum satisfiability as the function

$$\textbf{max-sat}(\mathcal{F}) = \begin{cases} nil & \text{if } \textbf{sat}(\mathcal{H}) = \mathbf{0}, \\ \underset{\alpha \in \mathcal{A}(Var)}{\textbf{arg max}} \Big(\alpha(\mathcal{H}) \cdot \big(\sum_{(\mathcal{C}, w_\mathcal{C}) \in \mathcal{S}} \alpha(\mathcal{C}) \cdot w_\mathcal{C} \big) \Big) & \text{otherwise.} \end{cases}$$

max-sat$(\mathcal{F})$ returns *nil* if the problem has no solution. Otherwise it returns the truth assignment satisfying all hard clauses that maximises the sum of weights of the satisfied soft clauses. In our approach there is a one-to-one correspondence between the path pay-off resulting from following a strategy α_{Agt} and the sum of weights of soft clauses satisfied by an assignment α. Therefore, we also define the pay-off as a function ρ on truth assignments α and WCNF formulas $\mathcal{F} = \mathcal{H} \wedge \mathcal{S}$:

$$\rho(\alpha, \mathcal{F}) = \alpha(\mathcal{H}) \cdot \big(\sum_{(\mathcal{C}, w_\mathcal{C}) \in \mathcal{S}} \alpha(\mathcal{C}) \cdot w_\mathcal{C} \big).$$

As it can be seen, the pay-off of assignments α that do not satisfy all hard clauses $\mathcal{H}$ will be always 0, and the pay-off of assignments that satisfy all hard clauses will be the sum of weights of satisfied soft clauses.

The encoding of the strategy synthesis problem $[M, s_0 \models \langle\langle Agt \rangle\rangle\, \varphi]_{Opt}$ for once-off goal-achievability along k-bounded path prefixes, as introduced in [23], is a WCNF formula

$$\mathcal{F}_{Agt} = [\langle\langle Agt \rangle\rangle\,] \wedge [M_k] \wedge [\varphi] \wedge [Opt_{Agt}]$$

where $[\langle\langle Agt \rangle\rangle]$ encodes that all agents must adhere to the protocol, $[M_k]$ encodes all k-bounded path prefixes of the system that start in the initial state, and $[\varphi]$ is a constraint that restricts the path prefixes to those that satisfy $\varphi = \bigwedge_{a \in Agt} (\mathbf{F} a.goal)$. Moreover, $[Opt_{Agt}]$ encodes all possibilities of agents being in a state where their individual goal is achieved, i.e., states in which their pay-off is 1. The sub-formula $[\langle\langle Agt \rangle\rangle] \wedge [M_k] \wedge [\varphi]$ consists of hard clauses whereas $[Opt_{Agt}]$ consists of soft 'pay-off' clauses with a weight of 1 each. If **max-sat**$(\mathcal{F}Agt) = \alpha$, and α_{Agt} is the joint strategy corresponding to α, then following α_{Agt} yields a k-bounded path prefix with an optimal overall pay-off. However, this approach neither ensures that the optimality persists for any infinite extension of the prefix, nor does it guarantee repetitive goal-achievability for all agents.

6 Optimal Strategy Synthesis for Infinite Runs

We now introduce an extended encoding that overcomes the previous limitations and allows to synthesise strategies resulting in infinite paths with optimal goal-achievability along the loop. The overall encoding is of the form

$$\mathcal{F}_{Agt}^{\infty} = [\langle\langle Agt \rangle\rangle] \wedge [M_{loop}] \wedge [\varphi^{\infty}] \wedge [Opt_{Agt}^{\infty}]$$

where $[\langle\langle Agt \rangle\rangle]$ encodes that in their uniform strategic decisions agents must adhere to the protocol at all times, $[M_{loop}]$ encodes all loops of the system, and $[\varphi^{\infty}]$ is a constraint that restricts the loops to those that satisfy φ^{∞}. Moreover, $[Opt_{Agt}^{\infty}]$ encodes all possibilities of agents being in a state where their individual goal is achieved, associated with a pay-off relative to the size of the loop. In the encoding, we still make use a 'bound' k, set to the maximum possible loop size for the considered MRA, thereby ensuring that all possible loops are taken into account.

The sub encoding $[\langle\langle Agt \rangle\rangle]$ is the same as in $\mathcal{F}_{Agt}$. It encodes all feasible strategies. We now discuss the further parts of the overall encoding that will restrict the synthesised strategy to one that ensures optimal goal-achievability along an infinite path.

6.1 Loop Detection

The encoding of loops is

$$[M_{loop}] = [Valid]_0 \wedge \bigwedge_{t=0}^{k-1} [Evolution]_{t,t+1} \wedge [Looped] \wedge [Aux_{loopClosed}]$$

where $[Valid]_0$ encodes that a loop starts in a *valid* state of M, meaning that each resource is either unallocated or allocated by a unique agent that has access to this resource, and no agent holds an amount of resources that exceeds its demand (see Appendix for the formal definition of $[Valid]_0$). $[Evolution]_{t,t+1}$ encodes the state evolution of the system from time step t to step $t+1$, as defined in [23].

Moreover, $[Looped]$ is a sub encoding that allows to detect whether there exists a time step t where the system is in the same state as at time step 0:

$$[Looped] = \bigvee_{t=1}^{k} [s_t = s_0] \quad \text{(see Appendix for the formal definition of } [s_t = s_0]\text{).}$$

Finally, $[Aux_{loopClosed}]$ is an auxiliary encoding that introduces Boolean variables $loopClosed_t$ with $0 \leq t \leq k$ that will evaluate to *false* for the time steps *before* the repeated state occurred and evaluate to *true* for the time steps *thereafter*:

$$[Aux_{loopClosed}] = \neg loopClosed_0 \wedge \bigwedge_{t=1}^{k} \Big(loopClosed_t \leftrightarrow (loopClosed_{t-1} \vee [s_t = s_0]) \Big)$$

A truth assignment α that satisfies $[M_{loop}]$ characterises a sequence of states $s_0 \ldots s_{t-1} s_t \ldots s_k$, in line with the evolution of M, where $s_t = s_0$. The truth assignment will set the *loopClosed* variables associated with the states s_0 to s_{t-1} *false* and the *loopClosed* variables associated with the states s_t to s_k *true*. We can conclude that $(s_0 \ldots s_{t-1})^\omega$ is a valid loop of the system and we can neglect the remaining states s_t to s_k. Fig. 1 graphically depicts how a loop is derived.

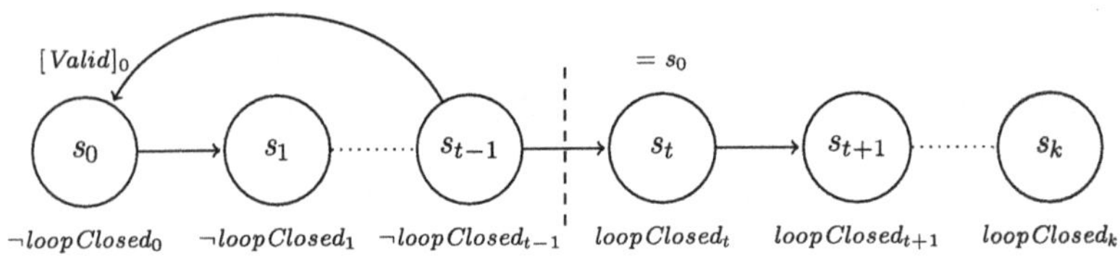

Fig. 1. Detected $(s_0 \ldots s_{t-1})^\omega$-loop.

6.2 Loops with Repetitive Goal-Reachability

In our overall encoding, $[M_{loop}]$ is conjuncted with $[\langle\langle Agt \rangle\rangle\,]$, which restricts loops to those that arise when agents make uniform strategic decisions. This also ensures that each state can occur at most once along a loop. Next, we extend the encoding by $[\varphi^\infty]$, ensuring that only loops on which each agent reaches its goal will be detected:

$$[\varphi^\infty] = \bigwedge_{a \in Agt} \Big(\bigvee_{t=0}^{k-1} ([a.goal]_t \wedge \neg loopClosed_t) \Big)$$

Here $[a.goal]_t$ encodes that agent a achieves its goal at the state at time step t, as defined in [23]. Additionally, we have the condition that the goal-achievement must happen at a time step *before* the loop is closed. Hence, $[\langle\langle Agt \rangle\rangle\,] \wedge [M_{loop}] \wedge [\varphi^\infty]$ evaluates to *true* for truth assignments that characterise loops, resulting from agents following a uniform strategy, for which $\bigwedge_{a \in Agt} (\mathbf{GF} a.goal)$ holds.

6.3 Loops with Optimal Frequency Pay-Off

Next, we extend our encoding such that the frequency in which the agents achieve their goals along the loop gets maximised. Computing and maximising the frequency requires information about the size of the loop. For this, we introduce the auxiliary encoding $[Aux_{loopSize}]$ that introduces Boolean variables $loopSize_t$ with $t \leq t \leq k$ such that $loopSize_t$ solely evaluates to *true* for truth assignments that characterise loops of size t.

$$[Aux_{loopSize}] \;=\; \bigwedge_{t=1}^{k} \left(loopSize_t \leftrightarrow (\neg loopClosed_{t-1} \wedge loopClosed_t)\right)$$

In this encoding we make use of the previously introduced *loopClosed* variables and the fact that the loop size is t if and only if the loop is *not* closed at time step $t-1$ but closed at step t.

If the loop size is t, then for each time step $t' < t$ where an agent a achieves its goal it shall be awarded a pay-off of $1/t$. For this, we define a further auxiliary encoding $[Aux_{goal}]$ that introduces Boolean variables ${}_{a}goal^{t}_{t'}$ indicating goal-achievement of agent a at time step t', assuming a loop of size t.

$$[Aux_{goal}] \;=\; \bigwedge_{a\in Agt} \bigwedge_{t=1}^{k} \bigwedge_{t'=0}^{t-1} \left({}_{a}goal^{t}_{t'} \leftrightarrow ([a.goal]_{t'} \wedge loopSize_t)\right)$$

In the frequency optimisation encoding $[Opt^{\infty}_{Agt}]$ we introduce a *pay-off clause* $({}_{a}goal^{t}_{t'}, \frac{1}{t})$ for each agent, each possible loop size and each time step before the loop size is reached:

$$[Opt^{\infty}_{Agt}] = [Aux_{loopSize}] \wedge [Aux_{goal}] \wedge \bigwedge_{a\in Agt} \bigwedge_{t=1}^{k} \bigwedge_{t'=0}^{t-1} \left({}_{a}goal^{t}_{t'}, \frac{1}{t}\right)$$

As it can be seen, the pay-off clauses are soft clauses with a weight of $1/t$. This completes the definition of our overall encoding $\mathcal{F}^{\infty}_{Agt}$. Solving the associated maximum satisfiability problem will return a truth assignment α that maximises the sum of weights of satisfied pay-off clauses. From α we can directly derive a corresponding strategy α_{Agt} [23]. Following α_{Agt} results in a loop with collectively optimal pay-off in terms of goal-achievement frequency.

6.4 From Loops to Looped Paths

Our approach allows to synthesise strategies that result in collectively optimal loops in the state space of an MRA. The initial state where all resources are unallocated may not be part of the loop and therefore, the synthesised strategy may only be a partial strategy. However, such a strategy can be straightforwardly extended to a complete one, defined for all states that will be reached when following it from the initial state.

Let $\alpha_{Agt} = (\alpha_a)_{a \in Agt}$ be a partial strategy derived from a satisfying truth assignment of an encoding $\mathcal{F}^{\infty}_{Agt}$ and let $s_0 \dots s_{t-1}$ be the corresponding sequence of states along the loop. Then α_{Agt} can be extended to a complete strategy according to the following procedure:

1. *Select state s along $s_0 \dots s_{t-1}$ with the smallest amount of allocated resources.*
2. *If s is the initial state of the MRA, then terminate.*
3. *Else, construct an action profile ap that results in s:*
   (a) *For each agent a in Agt:*
      i. *If a does not hold any resource in s, then set $ap(a) := idle^a$.*
      ii. *Else, select resource r_j with the smallest identifier j that agent a holds in s and set $ap(a) := req^a_{r_j}$.*
   (b) *Determine the state q for which $\delta(q, ap, s)$ holds.*
   (c) *For each agent a in Agt: set $\alpha_a((q)_a) := ap(a)$.*
4. *Set $s := q$ and go to Step 2.*

The procedure will extend any loop to an infinite path $\pi = \pi[0, l-1] \cdot \pi[l, q]^{\omega}$ that starts in the initial state of the MRA. Moreover, it will extend the strategy α_{Agt} such that if the agents follow α_{Agt} from the initial state, then this will result in π. Since in an infinite run the frequency pay-off only depends on the loop, adding a finite prefix does not affect the pay-off.

6.5 Properties of the Encoding

The major property of our encoding is that it allows to perform the synthesis of collectively optimal strategies via maximum satisfiability solving. Following the synthesised strategy results in an infinite run of the MRA with collectively optimal pay-off in terms of the frequency of achieving goals.

Theorem 1 (Optimal Strategy Synthesis).
Let $[M, s_0 \models \langle\langle Agt \rangle\rangle \varphi^{\infty}]_{Opt}$ be an optimal strategy synthesis problem and let $\mathcal{F}^{\infty}_{Agt}$ be its WCNF encoding. Then the following properties hold:

1. *If* ***max-sat***$(\mathcal{F}^{\infty}_{Agt}) = nil$*, then there does not exist a winning strategy for the grand coalition Agt to achieve φ^{∞}.*
2. *If* ***max-sat***$(\mathcal{F}^{\infty}_{Agt}) = \alpha$ *and α_{Agt} is the joint strategy corresponding to α, then α_{Agt} is a collectively optimal winning strategy.*

Proof sketch.
We have $\mathcal{F}^{\infty}_{Agt} = \mathcal{H} \wedge \mathcal{S}$ where $\mathcal{H} = [\langle\langle Agt \rangle\rangle\,] \wedge [M_{loop}] \wedge [\varphi^{\infty}] \wedge [Aux_{loopSize}] \wedge [Aux_{goal}]$ are the hard clauses and $\mathcal{S} = \bigwedge_{a \in Agt} \bigwedge_{t=1}^{k} \bigwedge_{t'=0}^{t-1} \left({}_a goal^t_{t'}, \frac{1}{t}\right)$ are the soft clauses of the encoding.

Property 1:
max-sat$(\mathcal{F}^{\infty}_{Agt}) = nil$ implies **sat**$([\langle\langle Agt \rangle\rangle\,] \wedge [M_{loop}] \wedge [\varphi^{\infty}] \wedge [Aux_{loopSize}] \wedge [Aux_{goal}]) = \mathbf{0}$ (Definition of **max-sat** for WCNF formulas). The sub formula $[Aux_{loopSize}] \wedge [Aux_{goal}]$ only introduces auxiliary variables, and thus, cannot be the cause of unsatisfiability. Hence, **sat**$([\langle\langle Agt \rangle\rangle\,] \wedge [M_{loop}] \wedge [\varphi^{\infty}]) = \mathbf{0}$. This

implies that $[M, s_0 \models \langle\langle Agt \rangle\rangle \varphi^\infty]$ does not hold ([23] and definition of $[M_{loop}]$ and $[\varphi^\infty]$). We can conclude that there does not exist a winning strategy for the grand coalition Agt to achieve φ^∞.

Property 2:
max-sat$(\mathcal{F}^{\infty}_{Agt}) = \alpha$ implies that the assignment α satisfies all hard clauses of the encoding. We can conclude that α characterises a strategy α_{Agt} that results in a loop for which φ^∞ holds. According to the definition of **max-sat**, out of all truth assignments that satisfy all hard clauses, α is the assignment that maximises the sum of weights of the satisfied soft clauses. Let w_α be the sum of weights of the soft clauses satisfied by α. Then for all other truth assignments α' that satisfy all hard clauses we have that $w_\alpha \geq w_{\alpha'}$. The definition of $[Aux_{loopSize}]$ ensures that there exists exactly one t with $\alpha(loopSize_t) = \mathbf{1}$, and for all $t' \neq t : \alpha(loopSize_{t'}) = \mathbf{0}$. This t is the size of the loop $(s_0 \ldots s_{t-1})^\omega$ characterised by α. $\alpha({}_agoal^t_{t'}, \frac{1}{t}) = \mathbf{1}$ if and only if agent a reaches its resource goal at time step t' along $(s_0 \ldots s_{t-1})^\omega$ (Definition of $[Aux_{goal}]$). Hence, $\rho_{Agt}(s_0 \ldots s_{t-1}) = w_\alpha$ (Definition 14). Based on a similar argumentation, we can show that each alternative truth assignment α' that satisfies all hard clauses characterises a loop with a pay-off $w_{\alpha'}$. We already argued that $w_\alpha \geq w_{\alpha'}$ for all alternative assignments α'. Thus, we can conclude that α characterises a joint winning strategy α_{Agt} that is collectively optimal.

7 Implementation and Experiments

We developed the tool SATMAS[1], which implements our technique for synthesising optimal strategies for infinite runs of MRAs. SATMAS takes an MRA M as input, encodes the associated strategy synthesis problem into propositional logic, converts the encoding into weighted conjunctive normal form (WCNF), and outputs it in DIMACS format. The Max-SAT solver Open-WBO [20] then processes the DIMACS file to generate a maximum-satisfying truth assignment. From this assignment, a corresponding collectively optimal strategy and the resulting infinite run of the MRA are derived. SATMAS supports two synthesis modes: a monolithic approach, which employs a single encoding of the entire problem, and an incremental approach, which iteratively considers different loop sizes. In each iteration of the incremental mode, the encoding is restricted to a fixed loop size, significantly reducing the complexity of the synthesis process.

In our experiments using the incremental mode, we successfully synthesised strategies for MRAs with up to five agents and five resources. The experiments were conducted on an Apple M3 Pro system with a 12-core CPU and 18 GB of RAM. Overall results showed that the primary factor affecting solving time was the bound on the loop sizes. Completeness is guaranteed when this bound equals the number of states in the MRA. However, since our objectives are universal—requiring that *all* agents achieve their goals infinitely often and that the *overall* pay-off is maximised—only those states that are *distinguishable* with respect

[1] Available at https://github.com/TuksModelChecking/Satmas.

to these objectives need to be considered. Based on symmetry arguments and Burnside's lemma [21], the number of distinguishable states of an MRA can be computed and used as a completeness-guaranteeing bound.

In the first set of experiments, we considered MRA implementations of the *Dining Philosophers* problem, which exhibits significant symmetry. The results for this case study are shown in Table 1(a). The *Scenario* column specifies the number of agents in *Agt*, the number of resources in *Res*, and each agent's demand $\mathcal{D}$ and number of accessible resources $\mathcal{ACC}$. While no uniform winning strategy existed for the 2-philosopher scenario, SATMAS successfully synthesised collectively optimal strategies and corresponding loops for the 3- and 4-philosopher scenarios in under 30 s. In the second experimental set, we varied the number of resources and the agents' demands (Table 1(b)). An increasing number of resources enlarged the state space and consequently the range of possible loop sizes, leading to longer solving times for larger instances. We observed a similar trend in the third experimental set, where increasing the number of agents led to higher bounds on loop sizes and thus longer solving times (Table 1(c)).

Our current implementation processes iterations over different loop sizes sequentially. However, since each iteration solves an independent sub problem, *parallel solving* is feasible and could significantly reduce total solving time, allowing larger scenarios to be considered. A parallel version of the iterative approach is currently under development.

Table 1. Experimental results.

(a) Dining Philosophers				
Scenario	Bound	Size of Optimal Loop	Optimal Pay-Off	Solving Time
$\lvert Agt\rvert = 2, \lvert Res\rvert = 2, \mathcal{D} = 2, \mathcal{ACC} = 2$	6	N/A	N/A	0.0106s
$\lvert Agt\rvert = 3, \lvert Res\rvert = 3, \mathcal{D} = 2, \mathcal{ACC} = 2$	9	8	4/8	0.0651s
$\lvert Agt\rvert = 4, \lvert Res\rvert = 4, \mathcal{D} = 2, \mathcal{ACC} = 2$	16	6	4/6	29.235s
(b) Increased Number of Resources and Demand				
Scenario	Bound	Size of Optimal Loop	Optimal Pay-Off	Solving Time
$\lvert Agt\rvert = 2, \lvert Res\rvert = 2, \mathcal{D} = 1, \mathcal{ACC} = 2$	4	N/A	N/A	0.0113s
$\lvert Agt\rvert = 2, \lvert Res\rvert = 3, \mathcal{D} = 2, \mathcal{ACC} = 3$	9	4	2/4	0.0893s
$\lvert Agt\rvert = 2, \lvert Res\rvert = 4, \mathcal{D} = 3, \mathcal{ACC} = 4$	16	3	2/3	8.3422s
$\lvert Agt\rvert = 2, \lvert Res\rvert = 5, \mathcal{D} = 4, \mathcal{ACC} = 5$	25	6	4/6	128.52s
(c) Increased Number of Agents				
Scenario	Bound	Size of Optimal Loop	Optimal Pay-Off	Solving Time
$\lvert Agt\rvert = 2, \lvert Res\rvert = 2, \mathcal{D} = 1, \mathcal{ACC} = 2$	4	2	2/2	0.0135s
$\lvert Agt\rvert = 3, \lvert Res\rvert = 2, \mathcal{D} = 1, \mathcal{ACC} = 2$	7	4	3/4	0.1302s
$\lvert Agt\rvert = 4, \lvert Res\rvert = 2, \mathcal{D} = 1, \mathcal{ACC} = 2$	11	4	4/4	6.7192s
$\lvert Agt\rvert = 5, \lvert Res\rvert = 2, \mathcal{D} = 1, \mathcal{ACC} = 2$	16	6	6/6	878.01s

8 Conclusion and Future Work

We presented a Max-SAT-based technique for synthesising collectively optimal strategies for *infinite* runs of multi-agent systems for resource allocation (MRAs). By encoding feasible loops within the system's state space and integrating constraints that ensure *repetitive* goal achievement, we established a method for deriving collectively optimal strategies in infinite settings. The proposed approach, implemented in our SATMAS tool, demonstrated effectiveness across various MRA instances, providing both monolithic and incremental synthesis modes. The incremental approach enables efficient use of parallel computation. In future work, we will focus on extending the framework to support the synthesis of Nash equilibrium strategies with respect to agents' quantitative objectives. This can be achieved through a step-by-step refinement of an initially synthesised collectively optimal strategy, until no agent can improve its pay-off through unilateral deviation.

Appendix

Definition 18 (Encoding of Valid States). *The encoding of valid states of an MRA M at time step 0 is $[Valid]_0 = [Access]_0 \wedge [Unique]_0 \wedge [Demand]_0$ where*

$$[Access]_0 = \bigwedge_{a \in Agt} \bigwedge_{r \in Res \setminus Acc(a)} [r \neq a]_0$$

encodes that in valid states resources may only be allocated by agents that have access to them, and

$$[Unique]_0 = \bigwedge_{r \in Res} \bigvee_{a \in Agt^+} ([r = a]_0)$$

encodes that in valid states each resource is either allocated by some agent or unallocated, and

$$[Demand]_0 = \bigwedge_{a \in Agt} \bigvee_{\substack{R \subseteq Acc(a) \\ |R| = |Acc(a)| - d(a)}} \Big(\bigwedge_{r \in R} [r \neq a]_0\Big)$$

encodes that in valid states no agent may hold an amount of resources that exceeds its demand. The sub encodings $[r = a]_0$ and $[r \neq a]_0$ have been defined in [23].

Definition 19 (Encoding of Identical States). *Let M be an MRA. Then*

$$[s_t = s_0] = \bigwedge_{r \in Res} \bigwedge_{a \in Agt} ([r = a]_t \leftrightarrow [r = a]_0)$$

encodes that the resource state at time step t is identical to the resource state at time step 0. The sub encoding $[r = a]_t$has been defined in [23].

References

1. Almagor, S., Kupferman, O., Perelli, G.: Synthesis of controllable Nash equilibria in quantitative objective game. In: IJCAI, vol. 18, pp. 35–41 (2018)
2. Asarin, E., Maler, O., Pnueli, A., Sifakis, J.: Controller synthesis for timed automata. IFAC Proceedings Volumes 31(18), 447–452 (1998), 5th IFAC Conference on System Structure and Control 1998 (SSC'98), Nantes, France, 8-10 July
3. Bacchus, F., Järvisalo, M., Martins, R.: Maximum satisfiability. In: Handbook of Satisfiability, pp. 929–991. IOS Press (2021)
4. Biere, A.: Bounded model checking. In: Handbook of satisfiability, pp. 739–764. IOS press (2021)
5. Bouyer, P., Fahrenberg, U., Larsen, K.G., Markey, N., Srba, J.: Infinite runs in weighted timed automata with energy constraints. In: Cassez, F., Jard, C. (eds.) FORMATS 2008. LNCS, vol. 5215, pp. 33–47. Springer, Heidelberg (2008). https://doi.org/10.1007/978-3-540-85778-5_4
6. Bouyer, P., Kupferman, O., Markey, N., Maubert, B., Murano, A., Perelli, G.: Reasoning about quality and fuzziness of strategic behaviors. ACM Trans. Comput. Log. **24**(3), 1–38 (2023)
7. Brenguier, R., Pérez, G.A., Raskin, J.F., Sankur, O.: Admissibility in quantitative graph games. arXiv preprint arXiv:1611.08677 (2016)
8. Brice, L., Raskin, J.F., Bogaard, M.V.D.: Subgame-perfect equilibria in mean-payoff games. arXiv preprint arXiv:2101.10685 (2021)
9. Brihaye, T., Bruyère, V., De Pril, J.: On equilibria in quantitative games with reachability/safety objectives. Theory Comput. Syst. **54**, 150–189 (2014)
10. Bruyère, V.: Synthesis of equilibria in infinite-duration games on graphs. ACM SIGLOG News **8**(2), 4–29 (2021)
11. Bruyère, V., Meunier, N., Raskin, J.F.: Secure equilibria in weighted games. In: Proceedings of the Joint Meeting of the Twenty-Third EACSL Annual Conference on Computer Science Logic (CSL) and the Twenty-Ninth Annual ACM/IEEE Symposium on Logic in Computer Science (LICS), pp. 1–26 (2014)
12. Bulling, N., Goranko, V.: Combining quantitative and qualitative reasoning in concurrent multi-player games. AAMAS **36**(1), 1–33 (2022)
13. Cohen, M., Dam, M., Lomuscio, A., Qu, H.: A symmetry reduction technique for model checking temporal-epistemic logic. In: Twenty-First International Joint Conference on Artificial Intelligence. Citeseer (2009)
14. De Masellis, R., Goranko, V., Gruner, S., Timm, N.: Generalising the dining philosophers problem: competitive dynamic resource allocation in multi-agent systems. In: European Conference on Multi-Agent Systems, pp. 30–47. Springer (2018)
15. Dimitrova, R., Ghasemi, M., Topcu, U.: Reactive synthesis with maximum realizability of linear temporal logic specifications. Acta Informatica **57**(1), 107–135 (2020)
16. Finkbeiner, B., Hahn, C., Torfah, H.: Model checking quantitative hyperproperties. In: International Conference on Computer Aided Verification, pp. 144–163. Springer (2018)
17. Gutierrez, J., Harrenstein, P., Wooldridge, M.: From model checking to equilibrium checking: Reactive modules for rational verification. Artif. Intell. **248**, 123–157 (2017)
18. Gutierrez, J., Najib, M., Perelli, G., Wooldridge, M.: On computational tractability for rational verification. In: Proceedings of the Twenty-Eighth International Joint Conference on Artificial Intelligence, IJCAI-19, pp. 329–335. International Joint Conferences on Artificial Intelligence Organization (7 2019)

19. Liao, X.: Maximum Satisfiability Approach to Game Theory and Network Security. Ph.D. thesis, Kyushu University (2014)
20. Martins, R., Manthey, N., Terra-Neves, M., Manquinho, V., Lynce, I.: Open-WBO@ MaxSAT evaluation 2020. MaxSAT Evaluation **2020**, 24 (2021)
21. Nasseef, M.T.: Counting symmetries with burnside's lemma and polya's theorem. Europ. J. Pure Appl. Math. **9**(1), 84–113 (2016)
22. Svoreňová, M., Kwiatkowska, M.: Quantitative verification and strategy synthesis for stochastic games. Eur. J. Control. **30**, 15–30 (2016)
23. Timm, N., Botha, J., Jordaan, S.: Max-SAT-based synthesis of optimal and Nash equilibrium strategies for multi-agent systems. Sci. Comput. Program. **228**, 102946 (2023)
24. Timm, N., Gruner, S., Harvey, M.: A bounded model checker for three-valued abstractions of concurrent software systems. In: Ribeiro, L., Lecomte, T. (eds.) Formal Methods: Foundations and Applications, pp. 199–216. Springer, Cham (2016)
25. Wooldridge, M., Gutierrez, J., Harrenstein, P., Marchioni, E., Perelli, G., Toumi, A.: Rational verification: From model checking to equilibrium checking. In: Proceedings of the AAAI Conference on Artificial Intelligence, vol. 30 (2016)

Allocating Resources Among Non-cooperative Agents with Leontief Utilities

Ioannis Caragiannis[1] and Nicos Protopapas[2(✉)]

[1] Department of Computer Science, Aarhus University, Åbogade 34, 8200 Aarhus, Denmark
iannis@cs.au.dk

[2] Archimedes, Athena Research Center, Artemidos 1, 15125 Marousi, Greece
nikosfprotopapas@gmail.com

Abstract. We study the allocation of multiple divisible resources to strategic agents in settings with strong complementarities, a structure common in applications such as cloud computing and wireless communication networks. Each agent demands resources in fixed relative proportions—a preference model known as Leontief utilities—and evaluates the resulting bundle via a monotone, concave valuation function on the fraction of the dominant resource she is allocated. To ensure low communication overhead, we consider mechanisms that use limited expressiveness and require agents to submit single scalar signals (rather than complete valuation reports) and charge them accordingly. We study the strategic games defined and prove that their price of anarchy depends linearly on the number of resources. Extensive simulation results suggest even better performance in practical scenarios.

1 Introduction

The need for efficient resource allocation often arises in environments where users demand combinations of multiple heterogeneous resources. In settings such as cloud computing platforms and 5G network services, users (or applications) typically have structured demands. For instance, a cloud computing task may require a predetermined ratio of CPU, memory, and bandwidth, while a 5G service slice may need a specific combination of spectrum, compute, and transport resources to operate effectively. In such contexts, a critical challenge is to design mechanisms that allocate limited resources efficiently across users with diverse but rigid consumption patterns.

Motivated by these practical scenarios, we study *simple mechanisms* for allocating divisible resources to strategic users with fixed bundle requirements. Each user is characterized by a fixed proportion in which she wishes to consume the available resources and derives value only from allocations that fully respect this structure. Users are asked to submit bids indicating their willingness to pay, and the mechanism computes both a resource allocation and corresponding payments. Since users act strategically, they participate in a game where they choose

M. Baldoni et al. (Eds.): EUMAS 2025, LNAI 16259, pp. 52–67, 2026.
https://doi.org/10.1007/978-3-032-22820-8_4

bids to maximize their utility—that is, the value derived from the allocated resources minus their payment to the mechanism. Our goal is to design mechanisms that compute efficient allocations in such non-cooperative settings, tailored to environments where users derive value only when allocated specific combinations of resources in fixed proportions rather than from individual resources independently.

We consider an abstract setting with a number of agents competing for multiple heterogeneous resources. Each agent has a fixed pattern in which they want to consume these resources, captured by a vector of relative demands. One of the resources is designated as the agent's *dominant resource* and is normalized to one, while the remaining demands are fractions between zero and one. An allocation simply specifies what share of each resource is given to each agent. Agents derive value from the allocated resources only if they are received in the exact proportions specified by their demand vector—a characteristic known as *Leontief preferences*. Receiving more of a single resource is not useful unless the other resources are also increased proportionally. Therefore, an agent's allocation can be conveniently described by the fraction of their dominant resource they receive; the amounts of the other resources are then determined by scaling their demand vector accordingly.

In addition to their demand vectors, each agent has a valuation function that captures how much they benefit from an allocation. This function depends only on the fraction of the dominant resource the agent receives and is assumed to be concave, reflecting diminishing returns. The total value generated by an allocation—known as the *social welfare*—is simply the sum of the agents' individual values. We are interested in mechanisms that determine how resources are allocated and how much each agent should pay. These mechanisms take as input the demand vectors and a report submitted by each agent. While the demand vectors are assumed to be public information, the valuation functions are private and not directly observable by the mechanism. To keep things simple and practical, we focus on a setting where agents communicate only a single scalar bid, which serves as a proxy for their private valuation.

Agents are strategic and aim to maximize their own utility, which is the value they get from the allocated resources minus the payment they are charged. We evaluate the outcome of a mechanism at *equilibrium*—that is, when no agent can improve their utility by unilaterally changing their bid, given the bids of the other agents. We measure the efficiency of a mechanism using the notion of the *price of anarchy*, which is defined as the ratio between the maximum possible social welfare (i.e., under an optimal allocation) and the social welfare achieved at the worst-case equilibrium.

1.1 Our Contribution

We propose a new mechanism that extends the proportional allocation paradigm introduced by Kelly [9] in settings with a single resource. The mechanism allocates to each agent the *maximum feasible amount of resources*, subject to proportionality based on their bid and demand vector. Despite this simplicity, the mechanism achieves strong efficiency guarantees. Specifically, we show that any equilibrium results in a social welfare that is at most a $(1+h^*)$-factor away from the optimum, where h^* is the optimal total *dominant share* – the sum of resources allocated to the most important resource in each bidder's demand. Moreover, we prove that this bound is *asymptotically tight*: there exist instances with linear valuation functions and binary demands where the price of anarchy is at least $h^*/2$. The quantity h^* is always smaller than both the number of agents n and the number of resources m, so a slightly weaker upper bound on the price of anarchy is $1 + \min\{n, m\}$.

We complement our theoretical analysis with an extensive experimental evaluation of several simple resource allocation mechanisms. Our main focus is the proportional mechanism along with natural variants and modifications. We also propose a greedy mechanism inspired by combinatorial auction theory [1], which prioritizes agents based on their bid-to-demand ratio. Across a diverse set of synthetic instances, we simulate the best-response dynamics of the mechanisms and measure their social welfare at equilibrium. Our results reveal that some of the proposed variants consistently outperform the baseline proportional mechanism in practice.

1.2 Related Work

The *proportional mechanism* was first introduced by Kelly [9] (see also the related discussion in [10]) as a simple and decentralized approach to resource sharing in networks, especially for elastic traffic such as bandwidth. It assumes that agents with concave utilities over a single divisible resource submit scalar bids, and a fraction of the resource that is proportional to each agent's bid is allocated accordingly. When agents are *price-anticipating*—that is, aware that their bids influence the market—strategic behavior may lead to inefficiency. Johari and Tsitsiklis [7] showed that, in such settings, the worst-case efficiency loss at equilibrium is bounded by a small constant: the price of anarchy is at most 4/3. A good introduction to the mechanism is given in [6], and its usage is further explained in [13]. Caragiannis and Voudouris [3] consider variations with incomplete information and present bounds on the price of anarchy over Bayes-Nash equilibria. Christodoulou et al. [4] extend this study to settings with multiple resources; they do not consider Leontief utilities, though.

The non-cooperative setting studied by Johari and Tsitsiklis [7] has received much attention. A first apparent question has been whether improved price of anarchy bounds are possible by changing the allocation function, but keeping the simple pay-your-bid payment rule. Sanghavi and Hajek [15] showed that no such mechanism has price of anarchy better than 8/7, designed an allocation function that achieves this bound for two players, and provided strong experimental evidence that a slightly inferior bound holds for arbitrarily many players. Surprisingly, full efficiency at equilibria (i.e., a price of stability equal to 1) is possible via different allocation/payment functions. This discovery was made in three independent papers by Maheswaran and Basar [12], Yang and Hajek [16], and Johari and Tsitsiklis [8]. The mechanism of Maheswaran and Basar [12] uses proportional allocation (but a different payment). Unfortunately, extending the mechanism to our setting seems very challenging. The mechanisms of Johari and Tsitsiklis [8] and Yang and Hajek [16] are adaptations of the well-known VCG paradigm (see also the survey by Johari [6] on these results). As such mechanisms have very inefficient equilibria (with unbounded price of anarchy), we do not consider them here.

Closely connected to our work is the literature on *dominant resource fairness (DRF)* [5], a prominent allocation rule in multi-resource settings. DRF is designed to ensure fairness by equalizing agents' shares of their most demanded (i.e., dominant) resource and has seen widespread adoption in cluster computing systems. In comparison, we consider mechanisms for high social welfare in non-cooperative settings with more complex preferences, where monetary transfers play a central role.

Also relevant to our work are recent papers that design optimal mechanisms for agents with Leontief preferences. The paper by Plaut [14] introduces a family of mechanisms that optimize a broad class of welfare functions under a relaxed form of Leontief preferences. However, their setting excludes the standard utilitarian social welfare objective, which is the focus of our work. Similarly, Brânzei et al. [2] study mechanisms for maximizing the Nash social welfare with Leontief utilities, which captures a balance between efficiency and fairness. Both of these approaches assume a different utility model from ours: the mechanisms operate with an artificial currency internal to the system, which has no external value for the agents. Our setting involves real money and is thus more aligned with market-based scenarios.

1.3 Roadmap

The rest of the paper is structured as follows. We begin with formal definitions in Sect. 2. We present the adaptation of the proportional mechanism to our setting in Sect. 3. The price of anarchy analysis follows in Sect. 4. We present our experimental analysis in Sect. 5. We conclude in Sect. 6.

2 Preliminaries

We denote vectors and matrices in boldface, using notation such as $\mathbf{b}$ (for bid vectors), $\mathbf{d}$ (for demand vectors), and $\mathbf{x}$ (for allocations). The ith component of a vector, e.g., $\mathbf{b}$ is written as b_i. For matrices, we use $\mathbf{d}_i$ to denote the ith row of $\mathbf{d}$, and d_{ij} to denote the entry in row i, column j.

Let $N = [n]$ and $M = [m]$ denote the sets of agents (or bidders) and resources, respectively. Each resource $j \in M$ is divisible and has a total supply of one unit. An allocation of resources to agents is an $n \times m$ matrix $\mathbf{x}$, where $x_{ij} \in [0, 1]$ denotes the fraction of resource j allocated to agent i. We denote by $\mathbf{x}_i$ the vector containing the fractions of resources agent i uses in allocation $\mathbf{x}$. An allocation $\mathbf{x}$ is feasible if $\sum_{i \in N} x_{ij} \leq 1$ for every resource $j \in M$ (i.e., no more than one unit in total of each resource is used).

Each agent $i \in N$ has a valuation function $v_i\colon [0,1]^m \to \mathbb{R}_{\geq 0}$, mapping each allocation $\mathbf{x}_i \in [0,1]^m$ to a non-negative value. We focus on the special case of *concave extensions of Leontief preferences* (CLP), where valuations take the form:

$$v_i(\mathbf{x}_i) = w_i\left(\max\{y \geq 0 : x_{ij} \geq y \cdot d_{ij}\ \forall j \in M\}\right),$$

with concave, nondecreasing functions w_i satisfying $w_i(0) = 0$, and demand vector $\mathbf{d}_i = (d_{i1}, \ldots, d_{im}) \in [0,1]^m$. For agents with Leontief preferences, we can assume, without loss of generality, that the demand vector is normalized, i.e., for each agent i there always exists some resource j such that $d_{ij} = 1$. We call such a resource a *dominant resource*[1] of agent i. It is not hard to see that $v_i(\mathbf{x}_i)$ is exactly the value agent i has for the proportion of its dominant resource under the allocation $\mathbf{x}$.

A mechanism takes as input the demand vectors $\mathbf{d} = (\mathbf{d}_1, ..., \mathbf{d}_n)$ and a bid vector $\mathbf{b} = (b_1, ..., b_n)$ consisting of the bid b_i that the mechanism elicits from each agent $i \in N$, and returns a feasible allocation $\mathbf{x}(\mathbf{b};\mathbf{d}) \in [0,1]^{n\times m}$. When the demands $\mathbf{d}$ are clear from context, we simply write $\mathbf{x}(\mathbf{b})$. We consider mechanisms which require each agent to pay their bid. Then, the utility of agent i is $u_i(\mathbf{b}) = v_i(x_i(\mathbf{b})) - b_i$.

A *pure Nash equilibrium (PNE)* of mechanism $x(\cdot)$ is a bid vector $\mathbf{b}$ satisfying

$$u_i(x_i(b_i, \mathbf{b}_{-i}; \mathbf{d})) \geq u_i(x_i(b_i', \mathbf{b}_{-i}; \mathbf{d})), \quad \forall b_i' \geq 0, \forall i \in N.$$

We usually refer to pure Nash equilibria simply as Nash equilibria. The set of Nash equilibria induced by instance I using mechanism x is denoted $E(I, x)$.

Given an allocation $\mathbf{x}$ and family of valuation functions $\mathcal{V} = \{v_i(\cdot)\}$, the *Social Welfare* is defined as $\mathrm{SW}(\mathbf{x}; \mathcal{V}) = \sum_{i \in N} v_i(\mathbf{x}_i)$. An allocation $\mathbf{x}^*$ is *socially optimal* if it maximizes the social welfare, i.e.,

$$\mathrm{SW}(\mathbf{x}^*; \mathcal{V}) = \max_{\mathbf{x} \in [0,1]^{n\times m}} \mathrm{SW}(\mathbf{x}; \mathcal{V}).$$

When valuations are clear from context, we write $\mathrm{SW}(\mathbf{x})$ instead of $\mathrm{SW}(\mathbf{x}, \mathcal{V})$.

The *price of anarchy (PoA)* of mechanism x is defined as

$$\mathrm{PoA} = \max_{I \in \mathcal{J}} \max_{\mathbf{b} \in E(I,x)} \frac{\mathrm{SW}(\mathbf{x}^*)}{\mathrm{SW}(\mathbf{x}(\mathbf{b}))}.$$

It quantifies the worst-case efficiency loss over all Nash equilibria and all instances.

Problem Definition. At this point, we are ready to define our problem formally. We are given a vector of bids $\mathbf{b}$ and matrix of demands $\mathbf{d} = (\mathbf{d}_1, ..., \mathbf{d}_n)$, and we want to find an allocation of the resources $\mathbf{x}(\mathbf{b}, \mathbf{d})$ with as low PoA as possible. Crucially, we lack knowledge of the concave functions $w_i(\cdot)$, and as a result, the true utility functions of the agents.

[1] Note that an agent might have multiple dominant resources; in that case, the agent should receive the same share for all of them.

For an instance $I = (N, M, \mathcal{V}, \mathbf{d})$ and an allocation $\mathbf{x} \in [0,1]^{n \times m}$, we define $\lambda_i(\mathbf{x}) = \min_j \frac{x_{ij}}{d_{ij}}$. Notice that $v_i(\mathbf{x}) = w_i(\lambda_i(\mathbf{x}_i))$. We will refer to $\lambda_i(\mathbf{x})$ as the *dominant resource share* of agent i. Of particular interest is also the quantity $\lambda_i^* = \lambda_i(\mathbf{x}^*)$, i.e., the dominant resource share of agent i at the socially optimal allocation. We will express the upper bound on the price of anarchy of the proportional mechanism in terms of the quantity h^* which denotes the sum of the dominant resource shares of all agents in the socially optimal allocation. We have

$$h^* = \sum_{i \in N} \lambda_i(\mathbf{x}^*) \leq n$$

and, denoting by r_i the dominant resource of agent i,

$$h^* = \sum_{i \in N} \lambda_i(\mathbf{x}^*) \leq \sum_{i \in N} x^*_{ir_i} = \sum_{j \in M} \sum_{i \in N : r_i = j} x^*_{ij} \leq m.$$

Hence, $h^* \leq \min\{n, m\}$. Intuitively, h^* is the total allocation that agents receive on their most demanded resources under the socially optimum allocation.

3 The Proportional Mechanism

In this section, we adapt the proportional mechanism to our setting with multiple resources. Given the demand vector $\mathbf{d} = (\mathbf{d}_1, ..., \mathbf{d}_n)$ and bid vector $\mathbf{b} = (b_1, ..., b_n)$, the mechanism computes the allocation $\mathbf{x}(\mathbf{b}; \mathbf{d})$ as follows (from now on, we use x_{ij} instead of $x_{ij}(\mathbf{b}; \mathbf{d})$):

$$x_{ij} = \alpha \frac{b_i \cdot d_{ij}}{\sum_{r \in N} b_r}, \tag{1}$$

where α is a scaling factor defined as

$$\alpha = \min_{k \in M} \frac{\sum_{i \in N} b_i}{\sum_{i \in N} b_i \cdot d_{ik}}. \tag{2}$$

Example 1. Let $\mathbf{b} = (2, 1, 1)$, $\mathbf{d}_1 = (1, 1, 1)$, $\mathbf{d}_2 = (1, 1/3, 0)$ and $\mathbf{d}_3 = (0, 1, 1)$. Then, the proportional mechanism sets $\alpha = 6/5$, assigns fractions $3/5$, $3/10$, and $3/10$ to the dominant resources of the three agents, and fractions scaled appropriately according to the demands in the other resources. The allocation is depicted in Table 1.

The following observations are simple yet useful for the technical parts of the upcoming sections.

Observation 1. *Any allocation returned by the proportional mechanism is feasible.*

Table 1. The allocation returned by the proportional mechanism for $\mathbf{b} = (2, 1, 1)$ and $\mathbf{d}_1 = (1, 1, 1)$, $\mathbf{d}_2 = (1, 1/3, 0)$, $\mathbf{d}_3 = (0, 1, 1)$. The fraction of the dominant resources the agents get are proportional to their bids.

	resource 1	resource 2	resource 3
agent 1	$\frac{3}{5}$	$\frac{3}{5}$	$\frac{3}{5}$
agent 2	$\frac{3}{10}$	$\frac{1}{10}$	0
agent 3	0	$\frac{3}{10}$	$\frac{3}{10}$

Proof. Let $j \in M$ be a resource. Then, by the definition of the proportional mechanism, we have

$$\sum_{i \in N} x_{ij} = \alpha \cdot \sum_{i \in N} \frac{b_i \cdot d_{ij}}{\sum_{r \in N} b_r} = \min_{k \in M} \frac{\sum_{i \in N} b_i}{\sum_{i \in N} b_i \cdot d_{ik}} \cdot \sum_{i \in N} \frac{b_i \cdot d_{ij}}{\sum_{r \in N} b_r} \leq 1,$$

as desired. □

Observation 2. *The scaling factor α is always at least 1.*

Proof. Since $d_{ik} \leq 1$ for all $i \in N, k \in M$, it follows that $\sum_{i=1}^{n} b_i d_{ik} \leq \sum_{i=1}^{n} b_i$. Substituting into Eq. (2) gives $\alpha \geq 1$. □

Observe that $\alpha = 1$ specifically when

$$\max_{k \in M} \sum_{i \in N} b_i \cdot d_{ik} = \sum_{i \in N} b_i,$$

i.e., when all agents have the same resource as dominant, in which case the proportional mechanism reduces to the single-resource proportional mechanism.

Observation 3. *For bidders with CLP preferences, the utility at bids* $\mathbf{b}$ *satisfies*

$$v_i(\mathbf{x}(\mathbf{b})) = w_i\Big(\alpha \frac{b_i}{\sum_{r \in N} b_r}\Big). \tag{3}$$

Proof. Recall that, for CLP valuations, it holds

$$v_i(\mathbf{x}) = w_i\Big(\max\{y \geq 0 : x_{ij} \geq y \cdot d_{ij},\ \forall j \in M\}\Big).$$

Substituting $x_{ij} = \alpha \cdot \frac{b_i \cdot d_{ij}}{\sum_{r \in N} b_r}$, we get

$$\max\{y \geq 0 : \alpha \cdot \frac{b_i \cdot d_{ij}}{\sum_{r \in N} b_r} \geq y \cdot d_{ij},\ \forall j \in M\} = \alpha \cdot \frac{b_i}{\sum_{r \in N} b_r},$$

and the claim follows. □

We remark that an alternative way to see why Observation 3 is true is to show that $\lambda_i = \alpha \cdot \frac{b_i}{\sum_{r \in N} b_r}$.

4 Price of Anarchy Analysis

In this section, we prove the upper and lower bound on the price of anarchy of the proportional mechanism. We begin with the upper bound.

Theorem 4. *The proportional mechanism achieves a price of anarchy of at most* $1 + h^* \leq 1 + \min\{n, m\}$ *for the family of CLP valuation functions.*

Proof. Let $\mathbf{b} \in E(I)$ be a pure Nash equilibrium of the proportional mechanism at the instance I and denote by $\mathbf{x}(\mathbf{b}; \mathbf{d})$ the returned allocation. Let $\mathbf{x}^*$ be the socially optimal allocation. Recall that λ_i^* is the dominant resource share of agent $i \in N$ in the socially optimal allocation and that $\sum_{i \in N} \lambda_i^* = h^*$.

We define $B = \sum_{i \in N} b_i$ and $B_{-i} = B - b_i$ for $i \in N$. Consider the deviating bid for agent i defined as $b_i' = \frac{\lambda_i^*}{h} \cdot B_{-i}$. Since $\mathbf{b}$ is a Nash equilibrium, no agent $i \in N$ has any incentive to deviate unilaterally to strategy b_i', i.e.,

$$u_i(b_i, \mathbf{b}_{-i}) \geq u_i(b_i', \mathbf{b}_{-i}) = u_i\Big(\lambda_i^* \cdot \tfrac{B_{-i}}{h^*}, \mathbf{b}_{-i}\Big), \tag{4}$$

for every agent $i \in N$. Let $a_i = \alpha(b_i', \mathbf{b}_{-i})$ be the scaling factor for the bidding profile $(b_i, \mathbf{b}_{-i})$. By the definition of the proportional mechanism and agent utility, we have

$$\begin{aligned} u_i\Big(\lambda_i^* \cdot \tfrac{B_{-i}}{h^*}, b_{-i}\Big) &= w_i\Big(a_i \cdot \tfrac{\lambda_i^* B_{-i}/h^*}{\lambda_i^* B_{-i}/h^* + B_{-i}}\Big) - \frac{\lambda_i^* B_{-i}}{h^*} \\ &= w_i\Big(a_i \cdot \tfrac{\lambda_i^*/h^*}{\lambda_i^*/h^*+1}\Big) - \frac{\lambda_i^* B_{-i}}{h^*} \\ &\geq w_i\Big(\tfrac{\lambda_i^*/h^*}{\lambda_i^*/h^*+1}\Big) - \frac{\lambda_i^* \cdot B}{h^*} \end{aligned} \tag{5}$$

The last inequality follows by monotonicity of the function w_i and since $a_i \geq 1$ by Observation 2, and since $B_i \leq B$.

Now, notice that the social welfare of the allocation $\mathbf{x}$ returned by the proportional mechanism can be expressed as the sum of all agents' utilities and bids. Thus, using inequalities (4) and (5), the fact $\sum_{i \in N} \lambda_i^* = h^*$, and the definition of B, we get

$$\begin{aligned} \mathrm{SW}(\mathbf{x}) &= \sum_{i \in N} u_i(b_i, \mathbf{b}_{-i}) + \sum_{i \in N} b_i \\ &\geq \sum_{i \in N} w_i\Big(\tfrac{\lambda_i^*/h^*}{\lambda_i^*/h^*+1}\Big) - \sum_{i \in N} \frac{\lambda_i^* \cdot B}{h^*} + \sum_{i \in N} b_i \\ &= \sum_{i \in N} w_i\Big(\tfrac{\lambda_i^*/h^*}{\lambda_i^*/h^*+1}\Big). \end{aligned} \tag{6}$$

Using Eq. (6), inequality (5) yields

$$\mathrm{SW}(\mathbf{x}) \geq \frac{1}{h^*+1} \cdot \sum_{i \in N} w_i(\lambda_i^*) = \frac{1}{h^*+1} \cdot \mathrm{SW}(\mathbf{x}^*),$$

which, along with the fact that $h^* \leq \min\{n, m\}$, completes the proof. □

We now present our lower bound, which shows that the analysis of the previous theorem is tight up to a constant factor.

Theorem 5. *The proportional mechanism has a price of anarchy of at least $m/2$.*

Proof. We show that the following construction leads to a price of anarchy of at least $m/2$. The lower bound construction uses linear valuation functions over Leontief preferences and normalized demands $d_{ij} \in \{0,1\}$ for all $i \in N, j \in M$. Hence, the valuation can be expressed as a multiplicative weight over the dominant resource.

In the construction, we consider a set L of m bidders who are single-minded, i.e., they want a single resource and only that resource. More precisely, for each $i \in L$, the demand vector satisfies $d_{i,i} = 1$ and $d_{i,j} = 0$ for any $j \neq i$. The valuation for these bidders is $v_i = 1$.

A second set S of k bidders each wants all resources, i.e., for each $i \in S$, the demand vector is $d_{i,j} = 1$ for all $j \in [k]$. These bidders have a common valuation $v_i(y) = v \cdot y$ for some $v \in [0,1)$.

Let $\mathbf{b}$ be a pure Nash equilibrium of the proportional mechanism on the instance described above. Due to symmetry, we can assume that all bidders in L bid b_L, and all bidders in S bid b_S. We can safely break this game into m parallel games, one per resource: in each of these games, one bidder in L and all bidders in S compete for the i-th resource.

Consider a bidder $i \in S$. Then,

$$u_i(b_i, \mathbf{b}_{-i}) = v \cdot \frac{b_i}{b_i + b_L + (k-1)b_S} - b_i.$$

Taking the derivative with respect to b_i and setting it to 0,

$$\frac{v \cdot (b_L + (k-1)b_S)}{(b_L + kb_S)^2} - 1 = 0 \quad \Rightarrow \quad \frac{v \cdot b_L}{(b_L + kb_S)^2} = 1. \tag{7}$$

Now consider a bidder $i \in L$. We have

$$u_i(b_i, \mathbf{b}_{-i}) = \frac{b_i}{b_i + kb_S} - b_i.$$

Taking the derivative with respect to b_i and setting it to 0, we get

$$\frac{kb_S}{(b_i + kb_S)^2} - 1 = 0 \quad \Rightarrow \quad \frac{b_L}{b_L + kb_S} = \frac{1}{\sqrt{kb_S}} \tag{8}$$

Solving the two Eqs. (7) and (8), we get that the equilibrium bids are

$$b_L = z, \quad b_S = \frac{v}{k + v - kv} \cdot z$$

for some $z \neq 0$. This implies that

$$\lambda_i = \frac{b_S}{kb_S + b_L} = \frac{z \cdot \frac{v}{k+v-kv}}{kz \cdot \frac{v}{k+v-kv} + z} = \frac{v}{k+v}$$

for any $i \in S$, and

$$\lambda_i = \frac{b_L}{b_L + kb_S} = \frac{z}{z + kz \cdot \frac{v}{k+v-kv}} = \frac{k+v-kv}{k+v},$$

for $i \in L$.

Notice that due to the proportional allocation of the mechanism, the term z cancels out and does not affect the allocation. For $\mathbf{b}$ to be an equilibrium, however, we need to ensure that $u_i(\mathbf{b}) \geq 0$ for all agents; otherwise, it is better for any agent to bid 0. That is, for any agent $i \in S$:

$$u_i(\mathbf{b}) = v \cdot \lambda_i - b_S = v \cdot \frac{v}{k+v} - \frac{v}{k+v-kv} \cdot z \geq 0$$

which implies, by rearrangement:

$$z \leq \frac{v(k+v-kv)}{k+v} = v \cdot \lambda_L$$

Similarly, for any $i \in L$:

$$u_i(\mathbf{b}) = \lambda_i - b_L = \frac{k+v-kv}{k+v} - z$$

which by rearrangement implies:

$$z \leq \frac{k+v-kv}{k+v} = \lambda_L$$

Since $v < 1$, the value z must lie in $(0, \lambda_L]$.

Hence, the social welfare at equilibrium is:

$$\begin{aligned} \mathrm{SW}^{\mathrm{EQ}} &= \sum_{i \in S} v \cdot \lambda_i + \sum_{i \in L} \lambda_i = k \cdot \frac{v^2}{k+v} + k \cdot \frac{k+v-kv}{k+v} \\ &= \frac{kv^2 + k(k+v-kv)}{k+v} \end{aligned}$$

We can bound the optimum social welfare by considering the allocation in which all bidders in L are assigned a whole resource each, i.e., $\mathrm{SW}^* \geq m$. Hence,

$$\mathrm{PoA} = \frac{\mathrm{SW}^*}{\mathrm{SW}^{\mathrm{EQ}}} \geq \frac{m}{\frac{kv^2+k(k+v-kv)}{k+v}} = \frac{m(k+v)}{kv^2 + k(k+v-kv)}$$

Setting $v = 1 - \frac{1}{m^2}$ and $k = m$, the price of anarchy becomes:

$$\mathrm{PoA} = \frac{m^2(m^3 + m^2 - m)}{2m^4 + m^3 - 3m^2 + 1} \geq m/2,$$

and the theorem follows. □

We remark that the particular construction in the proof of Theorem 5 satisfies $h^* = m$ and, hence, the proof implies an asymptotically optimal lower bound of $h^*/2$ on the price of anarchy.

5 Experimental Analysis

In this section, we present an experimental analysis[2] of our proposed mechanism and some natural extensions. The results indicate that the proportional mechanism often performs better in practice than its worst-case guarantees suggest. Additionally, we identify a natural extension that consistently outperforms the standard proportional mechanism across most scenarios.

5.1 Experimental Design

In our experiments, we test the performance of several mechanisms following a pay-your-bid strategy, with respect to price of anarchy, over a set of randomly generated inputs. Each input $I_{n,m,k}$ is parameterized by the number of agents n, the number of resources m, and a repetition index $k \in \{1, \dots, 50\}$, corresponding to independent random draws. For each fixed pair (n, m), we compute the price of anarchy for each of the 50 instances and report the average across all values.

To measure the price of anarchy, we simulate best-response dynamics. Agents are updated sequentially: at each step, a single agent chooses the bid that maximizes her utility. When no agent can further improve, the process converges to a pure Nash equilibrium. We discard instances where best-response dynamics fail to converge within a fixed iteration limit. Then, for each instance, we compute the optimal welfare by solving a convex program using agents' true utility and demand vectors.

5.2 Mechanisms

We evaluate the performance of several mechanisms, including the standard proportional mechanism, some natural extensions, and a greedy baseline.

The first mechanism we compare against is the proportional mechanism, exactly as described in Sect. 3. In addition, we evaluate two natural variants, which we refer to as proportional to squares and proportional to square roots. More precisely, in these two versions, the allocation becomes:

$$x_{ij} = \alpha \frac{b_i^2}{\sum_{r=1}^n b_r^2} d_{ij} \quad \textbf{and} \quad x_{ij} = \alpha \frac{b_i^{1/2}}{\sum_{r=1}^n b_r^{1/2}} d_{ij},$$

respectively. All other elements of the mechanism, including the scaling factor α and the payment rule, remain identical to those of the proportional mechanism.

Second, we expand the proportional mechanism towards demand-inspired discounts on their bid. Let $c_i \geq 1$ be a discounting factor per agent, which we will specify in a moment. The proportional mechanism with discounts allocates

$$x_{ij} = \alpha \frac{b_i/c_i}{\sum_{r=1}^n b_r} d_{ij}, \text{ with } \alpha = \min_{k \in M} \left\{ \frac{\sum_{i=1}^n b_i}{\sum_{i=1}^n b_i \cdot \frac{d_{ik}}{c_i}} \right\}$$

[2] The code used for the analysis is hosted in https://tinyurl.com/Proportional Leontief.

and the agents pay their bid b_i. Observe that the scaling factor α differs slightly from the proportional mechanism. We explore three versions: (1) $c_i = \sum_{j=1}^{m} d_{ij}$, (2) $c_i = \sqrt{\sum_{j=1}^{m} d_{ij}}$, and (3) $c_i = \sqrt{\sum_{j=1}^{m} d_{ij}^2}$. The first option discounts bids by the agent's total demand, the second applies a softer discount via the square root of the total demand, and the third scales bids according to the agent's ℓ_2 norm of demand.

As a third option, we develop a greedy idea, inspired by a celebrated result of Lehmann et al. [11] for combinatorial auctions. The core idea is to prioritize agents who bid high, relative to their overall demand. Specifically, agents are ranked in descending order of the ratio

$$\frac{b_i}{\sum_{j=1}^{m} d_{ij}},$$

which reflects how much value each agent offers per unit of total demand. The algorithm visits agents in this order and allocates to each the *maximum feasible multiple* λ_i of their demand vector $\mathbf{d}_i$, given the current availability of resources. That is, each agent receives the largest allocation $\lambda_i \cdot \mathbf{d}_i$ such that no resource constraint is violated. The available resources are updated accordingly, and the process continues with the next agent. Each agent receiving non-zero quantity pays their bid, while the rest pay 0.

5.3 Instances

We implement a variety of instance types using synthetic data to capture different scenarios. We create the data using two independent procedures. At first we create valuation functions for the agents. We have opted to use only linear valuation functions (i.e. of the form $w_i \cdot x_i$) in our experiments due to their simplicity, the cleaner and faster code they induce and the fact that they are known to be worst-case in the proportional mechanism[3]. For the sake of simplicity we sample weights w_i uniformly in $[0, 50]$.

Our second—and more elaborate—data generation procedure concerns the construction of the demand vectors $\mathbf{d}_i$. The first scenario is again the uniform creation of such demands, i.e. each $\mathbf{d}_i \in [0,1]^m$ with equal probability. A second scenario we implement is inspired by the worst-case instance we have found for the proportional mechanism. Hence, we implement *wide* $\mathbf{d}_i$, whose demand for all resources is high and *narrow* $\mathbf{d}_i$ which have high demand for few resources and very low demand for the rest. We have two versions of the narrow demands – a case where the number of large demands is selected uniformly at random, and the case where the number of large elements is a fixed percentage of m. In both cases, the exact resources with high and low demand are selected independently and uniformly at random.

[3] Johari and Tsitsiklis [7] have proven this formally for the case of a single resource, and our worst-case scenario also uses valuation functions.

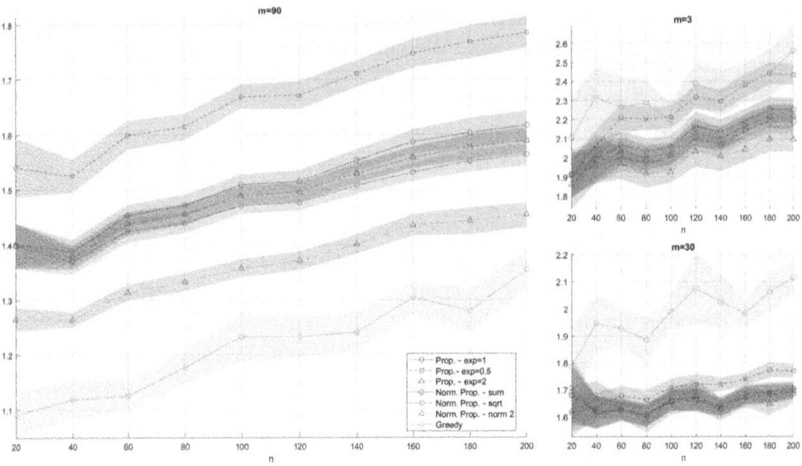

Fig. 1. Average price of anarchy (PoA) as a function of the number of agents n, under uniform demands. Results are averaged over 50 random instances. The y-axis shows PoA (lower is better); the x-axis shows the number of agents. Error bars represent 95% confidence intervals. Number of resources: $m = 90$ (large graph), $m = 30$ (small graph, bottom), and $m = 3$ (small graph, top).

5.4 Best Response Dynamics

We implement best-response dynamics using a grid-based method. In each iteration, agents are visited in random order. When an agent is selected, they evaluate their utility across a fixed set of bid values, chosen uniformly from the interval $[0, v_i]$, where v_i is the agent's valuation. The agent then selects the bid that yields the highest utility among the grid points, provided it improves their current utility by more than a small threshold. The process repeats until no agent can improve their utility significantly, or a maximum number of iterations is reached. This method guarantees that each update corresponds to a best response within the discretized bid space. We (informally) argue that the interval $[0, v_i]$ contains all possible equilibrium strategies for any agent in all the mechanisms we use. First, by convention we can set any $b_i < 0$ to yield zero utility to any agent. Also, notice that any bid $b_i > v_i$ is dominated by $b_i = 0$, since the best utility an agent can ever expect is v_i, and such a large bid will ensure negative utility, while bidding $b_i = 0$ yields a utility of 0. A high-level pseudocode of this procedure is shown in Algorithm 1.

5.5 Evaluation

We evaluate the mechanisms experimentally with respect to the price of anarchy of the equilibria reached. We present indicative results in Fig. 1. Due to space restrictions, most experiments are deferred in the full version of the paper. The mechanisms fall into three groups, which we also use to guide our visualizations.

Algorithm 1. Best-Response Dynamics

Require: Profile $\mathbf{d}$; valuations $\mathbf{v} \in \mathbb{R}^n_{\geq 0}$; integers K (max iterations), G (grid points); tolerance $\tau > 0$

Ensure: Final bids $\mathbf{b}^\star$, final allocation $\mathbf{x}^\star$, convergence flag

```
Initialize feasible bids b ∈ [0, max_{i∈N} v_i]^n        ▷ e.g., uniformly at random in [0, v_i]
x ← ApplyMechanism(b; d);   u ← ComputeUtility(x, d, v)
converged ← FALSE
for k = 1 to T do
    updates ← 0;   π ← random permutation of {1, ..., n}
    for each i ∈ π do
        T_i ← uniform grid over [0, v_i] with G points
        u^best ← u_i;   t^best ← b_i
        for each t' ∈ T_i do
            b^tmp ← b;   b_i^tmp ← t'
            x' ← ApplyMechanism(b^tmp; d) ; u' ← ComputeUtility(x', d, v)
            if u'_i − u^best > τ then
                u^best ← u'_i;   t^best ← t'                  ▷ possible best response
            end if
        end for
        if u^best − u_i > τ then
            b_i ← t^best                                      ▷ best response found
            x ← ApplyMechanism(b; d);   u ← ComputeUtility(x, d, v)
            updates ← updates + 1
        end if
    end for
    if updates = 0 then
        converged ← TRUE; break                               ▷ PNE found and exit
    end if
end for
b* ← b, x* ← x
```

The first group, shown in blue tones, includes the proportional mechanism and its two nonlinear variants: proportional to squares and proportional to square roots. The second group, shown in red tones, consists of three discounted versions of the proportional mechanism, where bids of agents with large demand vectors are scaled down. Finally, the third group includes the Greedy mechanism described earlier, shown in yellow tones. For each mechanism, we simulate best-response dynamics over three scenarios. We fix the number of resources to three representative values: $m = 3$, $m = 30$, and $m = 90$. We plot the average, over the iterations, PoA for instances of the same number of agents.

Our experimental evaluation supports and complements the theoretical findings. In particular, the observed average price of anarchy (PoA) for the proportional mechanism consistently remains well below the conservative upper bound of $1 + \min\{n, m\}$, especially as the number of agents or resources increases.

Our experiments also highlight several broader insights. While it is not surprising that different mechanisms perform better in different types of instances, our results provide concrete illustrations of these trade-offs. The proportional with discounts family of mechanisms shows remarkably stable performance across all experimental settings. Within the proportional mechanism family, we find that the proportional to squares variant consistently outperforms the others across all scenarios, and it is never outperformed. On the other hand, the proportional to square root mechanism tends to under-perform relative to the rest, regardless of the instance type. Finally, the Greedy mechanism performs quite well in the uniform instances, especially when resources are few compared to the number of agents, indicating a possible mechanism for further exploration.

6 Discussion and Open Problems

In this work, we extended the proportional mechanism to multi-resource settings with Leontief preferences, which naturally capture complementarities among resources. We established that the mechanism's price of anarchy is proportional to h^*, the sum of all agents' dominant shares in the socially optimal solution. Our experiments further showed that, although the theoretical bounds can be pessimistic, the original mechanism and several natural variants can be much more efficient in practice.

Several directions remain open. A central challenge is to determine whether mechanisms with sublinear price of anarchy—either in the number of agents or in the number of resources—are possible, or whether strong impossibility results rule them out under limited expressiveness. Another important direction is to tighten the analysis of the proportional mechanism itself: our current bounds leave a constant gap that likely requires more refined arguments to close. Finally, extending the experimental evaluation to real-world data would help assess the practical relevance of our findings and highlight concrete application domains.

Acknowledgments. This work has been partially supported by project MIS 5154714 of the National Recovery and Resilience Plan Greece 2.0 funded by the European Union under the NextGenerationEU Program. It has also been supported by the Hellenic Foundation for Research and Innovation (H.F.R.I.) under the "2nd Call for H.F.R.I. Research Projects to support Faculty Members & Researchers" (Project Number: 02440).

References

1. Blumrosen, L., Nisan, N.: Combinatorial auctions. In: Nisan, N., Roughgarden, T., Tardos, E., Vazirani, V.V. (eds.) Algorithmic Game Theory, pp. 267–300. Cambridge University Press (2007)
2. Brânzei, S., Gkatzelis, V., Mehta, R.: Nash social welfare approximation for strategic agents. Oper. Res. **70**(1), 402–415 (2022)
3. Caragiannis, I., Voudouris, A.A.: Welfare guarantees for proportional allocations. Theory Comput. Syst. **59**(4), 581–599 (2016)

4. Christodoulou, G., Sgouritsa, A., Tang, B.: On the efficiency of the proportional allocation mechanism for divisible resources. Theory Comput. Syst. **59**(4), 600–618 (2016)
5. Ghodsi, A., Zaharia, M., Hindman, B., Konwinski, A., Shenker, S., Stoica, I.: Dominant resource fairness: fair allocation of multiple resource types. In: Proceedings of the 8th USENIX Symposium on Networked Systems Design and Implementation (NSDI), Boston, MA, USA (2011)
6. Johari, R.: The price of anarchy and the design of scalable resource allocation mechanisms. In: Nisan, N., Roughgarden, T., Tardos, É., Vazirani, V.V. (eds.) Algorithmic Game Theory, pp. 543–568. Cambridge University Press (2007)
7. Johari, R., Tsitsiklis, J.N.: Efficiency loss in a network resource allocation game. Math. Oper. Res. **29**(3), 407–435 (2004)
8. Johari, R., Tsitsiklis, J.N.: Efficiency of scalar-parameterized mechanisms. Oper. Res. **57**(4), 823–839 (2009)
9. Kelly, F.: Charging and rate control for elastic traffic. Eur. Trans. Telecommun. **8**(1), 33–37 (1997)
10. Kelly, F.P., Maulloo, A.K., Tan, D.K.H.: Rate control for communication networks: shadow prices, proportional fairness and stability. J. Oper. Res. Soc. **49**(3), 237–252 (1998)
11. Lehmann, D., O'Callaghan, L.I., Shoham, Y.: Truth revelation in approximately efficient combinatorial auctions. J. Assoc. Comput. Mach. **49**(5), 577–602 (2002)
12. Maheswaran, R.T., Başar, T.: Efficient signal proportional allocation (ESPA) mechanisms: decentralized social welfare maximization for divisible resources. IEEE J. Sel. Areas Commun. **24**(5), 1000–1009 (2006)
13. Ozdaglar, A., Srikant, R.: Incentives and pricing in communications networks. In: Nisan, N., Roughgarden, T., Tardos, É., Vazirani, V.V. (eds.) Algorithmic Game Theory, pp. 571–592. Cambridge University Press (2007)
14. Plaut, B.: Optimal Nash equilibria for bandwidth allocation. In: Web and Internet Economics - 16th International Conference (WINE), Beijing, China (2020)
15. Sanghavi, S., Hajek, B.E.: Optimal allocation of a divisible good to strategic buyers. In: 43rd IEEE Conference on Decision and Control (CDC), pp. 2748–2753. IEEE (2004)
16. Yang, S., Hajek, B.E.: VCG-Kelly mechanisms for allocation of divisible goods: adapting VCG mechanisms to one-dimensional signals. IEEE J. Sel. Areas Commun. **25**(6), 1237–1243 (2007)

Explaining Why Fair Roommate Matchings Do Not Exist

Wassila Ouerdane, Francesco Sabatino(✉), and Anaëlle Wilczynski

MICS, CentraleSupélec, Université Paris-Saclay, Gif-Sur-Yvette, France
{wassila.ouerdane,francesco.sabatino,
anaelle.wilczynski}@centralesupelec.fr

Abstract. In this article, we investigate the explainability of the fair roommate matching problem, where pairs of agents must be formed based on their ordinal preferences and where the existence of a fair matching is not guaranteed. We focus on explaining instances where rank-envy-free matchings—a relaxation of envy-freeness—do not exist. Our goal is to provide short and easy-to-understand explanations for users. To this end, we propose three formulations of our roommate problem as instances of the Boolean satisfiability problem (SAT) and compare their properties. We then generate explanations derived from Minimal Unsatisfiable Subsets (MUSes) for all formulations by adapting an existing explainability procedure recently introduced in the context of a fair division problem. Our adaptation uses a sequential algorithm to avoid redundant arguments in the explanation that can happen in the initial procedure, but its efficiency depends on chosen arguments at each step. These choices are guided by proposed heuristics. We conduct experiments to empirically evaluate our heuristics, compare our SAT formulations as well as the MUSes we choose to derive explanations.

Keywords: Roommate matching · Fairness · Explainability

1 Introduction

Many real-life problems involve collective decisions affecting people's lives, such as elections, task or resource allocation in organizations, and student-university assignments. These decisions are usually centralized, with a central authority collecting agents' preferences, computing a solution, and communicating the outcome. Two key aspects are crucial in this process: ensuring the solution is *fair* according to agents' preferences, and providing clear *explanations* to build trust and acceptance. As AI increasingly drives decision-making, explainability becomes essential to maintain users' confidence in algorithmic outcomes [1].

Explaining the decisions of AI systems has become a central goal of Explainable AI (XAI) [16], aiming to make the reasoning behind algorithmic outcomes understandable, as users increasingly ask 'Why?'. While much of the focus has been on machine learning systems [1,5], explainability is equally crucial in

M. Baldoni et al. (Eds.): EUMAS 2025, LNAI 16259, pp. 68–86, 2026.
https://doi.org/10.1007/978-3-032-22820-8_5

other domains. In particular, collective decision making—where outcomes affect groups of agents—raises growing concerns about transparency, accountability, and shared understanding in social choice contexts [26,31].

Matching under Preferences [21] are pervasive problems in collective decision making, with applications in project assignment, housing and job markets, or school choice. In this article, we focus on the *roommate matching* problem [20], where the goal is to form pairs of agents while considering their preferences over potential partners. Such scenarios arise naturally when pairing students or employees for group work, or when assigning roommates in student housing. While stability issues have been extensively studied since the seminal work of Irving [20], fairness is also a key requirement—especially when agent communication is limited—to mitigate dissatisfaction from perceived inequality or exclusion. A classical fairness concept is *envy-freeness* [14], which imposes that each agent weakly prefers her own partner over any other agent's partner. However, in the context of roommate matchings with strict ordinal preferences, this condition becomes overly demanding, effectively requiring each agent to be matched with her top choice. A suitable relaxation in this setting is to avoid rank-based envy: no agent should prefer another agent's partner over her own if she has ranked that partner higher in her preference list. This notion has been explored in several matching contexts [17,22,29], and was formally introduced as a fairness criterion under the name *rank-envy-freeness* by Belahcene et al. [2] for ordinal fair division, and later extended to roommate matchings by Coutance et al. [12].

Explainability in collective decision making has been mainly investigated for voting problems [6,7,11,27]. The aim is to produce human-readable explanations that trace outcomes back to underlying assumptions (axioms) [28], or to use axioms to determine whether a decision is even entailed [30]. More recently, explainability has also been explored in the context of fair division [4,18,25,33]. In particular, Beynier et al. [4] focus on the specific matching problem of house allocation, where agents are assigned individual items. Their study investigates how to explain why no allocation can satisfy local envy-freeness [3]—a graph-based relaxation of envy-freeness. In contrast, to the best of our knowledge, explainability in agent matchings has received little attention. Notable exceptions include Loustalot [23], who studied justifications in the two-sided marriage setting, and Cabalar et al. [10], who proposed a preliminary taxonomy of explanations for the stable roommates problem.

In this article, we investigate the explainability of rank-envy-freeness in roommate matchings, focusing on cases where no rank-envy-free matchings exist. Although the decision problem for the existence of rank-envy-free matchings is already guided by axioms [28], as common in computational social choice [9], it does not directly provide an explanation which is understandable by human users. Therefore, we aim to derive explanations that are compact, easy-to-understand, and natural for human agents. Our approach takes inspiration from Beynier et al. [4], by encoding both structural and rank-envy-freeness constraints as a Boolean satisfiability (SAT) problem. When the instance is unsatisfiable, we extract a minimal unsatisfiable subset (MUS), which we represent using a graph structure that highlights the implication relationships between its clauses. We propose three different SAT formulations for our fair roommate matching problem and adapt the algorithm of Beynier et al. [4] to derive an explanation from the MUS graph. Our algorithm sequentially generates explanations by activating" selected graph nodes associated with clauses in the MUS. This approach reduces redundancy in the textual output but relies on the strategy used for node selection. We propose several heuristics to guide this process and empirically evaluate them on synthetic data, considering the different SAT formulations and multiple MUS selection strategies.

Our approach aligns with a broader tradition of applying Boolean satisfiability (SAT) solvers to prove impossibility theorems in social choice theory [15,32]. Recent studies have also examined the complexity of generating explanations based on logical formulations [6,8,27], or use heuristic methods to efficiently derive explanations [24]. However, to our knowledge, no one has yet focused on the roommate matching setting. Note nevertheless that, beyond explainability, Erdem et al. [13] have used a logical programming paradigm by encoding the stable roommates problem into Answer Set Programming.

2 SAT Formulation of Rank-Envy-Freeness

For any positive integer k, let $[k]$ denote the set $\{1, \ldots, k\}$. We are given a set $N := [n]$ of n agents, where n is even. Each agent $i \in N$ has strict ordinal preferences over the other agents expressed as a linear order $\succ_i$ over $N \setminus \{i\}$. The set of all agents' preference orders is called a preference profile, denoted by $\succ$. A roommate instance is given as a pair $(N, \succ)$. Our goal is to find a complete matching over the agents given as an involution $\sigma : N \to N$ where $\sigma(i) \in N \setminus \{i\}$ is the assigned partner of agent i in matching σ.

In this article, our focus is on *fair* matchings. As a measure of fairness, we propose to consider a relaxation of *envy-freeness*—where no agent should prefer the partner of another agent—by taking into account the rank of the envied partner in the justification of envy. For each agent $i \in N$, the rank of agent $j \in N \setminus \{i\}$ in agent i's preferences is denoted by $r_i(j)$ and is given by $r_i(j) := |\{\ell \in N \setminus \{i\} : \ell \succeq_i j\}|$. Moreover, for each agent $i \in N$, the set of agents ranking agent i as their most preferred agent is denoted by $top(i)$, i.e., $top(i) := \{j \in N \setminus \{i\} : r_j(i) = 1\}$. We denote by T the set of agents who are ranked first by at least one agent, i.e., $T := \{i \in N : top(i) \neq \emptyset\}$. More precisely, we will use the notion of *rank-envy-freeness* [2,12], which forbids situations with *rank-envy*, where an agent i prefers the partner of another agent j to her own partner, whereas i has ranked the partner of j better than what j does.

Definition 1 (Rank-envy-freeness (r-EF)). *A matching σ is said to be rank-envy-free (r-EF) if $\sigma(i) \succ_i \sigma(j)$ or $r_j(\sigma(j)) \leq r_i(\sigma(j))$, for all agents $i, j \in N$.*

An r-EF roommate matching does not always exist, and the associated decision problem is NP-complete [12]. We propose to formulate the problem of the existence of an r-EF roommate matching as a satisfiability problem. We consider $\frac{n(n-1)}{2}$ Boolean variables x_{ij} to represent a roommate matching σ, i.e., $x_{ij} = \top$ iff $\sigma(i) = j$, for every $i, j \in [n]$ where $i < j$. We directly incorporate the symmetry property of roommate matchings, i.e., $\sigma(i) = j$ implies $\sigma(j) = i$, in the definition of the variables by only defining x_{ij} and not x_{ji}, which allows us to reduce the number of variables and clauses. We nevertheless abuse of the notation by interchangeably writing x_{ij} or x_{ji} to refer to x_{ij} where $i < j$.

We first encode the structural constraints of bijection for roommate matchings: each agent should be assigned to at least one partner and an agent cannot be assigned to more than one partner.

$$\phi_N^{atleast} := \bigwedge_{i\in N} \phi_N^{atleast}(i) \text{ and } \phi_N^{atmost} := \bigwedge_{i\in N}\ \bigwedge_{j\in N, i<j}\ \bigwedge_{p\in N\setminus\{i,j\}} \phi_N^{atmost}(\{i,j\},p)$$

$$\text{with} \quad \phi_N^{atleast}(i) := \bigvee_{j\in N\setminus\{i\}} x_{ij} \text{ and } \quad \phi_N^{atmost}(\{i,j\},p) := (\neg x_{ip} \vee \neg x_{jp})$$

Then, we propose three different formulations to represent rank-envy-freeness.

Direct formulation.

$$\phi_{(N,\succ)}^{direct} := \bigwedge_{i\in N}\ \bigwedge_{j\in N\setminus\{i\}}\ \bigwedge_{p\in N\setminus\{i,j\}}\ \bigwedge_{\substack{q\in N\setminus\{i,j,p\}\\ (q\succ_i p)\wedge(r_i(q)<r_j(q))}} \phi_{(N,\succ)}^{direct}(i,j,p,q)$$

with $\phi_{(N,\succ)}^{direct}(i,j,p,q) := (\neg x_{ip} \vee \neg x_{jq})$. The direct formulation explicitly forbids rank-envy configurations. More precisely, when $\phi_{(N,\succ)}^{direct}(i,j,p,q)$ is defined, it means that agent i would be rank-envious towards agent j if $\sigma(i) = p$ and $\sigma(j) = q$, which is thus forbidden by this clause. We state below that this direct formulation adequately captures rank-envy-freeness in roommate matchings.

Proposition 1. *There exists an r-EF matching in instance $(N, \succ)$ iff formula $\phi_N^{atleast} \wedge \phi_N^{atmost} \wedge \phi_{(N,\succ)}^{direct}$ is satisfiable.*

Restriction Formulation.

$$\phi_{(N,\succ)}^{restrict} := \bigwedge_{i\in N}\ \bigwedge_{j\in N\setminus\{i\}}\ \bigwedge_{\substack{p\in N\setminus\{i,j\}\\ r_i(p)>r_j(p)}} \phi_{(N,\succ)}^{restrict}(i,j,p)$$

$$\text{with} \quad \phi_{(N,\succ)}^{restrict}(i,j,p) := (\neg x_{ip} \vee \bigvee_{\ell\in N\setminus\{i\},\ \ell\succ_j p} x_{j\ell}).$$

While the direct formulation explicitly forbids matched pairs, here we restrict the set of possible partners for agents to avoid rank-envy. More precisely, when $\phi_{(N,\succ)}^{restrict}(i,j,p)$ is defined, it means that agent j ranks agent p better than what agent i does. Therefore, to avoid rank-envy, this clause imposes that if agent i is matched with agent p, then agent j should be matched with an agent ℓ she prefers to p. This alternative formulation still adequately captures rank-envy-freeness.

Proposition 2. *There exists an r-EF matching in instance $(N, \succ)$ iff formula $\phi_N^{atleast} \wedge \phi_N^{atmost} \wedge \phi_{(N,\succ)}^{restrict}$ is satisfiable.*

Characterization Formulation.

$$\phi^{charact}_{(N,\succ)} := \bigwedge_{p\in T} \phi^{toprk}_{(N,\succ)}(p) \wedge \bigwedge_{p\in N\setminus T}\ \bigwedge_{\ell=2}^{n-1}\ \bigwedge_{\substack{i\in N\setminus\{p\}\\ r_i(p)=\ell}} \phi^{rk}_{(N,\succ)}(p,\ell,i) with$$

$$\phi^{toprk}_{(N,\succ)}(p) := (\bigvee_{i\in top(p)} x_{ip}) \text{ and } \phi^{rk}_{(N,\succ)}(p,\ell,i) := (\bigvee_{\substack{q\in N\setminus\{i\}\\ r_i(q)<\ell}} x_{iq} \vee \bigvee_{\substack{j\in N\setminus\{p,i\}\\ r_j(p)\leq\ell}} x_{jp} \vee x_{ip})$$

This formulation relies on the characterization of r-EF provided by Coutance et al. [12]. Informally, this characterization states that a matching is r-EF iff every agent who is ranked first by some agent is matched with such an agent, every agent who is ranked second by some agent who did not get her first choice is matched with such an agent, and so on. The clauses of the characterization formulation impose that: (1) each agent p who is ranked first by some agent is matched with such an agent (the $\phi^{toprk}_{(N,\succ)}(p)$ clause), and (2) each agent p who is never ranked first is matched with an agent who ranks her at rank smaller or equal to ℓ, for $\ell \in \{2,\dots,n-1\}$, if none of these agents are matched with an agent they prefer (the $\phi^{rk}_{(N,\succ)}(p,\ell,\cdot)$ clauses).

These new clauses capture several aspects of fair matchings: the r-EF requirement but also the structural constraints imposing at least one partner to each agent, making the at-least clauses from structural constraints redundant.

Proposition 3. *There exists an r-EF matching in instance $(N,\succ)$ iff formula $\phi^{atmost}_N \wedge \phi^{charact}_{(N,\succ)}$ is satisfiable.*

One can observe that some $\phi^{direct}_{(N,\succ)}$, $\phi^{restrict}_{(N,\succ)}$, or $\phi^{charact}_{(N,\succ)}$ clauses defined for different agents can be redundant. Therefore, for each formula ϕ expressing rank-envy-freeness, for $\phi \in \{\phi^{direct}_{(N,\succ)}, \phi^{restrict}_{(N,\succ)}, \phi^{charact}_{(N,\succ)}\}$, we consider the smaller formula ϕ' where ϕ' denotes the set of ϕ clauses where redundant clauses as well as clauses which include others have been removed. Note that this simplification does not impact the satisfiability of the formula. Hence, from now on, when referring to a given formula ϕ, we will always consider its minimal version ϕ'.

Note that a clause $\phi^{restrict}_{(N,\succ)}(i,j,p) = (\neg x_{ip})$ is also included in all clauses $\phi^{atmost}_N(\{i,\ell\},p)$ and $\phi^{atmost}_N(\{p,\ell\},i)$, for $\ell \in N\setminus\{i,p\}$. Yet, we choose not to remove ϕ^{atmost}_N clauses to keep these—easy to interpret—structural clauses. Let us illustrate our three SAT formulations on the following simple example.

Example 1. Let us consider a roommate instance with $n = 4$ agents who have the following preferences: $3 \succ_1 2 \succ_1 4$, $3 \succ_2 1 \succ_2 4$, $4 \succ_3 2 \succ_3 1$, $1 \succ_4 2 \succ_4 3$.

Since structural clauses $\phi^{atleast}_N$ and ϕ^{atmost}_N are rather simple and not dependent on the chosen formulation, we only present below the clauses used to represent r-EF in their simplified version (i.e., without redundant clauses).

Direct form. $\phi^{direct'}_{(N,\succ)}$	Restriction form. $\phi^{restrict'}_{(N,\succ)}$	Characterization form. $\phi^{charact'}_{(N,\succ)}$
$\phi^{direct}_{(N,\succ)}(1,4,2,3) = (\neg x_{12} \vee \neg x_{34})$	$\phi^{restrict}_{(N,\succ)}(1,3,4) = (\neg x_{14})$	$\phi^{toprk}_{(N,\succ)}(1) = (x_{14})$
$\phi^{direct}_{(N,\succ)}(2,3,4,1) = (\neg x_{24} \vee \neg x_{13})$	$\phi^{restrict}_{(N,\succ)}(4,1,3) = (\neg x_{34})$	$\phi^{toprk}_{(N,\succ)}(3) = (x_{13} \vee x_{23})$
$\phi^{direct}_{(N,\succ)}(3,1,2,4) = (\neg x_{23} \vee \neg x_{14})$	$\phi^{restrict}_{(N,\succ)}(2,3,4) = (\neg x_{24})$	$\phi^{toprk}_{(N,\succ)}(4) = (x_{34})$
	$\phi^{restrict}_{(N,\succ)}(2,4,1) = (\neg x_{12})$	
	$\phi^{restrict}_{(N,\succ)}(3,4,1) = (\neg x_{13})$	

3 Deriving an Explanation from a MUS

When our SAT formulations are not satisfiable, it means that there exists no rank-envy-free matching in the associated roommate instance. Our goal is to provide an explanation to understand why there exists no rank-envy-free matching in a given roommate instance. For this purpose, we extract from the SAT formulation a *minimal unsatisfiable subset (MUS)*, which is an unsatisfiable subset of clauses from a Boolean formula such that removing any clause from it will make it satisfiable. In this section, we will adapt a technique from Beynier et al. [4] to derive an explanation from a MUS, which consists in a dynamic explanation process which is defined over a so-called satisfiability implication graph.

3.1 Dynamic Process over the Satisfiability Implication Graph

Let us first quickly recall the explanation process of Beynier et al. [4] to derive an explanation from a MUS. They use a structure called *satisfiability implication graph* to represent the implication connections between the clauses of an unsatisfiable subset of clauses, from which a proof can be constructed. Given an unsatisfiable subset of clauses ψ, the satisfiability implication graph is a directed bipartite graph $G^{\psi} = (V^{\psi}, E^{\psi})$ where the set of nodes V^{ψ} is divided in two types: the *clause nodes* contain all clauses of ψ, and the *variable nodes* contain all variables of ψ, as well as nodes $\top$ and $\bot$. In general, any clause can be written as an implication between a conjunction of positive literals (or $\top$) and a disjunction of positive literals (or $\bot$). The arcs in E^{ψ} represent these implications as follows: for each clause C of ψ, there is an arc from each variable node representing a positive literal in the implicant part of C and the clause node associated with C, and there is an arc from this clause node to each variable node representing a positive literal in the implied part of C.

Beynier et al. [4] associate with the satisfiability implication graph an *activation function* $v : V^{\psi} \to \{0,1\}$ where a node $x \in V^{\psi}$ is said to be active if $v(x) = 1$. An active variable node means that the corresponding variable is set to true, while an active clause node means that the implicant part is set to true, and thus the implied part must be true. *Activation states* are defined successively where each activation state represents a feasible valuation of v. Initially,

Table 1. Semantics of nodes in our r-EF satisfiability implication graphs

Node	Semantics
x_{ij}	Suppose agents i and j are matched.
$\phi_N^{atleast}(i)$	Agent i must be matched with at least one agent.
$\phi_N^{atmost}(\{i,j\},p)$	Agent p cannot be matched with both agents i and j.
$\phi_{(N,\succ)}^{direct}(i,j,p,q)$	Agent i cannot be matched with agent p in the same time agent j is matched with agent q, otherwise i would rank-envy j.
$\phi_{(N,\succ)}^{restrict}(i,j,p)$	To avoid rank-envy from agent j towards agent i when i is matched with agent p, j must be matched with a partner she prefers to p.
$\phi_{(N,\succ)}^{toprk}(p)$	Since agent p is ranked first by some agents, p must be matched with an agent who ranks her first. over p. Else, to avoid envy, p should be matched to an agent who ranks them better than i.
$\phi_{(N,\succ)}^{rk}(p,\ell,i)$	Agent p is ranked by agent i at rank ℓ therefore, to avoid rank-envy, if i is not matched with a partner she prefers to p, then p must be matched with an agent who ranks her at a rank smaller or equal to ℓ.

the activation state v^0 is defined where only node $\top$ is active. Then, a new activation state $v' \neq v$ is defined as a *successor* of v if: (1) for every node $x \in V^\psi$, if $v(x) = 1$ then $v'(x) = 1$; (2) if x is a clause node such that all its predecessors are activated in v then $v'(x) = 1$; (3) if x is a clause node that becomes activated in v then one of its successors becomes activated in v'.

An activation path is a sequence of successive activation states which ends in an activation state with no successors. Beynier et al. [4] have proved that all activation paths defined over a satisfiability implication graph G^ψ eventually activate node $\bot$ iff ψ is unsatisfiable. In order to derive a proof for the lack of fair solutions in their setting, Beynier et al. [4] use a depth-first-search algorithm over all defined activation states, starting from v^0 and ending a path when node $\bot$ is activated, by printing the semantics of a node of the graph each time it becomes activated. The node semantics corresponding to our problem are described in Table 1. We illustrate below the previously described explanation process.

Example 1 (continued). Let us consider the roommate instance given in Example 1 where there is no rank-envy-free matching. We will consider the following MUSes (one for each formulation); they have a minimum number of clauses:

ψ^1 for direct form.	ψ^2 for restriction form.	ψ^3 for characterization form.
$\phi_N^{atleast}(2), \phi_N^{atleast}(3), \phi_N^{atleast}(4)$	$\phi_N^{atleast}(4)$	$\phi_{(N,\succ)}^{toprk}(1), \phi_{(N,\succ)}^{toprk}(4)$
$\phi_N^{atmost}(\{2,3\},4), \phi_N^{atmost}(\{3,4\},2), \phi_N^{atmost}(\{2,4\},3)$	$\phi_{(N,\succ)}^{restrict}(1,3,4)$	$\phi_N^{atmost}(\{1,3\},4)$
$\phi_N^{atmost}(\{3,4\},1), \phi_{(N,\succ)}^{direct}(2,3,4,1)$	$\phi_{(N,\succ)}^{restrict}(2,3,4)$	
$\phi_{(N,\succ)}^{direct}(3,1,2,4), \phi_{(N,\succ)}^{direct}(1,4,2,3)$	$\phi_{(N,\succ)}^{restrict}(4,1,3)$	

We construct in Fig. 1 the satisfiability implication graph associated with each MUS, from which a textual explanation can be derived, according to the depth-first-search algorithm of Beynier et al. [4].

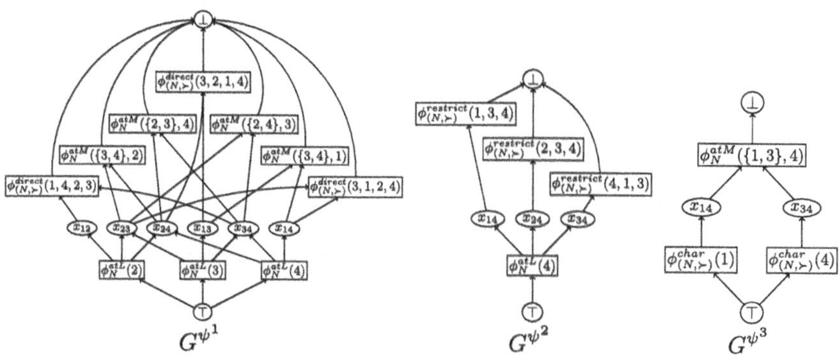

Fig. 1. Satisfiability implication graph for the MUSes considered in Example 1.

Observe that the depth-first-search algorithm over activation states of Beynier et al. [4] enumerates all combinations of possible assignments, when several clause nodes are activated in the same time. This can lead to many redundant arguments and an overcomplicated explanation. We thus propose a simpler algorithm in the next subsection in order to derive a more compact explanation.

3.2 Sequential Algorithm for Explanation

Instead of dealing with activation states as an additional component of a satisfiability implication graph, we will simply activate the nodes in the graph in a sequential manner, and print the corresponding semantics (see Table 1). The new process is described in Algorithm 1. This recursive algorithm is initially called with $Sequential(G^{\psi}, activ = \{\}, toActiv = \{\top\})$, where *activ* denotes the set of activated nodes and *toActiv* is the set of nodes which can be activated.

At each recursive call of the algorithm, an activatable node is chosen to be activated by the function $Pop^H(G^{\psi}, activ, toActiv)$, detailed in Algorithm 2, according to a given heuristic H. As a standard notation, $\Gamma_G^+(x)$ (resp., $\Gamma_G^-(x)$) refers to the set of successors (resp., predecessors) of node x in the directed graph $G = (V, E)$, i.e., $\Gamma_G^+(x) := \{y \in V : (x, y) \in E\}$ (resp., $\Gamma_G^-(x) := \{y \in V : (y, x) \in E\}$). This new algorithm is illustrated below for our running example.

Algorithm 1: $Sequential(G^\psi, activ, toActiv)$

Input: Satisfiability implication graph $G^\psi = (V^\psi, E^\psi)$, Set of activated nodes $activ \subseteq V^\psi$, Set of activatable nodes $toActiv \subseteq V^\psi$

if $\bot \in toActiv$ **then** print("Contradiction."); **return**;
$x \leftarrow Pop^H(G^\psi, activ, toActiv)$ ▷ Chooses a node x to activate;
if $x \neq \top$ **then** print(Semantics(x));
if *x is a clause node* **then**
  foreach $y \in \Gamma_{G^\psi}^+(x)$ **do** $Sequential(G^\psi, activ \cup \{x\}, toActiv \cup \{y\})$;
else $Sequential(G^\psi, activ \cup \{x\}, toActiv \cup \{y \in \Gamma_{G^\psi}^+(x) : \Gamma_{G^\psi}^-(y) \subseteq activ \cup \{x\}\})$;

Algorithm 2: $Pop^H(G^\psi, activ, toActiv)$ for a given heuristic H

if $\exists x \in toActiv \cap (\phi_N^{atmost} \cup \phi_{(N,\succ)}^{direct} \cup \{y \in \phi_{(N,\succ)}^{restrict} : |y| = 1\})$ **then** Remove x from $toActiv$; **return** x ▷ Clause node x directly leads to a contradiction;
if $\exists$ *variable node* $x \in toActiv$ **then** Remove x from $toActiv$; **return** x;
return $H(G^\psi, activ, toActiv)$

Example 1 (continued). Let us focus on the MUS ψ^1 for the direct formulation, whose satisfiability implication graph is given in Fig. 1. By running Algorithm 1, we can provide, e.g., the following excerpt of explanation:
Agent 4 must be matched with at least one agent.

1. *Suppose agents 1 and 4 are matched. Agent 3 must be matched with ≥ 1 agent.*
   (a) *Suppose agents 1 and 3 are matched. Agent 1 cannot be matched with both agents 3 and 4. Contradiction.*
   (b) *Suppose agents 2 and 3 are matched. Agent 3 cannot be matched with agent 2 in the same time agent 1 is matched with agent 4, otherwise 3 would rank-envy 1. Contradiction.*
   (c) *Suppose agents 3 and 4 are matched. Agent 2 must be matched with ≥ 1 agent.*
      i. *Suppose agents 1 and 2 are matched. Agent 1 cannot be matched with agent 2 in the same time agent 4 is matched with agent 3, otherwise 1 would rank-envy 4. Contradiction.*
      ii. *Suppose agents 2 and 3 are matched. Agent 3 cannot be matched with both agents 2 and 4. Contradiction.*

iii. *Suppose agents* 2 *and* 4 *are matched. Agent* 4 *cannot be matched with both agents* 2 *and* 3*. Contradiction.*

One can proceed in a similar way to justify the impossibility of matching agent 4 to agents 2 and 3.

One can assume that structural constraints for matchings are pretty natural for a user. In contrast, the explanation provided by Algorithm 1 on a MUS may still appear a bit more complicated than necessary. E.g., in the previous explanation on Example 1, assuming that agents 1 and 4 are matched, as well as agents 3 and 4, already makes the matching trivially unfeasible for a normal user, without the need of the $\phi_N^{atleast}(2)$ clause to reach a contradiction.

Therefore, we enrich a chosen MUS ψ with all ϕ_N^{atmost} clauses which concern two variables present in ψ, to obtain a new unsatisfiable subset of clauses ψ^* (which is thus not a MUS anymore). In general, for every MUS ψ, let us denote by ψ^* its augmented version with ϕ_N^{atmost} clauses. Then, we run Algorithm 1 on G^{ψ^*} and we select in priority in line 2 of Algorithm 1 a clause node related to an ϕ_N^{atmost} clause for activation, as detailed in Algorithm 2. With this new simplification, the previous textual explanation on Example 1 would reach a contradiction after (1c) and not need the arguments (1(c)i)–(1(c)iii).

Nevertheless, even with this simplification, the compactness of the explanation provided by Algorithm 1 is highly dependent on the choice of the node to activate (line 2). We provide, in Algorithm 2, some priority rules to choose nodes to activate from *toActiv*:

1. We choose in priority clause nodes which directly lead to a contradiction, i.e., whose unique successor is $\bot$; by definition, the associated clauses only contain negative literals. In our formulations, this concerns ϕ_N^{atmost} clauses, $\phi_{(N,\succ)}^{direct}$ clauses and $\phi_{(N,\succ)}^{restrict}$ clauses of size 1. If such clause nodes are in *toActiv*, the current partial assignment is already impossible, so only arguments directly leading to a contradiction are needed.
2. We then prioritize variable nodes to advance the completion of the current partial assignment and preserve the explanation's logical flow. If a variable node is in *toActiv*, it indicates that a clause node introducing it was previously activated. For example, in line (1a) of our textual explanation in Example 1, we activate x_{13} immediately after activating $\phi_N^{atleast}(3)$.

If these two priority rules cannot be applied, then the *toActiv* set only contains clause nodes that do not directly lead to a contradiction. The choice of the next clause node to activate can thus be guided by a given heuristic $H(G^\psi, activ, toActiv)$.

3.3 Measuring the Complexity of an Explanation

Beynier et al. [4] have proposed several metrics to evaluate the complexity of an explanation; some of those are based on the satisfiability implication graph:

- the *depth* D^ψ of the explanation produced by the MUS ψ, defined as the maximal length of an activation path in the dynamic explanation process associated with G^ψ, i.e., for each considered partial matching, we reach a contradiction in at most D^ψ steps;
- the *length* L^ψ of the explanation produced by the MUS ψ, defined as the number of feasible activation states in the dynamic explanation process associated with G^ψ, i.e., the depth-first search algorithm proposed by Beynier et al. [4] to derive an explanation takes L^ψ steps.

We will focus on the length as it represents the number of steps of the explanation when using the initial algorithm of Beynier et al. [4].

For the sake of comparison, we define the *sequential length* of an explanation, denoted by $LSeq^{\psi,S}$, as the total number of steps of our sequential algorithm (Algorithm 1), according to a given feasible sequence S of chosen nodes to activate in line 2 for each recursive call to Algorithm 1. A sequence S of nodes from G^ψ is feasible if, for each $k \in [|S|]$, the kth node of S is in the *toActiv* set of the kth recursive call to Algorithm 1, when in all previous ℓ^{th} recursive calls to Algorithm 1 (for $\ell \in [k-1]$) the ℓth node of S has been chosen in line 2. Note that the length L^ψ of an explanation associated with a MUS ψ does not measure the same thing as the sequential length $LSeq^{\psi,S}$ for a given sequence of activated nodes S. Indeed, the length L^ψ measures the number of activation states, where multiple clause nodes may be activated simultaneously, each representing a separate "single argument". In contrast, the sequential length $LSeq^{\psi,S}$corresponds to a specific run of the sequential algorithm and counts each newly activated node individually, with each activation representing a single argument. Hence, there exist instances where the length is longer than the sequential length and others where the reverse holds.

4 Structural Properties of Explanations Based on MUSes

Since we derive explanations from MUSes, we will analyze their structure.

4.1 Explanation via Direct Formulation

Let us first analyze explanations provided by the direct formulation. By construction, only $\phi_N^{atleast}$ clauses can contain positive literals; ϕ_N^{atmost} and $\phi_{(N,\succ)}^{direct}$ clauses contain only negative literals, and thus their associated clause nodes in the satisfiability implication graph directly point to $\bot$, i.e., they directly lead to a contradiction. It follows that every activation path has a length equal to 4, implying that the depth of the explanation D^ψ is always equal to 4, for every MUS ψ.

However, the fact that several $\phi_N^{atleast}$ clauses can be present in a MUS impacts the complexity of the explanation, as measured by its length.

Proposition 4. *For every MUS ψ of the direct formulation, the length of the explanation L^ψ is in $\Theta(n^{|\psi^{atL}|})$, where ψ^{atL} denotes the $\phi_N^{atleast}$ clauses of ψ.*

It follows that we can minimize the length of the explanation by choosing a MUS with a minimum number of $\phi_N^{atleast}$ clauses.

Consequently, we will now study the number of $\phi_N^{atleast}$ clauses in a MUS. We first establish that each MUS contains at least 3 $\phi_N^{atleast}$ clauses.

Proposition 5. *Under the direct formulation, the tight lower bound for the number of $\phi_N^{atleast}$ clauses in a MUS is equal to* 3.

Note first that the tight lower bound of 3 given in Proposition 5 can always be achieved when there are only four agents, as stated below.

Proposition 6. *The maximum, over all instances with $n = 4$ agents, of the minimum number of $\phi_N^{atleast}$ clauses in a MUS of the direct formulation is* 3.

However, in general, this bound cannot be achieved for all instances. Therefore, for a given instance, even in the best case, we may not always find a MUS with only a few $\phi_N^{atleast}$ clauses. It follows that the decision on which $\phi_N^{atleast}$ clause nodes to activate in our sequential algorithm may not be efficient, emphasizing the need for efficient heuristics.

4.2 Explanation via Restriction Formulation

Let us now analyze the restriction formulation. Unlike the direct formulation, its depth is not necessarily bounded by 4, as $\phi_{(N,\succ)}^{restrict}$ clauses may not directly lead to a contradiction but instead introduce disjunctions of positive literals. Consequently, the length of the explanation derived from a MUS depends not only on the number of $\phi_N^{atleast}$ clauses, but also on the number and size of the $\phi_{(N,\succ)}^{restrict}$ clauses. In particular, the length of the explanation is not necessarily minimal when minimizing the number of $\phi_N^{atleast}$ clauses in the MUS. In consequence, we investigate lower bounds for the clauses of a MUS. Note that the lower bound on the number of $\phi_N^{atleast}$ clauses can always be reached with four agents.

Proposition 7. *Under the restriction formulation, we have the following tight lower bounds in a MUS:* 1 *$\phi_N^{atleast}$ clause,* 0 *ϕ_N^{atmost} clauses, $n-1$ $\phi_{(N,\succ)}^{restrict}$ clauses, and n for the total number of clauses.*

Proposition 8. *The maximum, over all instances with* 4 *agents, of the minimum number of $\phi_N^{atleast}$ clauses in a MUS of the restriction formulation is* 1.

However, in general, this lower bound cannot be achieved for all instances. Nevertheless, we conjecture that for every instance, we can always find a MUS with only two $\phi_N^{atleast}$ clauses. Yet, even if such a property holds, there is no guarantee to reach a short explanation via the sequential algorithm, because of the role of $\phi_{(N,\succ)}^{restrict}$ clauses. Therefore, there is still a need to design good heuristics for the choice of which $\phi_N^{atleast}$ or $\phi_{(N,\succ)}^{restrict}$ clause nodes to activate.

4.3 Explanation via Characterization Formulation

Let us finally analyze the characterization formulation. As in the direct formulation, only ϕ_N^{atmost} clauses can contain negative literals and they contain only negative literals. Therefore, every activation path has a length equal to 4, implying that the depth of the explanation is always equal to 4. However, in contrast with the direct formulation for the $\phi_N^{atleast}$ clauses, not all $\phi_{(N,\succ)}^{charact}$ clauses—which only contain positive literals—have the same size.

Observe first that there is one clause $\phi_{(N,\succ)}^{toprk}$ for each agent $i \in T$, and $n - 1$ clauses $\phi_{(N,\succ)}^{rk}$ for each agent $i \in N \setminus T$, and thus in total $|T| + (n-1) \cdot |N \setminus T|$ clauses in $\phi_{(N,\succ)}^{charact}$. In general, there are thus $O(n^2)$ clauses in $\phi_{(N,\succ)}^{charact}$. Concerning the size of the clauses, when $i \in T$, we have $1 \leq |\phi_{(N,\succ)}^{toprk}(i)| \leq n-1$ and, when $i \in N \setminus T$, we have $2 \leq |\phi_{(N,\succ)}^{rk}(i,\cdot,\cdot)| \leq 2n - 3$. Therefore, in general, the clauses are of size $O(n)$ in $\phi_{(N,\succ)}^{charact}$. Consequently, for every MUS ψ of the characterization formulation, the length of the explanation L^ψ is given by $\Theta(\prod_{c \in \phi_{(N,\succ)}^{charact} \cap \psi} |c|)$ and thus is in $O(n^{n^2})$. It follows that both the number and the size of $\phi_{(N,\succ)}^{charact}$ clauses impact the length of the explanation.

Proposition 9. *Under the characterization formulation, we have the following tight lower bounds in a MUS: 2 for the number of $\phi_{(N,\succ)}^{charact}$ clauses, 1 for the number of ϕ_N^{atmost} clauses, 3 for the total number of clauses.*

Note that the tight lower bound of 2 $\phi_{(N,\succ)}^{charact}$ clauses given in Proposition 9 can always be achieved when there are only four agents, as stated below.

Proposition 10. *The maximum, with $n = 4$ agents, of the minimum number of $\phi_{(N,\succ)}^{charact}$ clauses in a MUS of the characterization formulation is 2.*

In general, this bound cannot be achieved for all instances. Therefore, the decision on which $\phi_{(N,\succ)}^{charact}$ clause nodes to activate in our sequential algorithm may not be efficient, which emphasizes a need for good heuristics.

5 Experimentally Shortening Explanations via Heuristics

Finally, we evaluate the quality of the explanations produced by our sequential algorithm (Algorithm 1). These explanations depend on the order in which nodes are activated. By definition, the algorithm gives priority to clause nodes that directly lead to a contradiction, as well as to variable nodes (see Algorithm 2). When no such nodes are available, a heuristic $H(G^\psi, activ, toActiv)$ is used to select the next nodes to activate, based on the graph G^ψ, the current set of activated nodes *activ*, and the set *toActiv* of nodes eligible for activation, where *toActiv* only contains clause nodes. We propose several heuristics H to choose clause nodes to activate according to a given metric (ties are arbitrarily broken).

- *MaxVarConnect*$^{\Sigma}$ (resp., *MaxVarConnect*$^{\min}$): We choose a clause node which maximizes the sum (resp., min) of the number of successors in G^{ψ} of the variables nodes associated with the variables of the clause:

$$\arg \max_{C \in toActiv} \{\sum_{v \in C} / \min_{v \in C}\} |\Gamma^{+}_{G^{\psi}}(v)|$$

These heuristics are specifically designed for the direct formulation, where choices are made on $\phi_N^{atleast}$ clause nodes whose successors are always direct predecessors of $\perp$. Thus, the more interconnected these successors are, the more likely they are to directly lead to a contradiction.
- *MinContrad*: We choose a clause node which minimizes the number of variables missing to reach a contradiction in the best case, by considering the current partial assignment augmented by the variables of the clause:

$$\arg \min_{C \in toActiv} \min_{C' \in \psi,\ \perp \in \Gamma^{+}_{G^{\psi}}(C')} |\{\neg x \in C' : x \notin (activ \cup C)\}|$$

The idea is to favor clauses that need less matching variables to assign afterwards in order to reach a contradiction.
- *MaxRankEnvy*: We choose a clause node maximizing the number of its variables matching agents in a rank-envious way w.r.t. the current assignment:

$$\arg \max_{C \in toActiv} |\{x_{ik} \in C : \exists j, \ell, x_{j\ell} \in activ,\ r_i(j) < \min(r_\ell(j), r_i(k)\}|$$

The idea is to generate more partial assignments that do not satisfy r-EF, to need less additional ones from other clauses to reach a contradiction.
- *MinClause*: We choose a clause node whose associated clause is the smallest:

$$\arg \min_{C \in toActiv} |C|$$

This heuristic is thought for the restriction and characterization formulations, as they are the only ones whose clause nodes to choose vary in their size. A small number of variables suggests a small number of additional partial assignments needed to reach a contradiction.
- *MaxMatched*: We choose a clause node with the most variables corresponding to at least one agent already matched in the current partial assignment:

$$\arg \max_{C \in toActiv} |\{x_{ij} \in C : \exists k \in [n], \{x_{ik}, x_{jk}\} \cap activ \neq \emptyset\}|$$

The idea is to reach more situations where an agent is matched with two different agents, thus triggering an ϕ_N^{atmost} clause node.

To evaluate the efficiency of our heuristics, we conduct an experimental study through computer simulations on 1,000 randomly generated preference profiles with $n = 8$ agents and no rank-envy-free matching. For each instance, we generate a MUS ψ and compute its sequential length $LSeq^{\psi,S}$ obtained by a single iteration of Algorithm 1, where each proposed heuristic defines the sequence

Table 2. Average of sequential lengths obtained via Algorithm 1 for different heuristics and chosen MUSes, for 1,000 iterations with $n = 8$ agents

	Direct Form.		Restriction Form.			Characterization Form.		
Heuristic	$LSeq^1$	$LSeq^2$	$LSeq^1$	$LSeq^2$	$LSeq^3$	$LSeq^1$	$LSeq^2$	$LSeq^3$
MaxMatched	91173.9	833.9	36	28.3	23.5	38.7	14.0	10.3
MaxRankEnvy	40008.7	632.4	35.4	28.3	23.5	39.0	14.2	10.6
MaxVarConnect$^{\min}$	15368.5	557.0	35.8	28.3	23.5	19.4	11.7	9.4
MaxVarConnect$^{\Sigma}$	13069.9	553.3	35.4	28.3	23.4	37.1	14.7	10.8
MinClause	49802.0	746.8	31.5	28.1	23.3	16.7	11.1	9.2
MinContrad	49802.0	746.8	31.5	28.1	23.3	16.7	11.1	9.2
random	53993.9	725.2	33.6	28.2	23.4	28.3	13.2	10.5
10random	31828.7	529.7	31.7	28.1	23.2	17.8	10.9	8.8
Length L	1188617.4	1276.9	61.1	28.5	23.9	121.0	12.1	9.0

S of clause nodes to activate. We then average the results over all instances. For comparison, we also compute the average sequential length using a random choice of clause nodes at each step (denoted by *random*), the average of the best sequential lengths over 10 iterations with random choice (*10random*), and the average of lengths L^{ψ} directly computed from the graph G^{ψ}.

For each instance, we derive explanations from several MUSes with particular characteristics. For this matter, we use the PySAT module [19] to define the SAT encoding of our formulations, and the OptUx solver to choose MUSes that optimize the number of clauses of a given type. We denote by $LSeq^1$ the average of the sequential lengths when using a random MUS–which serves as a base case–, by $LSeq^2$ the one when using a MUS with a minimum number of $\phi_N^{atleast}$ (resp., $\phi_{(N,\succ)}^{charact}$) clauses for the direct and restriction (resp., characterization) formulations, and by $LSeq^3$ the one when using a MUS with a minimum number of positive literals. Our results are reported in Table 2.

Comparing Heuristics for Each Formulation. For the direct formulation, MaxVarConnect$^{\min/\Sigma}$ seem to provide the best results as they provide on average an explanation two times shorter in sequential length than the best of 10 random iterations of the sequential activation. The most important factor to shorten the explanation is choosing a MUS of minimal length, as we can see that choosing a MUS with a minimal number of $\phi_N^{atleast}$ clauses will produce explanations significantly shorter in sequential length than random MUSes.

For a random MUS in the restriction formulation, the heuristics MinClause and MinContrad yield slightly better results than the others, which aligns with their underlying intuition. While the sequential activation procedure consistently produces shorter explanations than the initial algorithm of Beynier et al. [4]—whose size corresponds to the MUS length—we observe that the heuristics perform comparably to random clause selection. This suggests that, in this formulation, the specific choice of clause nodes may not have a significant impact on explanation length. Explanations tend to become more compact when selecting MUSes that minimize either the number of $\phi_N^{atleast}$ clauses or the number of positive literals, with a slight improvement observed across all heuristics. However, we also find that the original algorithm of Beynier et al. [4] achieves similar explanation sizes in these cases. This can likely be attributed to the structural properties of the restriction formulation, where many instances yield a MUS containing only a single $\phi_N^{atleast}$ clause, rendering both procedures structurally close. For the characterization formulation, the MinClause and MinContrad heuristics seem to generate more compact explanations than other heuristics, even though a few iterations of random clause choices can reach similar sequential lengths, which could suggest that not many possibilities of choices are involved. Interestingly, the explanation sizes produced by the sequential activation procedure closely match those of the initial algorithm of Beynier et al. [4] when minimizing the number of $\phi_{(N,\succ)}^{charact}$ clauses or the number of positive literals.

Comparing Formulations. Unsurprisingly, the direct formulation often yields significantly longer explanations than the others, as it must enumerate all possible assignments to demonstrate the absence of an r-EF matching. In contrast, the restriction and characterization formulations benefit from clauses that suggest alternative assignments to eliminate potential envy between agents, though this can result in explanations that are harder to interpret. Particularly, alternative assignments proposed by fairness clauses in the restriction formulation can imply other fairness clauses, which will complexify the reasoning from the user to understand why no fair assignment exists. Moreover, the direct and characterization formulations both have bounded depth, which means that when assumptions are made about assignments, they quickly lead to contradictions. Notably, the characterization formulation not only enjoys this bounded depth but also experimentally yields shorter explanations than the direct one. This likely stems from its closer alignment with the underlying fairness concept, as it is based on a meaningful characterization. However, its semantics may be less straightforward to interpret.

6 Conclusion

In this paper, we addressed why a certain notion of fairness cannot be achieved in roommate matchings. Inspired by similar work in fair division [4], we proposed three SAT formulations of the fair roommate matching problem and adapted an existing procedure [4] to generate textual explanations from MUSes. Our adaptation yields more compact explanations, though some steps rely on heuristic choices. We introduced several heuristics and MUS selection metrics to improve explanation compactness and efficiency. A natural extension is to investigate the computational complexity of selecting the optimal node activation sequence in our sequential algorithm to minimize explanation length. More broadly, future work could explore explainability for justifying solutions users may perceive as unfair. While we focused on rank-envy-freeness, other fairness criteria could be studied. Local explanations, specific to individual users, may also be valuable.

Acknowledgments. This work is supported by the ANR project APPLE-PIE (grant ANR-22-CE23-0008-01).

Disclosure of Interests. The authors have no competing interests to declare that are relevant to the content of this article.

References

1. Barredo Arrieta, A., et al.: Explainable artificial intelligence (XAI): concepts, taxonomies, opportunities and challenges toward responsible AI. Inform. Fusion **58**, 82–115 (2020)
2. Belahcene, K., Mousseau, V., Wilczynski, A.: Combining fairness and optimality when selecting and allocating projects. In: Proceedings of the 30th International Joint Conference on Artificial Intelligence (IJCAI-21), pp. 38–44 (2021)
3. Beynier, A., Chevaleyre, Y., Gourvès, L., Harutyunyan, A., Lesca, J., Maudet, N., Wilczynski, A.: Local envy-freeness in house allocation problems. Auton. Agent. Multi-Agent Syst. **33**(5), 591–627 (2019). https://doi.org/10.1007/s10458-019-09417-x
4. Beynier, A., Mailly, J., Maudet, N., Wilczynski, A.: Explaining the lack of locally envy-free allocations. In: Proceedings of the 27th European Conference on Artificial Intelligence (ECAI-24), pp. 3477–3484 (2024)
5. Biran, O., Cotton, C.: Explanation and justification in machine learning: a survey. In: Proceedings of the IJCAI-17 workshop on explainable AI (XAI), pp. 8–13 (2017)
6. Boixel, A., Endriss, U.: Automated justification of collective decisions via constraint solving. In: Proceedings of the 19th International Conference on Autonomous Agents and MultiAgent Systems (AAMAS-20), pp. 168–176 (2020)
7. Boixel, A., Endriss, U., Haan, R.d.: A calculus for computing structured justifications for election outcomes. In: Proceedings of the 36th AAAI Conference on Artificial Intelligence (AAAI-22), vol. 36, pp. 4859–4866 (2022)
8. Boixel, A., de Haan, R.: On the Complexity of Finding Justifications for Collective Decisions. In: Proceedings of the 35th AAAI Conference on Artificial Intelligence (AAAI-21), vol. 35, pp. 5194–5201 (2021)
9. Brandt, F., Conitzer, V., Endriss, U., Lang, J., Procaccia, A.D. (eds.): Handbook of Computational Social Choice. Cambridge University Press (2016)
10. Cabalar, P., Erdem, E., Fidan, M., Muñiz, B.: A preliminary taxonomy of explanations in problem solving. In: Proceedings of the 15th European Symposium on Computational Intelligence and Mathematics (ESCIM-24), pp. 50–51 (2024)
11. Cailloux, O., Endriss, U.: Arguing about voting rules. In: Proceedings of the 15th International Conference on Autonomous Agents and Multiagent Systems (AAMAS-16), pp. 287–295 (2016)
12. Coutance, B., Maddila, P., Wilczynski, A.: Rank-envy-freeness in roommate matchings. In: Proceedings of the 26th European Conference on Artificial Intelligence (ECAI-23), pp. 493–500 (2023)
13. Erdem, E., Fidan, M., Manlove, D., Prosser, P.: A general framework for stable roommates problems using answer set programming. Theory Pract. Logic Program. **20**(6), 911–925 (2020)

14. Foley, D.K.: Resource allocation and the public sector. Yale Economic Essays **7**(1), 45–98 (1967)
15. Geist, C., Peters, D.: Computer-aided methods for social choice theory. In: Endriss, U. (ed.) Trends in Computational Social Choice, chap. 5, pp. 249–268. AI Access (2017)
16. Gunning, D., Vorm, E., Wang, J.Y., Turek, M.: Darpa's explainable AI (XAI) program: a retrospective. Appl. AI Letters **2**(4), e61 (2021)
17. Harless, P.: Immediate acceptance and weak priorities: An adaptation that preserves efficiency and respects rank. Working paper (2018)
18. Hosseini, H.: The fairness fair: Bringing human perception into collective decision-making. In: Proceedings of the 38th AAAI Conference on Artificial Intelligence (AAAI-24), vol. 38, pp. 22624–22631 (2024)
19. Ignatiev, A., Morgado, A., Marques-Silva, J.: PySAT: A Python toolkit for prototyping with SAT oracles. In: Proceedings of the 21st International Conference on Theory and Applications of Satisfiability Testing (SAT-18), pp. 428–437 (2018). https://doi.org/10.1007/978-3-319-94144-8_26
20. Irving, R.W.: An efficient algorithm for the "stable roommates" problem. J. Algorithms **6**(4), 577–595 (1985)
21. Klaus, B., Manlove, D.F., Rossi, F.: Matching under preferences. In: Handbook of Computational Social Choice, pp. 333–355. Cambridge University Press (2016)
22. Kojima, F., Ünver, M.U.: The "Boston" school-choice mechanism: an axiomatic approach. Econ. Theor. **55**(3), 515–544 (2014)
23. Loustalot Knapp, D.: Justification of Matching Outcomes. Master's thesis, University of Amsterdam (2022)
24. Nardi, O., Boixel, A., Endriss, U.: A graph-based algorithm for the automated justification of collective decisions. In: Proceedings of the 21st International Conference on Autonomous Agents and Multiagent Systems (AAMAS-22), pp. 935–943 (2022)
25. Nizri, M., Hazon, N., Azaria, A.: Explainable Shapley-based allocation (student abstract). In: Proceedings of the 36th AAAI Conference on Artificial Intelligence (AAAI-22), vol. 36, pp. 13023–13024 (2022)
26. Núñez, M.: Towards transparent mechanisms. In: The Future of Economic Design: The Continuing Development of a Field as Envisioned by Its Researchers, pp. 341–346. Springer (2019)
27. Peters, D., Procaccia, A.D., Psomas, A., Zhou, Z.: Explainable voting. In: Proceedings of the 34th Annual Conference on Neural Information Processing Systems (NeurIPS-20), vol. 33, pp. 1525–1534 (2020)
28. Procaccia, A.D.: Axioms should explain solutions. In: The Future of Economic Design: The Continuing Development of a Field as Envisioned by Its Researchers, pp. 195–199. Springer (2019)
29. Ramezanian, R., Feizi, M.: Stepwise ordinal efficiency for the random assignment problem. J. Math. Econ. **92**, 60–65 (2021)
30. Schmidtlein, M.C., Endriss, U.: Voting by axioms. In: Proceedings of the 22nd International Conference on Autonomous Agents and Multiagent Systems (AAMAS-23), pp. 2067–2075 (2023)
31. Suryanarayana, S.A., Sarne, D., Kraus, S.: Justifying social-choice mechanism outcome for improving participant satisfaction. In: Proceedings of the 21st International Conference on Autonomous Agents and Multiagent Systems (AAMAS-22), pp. 1246–1255 (2022)

32. Tang, P., Lin, F.: Computer-aided proofs of Arrow's and other impossibility theorems. Artif. Intell. **173**(11), 1041–1053 (2009)
33. Zahedi, Z., Sengupta, S., Kambhampati, S.: 'Why didn't you allocate this task to them?' Negotiation-aware task allocation and contrastive explanation generation. In: Proceedings of the 38th AAAI Conference on Artificial Intelligence (AAAI-24). vol. 38, pp. 10243–10251 (2024)

BOID for Smart Scheduling: Integrating Default Logic and Embedding Models for Interpretable Personalization

Stipe Pandžić[1(✉)], Fabio Dijkshoorn[2], and Jan Broersen[3]

[1] LUCI Lab, University of Milan, Milan, Italy
stipepandzic@gmail.com
[2] Department of Information and Computing Sciences, Utrecht University, Utrecht, The Netherlands
f.dijkshoorn@students.uu.nl
[3] Department of Philosophy and Religious Studies, Utrecht University, Utrecht, The Netherlands
j.m.broersen@uu.nl

Abstract. This paper presents a proof-of-concept implementation of the BOID logic in smart scheduling tasks. We leverage the potential of using embedding models as a foundation for building knowledge bases and 'mining' BOID rules with priorities. With this approach, we address the problems of extracting logic rules from the data on users and conference topics. Our rule mining method addresses a key pitfall of logic-based systems: their dependence on domain experts to generate logic rules. We apply the model to the domain of conference planning, where we build a personalized conference attendance schedule for users of the BOID app. In generating the schedule, we rely on the three main resources for decision making: rule-based reasoning (BOID), embedding models and human input. Each of the resources has some specific role in eliciting either of the Belief, Obligation, Intention and Desire components. This makes our model 'hybrid' in at least two different ways, namely, as a hybrid learning-reasoning model and as a hybrid human-AI model. One of the main advantages of our model is interpretability through tracing the BOID rules underlying each decision in generated schedules.

Keywords: BOID logic · Default rule mining · Process trees · Smart scheduling · Embedding models

1 Introduction

In the realm of artificial intelligence for personalization and planning, autonomous agents frequently encounter environments characterized by conflicting objectives, competing priorities, and evolving circumstances. The BOID algorithm, as an autonomous goal-generation architecture offers a structured framework for addressing the challenge of generating goals in the face of complex

M. Baldoni et al. (Eds.): EUMAS 2025, LNAI 16259, pp. 87–103, 2026.
https://doi.org/10.1007/978-3-032-22820-8_6

interactions between users' Beliefs, Obligations, Intentions and Desires. BOID agents reason by relying on informational (beliefs), social (obligations), goal-specific (intentions) and personal (desire) factors and, therefore, operationalize the decision-making processes that reflect inherent complexities of human decision-making.

This paper presents an application of BOID to the domain of conference planning and session recommendations. The existing **conference** scheduling assistants are highly data-driven machine learning algorithms. There are multiple benefits of machine learning, but one of the main downsides is that the data is taken in "bulk" and not qualified according to whether social, preferential, goal-driven or other factors are decisive in giving a recommendation. The BOID logic gives the upper hand in building a smart conference scheduling assistant with an inherently *explainable* algorithm based on labeled rules. Another opportunity for BOID-based scheduling is to generate recommendations without overly relying on predictions from the data on users' previous conference-attendance behavior. BOID uses data in a way analogous to human decision-making. In the current application, we rely on data primarily as a source for mental attitudes, creating BOID agents that mimic how humans use external inputs to reason with beliefs, obligations, intentions and desires in decision-making.

Applying the BOID algorithm to scheduling decisions can enhance usability by making the process more transparent and allowing users to trace recommendations back to their original "motivational" mental attitudes, as interpreted by the algorithm. This means individuals can understand how their personal preferences and desires directly influence their schedules. However, within the specific context of conference attendance, there currently exists no logical algorithm designed to plan such activities while incorporating individual preferences. A search for automated "conference attendance scheduling" yields few results for an algorithm that offers this level of personalized and traceable planning.

This paper aims to apply the BOID algorithm to a practical scenario, specifically conference attendance scheduling. From a broader research perspective, this study is a contribution to the area of using **agent architectures** to tackle real-world problems. A widely acclaimed research success in this domain is Shoham et al.'s [14] personal assistant app based on the database perspective on modeling intentions. This approach inspired the *Timeful* personal assistant app and led to its commercial success through Google's acquisition.

We first analyze the default theories of BOID logic and introduce a new operational semantics based on process trees. Following this, we introduce a formalized case study of personalized conference scheduling using BOID. In Sect. 3, we generate a BOID process tree and a corresponding conference schedule example to illustrate our BOID algorithm, enhanced by the use of an embedding model. Finally, the modeling decisions (including the role of embedding models) and algorithm are explained in more detail, together with the description of the software architecture. Finally, we focus on the most relevant related work using logics with mental attitudes for scheduling problems, before concluding the paper.

2 Background and Theoretical Foundations

In complex scheduling environments, making decisions that are both efficient and transparent can be a significant challenge. A logic-based approach offers a structured framework that enhances the clarity and rationality of the decision-making process. By explicitly defining rules and priorities, it becomes easier to understand and justify why certain scheduling choices are made, leading to greater transparency.

One possible logic-based framework for this purpose is BOID logic. BOID logic was introduced by Broersen et al. [4,5] as a way to elicit agent goals with an algorithm that takes agents' beliefs, obligations, intentions and desires as an input. The BOID has several advantages as a candidate logic. For example, working with the 'mental attitudes' such as obligations, desires etc. enables us to trace back the origin of a decision that has been made to its root motivational and informational content. Another advantage is that BOID allows for reasoning with default assumptions, which are statements that are generally accepted as true unless contradicted by other available information. This is useful for our implementation because it gives us flexibility to model uncertainty about schedules.

To fully understand how a logic-based approach like the BOID algorithm improves scheduling transparency, we first provide a novel *operational* semantics for the BOID logic. The semantics is based on the operational semantics for normal default logic [1, Ch. 4]. In the operational semantics, we can handle default assumptions in a way that enables straightforward control over the source BOID rule 'modalities'. This forms a foundation for a transparent and traceable integration of embedder-sourced content into BOID default rules, as well as their prioritization that underlies the BOID decision-making algorithm.

2.1 BOID Logic

This section introduces the logical framework that we later apply to the example of generating individualized conference schedules, namely, the BOID logic architecture. According to [4], BOID was developed out of the interest in the relation between goals on the one hand and desires, intentions and obligations on the other hand. The BOID algorithm takes four basic 'mental attitudes' as a basis of the goal generation process. Broersen et al. offer the following intuitions behind the four mental attitudes: beliefs represent the information about the current state of the world, obligations represent attitudes that reflect the social nature of agents, intentions are the generated goals that the agent has selected in its previous deliberation and desires are (long term) preferences.

The BOID rule is, at its core, a normal default rule with the added rule type label.

Definition 1 (BOID Rule). *A BOID rule δ has the following general form*

$$\phi \xrightarrow{X} \psi$$

where ϕ and ψ are formulas of a propositional language L and $X \in \{B, O, I, D\}$ and B stands for beliefs, O stands for obligations, I stands for intentions, and D stands for desires.

Prioritization among rules matters. A decision to prioritize some BOID rules over others results in different agent types in the BOID algorithm. The original BOID [5] can model general agent types such as 'realistic', 'social', 'selfish' etc. as a result of different priority orders among sets of rules representing mental attitudes. Suppose, for example, an agent who is obliged to attend a meeting but desires to go for lunch. Depending on the agent type, the generated goal could be either attending the meeting (for a social agent) or going to lunch (for a selfish agent). Agent types can involve more intricate prioritization requirements. For example, in the case of the BOID "stable" agent, intentions override obligations, intentions override desires, and obligations override desires, that is, $\{I \succ O, I \succ D, O \succ D\}$. Throughout this paper, we assume the straightforward $\{B \succ O \succ I \succ D\}$ rule ordering, that is, *Realistic*, *Unstable-O*, *Stable-D* (and *Social*).[1] The agent is *realistic* in prioritizing beliefs, unstable-O and stable-D in prioritizing obligations over intentions and intentions over desires and therefore social in prioritizing obligations over desires.

As mentioned above, BOID defaults are *normal*. This means that the BOID rule $\phi \xrightarrow{X} \psi$ is a shorthand for

$$\frac{\phi :_X \psi}{\psi},$$

where the ϕ is a *prerequisite* of the rule and ψ is both a *justification* and a *consequent* of the default. A BOID theory T is called *normal* iff all its rules are normal. We say that a rule $\phi \xrightarrow{X} \psi$ is *applicable* to a deductively closed set of formulas $S \subseteq L$ iff $\phi \in S$ and $\neg\psi \notin S$.

In contrast to the standard Reiter's default rules [12], BOID rules have an additional "modality" specification of the mental attitude that they represent. Moreover, Reiter's original syntax for default rules is based on first-order logic, and we need only the expressivity of propositional logic. With these preliminaries on default, we are ready to define BOID theories:

Definition 2 (BOID Theory). *For a propositional language L, a BOID theory is a tuple $T = \langle W, B, O, I, D, \rho\rangle$, where $W \subset L$ is a finite set of facts, B, O, I and D are sets of belief, obligation, (prior) intention and desire BOID rules, and ρ a function from $B \cup O \cup I \cup D$ to the integers representing an agent's type.*

Relative to the (agent type) function ρ of T, We say that a rule $\delta \in B \cup O \cup I \cup D$ is $\rho -$ *applicable* to a deductively closed set of formulas $S \subseteq L$ iff δ is *applicable* and there is no rule $\delta_i \in B \cup O \cup I \cup D$ such that δ_i is applicable to S and $\rho(\delta_i) < \rho(\delta)$.

---

[1] Later on, we allow for flexibility in the ordering of motivational attitudes based on the strength of embedding rules within the agent's profile.

An important component of default logic-based systems are extensions. Some default theories have no extensions. However, existence of extensions in BOID is guaranteed with our choice of normal default theories. In our implementation of BOID, we will work with normal and *supernormal* default rules. Supernormal defaults are similar to the above-defined normal BOID defaults, with the added condition of having only tautological prerequisite formulas. Normal default theories provide a structured and predictable way to manage goal generation and conflict resolution, which makes them suitable for our BOID implementation based on balancing and prioritizing mental attitudes [4].

The original BOID algorithm provides a clear goal generation procedure, which is technically an algorithm to generate extensions. The pseudo-code provided in [4] is purposeful for understanding the underlying logic, but its implementation poses challenges and it is not optimized for computational efficiency. One of the difficulties is that it includes two nested loops. Therefore, we employ *process trees* as a method for calculating extensions in BOID.

2.2 Process Trees and Goal Generation

An *extension* of a BOID default theory captures the set of formulas representing potentially competing *goals* that may arise from applying defaults to facts. We now turn to defining the operational semantics for goal generation, with the process trees at the core of the semantics. The operational semantics definitions for BOID theories are inspired by those given for standard default theories by Antoniou [1]. The core concept of process trees revolves around applying default rules as long as possible.

A process is a sequence of applied default rules determined by the order of application and the extent of applying defaults. A process is denoted by the Greek letter Π and, with each process Π, we associate a set $In(\Pi)$ that collects the information obtained by the application of the defaults in Π:

$$In(\Pi) = Th^L(W \cup \{\psi \mid \phi \xrightarrow{X} \psi \text{ is an element of } \Pi\})$$

Intuitively, the set $In(\Pi)$ represents the current *goal base*. The following is the formal definition of the BOID process:

Definition 3 (BOID Process). *Π is called a process of T iff δ_k is applicable to $In(\Pi[k])$, for each k such that δ_k occurs in Π*

The following two requirements of prioritization and closure need to be met by any extension-generating process Π of T:

- Π is *prioritized* iff for each δ_k in Π it holds that δ_k is $\rho -$ *applicable* to $In(\Pi[k])$ and
- Π is *closed* iff every $\delta \in B \cup O \cup I \cup D$ that is applicable to $In(\Pi)$ already occurs in Π.

Closed and prioritized processes are desiderata ensuring that an extension E is being maximal, while adhering to some extralogical conditions encoded in the priority function.

Finally, we are ready to give the formal definition of a BOID extension:

Definition 4 (BOID Extension). *For a BOID theory T, a set of formulas E is a* BOID extension *of T iff there is some closed and prioritized process Π of T such that $E = In(\Pi)$.*

One practical challenge in exploring extensions is to keep track of all the possible extension-generating processes. This can occur due to the complexity of default logic, where multiple extensions may arise, conflicts between defaults must be resolved and prioritization of rules can obscure alternative extensions. To address this, we can structure all potential processes in the fashion of [1, p. 34] within a structure called a *process tree* of a given BOID theory T. In this tree, each node is labeled with a set of formulae representing the current state of the theory. The edges represent the application of defaults, labeled with the specific default being applied. By following the paths from the root of the process tree, each path corresponds to a process of T, ensuring that all possible extensions are explored in a comprehensive way. This standard method for displaying default logic processes is adapted here for goal generation in the BOID logic. We will first show the workings behind the process tree on a (simplified) example from our domain of application of BOID, namely, an example of generating personalized conference schedule.

3 Application Example: Conference Attendance

With the preliminaries on BOID extensions and process trees completed, we are ready to explore a practical example that demonstrates these methods in action and advances us toward our target use case. Implementing process trees is a straightforward but potentially costly procedure. In Sect. 4.2, we explain how our adaptation of the BOID algorithm efficiently uses process trees. The rest of this section details the application of the algorithm to a use case. Throughout the example, we keep the descriptions aligned with the BOID logic terminology. However, the logical structure of the example closely aligns with the inner workings of the implemented hybrid 'BOID-Embedder' algorithm (see Sect. 4).[2]

In one of the original BOID papers, Broersen et al. [4] give an illustrative example of an agent traveling to a conference and deciding on a hotel to book. Through this example, Broersen et al. present the decision-making processes of different types of agents. But beyond this example lies another problem in the domain of planning and scheduling familiar to anyone who has ever attended a conference, namely, the struggle of navigating multiple presentations scheduled across overlapping time slots.

[2] The example draws from an actual execution but has been refined for presentation, resulting in some deviations from the algorithm's full behavior. It is intended as a (faithful) illustrative aid rather than a precise reproduction.

The agent likely has an obligation to attend certain presentations, especially those within its research domain. Yet, it also harbors a desire to attend sessions on topics it enjoys, or those presented by friends. Thus, a conflict arises. The agent must attend presentation A out of duty, but presentation B sparks its interest. With both presentations set for the same time, the agent must decide which to attend.

As mentioned in 2.1, BOID allows obligations and desires to be modeled as default rules. With these rules in place, a schedule can be generated, tailored to the specific type of agent. For instance, imagine an agent attending a 'generalist' artificial intelligence conference with multiple overlapping presentations. The agent has specific obligations and desires regarding which presentations it wants to attend. To explore this scenario further, a hypothetical conference is provided below (Table 1).

Table 1. Sample schedule of a conference

	Session 1	Session 2	Session 3
Time slot 1	Alphafold protein prediction	Propositional language for KR	Norms and normative MAS
Time slot 2	Attention is all you need	The story of logic	Social behavior emergence in MAS
Time slot 3	Norm enforcement	Low-rank adaptation of LLMs	Agency in the age of AI
Time slot 4	Do moral robots always fail		

We build the BOID theory T_1 over the sample schedule and the agent's research profile and input. Notice that we show only a part of the BOID theory as the entire calculation of the theory T_1 process tree with all the BOID rules quickly becomes unmanageable for representation.[3] We start by first extracting belief rules of the following type from the conference schedule:

$$\begin{aligned} &do\_moral\_robots\_always\_fail \xrightarrow{B} timeslot\_4\_123 \; (\rho = 6) \\ &alphafold\_protein\_prediction \xrightarrow{B} timeslot\_1\_1 \quad\;\; (\rho = 6) \ldots \end{aligned}$$

Belief defaults represent the uncertain information of an agent about the current state of the world. The subjects of the presentations are not "hardcoded" as givens in a set of facts. For example, the set of facts W_1 does not contain the formula $propositional\_language\_for\_KR \rightarrow timeslot\_2\_1$. This complies to the core idea of BOID rules with 'modalities', which assume that beliefs are based on incomplete information and, therefore, subject to errors.

The next step is to formalize the desires and obligations of the agent in this example. Suppose that our agent is part of a research group that is focused on the ethics of artificial intelligence. If the agent is a 'social' type (obligations are more important than desires), then it should go to the presentation about

[3] We also omit rule naming convention and restrict our attention to the content of the rules.

machine ethics and *norms*. However, the agent wants to learn more about *theories of action and agency*, *logic* and *machine learning*. Obligations and desires are formalized as default rules as follows.

$$\top \xrightarrow{O} machine\_ethics \quad (\rho = 5)$$
$$\top \xrightarrow{O} norms \quad (\rho = 5)$$
$$\top \xrightarrow{D} theories\_of\_action\_and\_agency \quad (\rho = 3)$$
$$\top \xrightarrow{D} logic \quad (\rho = 3)$$
$$\top \xrightarrow{D} machine\_learning \quad (\rho = 3)\ldots$$

In general, intentions, obligations, and desires are considered static since their role is to guide the agent in long-term behavior and decision-making. However, the use of defaults to represent them signals that these attitudes do not always materialize as chosen goals.

The general commitments and interests in supernormal defaults give rise to the more specific default rules. In Sect. 4 we detail how we mine such rules from users' profiles.

$$machine\_ethics \xrightarrow{O} do\_moral\_robots\_always\_fail \quad (\rho = 5)$$
$$norms \xrightarrow{O} social\_behavior\_emergence\_in\_MAS \quad (\rho = 5)$$
$$theories\_of\_action\_and\_agency \xrightarrow{D} agency\_in\_the\_age\_of\_ai \quad (\rho = 3)$$
$$machine\_learning \xrightarrow{D} alphafold\_protein\_prediction \quad (\rho = 4)\ldots$$

Before implementing BOID rules in the algorithm, we need to circumvent a critical pitfall of applying logical systems. If the BOID theory starts with an empty set of facts ($W = \emptyset$), then all the rules can be applied even if it is not possible in the real world, i.e., an agent cannot be at two places at the same time. In logic, an incompatibility of this type is called "material inconsistency".

To address material inconsistency, we use the concept of mutual exclusivity by inducing formulas of the type $\neg(\phi \wedge \psi)$. If these formulae are added to the belief set for each conflicting time slot, then presentations that are given in the same time slot will not be added to the belief set. In our example, the set of facts (the starting information W of the BOID theory T_1) will be initialized with the following type of formulas representing mutually exclusive program items:

$$\{\neg(timeslot\_1\_1 \wedge timeslot\_1\_2) \wedge \neg(timeslot\_1\_1 \wedge timeslot\_1\_3) \wedge \neg(timeslot\_1\_2 \wedge timeslot\_1\_3)\}.$$

Fig. 1 shows the process tree and the way in which extensions are built by applying the above-specified defaults (Fig. 2).

After applying all the default rules, the following two BOID goal extensions can be calculated:

$$E_1 = Th^L(W_1 \cup \{machine\_ethics, do\_moral\_robots\_always\_fail, timeslot\_4\_123, norms, \ldots, timeslot\_2\_3, \ldots, timeslot\_1\_3, \ldots, low\text{-}rank\_adaptation\_of\_LLMs, timeslot\_3\_1, \ldots\});$$
$$E_2 = Th^L(W_1 \cup \{machine\_ethics, do\_moral\_robots\_always\_fail, timeslot\_4\_123, norms, \ldots, timeslot\_2\_3, \ldots, timeslot\_1\_3, \ldots, low\text{-}rank\_adaptation\_of\_LLMs, timeslot\_3\_2, \ldots\}).$$

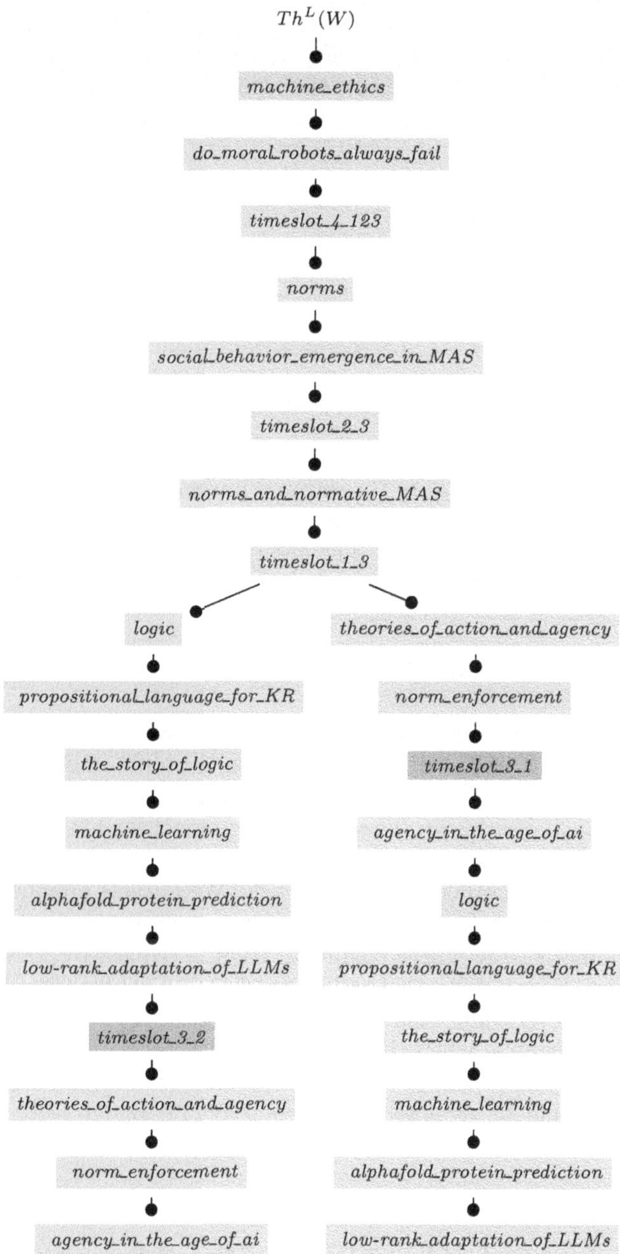

Fig. 1. Selected branches of the (prioritized) process tree of T_1.

According to the above sets, all subjects are included in the extensions. However, the agent is advised to attend only those time slots linked to the prioritized presentations that are part of both extensions. At this point, the schedule can be generated by working backward, identifying which presentations align with the designated time slots. As a result, the algorithm produces the personalized schedule in Table 2.

Table 2. Schedule output from the algorithm

	Session 1	Session 2	Session 3
Time slot 1	Alphafold protein prediction	Propositional language for KR	Norms and normative MAS
Time slot 2	Attention is all you need	The story of logic	Social behavior emergence in MAS
Time slot 3	Norm enforcement	Low-rank adaptation of LLMs	Agency in the age of AI
Time slot 4		Do moral robots always fail	

All the green-colored cells are the selected presentations the agent is advised to go to. The blue-colored cells highlight those presentations that are contained in some, but not all the extensions. The algorithm leaves it open to the users to resolve this type of conflict relying on their decision making.

4 Software Architecture and Implementation

The BOID system makes use of several different components, namely, an embedding model to gather BOID rules from the user's profile, the BOID-algorithm that uses the generated rules as an input to calculate the extensions, and, finally, a website to display the result. The embedding model facilitates the process of engaging with the user information to collect relevant rules. These components communicate with each other using websockets. Websockets provide a communication channel over a single, long-lived connection between a client and a server. Unlike traditional HTTP, where communication is request-response-based and typically unidirectional, websockets allow for real-time, bidirectional data transfer with minimal overhead. This can be useful since there can be splits in the process tree that happen when there are rules with the same priority and both can be applied. This, in turn, opens up the possibility of letting the user choose which *branch* should be explored. In normal HTTP based systems, it would be hard to communicate with the website if such a decision occurs, since it is unidirectional.

4.1 The Role of Embedding Models in Rule Mining and Specifying BOID Components

Embedding models have emerged as useful tools for practical tasks concerning semantic relations, but also as a resource for building knowledge bases. We will use them in the latter sense to provide information over which we extract default rules and to turn the relevant unstructured information into the format of default

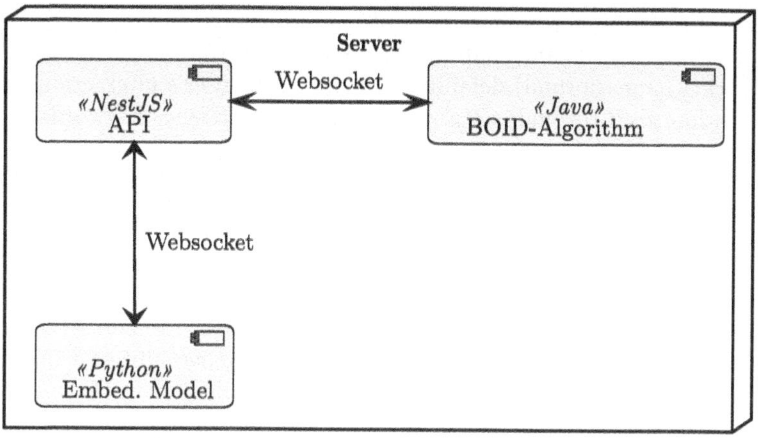

Fig. 2. BOID scheduler software architecture.

rules. This section details our use of embedding models to extract BOID rules, highlighting the advanced features of an open-source model E5-large-v2.

The E5 embedding model is a cutting-edge family of models designed for high-quality text embeddings. Thanks to its strong performance, E5 serves as a versatile, general-purpose embedding model for tasks requiring single-vector text representations, including retrieval, clustering, and classification, performing well in both zero-shot and fine-tuned scenarios [16]. These attributes make E5 (E5-large-v2) particularly well-suited for BOID rule mining because it can effectively analyze complex patterns, relationships, and behaviors within large datasets. With its robust natural language processing capabilities, E5-large-v2 facilitates the precise extraction and interpretation of BOID rules in our algorithm, aiding in the development of sophisticated agent-based models.

As argued by [8,11], large language models excel in understanding complex data when strengthened with a symbolic reasoning component. In the interest of increasing transparency of the system as a whole, we contend that one needs only to leverage one (important) component of large language models, namely *embedding models*. Tasks where embedding models can be particularly effective include unsupervised similarity estimation, capturing contextual nuances in large datasets, and extracting patterns and rules from text.

In our BOID scheduler, we build on embedding models' natural language processing capabilities that make them ideal for tasks requiring deep content understanding, such as extracting BOID rules. Our approach is anchored in the use of a frozen embedding model, applying a single encoding step to carefully formatted inputs, which are then compared to candidate vectors to enable zero-shot inference. The main steps involved in fostering rule mining through embedding model inference are:

- Detailing conference schedules in the JSON format to provide information on the time slots, topics, and speakers;

- Generating (supernormal) default *obligations* from keywords found in the user's scholar profile and matched to presentation topics;
- Gathering (supernormal) default *desires* from the user's interaction with the application itself through selecting a subset of conference keywords.

In mining BOID default rules, embedding models help in obtaining and formulating the initial set of supernormal defaults with a tautological antecedent. After mining an initial set of obligation and desire rules, the role of embedding models is to find out which keywords, be it either Google Scholar or user-indicated conference keywords, correspond to the paper entries in the conference program. This is the key step in connecting general topics from a user's profile to the actual conference program items. For example, a general interest in 'machine ethics' needs to be recognized as similar enough to the paper '*Do moral robots always fail*', which does not specifically mention either of the terms in the aforementioned keyword. The keyword-paper similarity measure relies on the cosine similarity measure between two vectors. This is a method in which state-of-the-art embedding models excel at finding semantic similarity in embedding vectors of two concepts or pieces of text.

The question of how to learn default generalizations has not been adequately addressed in the logic community, despite the tradition that default reasoning has in the knowledge representation research [9, p. 898]. We propose a practical answer to this question to generate BOID defaults. In our chosen domain of application, we generate defaults based on the mentioned semantic proximity of concepts. The process is constrained by requiring keywords to be connected to the paper topics in a significant way, where the similarity estimation grounds a 'default' once the cosine similarity measure surpasses a heuristic threshold. Our current method considers a keyword to be significantly connected to a paper topic if the similarity score exceeds a threshold that is set here to 0.75. This threshold was chosen to balance recall and precision, but alternative methods (e.g., via adaptive thresholds or reranker models) could further reduce arbitrariness in defining connections.[4]

Interpreting BOID Mental Attitudes Algorithmically. As indicated above, the process of extracting *obligations* and *desires* begins with analyzing the Google Scholar profile of the user and the user's selection of conferences keywords, respectively. This is the first step in *mining* defaults. The keywords available in the Google Scholar profile indicate relevant topics, suggesting that the user is likely required to attend presentations on similar subjects. We philosophically justify our interpretation of obligations in the following way. Any given research portfolio is a resource for extracting topics that stand as long-term commitments that a user has with respect to certain topics. Such long-term

[4] This is a sensitive part of the rule mining method via 'embedders'. For some models, setting a threshold as high as, e.g., 0.8 can compromise recall to the point of failing to mine the intuitively plausible rule $norms \xrightarrow{O} norm\_enforcement$.

commitments give rise to professional duties and obligations to deepen the knowledge of particular subjects. These commitments are external to the user in the sense that they are not changed on the whim of momentary wishes, in the way that obligations are external to moral agents.

Desires, on the other hand, are determined through a system where users have a liking for a certain number of conference keywords. If a user expresses interest in specific subjects, it can be inferred that they prefer attending presentations related to those topics. These preferences may overlap with the users' obligations, but not necessarily. We hereby leave space for situations in which a user wants to learn something about a topic that is further away from their usual topics of choice.

Once the first-layer identification of obligation and desire rules is completed, the embedding model matches their consequents to the topics of the conference presentations in the second layer of rule mining. This is done using a zero-shot embedding inference, where a conference schedule is provided with the extracted titles and abstracts for semantic similarity measurements. To finalize the second layer of rule mining, the identified obligations and desires from the schedule are converted into default rules using Python functions. To illustrate the second layer of rule mining, consider again the first-layer rule $\top \xrightarrow{O} machine\_ethics$, expressing the obligation to learn about the topic 'machine ethics'. This research commitment triggers the obligation to attend the presentation of the paper '*Do moral robots always fail*', that is, $machine\_ethics \xrightarrow{O} do\_moral\_robots\_always\_fail$.

It is important to note that the second layer defaults in principle inherit the priority order of the tautological rule, which has their antecedent as a consequent. This enables us to keep the priority ordering constrained by the chosen structure of the preset BOID agent type. However, we leave space for strengthening the priority value of a motivational attitude based on the fit with the user's researcher profile. The 'fit' with the research profile is fleshed out as a number of keywords from the user's Google Scholar profile that match a paper's topic. In this way, the priority value of a desire rule might, for example, increase to match or even surpass that of an obligation rule if the desire is strongly embedded in the interests indicated by the user. We find this decision justified with respect to our overall 'low-stakes' domain of application. Thus the actual adopted agent type is **flexible** $\{B \succ O \succ I \succ D\}$. In principle, we leave k integer values between the O rules with respect to the I rules and n integer values between the I rules and D rules, where the value of k and n indicate whether an agent is flexible or persistent with respect to its agent type.

4.2 Algorithm Implementation, Optimization and Inner Workings Based on Process Trees

The BOID algorithm utilizes a library called *Tweety*. According to its developers [15]:" *Tweety* is a collection of Java libraries that provides a general interface layer for doing research in and working with different knowledge representation formalisms such as classical logics, conditional logics, probabilistic logics, and computational argumentation". *Tweety* also has a Default Logic library, in specific. The package includes a reasoner that uses process trees to calculate extensions of default theories. This creates a starting point for implementing the BOID-algorithm, since it is possible to build upon the components provided by *Tweety*.

The initial step is populating the set of facts (W set of T), and checking whether the branch in the tree is already closed. As long as the branch remains open, it applies a default rule that has not yet been applied but is applicable and prioritized, that is, ρ-applicable. If the conditions are met, the rule is applied, thereby forcing closure of a process. Afterwards the algorithm checks if the branch qualifies as a process (see definition 3).

In the conference example, the rules are ordered in descending priority. The system interprets these components based on the user's predefined goals for attending the conference, as exemplified by the "motivational" components such as desires and obligations. However, there are cases where some rules share the same prioritization. This raises the question of which rule should be applied. The current implementation applies both rules, causing the tree to split into two new branches, both of which are explored. The approach could be seen as computationally suboptimal inasmuch as it applies multiple rules that have the same priority because this can cause the tree to grow significantly larger. To address this, a future enhancement will allow the user to select a default rule to apply if such a split occurs. The algorithm would then continue down that branch without considering the others. If this leads to an otherwise overruled branch (given some extralogical criteria), the algorithm will backtrack and inform the user that the other branch may be a better option.

API. The website is developed using NestJS, a progressive Node.js framework designed for building efficient, reliable, and scalable server-side applications. NestJS leverages TypeScript and a modular architecture, providing well-established design patterns and flexibility for structuring maintainable APIs. Built on top of Express.js (or optionally Fastify), it seamlessly integrates with databases, authentication mechanisms, and third-party services, making it a robust choice for modern application development.

In this implementation, NestJS serves as both the API and front end, ensuring a unified development experience. Communication between different components is facilitated through a WebSocket server, enabling real-time, bidirectional data exchange. NestJS primarily supports RESTful APIs, but it also includes built-in support for WebSockets via gateways—specialized classes that handle real-time communication between clients and servers. This approach enhances the application's responsiveness, making it well-suited for interactive and data-driven mobile experiences.

The decision to use NestJS is driven by its scalability, strong TypeScript support, and structured approach to back-end development. Its modular design allows for easy expansion and maintainability while ensuring optimal performance across different platforms.[5]

5 Conclusion and Discussion

This paper demonstrated how the BOID algorithm can be applied to enhance scheduling transparency and usability in the context of conference attendance. By integrating foundational concepts such as default logic, process trees and the prioritization of cognitive elements, the BOID architecture has shown to be effective for creating personalized and adaptive schedules based on user-defined preferences and priorities.

There are several academic personalization tools that are integrated in conference management systems. Among them, there is some available information that these tools are based on "talk similarity" ('*EasyChair*') [6], users' input ('*Ex Ordo*') [7] and semantic search and Microsoft Academic Graphs ('*Microsoft Academic*') [10]. These systems are very similar to the product or content recommender systems used by 'tech' companies in personalizing their offer and their primary use is not in session recommendations. There seem to be no available tools that use logical systems specifically for session scheduling.

One example of using BDI-like logics in scheduling is the 'Timeful' app that was developed by Shoham et al. [13,14]. The role of BDI logic in this system is, however, unclear to us and the app is not available any more after being purchased by *Google* in 2015 and (presumably) integrated into Google Calendar tools. The initial system, however, was based on a data model called the 'intention object' (IO), which is a feature vector capturing practical attributes of intentions such as time constraints, locations, and contextual execution conditions. Conceptually, the closest system that we are aware of is the work on 'levels of modality' in BDI logic [2,3]. The system incorporates qualitative modality levels for beliefs, desires, and intentions that enable a personal assistant agent to dynamically schedule tasks. The algorithm uses an ordering of tasks based on the confidence in beliefs, urgency of desires- etc., represented as numerical parameters. The system is thus capable of dealing with modality conflicts and assigning time slots. As indicated by the authors, "often it is not clear how many levels of the mentalistic notions are needed in a given application, and how to determine the division points" [2, p. 261]. To address the issue, the algorithm relies on domain expert knowledge to define these levels for specific applications. This brings us to the pitfall of logic-based applications that we mentioned above, namely, how exactly are we to extract rules and their priorities from data. The current BOID application use of embedding models gives one solution to this long-standing problem.

Our system currently does not include the iterative nature of the BOID algorithm that preserves intentions from an agent's previous deliberation, partially because our scheduling example focuses on a one-time decision procedure. In the

[5] Our source code is available on the website: https://anonymous.4open.science/r/BOID-Conference-00F5/README.md.

current algorithm, intentions are implemented as users' direct inputs of the time slots they decided to attend. The intention component can be elaborated further by incorporating users' intentions as higher-level goals for a specific conference elicited by a set of questions. Another venue for improving the algorithm is the user interface Q&A that gathers desires. Currently, the interface is very simplistic and has been made for the proof of concept. A more advanced way to get the desire component would be to present users with, for example, an interactive conference topics graph, which would allow users to rank their interests that we interpret as desires.

We, however, show a concrete implementation of the BOID logic algorithm within a software architecture, leveraging tools like an embedding model, a NestJS API, and a React Native app that support its practical applicability. By incorporating real-time decision-making through web sockets and extending the flexibility of process tree exploration, the system aligns technical feasibility with user-centered design. These advancements offer a promising avenue for deploying BOID logic in real-world applications, where decision transparency and adaptability are critical.

Future research in our group focuses on enhancing the user interaction with the system, particularly exploring how BOID types can be more effectively gathered from user input and user profiles. Investigating these aspects will provide better alignment of system-generated goals with individual user preferences, thereby improving the system's intuitiveness and practical value.

Acknowledgments. We would like to thank the Dutch Research Council (Nederlandse Organisatie voor Wetenschappelijk Onderzoek, NWO) for their support of the project "Empowering Human Intentions through Artificial Intelligence", and to the Human-centered Artificial Intelligence (HAI) 'focus area' of Utrecht University for supporting the project "Intention refinement for smart scheduling". The first author thanks the Italian Ministry of University and Research for the support of the "Reasoning with Data" (ReDa, G53C23000510001) project awarded to Prof. Hykel Hosni under the FIS1 Advanced Grant scheme.

References

1. Antoniou, G.: Nonmonotonic Reasoning. MIT Press, Cambridge, MA (1997)
2. Blee, J., Billington, D., Governatori, G., Sattar, A.: Levels of modality for BDI logic. J. Appl. Log. **9**(4), 250–273 (2011)
3. Blee, J., Billington, D., Sattar, A.: Reasoning with levels of modalities in BDI logic. In: Ghose, A., Governatori, G., Sadananda, R. (eds.) Agent Computing and Multi-Agent Systems: 10th Pacific Rim International Conference on Multi-Agents, PRIMA 2007, pp. 410–415. Springer (2009)
4. Broersen, J., Dastani, M., Hulstijn, J., van der Torre, L.: Goal generation in the BOID architecture. Cogn. Sci. Q. **2**(3–4), 428–447 (2002)
5. Broersen, J., Dastani, M., van der Torre, L.: Resolving conflicts between beliefs, obligations, intentions, and desires. In: Benferhat, S., Besnard, P. (eds.) European Conference on Symbolic and Quantitative Approaches to Reasoning and Uncertainty, pp. 568–579. Springer (2001)

6. EasyChair: Easychair smart program technology. https://easychair.org/smart_program. Accessed 15 Jan 2025
7. Ex Ordo: Conference management software. https://www.exordo.com/product/conference-management. Accessed 15 Jan 2025
8. Freedman, G., Dejl, A., Gorur, D., Yin, X., Rago, A., Toni, F.: Argumentative large language models for explainable and contestable decision-making (2024). https://arxiv.org/abs/2405.02079
9. Khan, R.A., Belle, V.: Abnormal predicates: Learning categorical defaults from probabilistic rules. In: Rocha, A.P., Steels, L., van den Herik, H.J. (eds.) 17th International Conference on Agents and Artificial Intelligence. vol. 3, pp. 892–900. SCITEPRESS (2025)
10. Microsoft Research: A fresh look: Microsoft academic website refresh. https://www.microsoft.com/en-us/research/articles/a-fresh-look-microsoft-academic-website-refresh/. Accessed 15 Jan 2025
11. Pan, L., Albalak, A., Wang, X., Wang, W.Y.: Logic-LM: Empowering large language models with symbolic solvers for faithful logical reasoning (2023). https://arxiv.org/abs/2305.12295
12. Reiter, R.: A logic for default reasoning. Artif. Intell. **13**(1–2), 81–132 (1980)
13. Shoham, Y.: Logical theories of intention and the database perspective. J. Philos. Log. **38**, 633–647 (2009)
14. Shoham, Y.: Why knowledge representation matters. Commun. ACM **59**(1), 47–49 (2015)
15. Thimm, M.: The tweety library collection for logical aspects of artificial intelligence and knowledge representation. KI-Künstliche Intelligenz **31**(1), 93–97 (2017)
16. Wang, L., et al.: Text embeddings by weakly-supervised contrastive pre-training. arXiv preprint arXiv:2212.03533 (2022)

Networks and Learning

Successful Misunderstandings: Learning to Coordinate Without Being Understood

Nikolaos Kondylidis[1(✉)], Anil Yaman[1], Frank van Harmelen[1], Erman Acar[2], and Annette ten Teije[1]

[1] Vrije Universiteit Amsterdam, Amsterdam, The Netherlands
{nikos.kondylidis,a.yaman,frank.van.harmelen,annette.ten.teije}@vu.nl
[2] University of Amsterdam, Amsterdam, The Netherlands
e.acar@uva.nl

Abstract. The main approach to evaluating communication is by assessing how well it facilitates coordination. If two or more individuals can coordinate through communication, it is generally assumed that they understand one another. We investigate this assumption in a signaling game where individuals develop a new vocabulary of signals to coordinate successfully. In our game, the individuals do not have common observations besides the communication signal and outcome of the interaction, i.e. received reward. This setting is used as a proxy to study communication emergence in populations of agents that perceive their environment very differently, e.g. hybrid populations that include humans and artificial agents. Agents develop signals, use them, and refine interpretations while not observing how other agents are using them. While populations always converge to optimal levels of coordination, in some cases, interacting agents interpret and use signals differently, converging to what we call **successful misunderstandings**. However, agents of population that coordinate using misaligned interpretations, are unable to establish successful coordination with new interaction partners. Not leading to coordination failure immediately, successful misunderstandings are difficult to spot and repair. Having at least three agents that all interact with each other are the two minimum conditions to ensure the emergence of shared interpretations. Under these conditions, the agent population exhibits this emergent property of compensating for the lack of shared observations of signal use, ensuring the emergence of shared interpretations.

Keywords: Emergent Communication · Successful Misunderstandings · Emergent Communication from Disjoint Observations · Robust Emergent Semantics

1 Introduction

The dynamic population aspect of Open Multi-Agent Systems (OMAS), does not guarantee an existing shared communication protocol. Nonetheless, agents may need to coordinate to achieve their goals. Furthermore, the system can exhibit robustness if it is possible to develop and maintain its communication

M. Baldoni et al. (Eds.): EUMAS 2025, LNAI 16259, pp. 107–123, 2026.
https://doi.org/10.1007/978-3-032-22820-8_7

system autonomously. Emergent semantics [5] describes how an agent population can develop a communication protocol in a decentralized manner from scratch. Agents communicate signals in task-oriented interactions and individually update their interpretation based on interaction satisfaction. Naturally, developing a shared semantics is expected to play a crucial role in aligning with other agents to achieve coordination. However, the decentralized nature of emergent semantics makes it challenging to verify the correct or shared use of emergent semantics. Successful coordination is usually assumed to suggest shared understandings or shared interpretations [3], especially when the internal representations of the agents are inaccessible or uninterpretable [10].

Communication emergence and language alignment have been studied between artificial agents [1,7,11,12,19] humans [8,15], and hybrid populations [10,13,14], although less in the last category. Evaluating interpretations solely on the basis of the interaction outcome may foster new risks, as reward-driven optimization could lead to unintended behaviors [17], due to phenomena such as shortcut learning [9]. Shortcut learning describes scenarios where machine learning models achieve high task performance but for the wrong reasons, giving us the wrong impression that they are trained correctly while failing to generalize. When it comes to language understanding, thought experiments, like the Chinese room [18] or the super intelligent octopus test [4], question whether humans and AI systems understand language in the same way. Is it safe to assume successful coordination is always a consequence of shared interpretations for emergent semantics in hybrid populations?

In emergent semantics, signals are interpreted in relation to the (perceived) situational context of their use. How are the emerged semantics affected in case the interacting agents have very different physiology and perception? Answering this question can bring insights for when applying emergent semantic methods in hybrid populations that include both humans and artificial agents. To computationally represent interaction between agents with very different perception, we take the extreme case where they exist in separate environments. We study what interpretations emerge in such a setting and answer 3 research questions:

- **RQ1:** *Is alignment always a by-product of coordination?*
- **RQ2:** *When do misaligned interpretations cause coordination failure?*
- **RQ3:** *What conditions ensure the emergence of shared interpretations?*

We apply an emergent communication method, inspired by language games [19], to study the affect of interacting agents existing in separate environments. An agent population develops a novel set of signals and aligns their interpretation by engaging in a Lewis signaling game [12] from separate environments. During an interaction, a Sender agent needs to communicate the environment's observed state to a receiver, who can perform an action. Existing in separate rooms, the Sender cannot observe the Receiver's action. The agents always receive equal reward, the value of which depends on the environment's state and the performed action. Which state-action combinations return positive reward is not given to the agents, otherwise they could infer unobserved information. Agents reinforce (weaken) signal interpretations that lead to (un)successful interactions.

To answer RQ1, we propose metrics to measure signal interpretation alignment between agents and compare it with coordination success. To answer RQ2, we design experiments that have two phases, i.e. i) the convergence phase and ii) the robustness test phase, to study the adaptability of converged semantics. Agent populations converge to signal interpretations that always lead to successfully coordination during the convergence phase. During the second phase, we allow agents to interact with new interaction partners, to test the robustness of the converged semantics. To answer RQ3, we identify necessary conditions during the convergence phase to ensure the emergence of shared semantics. We present in detail three experiments. In the first two, populations of 2 and 3 agents are joined by a new agent during the robustness test phase. In the third experiment, we apply interaction restrictions in populations of 3 agents during the convergence phase, which are lifted during the test phase.

Across all episodes, the agents converge to using signals in a way that always returns the best possible reward during the convergence phase of the experiments. In some cases, agents coordinate successfully, i.e. perform the action that gives them positive reward, without interpreting signals in the same way; answering RQ1. When agents coordinate successfully while interpreting the communicated symbol differently, we say that it is due to "**successful misunderstandings**". Communicating using successful misunderstanding does not cause coordination failure during the convergence phase. However, agents of populations that coordinate while interpreting signals differently, are not able to establish successful coordination during test phase with agents they have not interacted with during the convergence phase; answering RQ2. To ensure shared interpretation, we identify two conditions: i) the population has at least 3 agents, and ii) every agent can interact with any other agent; answering RQ3.

We show that agent coordination is not always a result of shared signal interpretation or use in emergent semantics between separate environments. Instead, agents can rely on successful misunderstandings that are not robust to new agent interaction pairings. Finally, we show an emergent property of populations that learn to communicate and include at least 3 agents that can all interact with each other. Such populations can compensate for the lack of observability of the environment and avoid the emergence of successful misunderstandings. This is crucial when agents assume shared interpretations to identify the reward function of the environment. Avoiding successful misunderstandings can offer insights for future research on hybrid populations that can learn to communicate.

The paper is structured as follows. In Sect. 2 we provide an overview of studies on (emergent) communication, showing that successful coordination is typically interpreted as evidence of shared understanding, identifying the literature gap. In Sect. 3 we present how agent populations interact and learn to interpret signals. In Sect. 4, we describe the experiments that allow us to answer our RQs. In Sect. 5, we present experiment results and answer our RQs. Finally, in Sect. 6 we conclude our study and suggest future directions.

2 Related Work

In this section, we present related studies on (emergent) communication in populations of artificial agents, humans, and hybrid populations. We identify the novelties of our study with respect to the related work.

2.1 Emergent Communication Between Artificial Agents

The study of emergent communication has been a focal point in multi-agent learning, where agents develop their own language-like protocols to facilitate coordination and task completion. [19] introduced the Naming Game, which shows how agents can self-organize vocabularies through reinforcement mechanisms. The agents engage in episodes playing referential games, having to use a word to refer to objects based on properties of the object, like its color. The agents operate using interpretable methods, demonstrating how the agents converge to a common vocabulary that the agents also interpret similarly. [11] studied communication emergence using deep learning methods in which the agents had to communicate which of the images presented was the correct. Agents learn to interpret a communication vocabulary by relating it with visual characteristics. The authors design the experimental setup in ways that would push the agents to relate the communicated symbols to known categories of the images. The study presents agents' internal representations, but does not make conclusive statements regarding their correct or shared interpretation. In [3], and other Ontology Alignment (OA) studies [2,6], task-oriented interactions are used as a means of establishing a shared understanding between agents. The fundamental hypothesis in [3] is that successful coordination suggests alignment, that is, shared interpretations. However, most studies do not investigate whether agents use shared interpretations, as long as they coordinate successfully [7,16]. In this work, we study whether emergent semantics between agents that communicated between separate environments are shared.

2.2 (Emergent) Communication Between Humans

An overview study on how humans interpret dialogue and recover from misaligned interpretations (misunderstandings) is presented in [15]. The overview suggests that conversation participants independently construct their own internal situational model that includes contextual information, useful for text production or comprehension. Furthermore, the study claims that "the linguistic representations that underlie coordinated dialogue come to be aligned". Translating the claim in computational terms, successful coordination suggests aligned internal representations and vice versa. Moreover, misalignment of participants' situational models can lead to misunderstandings and unsuccessful dialogue. In such a case, the participants align their situational models and reach a common ground through more dialogue. In [8], emergent semantics experiments are performed with humans. During each experiment, two participants need to develop a new sign system to co-navigate over a partially observable map of rooms.

They can only communicate using a modified seismograph, which requires them to develop a new set of signs and learn to interpret them in the same way to successfully coordinate. The study focuses in particular on the type of signals that humans create and how they assign meaning to them. The simple nature of the experiment allows for the interpretation of the new signs. Both signal forms and interpretations are related to either i) enumerating the rooms, or ii) describing their coordinates, or iii) describing visual characteristics of the rooms. By interpreting the emergent signs, we can also see that the participants learned to interpret the signs in the same way. This acts as further evidence of the common assumption that successful coordination leads to shared interpretations and vice versa. Our work investigates whether this assumption holds when the communicating parties perceive their environment very differently as if they exist in separate environments.

2.3 Emergent Communication in Hybrid Populations

The assumption that successful coordination is indirect evidence and the result of shared interpretations is extended also to hybrid populations [10] Following [3], they suggest that agents in hybrid populations can align their interpretations through task-oriented interactions that require coordination. This assumption is followed since in hybrid populations, agent's interpretations cannot be directly compared to evaluate similarity [10]. The same assumption is held in a demo [14], where humans can teach agents a grounded concept by playing the Naming Game. In [13], a human is teaching a robot to perform a collection of commands. Again, successful task performance is interpreted as correct task understanding. In this work, we investigate if this is indeed the case, when the interacting agents exist in separate environments, to computationally mimic interacting agents with very different perceptions.

2.4 Conclusion

All emergent semantics studies between artificial agents, humans, or hybrid populations follow the assumption that successful coordination suggests aligned representations. Our RQ1, i.e. "is alignment always a by-product of coordination?" investigates whether this claim is always true, or if consistent coordination can also be observed with misaligned semantics. To the best of our knowledge, this has not been studied before. In case RQ1 shows that misalignment can still lead to consistent coordination, we then explore RQ2 and RQ3 that study what are the limitations in this case and how to prevent this from happening, respectively.

3 Emergent Communication over Separate Environments

We perform communication emergence experiments on a population of artificial agents, following the experimental setup of Language Games [19]. In Language Games, an agent population develops a new signaling system through pairwise

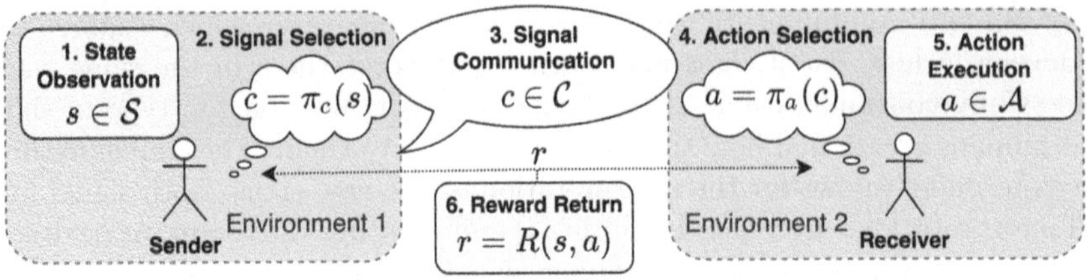

Fig. 1. The 6 steps of the signaling game between a Sender and Receiver that exist in separate environments.

participation in coordination games. In contrast to Language Games, the agents do not interact in the same environment, and have very few common observations. In addition to studying successful coordination, we are also recording to what extent the agents interpret the communication signals in the same way.

3.1 The Signaling Game Over Separate Environments

This section introduces the Lewis signaling game [12] in which two selected agents communicate within an episode to coordinate. One agent is assigned to the role of Sender, and the other to the role of Receiver. The game takes place in an environment, that is, in some state $s \in \mathcal{S}$. A set of actions ($\mathcal{A}$) can be performed in the environment. Depending on the combination of the environment state s, and the action performed ($a \in \mathcal{A}$), a reward $r \in \mathcal{R}$ is given to agents, based on the reward function $R : \mathcal{S} \times \mathcal{A} \to \mathcal{R}$. The reward function $R(s, a)$ is designed so that for each environment state s, there is exactly one action a that returns a positive reward. The agents always receive the same reward, making it a game of perfect common interest.

In our setting, the two agents play the coordination game from separate environments, as illustrated in Fig. 1. At the beginning of the episode, the environment's state (s) is randomly assigned and can only be observed by the Sender. Then, it decides which signal (c) to communicate, using its communication policy $\pi_c(s) : \mathcal{S} \to \mathcal{C}$. The Receiver is the only one that can select and perform an action (a). To do so, it uses its action selection policy $\pi_a(c) : \mathcal{C} \to \mathcal{A}$. The Sender does not know which actions are performed by the Receiver. Given the combination of state-action, the environment provides a reward value to the agents based on the reward function $R(s, a)$. The agents do not know the reward function of the environment $R(s, a)$. The two possible reward functions for an environment with two possible states and two actions is presented in Fig. 2. Finally the Sender and the Receiver update how they use the communicated signal based on the interaction outcome. Except for the signal communicated and the reward received, the agents have no other common observations.

3.2 Agent Policies

This section describes signal and action selection policies, and how agents learn from episodes.

Signal Utility Values and Interpretations Signals are used probabilistically, according to the total reward each interpretation has returned in the past. Agents are only aware of episodes they have participated in and only learn from them. For each signal, the agent stores the total reward, indexed by observed state $V(c, s)$ or performed action $V(c, a)$, depending on their role in that episode. Agents forget words they did not use in the last 20 episodes in which they participated.

Signal Selection Policy $\pi_c(s)$ Function $\pi_c(s)$ takes as input the observed state s and decides which signal c to communicate. First, the agent populates a set of candidate signals to communicate $\mathcal{C}_s$; its action set. The action set consists of all signals that have a higher utility value for the observed state than any other state; $c \in \mathcal{C}_s$, if $V(c, s) > V(c, s') \in S \setminus \{s\})$. The utility values of the candidate signals are normalized using the softmax function and treated as selection probabilities for the corresponding signals. To ensure that the agents explore enough and eventually converge to using an optimal policy, a probability mass equal to ϵ is evenly distributed among the candidate words. The value of ϵ decreases linearly from 0.2 to 0 during the first 5k episodes of the experiment. In case there are no candidate signals to communicate, i.e. $\mathcal{C}_s = \emptyset$, the agent creates and communicates a new signal.

Action Selection Policy $\pi_a(c)$ The Receiver observes the communicated signal c and retrieves the total returns per action this agent has received in the past when this word was sent, $V_r(c, a), \forall a \in \mathcal{A}$. Then, it normalizes these values using the softmax function and probabilistically selects one of them. Again, an ϵ value or probability mass is assigned to all possible actions $a \in \mathcal{A}$. Again, the value of ϵ decreases linearly from 0.2 to 0 during the first 5k episodes of the experiment.

Learning from Episodes At the end of the episode, the agents receive some reward based on the combination of the environment's state and the action performed by the Receiver, as defined by $r = R(s, a) \in \mathcal{R}$. The Sender updates the utility of the sent signal for the observed state, $V_s(c, s) = V_s(c, s) + r$. The Receiver does the same for the utility of the received signal and the performed action, $V_r(c, a) = V_r(c, a) + r$.

4 Experimental Setup

In this section, we describe the experimental setup that allows us to answer our 3 RQs. In Sect. 4.1, we introduce evaluation metrics that allow us to measure both coordination success and interpretation alignment in a population. To answer RQ1, whether interpretations that enable successful coordination are always shared, we just need one example where agents coordinate successfully with misaligned interpretations. To answer RQ2, whether useful but misaligned representations can cause coordination failure in the future, we perform experiments in two phases, described in Sect. 4.2. During the first phase of the experiment, i.e. the convergence phase, the population converges to using a common set of signals that allow them to achieve optimal coordination levels. During the second phase, i.e. the robustness test phase, we allow the agents to also interact with new interaction partners. Finally, in Sect. 4.3, we present an overview of the 3 experiments we perform and their conditions, which allows us to answer RQ3, i.e. what are the necessary conditions to ensure the emergence of shared interpretations?

4.1 Evaluation Metrics

We will now present the metrics that allow us to evaluate the agents' emerged semantics. We report average metric values over moving windows of 100 episodes for the findings to be more robust.

- **Reward**: The average reward reflects the ability of the agent population to coordinate successfully.
- **|Vocabulary|**: The agents' average signal vocabulary size. Reduction shows population semantics convergence.
- **Alignment**: Semantic alignment measures the ratio of the population that shares the dominant interpretation for each signal-role (Sender or Receiver) combination. It is calculated by the formula $\frac{|interpretation\_majority|-1}{|population|-1}$, and averaged over all signal-role combinations. The optimal value is 1, when every agent uses all signals in the same way for every roles.
- **Intent Met**: The ratio of episodes in which the Sender's intent was met, i.e. the Sender would select the same action as the receiver did, given the communicated signal.
- **Suc. Mis.**: The successful misunderstanding ratio of episodes, when agents receive positive reward while the Sender's intent was not met.

4.2 The 2-Phase Robustness Tests

To answer our second research question, i.e. are there negative consequences if the interactions are successful using misaligned representations, we perform experiments in two phases. In **Phase 1**, i.e., convergence phase, agents with no prior knowledge are interacting until they converge using signals that allow them to always coordinate successfully. Then, in **Phase 2**, i.e. robustness test phase, agents interact with new interaction partners and see if after enough interactions, they are able to converge again to always coordinating successfully. Each phase consists of 10k episodes, giving agents enough interactions to converge. We have two ways to make agents interact with new interaction partners in phase two, which gives us two experimental setups.

- **Population Increase**: Agents can interact with any other agent. A new agent with no knowledge is added to the population at the start of phase 2.
- **Initially Grouped**: In phase 1, agents are split into two groups and can only interact with agents from the other group. In phase 2, everyone interacts with everyone.

4.3 Overview of Presented Experiments

In this section, we describe the three experiments that we present in detail and allow us to answer our RQs. The first experiment starts with 2 agents in the first phase; named **2 agents**. In the second phase, we perform the population increase robustness test, by adding a third agent. Next, we conduct an experiment with three agents that form interaction pairs in an unrestricted way during the first phase; denoted as **3 Unrestricted**. During its test phase, we again apply the new population increase robustness test, adding a fourth agent. The third experiment, that is, **3 Restricted**, starts with 3 agents, but two of them belong to the same group and are not allowed to interact during the first phase. Thus, this experiment applies the "initially grouped" robustness test, and during the second phase, the two agents of the same group are also allowed to interact. This experiment is repeated with 4 agents in both phases, to further validate our observations. Table 1 provides an overview of these 3 experiments.

Table 1. Experimental setup overview of the three presented experiments.

Experiments		Phase 1: Convergence		Intervention	Phase 2: Robust. Test	
#	Name	Restricted	Agents	Robustness Test	Restricted	Agents
1	**2 Agents**	No (N/A)	2	Population Increase	No	3
2	**3 Unrestricted**	No	3	Population Increase	No	4
3	**3 Restricted**	Yes	3	Initially Grouped	No	3

Experiments are performed using environments with 2 states and 2 actions. Consequently, the only two possible reward functions are R_1 and R_2 for $\mathcal{R} = \{-1, 1\}$, which are presented in Fig. 2. To minimize the effect of random chance in

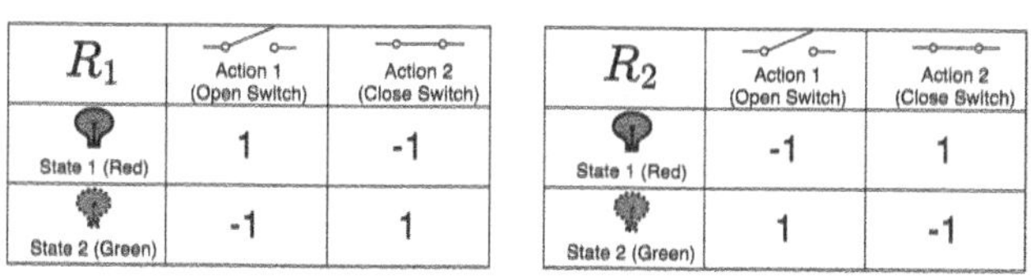

Fig. 2. The two possible reward functions (R_1, R_2) for a setting with 2 states and 2 actions.

the presented experiments, we repeat them 1000 times and report average values together with their Standard Deviation (SD) in parentheses. Each repetition of the experiment independently samples between using R_1 or R_2. The code for replicating the findings is available online[1].

5 Experiment Results

In this section, we present the experiment results, perform necessary analysis, and answer our 3 RQs. Experiments 1, 2, and 3, as described in Sect. 4.3, are presented in Sects. 5.1, 5.2, and 5.3, respectively. In Sect. 5.4 we identify the necessary conditions that ensure shared signal interpretations in emergent communication over separate environments. In Sect. 5.5, we mention performed experiments using more complicated reward functions that validate the generalizability of our findings.

5.1 Experiment 1: 2 Agents

Here, we will present the results of our first experiment. During the first phase, i.e. until episode 10k, populations of 2 agents exhibit clear signs of communication emergence convergence. As shown in Fig. 3, agents receive maximum reward while requiring approximately the least necessary number of signals. At the same time, i) semantic alignment score, ii) intent met ratio, and iii) successful misunderstandings ratio are on average around 50% at the end of the first phase, as Table 2 shows. This means that on average half the times i) the agents interpret the signals differently, ii) the Sender would behave differently had it acting as Receiver, and iii) the agents receive high reward for the wrong reasons. This answers our first research question, proving that emergent semantics that

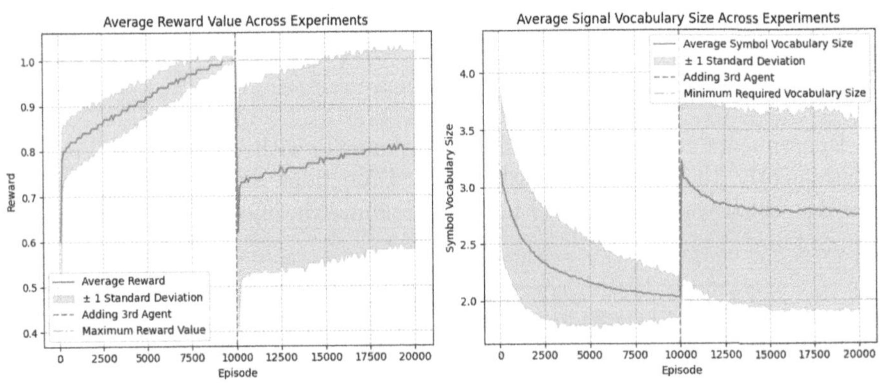

Fig. 3. Average reward (left) and signal vocabulary size (right) of the 2 Agents experiment.

[1] https://github.com/kondilidisn/eumas-successful-misunderstandings

Table 2. Evolution of the evaluation metric values over episodes of both phases, for the 1st experiment, i.e. "2 Agents". SD in parenthesis.

Episodes	Reward	|Vocabulary|	Alignment	Intent Met	Suc. Mis.
Convergence Phase: 2 agents					
100	0.60 (0.12)	3.14 (0.69)	0.49 (0.29)	0.49 (0.15)	0.51 (0.15)
500	0.81 (0.06)	2.85 (0.63)	0.48 (0.34)	0.49 (0.23)	0.51 (0.23)
5k	0.92 (0.04)	2.16 (0.37)	0.48 (0.46)	0.49 (0.39)	0.51 (0.39)
10k	1.00 (0.00)	2.03 (0.18)	0.48 (0.49)	0.49 (0.49)	0.51 (0.49)
Robustness Test Phase: 3 Agents (Unrestricted Partners)					
10k+100	0.62 (0.22)	3.22 (1.03)	0.73 (0.21)	0.59 (0.27)	0.41 (0.27)
10k+500	0.73 (0.21)	3.03 (0.87)	0.76 (0.21)	0.62 (0.29)	0.38 (0.29)
10k+5k	0.78 (0.23)	2.79 (0.85)	0.79 (0.21)	0.67 (0.31)	0.33 (0.31)
10k+10k	0.80 (0.22)	2.75 (0.85)	0.80 (0.21)	0.70 (0.31)	0.30 (0.31)

always lead to successful coordination do not always imply shared interpretations. Once a third agent is introduced in the test phase, the population cannot converge again to optimal behavior. Instead, it only manages to achieve 80% of the maximum reward, using more words than necessary. On the other hand, semantic alignment and Sender's intent met ratios have increased to 0.8 and 0.7, respectively.

Failure Analysis. There are two main questions raised from the experiment behavior presented in Table 2. First, how do agents coordinate successfully while misinterpreting each other during the convergence phase? Second, why do populations cannot converge to successfully coordinating during the second phase, when the third agent is introduced? To answer them, we present histograms of average evaluation metrics of individual experiments at the end of the two phases, i.e. episodes 10k and 20k, in Fig. 4. At the end of the convergence phase, Sender's intent was always met (0.9–1.0) at 40% of the experiments. For another 40% of the experiments, Sender's intent was never met (0.0-0.1). However, the agents were always communicating successfully. The 40% of the experiments where Sender's intent met was (>0.9) is still present at the end of the second phase. This demonstrates that populations with shared interpretations manage to reconverge to successfully coordinating after the fourth agent is introduced in the second phase. Instead, 40% of the experiments in which the agents converge to using successful misunderstandings in the first phase ((>0.9)) are scattered both in the Sender's intent met and in the reward histograms around random chance (0.5). This shows that agents of populations that converge to using misaligned interpretations are unable to adapt to interacting with new agents; responding to RQ2.

By investigating the performance of individual experiments in Fig. 4, we observe that our experimental setup has two Nash equilibria. One, is the

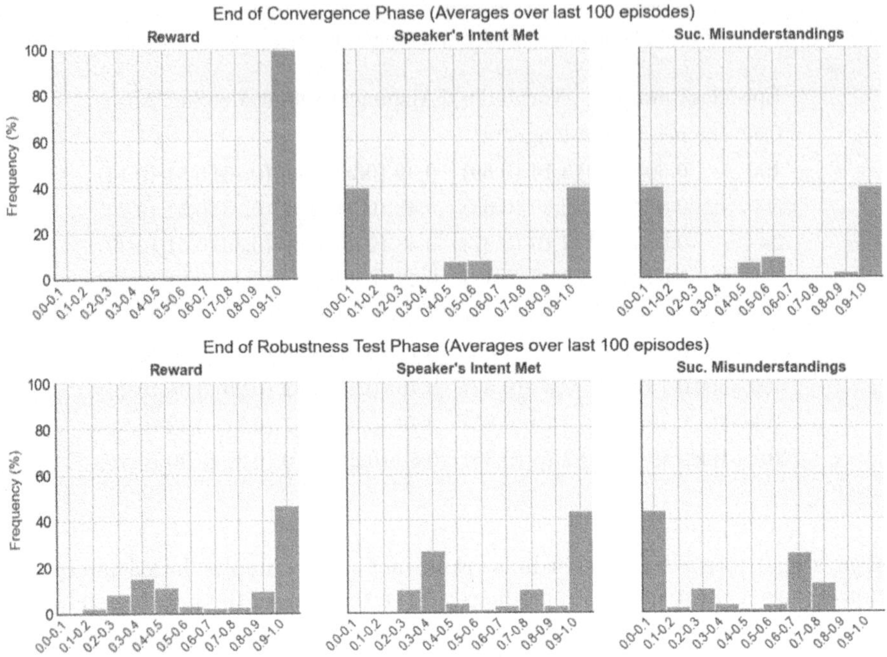

Fig. 4. Distribution of the individual experiments over value ranges for 3 evaluation metrics at the end of first (top) and second (bottom) phases of the 1st experiment, i.e. "2 Agents".

"expected one", when the agents interpret the signals in the same way, which is always the case for 40% of the experiments presented above. The second is when the agents use the signals exactly in the opposite way, which is the case for the other 40% of the experiments. When the agents converge to the second equilibrium, we say that they coordinate correctly using **successful misunderstandings**. Figure 5 explains this in detail.

5.2 Experiment 2: 3 Unrestricted Agents

We will now present the results of the second experiment, where the population consists of 3 agents from the beginning. An initial population of 3 agents approximates optimal communication behavior in terms of reward and vocabulary needed, at the end of both experiment phases, as Fig. 6 illustrates. Furthermore, populations are able to converge again to optimal behavior when a new agent is added at the beginning of phase 2 (red dashed lines), passing the robustness test. Agents almost always use communication signals in the same way, since both the alignment score and the Sender's intent met ratio are around 100%, as Table 3 shows.

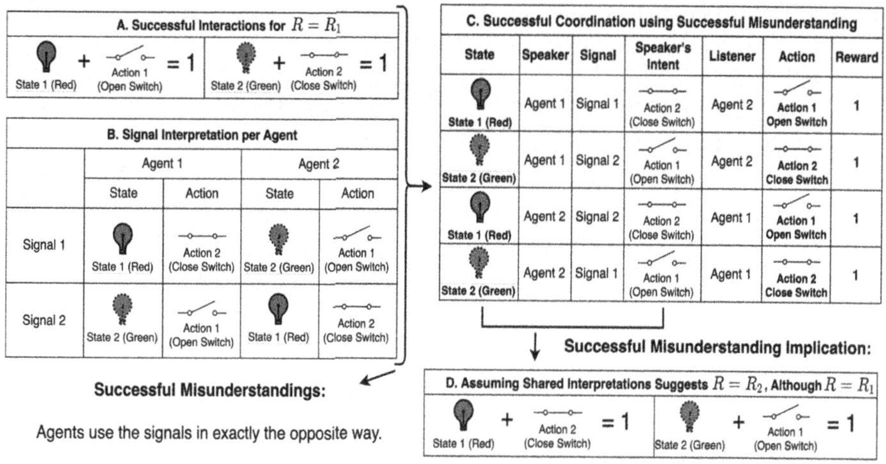

Fig. 5. A: Experiment reward function. B: Agent signal interpretation. C: Successful coordination due to successful misunderstandings in all 4 possible episodes. D: Inferred reward function, assuming common interpretations.

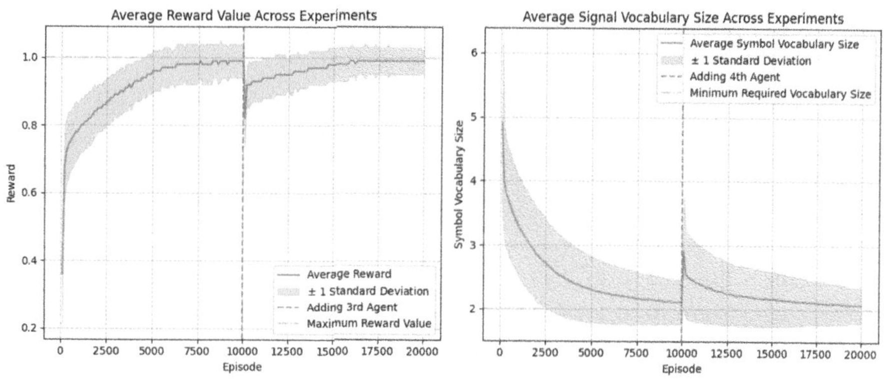

Fig. 6. Experiment "3 Unrestricted" showing successful communication convergence and passing the robustness test.

5.3 Experiment 3: 3 Restricted Agents

We present the results of the third experiment in Table 4, where interaction restrictions are applied to a population of 3 agents during phase 1. The emergent communication behavior of the experiment is similar to the one seen in the first experiment; see Sect. 5.1. Specifically, during phase 1, agents are able to coordinate successfully. At the same time, populations have an average semantic alignment score of 68%, i.e. equal to random change for 3 agent populations, and Sender's intent is only met half the times. This again causes the experiment to fail the robustness test during phase 2, achieving on average 0.71 reward by the end of the second phase, using 2.24 signals; see Table 4.

Table 3. Evolution of the evaluation metric values over episodes of both phases, for the 2nd experiment, i.e. "3 Unrestricted". SD in parenthesis.

Episodes	Reward	|Vocabulary|	Alignment	Intent Met	Suc. Mis.
Convergence Phase: 3 Agents (Unrestricted Partners)					
100	0.36 (0.15)	4.91 (1.26)	0.70 (0.13)	0.56 (0.08)	0.44 (0.08)
500	0.75 (0.09)	3.65 (0.83)	0.86 (0.11)	0.73 (0.11)	0.27 (0.11)
5k	0.96 (0.06)	2.31 (0.53)	0.96 (0.08)	0.94 (0.09)	0.06 (0.09)
10k	0.99 (0.05)	2.12 (0.34)	0.98 (0.07)	0.98 (0.08)	0.02 (0.08)
Robustness Test Phase: 4 Agents (Unrestricted Partners)					
10k + 100	0.82 (0.08)	2.91 (0.84)	0.86 (0.14)	0.88 (0.07)	0.12 (0.07)
10k + 500	0.93 (0.06)	2.48 (0.65)	0.94 (0.09)	0.92 (0.06)	0.08 (0.06)
10k + 5k	0.98 (0.05)	2.17 (0.43)	0.98 (0.06)	0.97 (0.05)	0.03 (0.05)
10k + 10k	0.99 (0.04)	2.08 (0.28)	0.99 (0.05)	0.99 (0.04)	0.01 (0.04)

Table 4. Evolution of the evaluation metric values over episodes of both phases, for the 3rd experiment, i.e. "3 Restricted".

Episodes	Reward	|Vocabulary|	Alignment	Intent Met	Suc. Mis.
Convergence Phase: 3 Agents (Restricted Partners)					
100	0.46 (0.14)	4.98 (1.41)	0.54 (0.15)	0.50 (0.12)	0.50 (0.12)
500	0.79 (0.07)	3.72 (0.83)	0.62 (0.17)	0.50 (0.21)	0.50 (0.21)
5k	0.95 (0.03)	2.75 (0.89)	0.65 (0.23)	0.50 (0.38)	0.50 (0.38)
10k	0.99 (0.02)	2.48 (0.82)	0.68 (0.25)	0.50 (0.45)	0.50 (0.45)
Robustness Test Phase: 3 Agents (Unrestricted Partners)					
10k + 100	0.69 (0.30)	2.47 (0.81)	0.74 (0.22)	0.65 (0.30)	0.35 (0.30)
10k + 500	0.70 (0.30)	2.44 (0.76)	0.74 (0.22)	0.65 (0.30)	0.35 (0.30)
10k + 5k	0.71 (0.31)	2.27 (0.53)	0.75 (0.23)	0.68 (0.31)	0.32 (0.31)
10k + 10k	0.71 (0.31)	2.24 (0.49)	0.76 (0.23)	0.69 (0.31)	0.31 (0.31)

Beyond Three Agents: Consistent Findings with a Fourth. We repeat the experiment with 4 agents (in both phases) to see if a larger population size is a sufficient condition for avoiding successful misunderstandings. Nevertheless, the findings are consistent with those presented in Table 4. Due to space limitation, we will only present key findings. During the convergence phase, all experiments converge to optimal communication, receiving maximum reward with the minimum required signal vocabulary size. However, in approximately half of the experiments, this is achieved using successful misunderstandings. During the second phase, when agent pairing restrictions are lifted, the populations do not converge to optimal levels of coordination. By the end of the second phase, the populations on average receive 0.68 (0.29) reward, uses 2.54 (0.68) signals, has a semantic alignment ratio of 0.68 (0.29), and the sender's intent is met 0.68%

(29%) of the times (standard deviation in parentheses). Interestingly, we observe that at the end of the first phase, agents that belong to the same group (who are not yet allowed to interact) use signals in a more similar way than when comparing agents from different groups. Specifically, each group of two agents has an average semantic alignment score of 0.86 (0.20), while the total population has a semantic alignment score of 0.64 (0.25).

5.4 Necessary Conditions to Avoid Successful Misunderstandings

Experiments "2 Agents" and "3 Restricted" allow the population to converge using successful misunderstandings during phase 1. On the other hand, experiment "3 Unrestricted" does not. We can therefore conclude that there are two necessary conditions for agents to develop shared interpretations when learning to communicate from separate environments and do not know the environment's reward function. First, the population must consist of at least 3 agents. Second, agents must be expected to interact with any other agent. In case we want to ensure shared emerged semantics between only two agents, we must initially include a third agent, who can later be removed. For larger populations, it is sufficient to have a "misunderstanding detection" team of 3 agents. When these 3 agents interact successfully with each other for any scenario, then they have shared interpretations. Subsequently, any agent that interacts successfully with one of these 3 agents, can be assumed to also share their interpretations.

5.5 Experiment Validation on More Complex Reward Functions

To validate the generalizability of our findings, we repeat our experiments for two additional settings that make coordination establishment more challenging. We present a possible reward function for each new setting in Fig. 7. In the first setting, i.e. $R_{Assymetric}$, reward functions are asymmetric, biasing the action selection of the receiver and making coordination establishment more challenging. In the second setting, i.e. $R_{3\times 3}$, the environment has 3 states and allows 3 actions, as opposed to 2 states and 2 actions used before. This leaves more room for possible misinterpretations and decreases the possibility of successful coordination due to chance. These additional experiments verify that having at least three agents and ensuring a fair chance that every agent interacts with any other agent are the two necessary conditions for shared emerged interpretations.

$R_{Assymetric}$	a_1	a_2
s_1	3	-3
s_2	-1	1

$R_{3\times 3}$	a_1	a_2	a_3
s_1	-1	1	-1
s_2	-1	-1	1
s_3	1	-1	-1

Fig. 7. Other reward functions used to validate our findings' generalisability.

6 Conclusions and Future Work

In this work, we extend emergent semantics experiments to interactions that take place between separate environments. The experiments presented allow us to answer our 3 RQs. By comparing measurements of coordination success and signal interpretation alignment between agents, we are able to answer RQ1, i.e. "Is alignment always a by-product of coordination?". The answer is "No", since we observe agent populations that converge to using successful misunderstandings, i.e. high levels of coordination using misaligned interpretations, at the end of phase 1 in both experiments 1 (Sect. 5.1) and 3 (Sect. 5.3). To answer RQ2, "When do misaligned interpretations cause coordination failure?", we study the robustness of successful misunderstandings. Agent populations that coordinated using successful misunderstandings were not able to learn to coordinate with new interaction partners, as seen in phase 2 of both experiments 1 (Sect. 5.1) and 3 (Sect. 5.3). Finally, to answer RQ3, i.e. "What conditions ensure the emergence of shared interpretations?", we conclude in Sect. 5.4 that populations need to have a group of at least 3 agents that interact with each other in all possible scenarios, i.e. environment states. This groups ensures the emergence of shared interpretations. The presented experiments are validated in environments that make coordination establishment more difficult, as presented in Sect. 5.5.

Future directions of this study can repeat experiments while including humans in agent populations. Moreover, identifying experimental setups that require unrestricted agent populations of 4 agents, instead of 3, to avoid successful misunderstandings, can lead towards developing a broader theory. Last but not least, future studies can focus on identifying possible misalignment and its consequences between humans and large language models.

Acknowledgments. This work was supported by "MUHAI - Meaning and Understanding in Human-centric Artificial Intelligence" project, funded by the European Union's Horizon 2020 research and innovation program under grant agreement No 951846.

References

1. Aberer, K., Cudré-Mauroux, P., Hauswirth, M.: The chatty web: Emergent semantics through gossiping. In: Proceedings of the 12th International Conference on World Wide Web, pp. 197–206 (2003)
2. Anslow, M., Rovatsos, M.: Aligning experientially grounded ontologies using language games. In: Croitoru, M., Marquis, P., Rudolph, S., Stapleton, G. (eds.) Graph Structures for Knowledge Representation and Reasoning, pp. 15–31. Springer International Publishing, Cham (2015)
3. Atencia, M., Schorlemmer, M.: An interaction-based approach to semantic alignment. Web Semantics: Sci. Serv. Agents World Wide Web s **12–13**, 131–147 (04 2012). https://doi.org/10.1016/j.websem.2011.12.001

4. Bender, E.M., Koller, A.: Climbing towards NLU: On meaning, form, and understanding in the age of data. In: Jurafsky, D., Chai, J., Schluter, N., Tetreault, J. (eds.) Proceedings of the 58th Annual Meeting of the Association for Computational Linguistics, pp. 5185–5198. Association for Computational Linguistics, Online (Jul 2020). https://doi.org/10.18653/v1/2020.acl-main.463, https://aclanthology.org/2020.acl-main.463/
5. Cudré-Mauroux, P.: Emergent Semantics, pp. 982–985. Springer US, Boston, MA (2009). https://doi.org/10.1007/978-0-387-39940-9_1311
6. Euzenat, J.: First experiments in cultural alignment repair (extended version). In: The Semantic Web: ESWC 2014 Satellite Events, pp. 115–130. Springer-Verlag, Berlin, Heidelberg (2014). https://doi.org/10.1007/978-3-319-11955-7_10, https://doi-org.vu-nl.idm.oclc.org/10.1007/978-3-319-11955-7_10
7. Foerster, J., Assael, I.A., de Freitas, N., Whiteson, S.: Learning to communicate with deep multi-agent reinforcement learning. In: Lee, D., Sugiyama, M., Luxburg, U., Guyon, I., Garnett, R. (eds.) Advances in Neural Information Processing Systems, vol. 29. Curran Associates, Inc. (2016)
8. Galantucci, B.: An experimental study of the emergence of human communication systems. Cogn. Sci. **29**, 737–67 (09 2005). https://doi.org/10.1207/s15516709cog0000_34
9. Geirhos, R., et al.: Shortcut learning in deep neural networks. CoRR **abs/2004.07780** (2020). https://arxiv.org/abs/2004.07780
10. Kondylidis, N., Tiddi, I., ten Teije, A.: A framework for establishing shared, task-oriented understanding in hybrid open multi-agent systems. Front. Artif. Intell. **Volume 8 - 2025** (2025). https://doi.org/10.3389/frai.2025.1440582, https://www.frontiersin.org/journals/artificial-intelligence/articles/10.3389/frai.2025.1440582
11. Lazaridou, A., Peysakhovich, A., Baroni, M.: Multi-agent cooperation and the emergence of (natural) language. CoRR **abs/1612.07182** (2016). http://arxiv.org/abs/1612.07182
12. Lewis, D.K.: Convention: A Philosophical Study. Wiley-Blackwell, Cambridge, MA, USA (1969)
13. Mohan, S., Laird, J.: Learning goal-oriented hierarchical tasks from situated interactive instruction. In: roceedings of the AAAI Conference on Artificial Intelligence vol. 28 (06 2014). https://doi.org/10.1609/aaai.v28i1.8756
14. Nevens, J., Van Eecke, P., Beuls, K.: Interactive learning of grounded concepts. In: BNAIC/BENELEARN (2019)
15. Pickering, M.J., Garrod, S.: Toward a mechanistic psychology of dialogue. Beha. Brain Sci. **27**(2), 169–190 (2004). https://doi.org/10.1017/S0140525X04000056
16. Rita, M., et al.: Emergent communication: Generalization and overfitting in lewis games (2022). https://arxiv.org/abs/2209.15342
17. Russell, S.: Human compatible: AI and the problem of control. Penguin UK (2019)
18. Searle, J.R.: Minds, brains, and programs. Behav. Brain Sci. **3**(3), 417–424 (1980). https://doi.org/10.1017/S0140525X00005756
19. Steels, L.: Experiments in Cultural Language Evolution. John Benjamins (2012). https://doi.org/10.1075/ais.3, luc Steels and Martin Loetzsch (2012). The Grounded Naming Game. pp. 41–59 (2012)

Adaptive Influence Maximization on Hypergraph Topologies

Vincenzo Auletta, Francesco Cauteruccio(✉), Diodato Ferraioli, and Grazia Ferrara

DIEM, University of Salerno, I84084 Fisciano, Italy
{auletta,fcauteruccio,dferraioli,grferrara}@unisa.it

Abstract. Influence maximization (IM) is a fundamental problem in computer and network science, with a plethora of applications. In this problem, you have to select a set of seeds to start an information diffusion campaign in order to maximize the number of influenced agents. In this paper, we consider the adaptive version of the problem where the campaign can be organized in several rounds and at the beginning of each round a different set of seeds can be selected, depending on the results of the previous rounds. The IM problem has been generally studied on networks, represented by graphs, where there are only binary relations among the nodes. However, real-world scenarios often involve more complex, multiway relationships, which can be better represented by hypergraphs rather than graphs. In this paper, we address these limitations by introducing the Adaptive Influence Maximization problem on Hypergraphs (AdaptHIM) which, to the best of our knowledge, has not been studied before. In particular, we introduce a formal framework to generalize it, and we propose a novel approach, based on the Elephant Herding Optimization algorithm, to address it, which we call `AdaptEHO`. This approach adaptively selects seeds by leveraging observed influence spread from prior rounds, and aims to balance exploration and exploitation. Through a comprehensive experimental campaign on real-world hypergraph datasets, we demonstrate that `AdaptEHO` outperforms baseline methods in influence spread while maintaining computational efficiency, thus resulting in a suitable trade-off for different scenarios of application.

Keywords: Adaptive Influence Maximization · Hypergraphs · Elephant Herding Optimization

1 Introduction

Influence maximization (IM) is a fundamental problem in computer science, and in particular in network science, with applications ranging from viral marketing and information dissemination to public health and opinion dynamics [3,5,10,11,34]. The aim of the problem is to identify a set of key entities, also called seeds, in a network whose activation leads to the maximum spread

M. Baldoni et al. (Eds.): EUMAS 2025, LNAI 16259, pp. 124–143, 2026.
https://doi.org/10.1007/978-3-032-22820-8_8

of influence under a given diffusion model. Traditional formulations assume that the underlying network is fully known and that seed selection is performed once, prior to any diffusion activity [7,22]. However, such assumptions are rarely met in real-world scenarios, where networks may be only partially observed and we learn their structure while interacting with it, and decisions should be made incrementally as feedback becomes available. Motivated by these limitations, in the last years there has been a growing interest in the adaptive setting of IM, that is, a paradigm that allows for sequential seed selection based on observed outcomes of previous activations [14,16,30]. This adaptive framework reflects realistic constraints in many applications, such as in the field of public health driven interventions, where influence maximization techniques are used to support community-driven interventions [33], and online influencer marketing campaigns, in which the marketers target a sub-population of influential people and the remaining potential of each of them must be taken into account when maximizing the influence [19].

Indeed, adaptivity introduces algorithmic and theoretical challenges, particularly in balancing exploration, i.e., gathering new information, and exploitation, i.e., leveraging current knowledge to make effective decisions [16]. Yet, a critical limitation persists in IM research: most models rely on graph-based representations, where edges encode pairwise interactions. While useful, such representations fail to capture higher-order relationships such as group discussions, team collaborations, or multi-user interactions, that define many real-world systems [8]. Hypergraphs, which generalize graphs by allowing edges (called hyperedges) to connect arbitrary subsets of nodes, provide a more accurate framework for these scenarios [9].

The emerging field of hypernetwork science has demonstrated that hypergraphs are essential for modeling social ecosystems, biological networks, and technological systems where group dynamics dominate [1,8]. Following this, in recent years, a thread of research has emerged that generalizes the IM problem from graphs to hypergraphs. In such a context, laying out the IM problem on hypergraphs surely poses new questions, as classical diffusion models must be adapted to account for group-level dynamics [23].

Despite its importance, IM in hypergraphs remains relatively underexplored. Most existing work either simplifies hypergraphs into graphs [2,4], losing crucial structural nuances, or focuses on non-adaptive settings [35,38] where all seeds are selected in a single step. This gap is particularly important in the adaptive IM paradigm, where sequential decision-making could leverage hypergraph topology to optimize exploration-exploitation trade-offs. For example, in a marketing campaign, observing how influence propagates through hyperedges, e.g., group purchases or shared content, could refine future seed selections dynamically.

More specifically, to the best of our knowledge, while there are some works studying the IM problem on hypergraphs, the adaptive setting of the problem has never been studied on such topologies yet. In light of this, in this paper, we aim to contribute to this setting by introducing a formal framework to represent the adaptive IM problem on hypergraphs, together with a novel algorithm to address it.

Related Literature. In what follows, we want to provide a bird's-eye view of the related literature, focusing on two strands, namely, the adaptive IM problem on graphs, and the IM problem on hypergraphs.

Early work by Golovin and Krause [14] introduced a theoretical framework for adaptive IM, proving a $(1-1/e)$-approximation guarantee for sequential seed selection ($b = 1$ per batch). However, their algorithm assumed exact computation of expected influence spreads, which is #P-hard in general [11]. Subsequent efforts by Vaswani and Lakshmanan [30] relaxed this requirement but imposed stringent accuracy constraints that remain impractical for large networks. The AdaptGreedy framework proposed by Han et al. [16], represented a significant advance by offering the first practical solution for adaptive IM with provable guarantees. Unlike prior work, AdaptGreedy accomodated batch sizes $b \geq 1$ and enabled the efficient instantiation with the state-of-the-art non-adaptive IM algorithms. This kind of framework allows for generalization across all pre-existing non-adaptive algorithms, and its performance depends on their efficiency. Additionally, Sun et al. [26] introduced the Multi-round Influence Maximization problem, where influence propagated in multiple rounds independently and from (possibly) different seed sets but, in contrast to the previous setting, the aim is to maximize the expected number of nodes that are activated in at least one round.

All these works rely on the possibility of observing the entire diffusion cascade, i.e., the *full-feedback* setting. This assumption is often unrealistic in large networks due to delays and computational costs. To address this limitation, weaker feedback models were introduced, namely myopic and partial feedback. For instance, when using the myopic feedback, only the status of the neighbors of the seed nodes is observed after each timestep t. While more practical, this model breaks the adaptive submodularity property, complicating theoretical analysis. Salha et al. [25] proposed a modified IC model where nodes retain activation status across timesteps, restoring submodularity and enabling a $(1-1/e)$-approximation guarantee for adaptive greedy policies. Their layered graph representation maps myopic observations to full-feedback equivalents, though adaptivity gaps remain bounded by $e/(e-1)$ [24]. Instead, when using the partial feedback, after activating a seed node at time t, we observe the propagation in the graph for d steps. Tong and Wang [28], formalized this as the (k, d)-AIM problem, where seeding decisions are made after d-step observations. Their greedy policy achieves $(a - e^{-1/\alpha})$-approximation, where α quantifies the regret of seeding immediately versus waiting for more information. For $d = 1$, it reduces to myopic feedback; for $d \to \infty$, it approaches full feedback. Yuan and Tang [36] introduced the α-greedy policy for partial feedback, dynamically triggering seed selection when the ratio of observed nodes exceeds a threshold α.

Other approaches [12,13,19,20,29,32] frame into the multi-armed bandit paradigm, learning diffusion parameters during the propagation campaigns, contributing to the field of Online Influence Maximization (OIM). This setting is closely related to adaptive IM, as both involve sequential decision-making under uncertainty. However, OIM typically assumes no prior knowledge of the network's diffusion parameters, while AIM often assumes partial knowledge (e.g., the graph structure) and focuses on adapting seed selection based on observed feedback during a single campaign.

The Influence Maximization problem on Hypergraphs has received increasing attention in recent years [2,4,6,15,23,35,38]. For instance, in [2], the authors represent a multimedia social network as a hypergraph, and to evaluate the spread of information, they transform the hypergraph into a bipartite graph and apply well-known algorithms to it. The work in [4] reasons similarly, and proposes four different heuristics to tackle the problem when a well-known diffusion process model, called Linear Threshold (LT), is considered. Instead, the work presented in [23] addresses the IM problem on hypergraphs by focusing on the HyperCascade diffusion model, which generalizes the standard Independent Cascade (IC) model.

The NP-hardness of the IM problem on hypergraphs has been shown in [38], where a sandwich approximation framework is proposed, and an algorithm preserving a $(1 - 1/e - \epsilon)$-approximation is presented. Furthermore, there are also some works addressing the problem by directly operating on hypergraphs rather than on bipartite graph representations. For instance, in [35] the authors study the problem under the Susceptible-Infected model with Contact Process diffusion model, which simplifies both the IC and the LT models. The authors then propose an algorithm called HADP to address it. This model is also taken into account in [15], where the authors introduce an algorithm called multi-hop influence estimation (MEI), which is based on transforming the hypergraph into a directed weighted graph. The authors also propose an adaptive neighborhood coefficient algorithm, called Adeff, a heuristic in which seed nodes are selected based on the ratio between their degree and hyperdegree. Finally, in [6], the authors present a general heuristics-based framework for addressing the problem, based on generalizing the problem by encompassing specializations of both the algorithms and the diffusion processes exploited.

Contribution of the Paper. In this paper, we propose a novel algorithmic framework that lies at the intersection of these two strands of research, and we provide the first formal definition of the adaptive influence maximization problem on hypergraphs.

Particularly, we propose an algorithmic framework that, thanks to its components, allows us to represent and generalize both this problem and possible approaches to tackle it. Then, within this framework, we provide a formal definition of the problem and state its aim. Finally, we propose an algorithm to tackle this new problem based on a metaheuristic called Elephant Herding Optimization. It is a population-based heuristic, inspired by the social behavior of elephant herds, where each individual is a solution. The algorithm is adaptive, in the sense that it enables the adaptive seed selection based on the observed outcomes of prior influence rounds. Summarizing, the main contributions of this work are as follows:

- We provide an algorithmic framework to represent and generalize the adaptive influence maximization problem on hypergraphs;
- Within the aforementioned framework, we provide a formal definition of the problem;
- We propose an algorithm to tackle the adaptive influence maximization problem on hypergraphs, based on a metaheuristic called Elephant Herding Optimization;
- We carry out an exhaustive experimental campaign in which we assess the goodness of our proposed approach.

To the best of our knowledge, this is the first formal definition of the adaptive influence maximization problem on hypergraphs, along with an algorithmic framework and an approach to address it. Our results demonstrate that this combination leads to more flexible and effective strategies for influence spread in higher-order networks when adaptivity is a desideratum.

Structure of the Paper. The rest of the paper is organized as follows. In Sect. 2 we provide some necessary background on the context. Then, in Sect. 3, we introduce the framework and we formally state the problem. Afterwards, in Sect. 4 we present our proposed algorithm, while in Sect. 5 we illustrate the experimental campaign. Finally, in Sect. 6, we draw our conclusion and highlight some future works.

2 Background

We start by formally defining the concept of a hypergraph. A *hypergraph* $H = (V, E)$ is a mathematical structure composed of a set $V = \{v_1, \ldots, v_n\}$ of elements, referred to as *nodes*, and a collection of subsets $E = (e_1, \ldots, e_m)$, known as *hyperedges* [9]. Each hyperedge represents a relationship among a subset of nodes in V, such that $e_j \subseteq V$ for all $j = 1, \ldots, m$. The *order* of a hypergraph corresponds to the total number of nodes, given by $n = |V|$, while its *size* refers to the number of hyperedges, expressed as $m = |E|$. Furthermore, the *size* of an individual hyperedge is defined by its cardinality, i.e., $|e_j|$. A node $v_i \in V$ is said to be a member of a hyperedge $e_j \in E$ if and only if $v_i \in e_j$, and e_j is said to contain v_i. The *degree* of a node v_i, denoted as $d(v_i)$, is defined as the number of its neighbors, where a node $v_l \in V$ is considered a neighbor of v_i if and only if there exists at least one hyperedge e_j that contains both v_l and v_i. In contrast, the *hyperdegree* of a node v_i, denoted as $d^H(v_i)$, represents the number of hyperedges to which v_i belongs. It is important to note that, in many instances within the literature, the term degree is often used to refer to the hyperdegree [1]. As an example, suppose we have $H = (V, E)$, with $V = \{v_1, v_2, v_3, v_4, v_5\}$, and $E = \{e_1, e_2, e_3\}$, where $e_1 = \{v_1, v_2\}$, $e_2 = \{v_2, v_3, v_4\}$, and $e_3 = \{v_1, v_3, v_5\}$. In this case we have that the order n of H is 5, while its size m is 3. Also, we have $d(v_2) = 3$ and $d^H(v_2) = 2$.

In the general context of the IM problem, one key component is the diffusion process model. Diffusion process models are theoretical frameworks designed to simulate how information spreads through a network. Lately, different diffusion process models have been reported in the hypergraph-related literature, and one of the most peculiar ones is the Susceptible-Infected with Contact Process (SICP) model [27]. In it, nodes can be either in a susceptible (S) or active (that is, infected) (I) state. An S-state node can be activated by each of its neighbors in the I-state with a given infection rate β. The model works as follows:

1. Nodes in the seed set are set to be active (I-state), and the remaining nodes are susceptible (S-state);
2. At each time step t, we find the I-state nodes. For each I-state node v_i, we find all hyperedges E_i containing the node v_i. Then, a hyperedge e_j is chosen from E_i uniformly at random, and each of the S-state nodes in e_j will be activated by v_i with probability β;
3. The process terminates after T steps.

We denote as influenced all nodes that are in the I-state when the process terminates. As mentioned above, various diffusion process models have been proposed in the literature [37,38]. While this paper focuses specifically on the SICP model, it is helpful to define a generic diffusion process formally. Accordingly, we denote by $\sigma_H(S)$ the set of nodes influenced at the end of a generic diffusion process operating on the hypergraph H and starting from the seed set S.

3 The Adaptive Influence Maximization Problem on Hypergraphs

In this section, we first introduce a formal framework to represent the adaptive influence maximization problem on hypergraphs (see Sect. 3.1). Then, building upon the framework, we provide a formal definition of the problem in Sect. 3.2.

3.1 Framework

We are now able to describe the problem, which we refer to as AdaptHIM. To do so, we design a formal framework encompassing all the components needed to represent the problem of adaptive influence maximization on hypergraph topologies. Thanks to this framework, we generalize the problem and possible approaches to it, while also defining it formally. Prior to introducing the framework, we provide a high-level overview of the problem itself, which seeks to select a *sequence of nodes* across multiple *rounds* in order to maximize the total number of influenced nodes. In each round, a subset of nodes is selected, initiating a *diffusion process* where influence spreads from the selected nodes to others according to the structure of the hypergraph. A node is considered influenced if it becomes activated through this spread of influence. The process is subject to a *budget* constraint, which limits the total number of nodes that can be selected across all rounds. The objective is to maximize the total number of influenced nodes by the end of the process.

We represent the framework as the tuple $\mathfrak{A} = \langle H, k, r, \sigma \rangle$. Here, the components are as follows:

- $H = (V, E)$ is the hypergraph we consider as input of the problem;
- $k \in \mathbb{N}^+$ represents the *budget*;
- $r \in \mathbb{N}^+$ represents the number of *rounds*;
- $\sigma(\cdot)$ is a diffusion process operating over the hypergrah H.

Pragmatically speaking, the framework represents an instance of the problem. H is the hypergraph we work on, while k and r are the two essential properties of the problem. The former, k, is the budget and represents the total number of nodes that can be selected across all rounds, while r is the total number of rounds. Note that the problem seeks to select a sequence of nodes, and such a selection induces an overall process representing the core of the adaptive influence maximization problem on hypergraphs. This process consists of the following flow, unfolding in r rounds:

1. At each round $1 \leq t \leq r$, a seed selection method $\rho(\cdot)$ selects a subset of nodes $S_t \subset V$;
2. The *expected influence*, that is, the number of influenced nodes, is now calculated by applying the diffusion process $\sigma(\cdot)$ on the hypergraph H starting from the nodes in S_t; at this step, the process records the set of influenced nodes, that is, the set of nodes influenced at the end of the diffusion process, as $\mathcal{O}_t = \sigma_H(S_t)$;
3. In the next round $t+1$, the seed selection algorithm ρ may now select the next nodes S_{t+1} based on the history of influenced nodes $\mathcal{H}_t = (\mathcal{O}_t, \mathcal{O}_{t-1}, \ldots, \mathcal{O}_1)$, that is the sequence of the sets of influenced nodes up to round t;
4. The process then continues until exactly k seed nodes are selected across r rounds, that is, $|\bigcup_{t=1}^{r} S_t| = k$. Eventually, the process outputs the overall set of influenced nodes $\mathcal{O}^* = \bigcup_{\mathcal{O}_j \in \mathcal{H}_r} \mathcal{O}_j$, which we also call influence spread.

It is essential to point out that the description of such a process introduces another aspect of great importance for the AdaptHIM problem, namely, the seed selection algorithm $\rho(\cdot)$. The seed selection method $\rho(\cdot)$ represents an algorithm which, sequentially, decides at each round $1 \leq t \leq r$ which subset of nodes $S_t \subseteq V$ to select. Similarly to what happens in the adaptive influence maximization problem on graphs, we refer to S_t as the seed set at round t, and each node in S_t is also called a seed [7]. Clearly, $\rho(\cdot)$ can be designed to select S_t in different ways, with the only constraint being that, at the end of all rounds, the total number of selected seeds must be equal to the budget k. In our setting, we assume that $\rho(\cdot)$ is designed to select S_t constrained to $|S_t| = \lfloor \frac{k}{r} \rfloor$, that is, exactly $\lfloor \frac{k}{r} \rfloor$ seeds are selected at each round. Furthermore, it is clear that, in the adaptive setting, an algorithm selecting the seed set S_t could benefit from exploiting the information regarding the history of observed influenced nodes $\mathcal{H}_t$, and the sequence of selected seed sets, especially. We denote and define the latter as $\mathcal{S}_r = (S_r, S_{r-1}, \ldots, S_1)$, that is, $\mathcal{S}_r$ is the sequence of selected seed sets up to round r. As it will be clear from the following, the sequence of selected seed sets plays an important role in the definition of the problem, as well as in a possible seed selection algorithm suitable for the problem at hand.

3.2 Problem Definition

Given the framework, we are now able to provide a formal definition of the AdaptHIM problem.

Definition 1 (The Adaptive Influence Maximization Problem on Hypergraphs). *Given an instance of the framework $\mathfrak{A} = \langle H, k, r, \sigma \rangle$, the adaptive influence maximization problem on hypergraphs (the AdaptHIM problem) consists in finding a sequence of selected seed sets $\mathcal{S}_r = (S_1, S_2, \ldots, S_r)$, where $S_t \subseteq V$, $1 \leq t \leq r$, and $|\bigcup_{t=1}^{r} S_t| = k$, such that expected number of influenced nodes $\mathbb{E}[|\mathcal{O}^*|]$ at the end of the process is maximized.*

In other words, given an instance of the problem, the objective is to find a sequence $\mathcal{S}_r$, constrained to the budget k and the number of rounds r, that maximizes the expected total influence. Therefore, we seek seed selection algorithms ρ that can find $\mathcal{S}_r$ effectively. In the next section, we will introduce such an algorithm based on the so called Elephant Herding Optimization algorithm.

4 An Adaptive Elephant Herding Optimization Algorithm

We propose an algorithm to tackle the AdaptHIM problem on hypergraphs based on a metaheuristics called Elephant Herding Optimization (EHO from now on). The EHO algorithm is a population-based metaheuristic inspired by the social behavior of elephant herds [21,31]. The population consists of a number of elephants (also called individuals), each representing a possible solution to the problem. These elephants are grouped into subgroups known as clans, where each clan is led by a matriarch, that is, the best-performing individual within that subgroup [17]. The algorithm simulates two main operators, namely, *(i)* the clan updating operator, and *(ii)* the separating operator, and its overall behavior unfolds over a certain number of iterations [31]. As far as the former operator is concerned, each elephant in a clan updates its position by moving toward the matriarch of the clan. Generally, the update rule for the j-th elephant in the i-th clan at a certain iteration t is defined as $x_{i,j}^{t+1} = x_{c,j}^{t} + \alpha \cdot (x_{c,j}^{t} - x_{i,j}^{t})$, where $x_{i,j}^{t}$ is the position of the j-th elephant in the i-th clan at iteration t, $x_{c,j}^{t}$ is the position of the matriarch (best individual) in the i-th clan, and $\alpha \in [0,1]$ is a scaling factor that controls the influence of the matriarch. As for the separating operator, to maintain diversity in the population and explore new regions of the search space, the worst-performing elephant in each clan is replaced with a new randomly generated individual. This operation is generally defined as $x_{\text{worst}}^{t+1} = x_{\min} + rng \cdot (x_{\max} - x_{\min})$, where x_{worst}^{t+1} is the new position for the worst-performing elephant, $x_{\min}$ and $x_{\max}$ define the search space boundaries, and rng is a uniformly distributed random number in $[0,1]$. Note that the population of elephants is divided into n_{clan} clans of equal size. Within each clan, all elephants update their positions according to the clan updating operator, except the worst one, which is reinitialized using the separating operator. This structure allows EHO to balance exploration, via the separating operator, and exploitation, via movement toward the matriarch, making it suitable for different optimization problems [17,21].

Algorithm 1. `AdaptEHO`

Input: Hypergraph $H = (V, E)$, budget k, number of rounds r, diffusion process model σ, number of elephants *elephants*, number of clans *clans*.
Output: Set of influenced nodes $\mathcal{O}^*$.

$\mathcal{O}^* \leftarrow \emptyset$
$\mathcal{P} \leftarrow$ `InitPopulation`$(H, elephants, clans)$
for $t = 1$ to r **do**
  $\mathcal{O}_t \leftarrow$ `EHOround`$(H, k, r, \sigma, \mathcal{P})$
  $\mathcal{O}^* = \mathcal{O}^* \cup \mathcal{O}_t$
  $H \leftarrow$ `UpdateHypergraph`$(H, \mathcal{O}^*)$
  $\mathcal{P} \leftarrow$ `UpdatePopulation`$(\mathcal{P}, \mathcal{O}^*)$
return $\mathcal{O}^*$

Here, we introduce an extension of EHO called `AdaptEHO`. The idea behind this extension is to make EHO suitable for tackling the AdaptHIM problem. The pseudocode of `AdaptEHO` is depicted in Algorithm 1. Here, the algorithm starts by defining the set $\mathcal{O}^*$, which will eventually contain the set of influenced nodes at the end of the process. Then, the population $\mathcal{P}$ is initialized via the function `InitPopulation`. This function works as follows: *clans* clans are created, each of which contains $\frac{elephants}{clans}$ elephants. An elephant is represented by a tuple $e = (\mathbf{v}, \mathcal{O})$, where $\mathbf{v} = [0,1]^{|V|}$ is a vector initialized with non-negative entries such that $\sum_{i=1}^{n} \mathbf{v}[i] = 1$; here, the i-th entry of $\mathbf{v}$ refers to the node $v_i \in V$. $\mathcal{O}$ is the set of influenced nodes, obtained by carrying out the diffusion process σ starting from a seed set selected by exploiting $\mathbf{v}$, and initially defined as $\mathcal{O} = \emptyset$. When it is clear from the context, for an elephant e we refer to these two values as $e_{\mathbf{v}}$ and $e_{\mathcal{O}}$, respectively. For a clan C, besides indicating the elephants contained in it, we also indicate with C_{e^*} the matriarch of the clan, e.g., the elephant $e^* \in C$ whose set $e^*_{\mathcal{O}}$ is the greatest among all elephants $e \in C$.

After these two preliminary definitions, the algorithm starts r rounds, and in each round, the following process is carried out.

First, the function `EHOround` is invoked to retrieve the best set of influenced nodes $\mathcal{O}_t$ obtained at round t. The pseudocode for `EHOround` is provided in Algorithm 2. Here, the function iterates *steps* times. In each iteration, it considers each clan C of the population, and for each elephant $e \in C$, we select the seed set S_e to be used for the diffusion process $\sigma_{S_e}(H)$ in order to obtain $e_{\mathcal{O}}$. Note that S_e is selected via the function `SelectSeeds`: this function is deliberately general, and can be implemented to exploit several strategies for selecting seeds. In our case, we select the top-$\lfloor \frac{k}{r} \rfloor$ nodes in V indicated by the corresponding highest entries in $e_{\mathbf{v}}$. At this point, `EHOround` implements the first operator of the EHO algorithm, that is, the clan updating operator. To do so, for the

Algorithm 2. `EHOround`

Input: Hypergraph $H = (V, E)$, budget k, number of rounds r, diffusion process model σ, elephants population $\mathcal{P}$, number of steps *steps*.
Output: Set of influenced nodes $\mathcal{O}_t$ at round t.

for $i = 1$ to *steps* **do**
  for $C \in \mathcal{P}$ **do**
    for $e \in C$ **do**
      $S_e \leftarrow$ `SelectSeeds`(H, k, r)
      $e_{\mathcal{O}} \leftarrow \sigma_{S_e}(H)$
    $C_{e^*} \leftarrow argmax_{e \in C}|e_{\mathcal{O}}|$ ▷ Clan updating operator
    for $e \in C \setminus \{C_{e^*}\}$ **do**
      `UpdateElephant`(e, C_{e^*})
    $e' \leftarrow argmin_{e \in C}|e_{\mathcal{O}}|$ ▷ Separating operator
    `InitElephant`(e')
$e^* \leftarrow$ `BestMatriarch`$(\mathcal{P})$
$\mathcal{O}_t \leftarrow e^*_{\mathcal{O}}$
return $\mathcal{O}_t$

clan C, we identify the matriarch e^*, that is, the best performing elephant of C. Then, all elephants in C, except for e^*, are updated to make their position closer to the matriarch. This operation is applied on the node vector $e_{\mathbf{v}}$ using the aforementioned rule, as originally proposed in [31], and it is implemented by the function `UpdateElephant`. Similarly, the separating operator is implemented by replacing the worst performing elephant e', i.e., the elephant exhibiting the smallest set of influenced nodes $e'_{\mathcal{O}}$ among all elephants in the clan, with a new initialization; that is, its vector $e'_{\mathbf{v}}$ is initialized with non-negative entries such that $\sum_{i=1}^{n} e'_{\mathbf{v}}[i] = 1$; this last step is carried out by the `InitElephant` function. Eventually, the `EHOround` function terminates and returns the set of influenced nodes $\mathcal{O}_t$, that is, the greatest set of influenced nodes identified among all elephants for each clan, which is given by the best performing matriarch among all clans.

At this stage, Algorithm 1 continues by updating the set of influenced nodes $\mathcal{O}^*$ with the ones obtained in the current round t, and then both the hypergraph H and the elephants population $\mathcal{P}$ are updated. Here, some details are in order. The function `UpdateHypergraph` simply updates H by removing from V all nodes contained in $\mathcal{O}^*$, that is, all influenced nodes will not be taken into account in the next rounds of the algorithm. Then, the function `UpdatePopulation` exploits the information regarding influenced nodes to update all elephants. In particular, the information about a particular node being removed from the hypergraph is injected into the representation of an elephant by setting the corresponding entry in the vector to 0. More formally, let e be an elephant belonging to the population $\mathcal{P}$. Then, for each $v \in \mathcal{O}^*$, $e_{\mathbf{v}}[v] = 0$. Eventually, the algorithm terminates, returning the set $\mathcal{O}^*$ of influenced nodes.

We note that, although not explicitly stated, the algorithm inherently computes the sequence of selected seed sets S_r, as these sets are instrumental in determining the influential nodes. Moreover, the concluding steps of the algorithm, and specifically, the update of the hypergraph structure and the adaptation of the population, serve a crucial role in endowing `AdaptEHO` with adaptive capabilities. By incorporating newly discovered information and discarding non-relevant nodes, the algorithm effectively evolves over each round. This adaptivity enables it to adjust to shifts in the underlying influence spread, maintain exploration of the search space, and incrementally refine its approximation of the optimal seed set.

5 Experiments

In this section, we present the results of a series of experiments conducted to evaluate the effectiveness of the proposed approach. We begin by providing a detailed description of the experimental setting, followed by an overview of the used datasets along with their key characteristics. Subsequently, we outline the baselines selected to perform the comparison. Finally, we report and discuss the results of three experiments conducted on real-world hypergraphs: a comparison of expected influence spread, a comparison of running time, and parameter tuning.

5.1 Setup

All experiments were conducted on a computer equipped with an Intel(R) Core(TM) i9-10980XE @ 3.00GHz processor, 64 GB of RAM, and a Windows operating system. The whole framework was implemented in Python 3.13[1]. For each configuration, experiments were repeated 100 times to account for variability, and the average influence spread and running time were used for evaluation purposes. In the evaluation of influence spread, each set of selected seeds was assessed over 100 simulations for each round of the adaptive execution. The running time was measured as the time required to complete the seed selection and diffusion evaluation. Randomness was controlled by independently sampling new diffusion processes for each trial, ensuring statistically robust results.

5.2 Datasets

We evaluated the proposed method on several real-world hypergraph datasets. Each dataset is represented as a hypergraph, where nodes correspond to entities and hyperedges capture higher-order relations among them. A summary of the key statistics of the datasets is provided in Table 1. To complement it, a brief description of each dataset is provided in the following:

[1] Source code and datasets are available at https://gitlab.com/core_lab/infmax-hypernetworks/adapthim.

Table 1. Properties of the selected datasets. n and m denote the order and size, respectively. $\overline{|e_j|}$ represents the average hyperedge size, while $\overline{d}$ and $\overline{d^H}$ denote the average degree and average hyperdegree, respectively.

Dataset	n	m	$\overline{\lvert e_j \rvert}$	$\overline{d}$	$\overline{d^H}$
Algebra	423	1268	6.52	78.90	19.53
Rest.-Rev	565	601	7.66	79.75	8.14
Geometry	580	1193	10.47	164.79	21.53
Music-Rev	1106	694	15.13	167.88	9.49
NDC	1161	1088	5.92	10.72	5.55
Bars-Rev	1234	1194	9.94	174.30	9.62
iAF1260b	1668	2351	3.87	13.26	5.46
iJO1366	1805	2546	3.94	16.92	5.55

- The *Restaurant-Rev* dataset (Rest.-Rev in the table) captures Yelp user reviews for different types of restaurants collected over the course of a month. In this dataset, nodes represent individual users, while hyperedges group together users who reviewed the same restaurant.
- The *Bars-Rev* dataset similarly consists of Yelp user reviews, specifically focused on bars located in Las Vegas, NV. As with Rest.-Rev, nodes correspond to Yelp users, and hyperedges connect users who reviewed the same venue.
- The *Music-Rev* dataset comprises Amazon user reviews related to specific categories of blues music within a monthly timeframe. Here, nodes represent Amazon users, and hyperedges aggregate users who reviewed items within the same music category.
- The *Algebra* and *Geometry* datasets are constructed from user interactions on the MathOverflow platform. These datasets predominantly capture discussions, queries, and solutions related to algebra and geometry topics, respectively. Nodes represent individual MathOverflow users, while hyperedges connect users who contributed to discussions within the same thematic category.
- The *NDC-classes* dataset (NDC in the table) represents a hypergraph where nodes correspond to class labels, and each hyperedge corresponds to a drug characterized by a specific combination of class labels.
- The *iAF1260b* and *iJO1366* datasets focus on metabolic reactions. In these hypergraphs, nodes represent metabolites, and hyperedges group metabolites that participate in the same reaction, ensuring no repetition of nodes within a hyperedge.

We selected these datasets as they capture a diverse range of interaction patterns, allowing us to assess how different structural properties impact the performance of the evaluated algorithms. It is also important to note that these datasets do not represent large-scale hypergraphs. This choice aligns with previous works in the literature [15,35], which also employ these datasets for experimental evaluation, thereby situating our contribution within a consistent experimental framework.

5.3 Selected Algorithms and Settings for Comparison

To assess the effectiveness of the proposed approach, we compare it against a set of baseline methods commonly employed in influence maximization problems. These baselines include both heuristic and greedy-based strategies, capturing a range of seed selection paradigms. To ensure a fair comparison, we employ their adaptive version obtained by embedding them within the AdaptGreedy framework presented in [16]. Here, we recall that the AdaptGreedy works as follows: at each round, it selects a batch of seed nodes that approximately maximizes the expected influence spread given the current state of the network, observes the diffusion outcome, and updates the network by removing activated nodes. Note that AdaptGreedy is defined for graphs only. Therefore, we had to extend it, together with the following baseline methods, to work on hypergraph topologies. We also extended a classical IM algorithm for hypergraphs, although it does not consider the adaptive scenario directly.

The baseline methods considered in our experimental evaluation are the following:

- A_{DEG} – It selects the top-k nodes based on their highest degree on the hypergraph.
- $A_{HYPERDEG}$ – This algorithm is similar to the A_{DEG} method but differs in the property used for node selection. Instead of the degree, it selects the top-k nodes based on their hyperdegree.
- A_{KKT} – This baseline is inspired by the well-known approach proposed by [18]. It iteratively selects the node with the maximal influence on the network until the desired number of seed nodes has been selected.
- A_{HADP} – It is one of the most recent algorithms proposed for the IM problem on hypergraphs [35]. It is an adaptive degree-based heuristic algorithm, whose aim is to iteratively select nodes with low influence overlap as seeds.

Moreover, to evaluate the effectiveness of the algorithms in spreading influence, we used the well-known Susceptible-Infected with Contact Process (SICP) diffusion model. The infection rate and the number of executed steps of the process were respectively $\beta = 0.01$ and $T = 25$. As far as it concerns the A_{KKT} algorithm, we set the number of Monte Carlo simulations of the seed selection algorithm to 100. Finally, for `AdaptEHO`, we started by considering a number of elephants, clans, and steps of respectively $elephants = 6$, $clans = 3$, and $steps = 20$. The update coefficient to move the elephants towards the matriarch in the `UpdateElephant` within the `EHOround` function is $\alpha = 0.5$. Additional experiments testing `AdaptEHO` parameters' quality are provided in Sect. 5.6. Initially, we set the number of rounds to $r = 5$, and for the total number of seeds k we experimented with the values $k = \{5, 10, 15, 20, 25\}$.

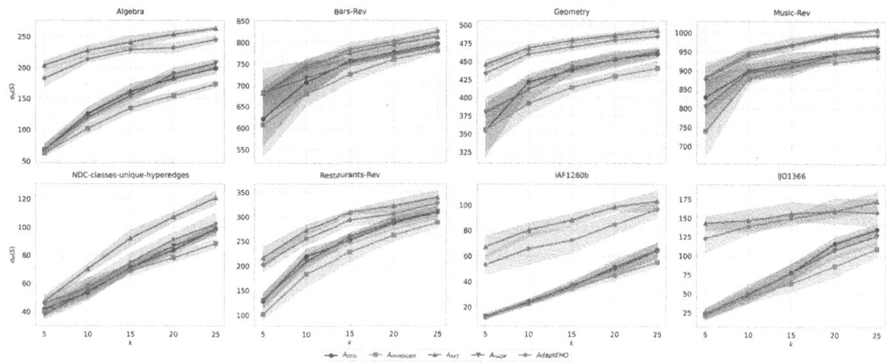

Fig. 1. Expected influence spread $\sigma_H(S)$ comparison between AdaptEHO and baseline methods across different seed set sizes ($k = 5$ to 25) and datasets. Results are averaged over 100 runs using SICP diffusion parameters $\beta = 0.01$ and $T = 25$, with AdaptEHO parameters $elephants = 6$, $clans = 3$, $steps = 20$, and $\alpha = 0.5$.

5.4 Expected Influence Spread Comparison

In this section, we evaluate the performance of our proposed algorithm in terms of influence spread, comparing it with the baselines and related settings introduced in Sect. 5.3.

The results of such a comparison are depicted in Fig. 1. From the analysis of this figure, we can observe how AdaptEHO consistently achieves higher performances than both degree- and hyperdegree-based approaches A_{DEG} and $A_{HYPERDEG}$, respectively, across all datasets with the budget k varying. These improvements are particularly notable in Algebra, Bars-Rev, Geometry, Music-Rev, Rest.-Rev, iAF1260b, and iJO1366 datasets. The same can be observed for A_{HADP}. We also see that A_{KKT} remains one of the strongest performers in terms of raw influence spread, achieving solid results across different settings. Nevertheless, it is important to point out, as we highlighted in the previous section, that the time complexity of A_{KTT}, being orders of magnitude way higher than all other algorithms, makes it not straightforwardly applicable in various contexts [16]; this will be also clear from the analysis of the running time comparison presented in Sect. 5.5. Indeed, AdaptEHO demonstrates competitive performance while avoiding the computational overhead of extensive simulations required by A_{KKT}. This trade-off highlights AdaptEHO as an effective and scalable alternative for influence maximization, especially in settings where running time efficiency is critical. Interestingly, we observe an unexpected behavior in the Bars-Rev dataset, where AdaptEHO marginally outperforms A_{KKT} at certain values of k. This result, while seemingly anomalous, can be attributed to several factors. First, AdaptEHO benefits from its population-based exploration strategy and environment adaptation, allowing it to uncover high-influence nodes that other approaches may overlook. Additionally, its mechanism of progressively removing influenced nodes and reinforcing solutions within clans introduces diversity and resilience to local optima. While this performance crossover is not observed in other datasets, it highlights the potential usefulness of adaptive metaheuristics in capturing higher-order topological patterns not easily exploitable by (possibly greedy) approaches. Furthermore, in Table 2, we depict the average expected influence $\sigma_H(S)$, obtained at the end of the abovementioned comparison. Here, we can see how the values support the previous discussion. In particular, we observe how `AdaptEHO` achieves higher values than other algorithms among all datasets, except for A_{KTT}, where only in the Bars-Rev dataset `AdaptEHO` achieves higher results, as also highlighted before.

Table 2. Quantitative comparison of influence spread performance between `AdaptEHO` and baseline methods. The table shows the expected influence spread $\sigma_H(S)$ achieved with different seed set sizes ($k \in \{5, 10, 15, 20, 25\}$) across all datasets. Results are averaged over 100 independent runs using the SICP diffusion model ($\beta = 0.01$, $T = 25$) and `AdaptEHO` parameters (*elephants* = 6, *clans* = 3, *steps* = 20, $\alpha = 0.5$).

Dataset	Algebra					Bars-Rev					Geometry					Music-Rev				
k	5	10	15	20	25	5	10	15	20	25	5	10	15	20	25	5	10	15	20	25
A_{DEG}	67	125	162	183	199	622	708	756	777	797	355	422	439	454	461	829	900	921	944	952
$A_{HYPERDEG}$	62	102	135	154	174	608	679	725	760	781	356	392	414	430	441	740	878	917	923	937
A_{KKT}	203	227	241	253	262	681	747	774	795	812	446	468	479	486	493	882	947	969	993	1008
A_{HADP}	68	120	154	190	207	683	718	751	772	792	380	411	442	453	464	804	897	908	943	957
`AdaptEHO`	183	214	229	232	245	681	740	783	802	826	434	461	471	480	485	879	940	967	990	994
Dataset	NDC					Rest.-Rev					iAF1260b					iJO1366				
k	5	10	15	20	25	5	10	15	20	25	5	10	15	20	25	5	10	15	20	25
A_{DEG}	42	54	71	84	99	128	220	251	288	310	12	24	36	52	65	24	49	78	116	135
$A_{HYPERDEG}$	40	58	69	78	88	101	183	227	262	289	13	23	35	45	55	21	47	63	87	110
A_{KKT}	47	70	91	107	120	216	272	308	322	339	67	80	88	98	103	142	146	156	159	172
A_{HADP}	38	54	71	86	98	131	209	258	291	311	13	24	37	50	64	23	49	78	108	127
`AdaptEHO`	46	57	75	91	102	202	255	293	306	328	53	66	72	85	97	123	139	150	160	158

5.5 Running Time Comparison

In this section, we analyze the running time of our proposed algorithm and compare it with the baselines. The running time comparison across datasets highlights a sharp contrast between the computational efficiency of heuristic approaches, namely, A_{DEG}, $A_{HYPERDEG}$, A_{KKT}, A_{HADP}, and `AdaptEHO`. As expected, A_{KKT} incurs significantly higher running time costs due to its reliance on repeated simulations for estimating marginal influence gains [16]. This approach does not scale efficiently with the budget k, resulting in super-linear growth behavior in running time. For instance, in Bars-Rev and Music-Rev, A_{KKT} exceeds 4000 s when $k = 25$, whereas all other approaches remain below 50 s.

Moreover, we can see how **AdaptEHO** achieves running time performances comparable to the other methods, despite its iterative and population-based nature. This is somewhat expected, due to the fact that **AdaptEHO** is designed to follow a round-based structure with an efficient influence evaluation; indeed, each round uses a relatively small, fixed population of elephants, i.e., candidate solutions, and a limited number of steps, avoiding possible costly exhaustive simulations. As a result, **AdaptEHO** exhibits near-linear scaling with respect to k and shows robust performance across all datasets.

This substantial efficiency advantage, combined with the competitive influence spread performance, depicted in Fig. 1 and Table 2, obtained by **AdaptEHO**, makes the latter a solid alternative to greedy algorithms, especially when computational resources or running time are constrained (Fig. 2).

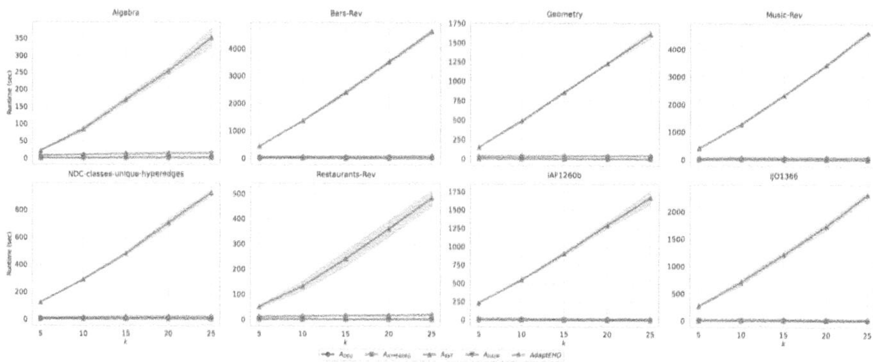

Fig. 2. Running time comparison between **AdaptEHO** and baseline methods across different seed set sizes ($k \in \{5, 10, 15, 20, 25\}$) and datasets. Results are averaged over 100 runs using SICP diffusion parameters $\beta = 0.01$ and $T = 25$, with **AdaptEHO** parameters *elephants* = 6, *clans* = 3, *steps* = 20, and $\alpha = 0.5$.

5.6 Parameter Tuning

Like many metaheuristic optimization methods, the **AdaptEHO** algorithm requires the configuration of several key parameters. Among these, the most critical are the population size, defined by the number of elephants (*elephants*), and the social structure, determined by the number of clans (*clans*). This study conducts a systematic investigation into the effects of varying these parameters by evaluating different combinations of *elephants* and *clans*, ensuring that the constraint $elephants \geq clans$ is maintained. The tested configurations include {(4,2), (6,2), (6,3), (8,2), (8,4), (10,2), (12,2), (12,3), (12,4), (20,4), (20,5), (30,5), (30,6), (50,5), (50,10)}. The experimental setup fixed the number of optimization steps at *steps* = 20, with a budget constraint of $k = 20$ and $r = 5$ rounds. For each parameter combination, the algorithm was executed over 100 independent trials, and the resulting seed sets were assessed using 100 simulations of the SICP diffusion model. Performance metrics included the average influence spread, standard deviation, and computational runtime. The findings indicate that configurations with 20 or more *elephants* generally achieve a higher influence spread, albeit with a modest increase in runtime. Figure 3 illustrates these results, plotting average influence spread (x-axis) against runtime in seconds (y-axis), with each data point representing a distinct parameter configuration. The analysis reveals a clear trend: larger elephant populations tend to yield greater influence, though with diminishing returns as population size increases. Notably, configurations with $elephants \in \{20, 30\}$ demonstrate an optimal balance between influence maximization and computational efficiency. These settings outperform those with fewer *elephants* in terms of influence while maintaining runtimes comparable to smaller populations (e.g., $elephants \in \{4, 6, 8, 10, 12\}$). In contrast, configurations with $elephants = 50$ exhibit only marginal gains in influence but require substantially more computational resources. Across most datasets, the runtime for configurations with 20 or 30 *elephants* remains below 40 s, reinforcing their suitability for practical applications where both performance and efficiency are critical.

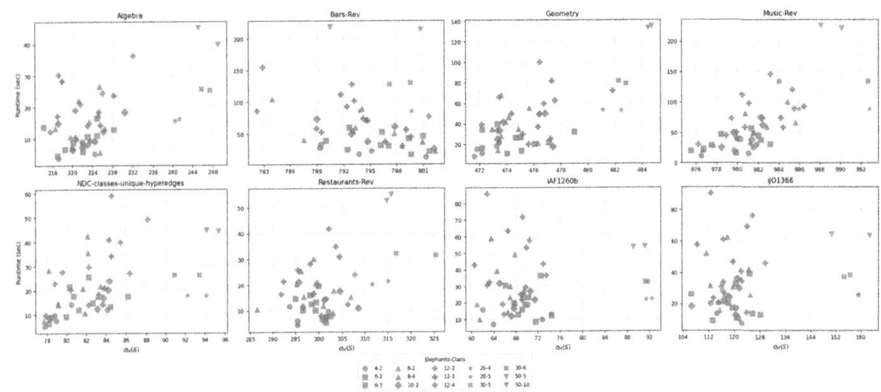

Fig. 3. Influence spread versus running time trade-off for different AdaptEHO parameter configurations (varying elephants *elephants* and clans *clans*) across datasets, with AdaptEHO parameters $steps = 20$ and $\alpha = 0.5$.

6 Conclusion

In this paper, we introduced the novel Adaptive Influence Maximization problem on Hypergraphs (AdaptHIM), formalizing it within a flexible formal framework that generalizes adaptive seed selection in networks exhibiting higher-order interactions. The problem consists of finding a sequence of selected seed sets over a certain number of rounds such that the number of influenced nodes at the end of the process is maximized. Along with the framework, we proposed a novel approach addressing the problem, called `AdaptEHO`, which is based on the Elephant Herding Optimization algorithms. It dynamically adjusts seed selection by leveraging feedback from prior influence rounds. We carried out a comprehensive experimental evaluation on different real-world hypergraphs, and demonstrated that `AdaptEHO` achieves solid influence spread compared to baseline methods while maintaining computational efficiency.

This paper does not represent an ending point, but rather a starting point for future research to deepen and extend the overall problem. First off, theoretical guarantees about the problem and possible approaches could be investigated. Also, it would be interesting to consider dynamic hypergraphs, i.e., hypergraphs whose structure may change during rounds. Moreover, different extensions could be studied, such as incorporating fairness or diversity in seed selection to align with real-world constraints.

Acknowledgments. This work is supported by the PNRR project FAIR—Future AI Research (PE00000013) under the NRRP MUR program funded by NextGenerationEU.

References

1. Aksoy, S.G., Joslyn, C., Ortiz Marrero, C., Praggastis, B., Purvine, E.: Hypernetwork science via high-order hypergraph walks. EPJ Data Sci. **9**(1), 1–34 (2020). https://doi.org/10.1140/epjds/s13688-020-00231-0
2. Amato, F., Moscato, V., Picariello, A., Sperlí, G.: Influence maximization in social media networks using hypergraphs. In: Proceedings of the GPC International Conference on Green, Pervasive, and Cloud Computing, pp. 207–221 (2017)
3. Amoruso, M., Anello, D., Auletta, V., Cerulli, R., Ferraioli, D., Raiconi, A.: Contrasting the spread of misinformation in online social networks. J. Artif. Intell. Res. **69**, 847–879 (2020)
4. Antelmi, A., Cordasco, G., Spagnuolo, C., Szufel, P.: Social influence maximization in hypergraphs. Entropy **23**(7), 796–810 (2021)
5. Auletta, V., Ferraioli, D., Greco, G.: On the complexity of reasoning about opinion diffusion under majority dynamics. Artif. Intell. **284**, 103288 (2020)
6. Auletta, V., Cauteruccio, F., Ferraioli, D.: Heuristics for the influence maximization problem on hypergraphs. In: Proceedings of the International Conference on Advances in Social Networks Analysis and Mining, pp. 255–262. ASONAM, Springer (2024)
7. Banerjee, S., Jenamani, M., Pratihar, D.K.: A survey on influence maximization in a social network. Knowl. Inf. Syst. **62**(9), 3417–3455 (2020). https://doi.org/10.1007/s10115-020-01461-4
8. Battiston, F., et al.: Networks beyond pairwise interactions: structure and dynamics. Phys. Rep. **874**, 1–92 (2020)
9. Bretto, A.: Hypergraph Theory: An Introduction. Springer (2013)
10. Castiglioni, M., Ferraioli, D., Gatti, N., Landriani, G.: Election manipulation on social networks: seeding, edge removal, edge addition. J. Artif. Intell. Res. **71**, 1049–1090 (2021)

11. Chen, W., Wang, C., Wang, Y.: Scalable influence maximization for prevalent viral marketing in large-scale social networks. In: Proceedings of the ACM SIGKDD International Conference on Knowledge Discovery and Data Mining, pp. 1029–1038 (2010)
12. Chen, W., Wang, Y., Yuan, Y.: Combinatorial multi-armed bandit: general framework, results and applications. In: Proceedings of the 30th International Conference on International Conference on Machine Learning - Vol. 28, pp. I–151–I–159. ICML'13, JMLR.org (2013)
13. Chen, W., Wang, Y., Yuan, Y., Wang, Q.: Combinatorial multi-armed bandit and its extension to probabilistically triggered arms. J. Mach. Learn. Res. **17**(1), 1746–1778 (2016)
14. Golovin, D., Krause, A.: Adaptive submodularity: theory and applications in active learning and stochastic optimization. J. Artif. Int. Res. **42**, 427–486 (2011)
15. Gong, X., Wang, H., Wang, X., Chen, C., Zhang, W., Zhang, Y.: Influence maximization on hypergraphs via multi-hop influence estimation. Inform. Process. Manage. **61**(3), 103683 (2024)
16. Han, K., Huang, K., Xiao, X., Tang, J., Sun, A., Tang, X.: Efficient algorithms for adaptive influence maximization. Proc. VLDB Endow. **11**, 1029–1040 (2018)
17. Ismaeel, A.A., Elshaarawy, I.A., Houssein, E.H., Ismail, F.H., Hassanien, A.E.: Enhanced elephant herding optimization for global optimization. IEEE Access **7**, 34738–34752 (2019)
18. Kempe, D., Kleinberg, J., Tardos, E.: Maximizing the spread of influence through a social network. In: Proceedings of the ACM SIGKDD International Conference on Knowledge Discovery and Data Mining, pp. 137–146 (2003)
19. Lagrée, P., Cappé, O., Cautis, B., Maniu, S.: Algorithms for online influencer marketing. ACM Trans. Knowl. Discov. Data **13**(1) (2018)
20. Lei, S., Maniu, S., Mo, L., Cheng, R., Senellart, P.: Online influence maximization. In: Proceedings of the 21th ACM SIGKDD International Conference on Knowledge Discovery and Data Mining, pp. 645–654. KDD '15, Association for Computing Machinery (2015)
21. Li, J., Lei, H., Alavi, A.H., Wang, G.G.: Elephant herding optimization: variants, hybrids, and applications. Mathematics **8**(9), 1415 (2020)
22. Li, Y., Fan, J., Wang, Y., Tan, K.L.: Influence maximization on social graphs: a survey. IEEE Trans. Knowl. Data Eng. **30**(10), 1852–1872 (2018)
23. MA, A., Rajkumar, A.: Hyper-imrank: Ranking-based influence maximization for hypergraphs. In: Proceedings of the ACM IKDD CODS and COMAD Joint International Conference on Data Science & Management of Data, pp. 100–104 (2022)
24. Peng, B., Chen, W.: Adaptive influence maximization with myopic feedback. In: Advances in Neural Information Processing Systems. Curran Associates, Inc. (2019)
25. Salha, G., Tziortziotis, N., Vazirgiannis, M.: Adaptive submodular influence maximization with myopic feedback. In: 2018 IEEE/ACM International Conference on Advances in Social Networks Analysis and Mining (ASONAM), pp. 455–462 (2018)
26. Sun, L., Huang, W., Yu, P.S., Chen, W.: Multi-round influence maximization. In: Proceedings of the 24th ACM SIGKDD International Conference on Knowledge Discovery & Data Mining, pp. 2249–2258. Association for Computing Machinery (2018)
27. Suo, Q., Guo, J.L., Shen, A.Z.: Information spreading dynamics in hypernetworks. XXPhys. A **495**, 475–487 (2018)
28. Tong, G., Wang, R.: On adaptive influence maximization under general feedback models. IEEE Trans. Emerg. Top. Comput. **10**(1), 463–475 (2020)

29. Vaswani, S., Kveton, B., Wen, Z., Ghavamzadeh, M., Lakshmanan, L.V., Schmidt, M.: Model-independent online learning for influence maximization. In: Proceedings of the 34th International Conference on Machine Learning - Volume 70, pp. 3530–3539. ICML'17, JMLR.org (2017)
30. Vaswani, S., Lakshmanan, L.V.S.: Adaptive influence maximization in social networks: Why commit when you can adapt? CoRR (2016)
31. Wang, G.G., Deb, S., Coelho, L.d.S.: Elephant herding optimization. In: 2015 3rd International Symposium on Computational and Business Intelligence (ISCBI), pp. 1–5. IEEE (2015)
32. Wen, Z., Kveton, B., Valko, M., Vaswani, S.: Online influence maximization under independent cascade model with semi-bandit feedback. In: Advances in Neural Information Processing Systems, vol. 30. Curran Associates, Inc
33. Wilder, B., et al.: End-to-end influence maximization in the field. In: Proceedings of the AAMAS International Conference on Autonomous Agents and Multiagent Systems, vol. 18, pp. 1414–1422 (2018)
34. Wilder, B., Vorobeychik, Y.: Controlling elections through social influence. In: Proceedings of the AAMAS International Conference on Autonomous Agents and Multiagent Systems, pp. 265–273 (2018)
35. Xie, M., Zhan, X.X., Liu, C., Zhang, Z.K.: An efficient adaptive degree-based heuristic algorithm for influence maximization in hypergraphs. Inform. Process. Manage. **60**(2), 103161 (2023)
36. Yuan, J., Tang, S.: No time to observe: Adaptive influence maximization with partial feedback. CoRR (2016)
37. Zhang, R., Qu, X., Zhang, Q., Xu, X., Pei, S.: Influence maximization based on threshold models in hypergraphs. Chaos: Interdisc. J. Nonlinear Sci. **34**(2), 1–16 (2024)
38. Zhu, J., Zhu, J., Ghosh, S., Wu, W., Yuan, J.: Social influence maximization in hypergraph in social networks. IEEE Trans. Netw. Sci. Eng. **6**(4), 801–811 (2018)

Adaptive Multi-agent System for Dynamic Preference Learning: Application to Mobility

Alexandre Perles[1(✉)], Valérie Camps[1], and Elsy Kaddoum[2]

[1] IRIT, Université de Toulouse, CNRS, Toulouse INP, Toulouse, France
{alexandre.perles,valerie.camps}@irit.fr
[2] IRIT, Université de Toulouse, CNRS, Toulouse INP, UT2, Toulouse, France
elsy.kaddoum@irit.fr

Abstract. The concept of MaaS (Mobility as a Service) consists of integrating various transport services into a single platform to support users in planning their journeys and encourage the use of sustainable transport. The acceptability of such systems depends on their ability to personalize services according to individual user needs and preferences.

This study is conducted within the framework of MaaS and focuses on users' mobility behavior to predict the mode of transport they are likely to choose for their next trip. The goal of this prediction is to guide users toward more sustainable alternatives while respecting their preferences.

This work proposes AMAS4PL, a system designed to learn and adapt individual mobility preferences based on their travel patterns. AMAS4PL relies on a multi-agent system for data stream clustering, called AMAS4DC, which can continuously learn evolving user travel patterns over time. Conducted experiments underline AMAS4PL better performances regarding baseline methods.

Keywords: Preference learning · Data stream · Multi-agent system · Mobility

1 Introduction

To achieve sustainable mobility, cities need to improve their public transport infrastructure, integrate new modes of transport (such as car-sharing, bike-sharing, on-demand services, car-pooling, etc.) and develop platforms that facilitate accessibility to all public and shared mobility options. The concept of Mobility-as-a-Service (MaaS) [13] is one solution to overcome these challenges.

MaaS aims to unify various mobility services offered by different providers into a single digital platform, enabling users to plan, book and pay for their journeys [13]. One of the long-term objective of MaaS is to gradually change the travel behavior of its users, encouraging them to make more sustainable transport choices. To support this, behavior change strategies [9] can be integrated into MaaS applications to encourage users to modify their travel habits.

M. Baldoni et al. (Eds.): EUMAS 2025, LNAI 16259, pp. 144–160, 2026.
https://doi.org/10.1007/978-3-032-22820-8_9

Anagnostopoulou et al. [2] carry out a systematic review of existing research on persuasive technologies applied to urban mobility and highlight the need to integrate the personalization aspect into systems aimed at promoting sustainable modes of transport.

In information systems, *personalization* is defined as *the automatic adaptation of information content, structure and presentation to an individual user* [23]. It considers the user's preferences and past habits in order to deliver relevant information or content at the most appropriate time [10], ideally without requiring explicit requests from the user [21]. Personalization serves a dual purpose; it plays a key role in encouraging, persuading and supporting the user in changing their behavior [24] while also improving the user's trust in the system [6]. To achieve this personalization, it is necessary to observe one individual in their activities in order to identify and learn both their regularities (i.e. what activities the individual regularly performs) and their preferences (i.e. how the individual performs these activities). The regularities learned can then be used to proactively offer services corresponding to the preferences learned from the regularities detected. Finally, to be truly effective, personalization must also take into account the evolution and potential changes in the user's behavior; in other words, it needs to be dynamic and adaptive. In the context of a MaaS, this personalization involves learning a user's regular itineraries in order to (i) anticipate their travel needs and (ii) proactively suggest itineraries using their preferred modes of transport. Over time, the MaaS can gradually introduce and promote more sustainable alternatives.

This study aims to predict the mode of transport a user is likely to choose for a given itinerary, with the goal of anticipating their needs and offering greener alternatives. An itinerary is defined as a travel from a point to another at a specific date and time using particular modes of transport. To predict modes of transport, classifications algorithms can be used to build a model based on learned data. This model is then used to predict the mode of transport for a given user and itinerary. Many classifiers require a large dataset to build a static model. These models often lack adaptability, and incorporating new training data requires a complete recalculation of the model, which can lead to significant computational and memory costs (due to the need to keep in memory all the training data).

In this article, we present AMAS4PL, a system for the adaptive learning of transport mode preferences of a given user, based on their regularity patterns. AMAS4PL uses a machine-learning approach to dynamically learn these preferences as the user travels. AMAS4PL is an extension of AMAS4DC (Adaptive Multi-Agent System for Dynamic Clustering), a multi-agent model for dynamic data stream clustering [22]. After presenting the main research related to user preference learning in Sect. 2, Sect. 3 outlines the objectives that a dynamic preference learning system should fulfill. It also proposes a formalization of the problem. The proposed extension of the AMAS4DC model, called AMAS4PL, is then detailed in Sect. 4. The evaluation of the proposed system, along with its comparison to the state-of-the-art algorithms, are presented in Sect. 5, before concluding in Sect. 6.

2 User Preferences: a Literature Review

We define a "behavior" as an observable action performed by an individual and a "regularity" as a repetition of behaviors. To observe user behavior and learn their preferences for each travel regularity, two major points must be addressed: the representation of user preferences (preference model) and how to learn these preferences (learning approach).

2.1 Preference Model

The preference model is used to provide a computational representation of user preferences. Liu et al. [16] compare different preference models used in recommender systems. In the linear function model, which is a utility function, user preferences are represented as vectors of weights assigned to each *element* (an entity that can be enjoyed by a user or recommended to a user). Other models, such as the polynomial function, the tree-based model and the conditional preference network (CP-Net) are also discussed in [16]. These models support the representation of conditional preferences offering greater expressiveness, but they often have a high computational cost.

Basile et al. [3] propose to model users' mobility preferences as a vector of relevance values. This model includes two sets of values indicating the important the user places on factors such as fitness, pleasure and productivity (i) in general and (ii) for each mode of transport. This approach is interesting because it takes into account user preferences both at a global level and at an itinerary level.

Georgakis et al. [11] propose to use user preferences to assess the relevance of itineraries and rank them accordingly. They build a user preference vector assigning a weight to each mode of transport at each time of day from the user's behavior history. They then compute the cosine similarity [7] between this user preference vector and feature vector of the itinerary, and use the resulting score to rank them accordingly. Their system gives good results, but it has two limitations: it requires storing in memory all behaviors history, and also asking the user's for their general preferences (i.e. what modes of transport the user generally prefers regardless of the itinerary).

All this research shows that representing user preferences as a feature vector is relevant because (i) it is simple to compute, (ii) features can easily be added or removed, and (iii) such a representation has shown good results in various applications.

In this study, we consider that each preference is independent of the others. Unlike existing approaches that consider preferences globally, the representation of each preference as a weight vector is relevant.

2.2 Learning Approach

Route choice modeling and imitation learning are both suitable approaches for learning user preferences in mobility. However, route choice modeling focuses more on the decision-making process of a user when choosing one route over another. Imitation learning can be used to observe user behavior and infer preferences from it. That said, both methods are generally not dynamic and often assume static user behavior. Recommender systems are widely used for learning user preferences from behavioral data. The idea is to observe the user's past behavior in order to predict future actions.

In the field of recommender systems, approaches can be grouped into two main categories: Content-Based Filtering and Collaborative Filtering. Collaborative filtering refers to approaches that use information from multiple users to make recommendations. This category can also be divided into two subcategories: memory-based and model-based filtering. Model-Based Filtering builds a model from historical user actions, without storing all user action. This model can be used to recommend new content. The model can be built using various methods such as K-nearest neighbors, neural networks or Naive Bayes. One well-performing method is the Random Forest algorithm [5]. It creates a set of decision trees from subsets of the training data and uses them for prediction. Despite a relatively long training process, this algorithm gives good prediction performances in terms of speed and quality and can incorporate temporal feature (date and time of the data). However, it lacks adaptability since all trees have to be rebuilt whenever new information is learned. To overcome this limitation, Domingos et al. [8] presented the Very Fast Decision Tree (or Hoeffding Tree) which incrementally builds a decision tree. Bitef et al. [4] and Manapragada et al. [17] proposed to improve this algorithm by respectively proposing the Hoeffding Adaptive Tree classifier algorithm which detects and replaces tree branches having a decreasing accuracy, and the Extremely Fast Decision Tree (or Hoeffding AnyTime Tree) algorithm in which processing time is reduced by rapidly creating decision trees and subsequently adjusting them if necessary. These algorithms have shown good performance while dynamically supporting model changes.

An alternative incremental method is the Mondrian Forest; it is an efficient online version of Random Forest proposed by Lakshminarayana et al. [15]. Mourtada et al. [20] and Khannouz et al. [14] introduced two variants: Aggregated Mondrian forests and Mondrian Forest under Memory Constraint, that perform well in a memory constrained environment. The main benefit of these models is their ability to ingest new data without full retraining. However, performance remains highly sensitive to hyperparameters, especially tree depth. The variety of data can impact the tree depth required to create a high-performance model. In order to avoid this problem, we propose to create one simple model for each regularity, thereby considerably reducing the learning process and its adaptation to changes.

In a previous work [22], we introduced the AMAS4DC agent-based model. Applied to the mobility domain, it effectively detected regularities in a user's itineraries from a data stream. Moreover, the use of a multi-agent system for learning preferences allows parallel computation due to its decentralization nature, and physically distribution of the workload across agents.

In this paper, we introduce AMAS4PL (Adaptive Multi-Agent System for Preference Learning), an extension of AMAS4DC designed to learn user preferences in terms of transport modes at the level of each detected itinerary regularity.

3 Dynamic Preference Learning Problem

Based on the studies presented above, a system designed to learn user preferences must have the following properties:

- model user preferences as a weighted feature vector where each feature is associated with a specific weight;
- adapt to changes in user behavior over time,
- perform preference learning at the level of each observed regularity.

Given these objectives, we define dynamic preference learning as a process consisting of:

1. observing user behavior expressed as a list of features concerning a given service;
2. learning regularities in user behavior by clustering them according to similarities between their characteristics (in our case, clustering is performed by AMAS4DC [22]);
3. then, learning, for each detected regularity, a vector of weighted features that reflects the user's preferences in the context of that regularity.

This article focuses on learning user preferences at the level of each regularity, which can be formalized by:

- a set of regularity clusters denoted $RC = \{R_1; R_2; \ldots; R_n\}$ where n is the number of learned regularities;
- each regularity R_i is associated with a centroid C and a weighted feature vector $WF = \{(w_1, f_1); (w_2, f_2); \ldots; (w_k, f_k)\}$ where k is the number of considered features and w_i represents the user's preference weight for feature f_i.

Figure 1 illustrates the link between the behaviors, the corresponding regularities and the associated weighted feature vectors. For each new observed behavior, the learning mechanism must adapt the feature weights of the corresponding regularity. If no corresponding regularity is found, a new cluster is added to the set RC with a vector of weighted features initialized according to the observed regularity. This vector will be adapted to future user behavior.

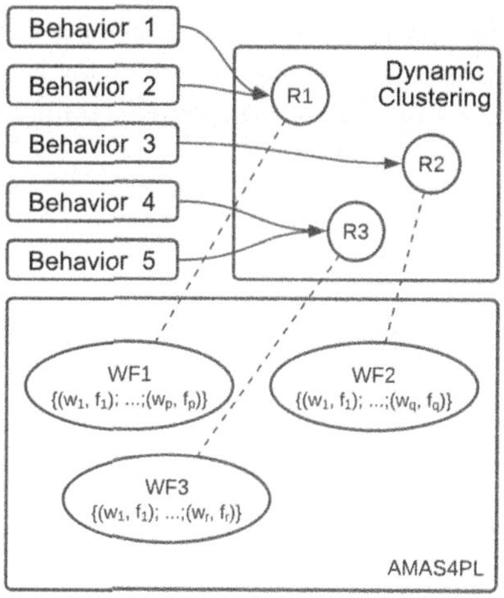

Fig. 1. Preference weights associated with regularities.

4 AMAS4PL: An Extension of AMAS4DC for Transport Mode Prediction

AMAS4DC is a multi-agent system developed to dynamically and adaptively create clusters representing regularities in a user's travel behavior [22].

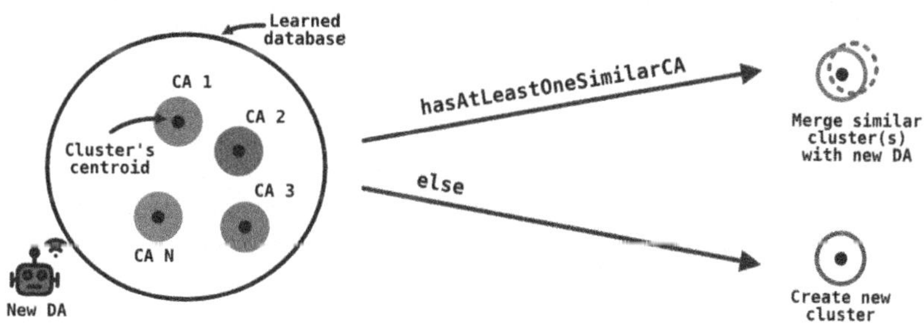

$$\textbf{hasAtLeastOneSimilarCA} := (\exists i \in \{1, ..., N\} \mid \textbf{sim}(CA_i, \textbf{newDA}) > \textbf{fusion\_threshold})$$

Fig. 2. AMAS4DC overview.

As presented in Fig. 2, it consists of two types of agent: a Data Agent (DA) and a Cluster Agent (CA). A DA represents an itinerary just completed by the user, and a CA represents a regularity. When a new DA is added to the system, it compares itself to existing CAs. If a CA calculates a similarity value (sim) above a certain threshold (fusion_threshold), the DA merges with that CA. Otherwise, the DA becomes a new CA, representing a new regularity. In this work, AMAS4PL extends the original AMAS4DC with:

1. the redefinition of the centroid representation of a CA in order to integrate weighted features representing user preferences for this cluster (regularity);
2. the revision of the fusion process to take into account this new representation.

Once learning is complete, the aim is to predict the mode of transport for an itinerary I. This is done by finding the most similar CA and returning the mode of transport having the highest weight in the CA representation (i.e. the user's preferred mode of transport for this regularity).

4.1 Representation of the Centroid of a Cluster Agents

In AMAS4DC, similarity between a centroid and an itinerary was computed as a binary value based on predefined criteria. The fusion between a centroid and an itinerary was performed with predefined domain-dependent rules. In this extension, we normalize input data in order to eliminate domain dependency and expert rules, but also to facilitate fair comparison with other approaches. The CA centroid is now represented by a vector of decimal numbers corresponding to the characteristics of an itinerary, namely:

- latitude and longitude of the starting point;
- latitude and longitude of the arrival point;
- day of the week, and
- departure time.

Each CA is also associated with a preference-weighted feature vector reflecting the user's transport mode preferences for that specific regularity. As the data in the vector representing the itinerary is normalized, the similarity function [22] is replaced by an Euclidean distance metric.

4.2 Fusion Process

To facilitate the merging process, we consider that a Data Agent (DA) is represented in the same way as a Cluster Agent (CA), with the difference that the DA's weighted feature vector is initialized by the mode of transport used in the corresponding itinerary, with a preference weight of 100% (for example, for an itinerary made by bus, the feature vector is $WF = \{1, Bus\}$).

The fusion process for 2 agents with this new representation is described in Algorithm 1. When two agents merge (their similarity is greater than the fusion_threshold hyperparameter), the new centroid C_{result} is computed as a weighted average of the two centroids; the new feature vector WF_{result} is calculated as a weighted average of the feature vectors of the two agents. These weights are calculated with the new fusion_speed hyperparameter, which indicates the importance of a new data point compared to an old one.

In the original version of AMAS4DC, when a DA perceived several similar CAs (similarity $> fusion\_threshold$), it would merge with only the most similar one, ignoring the others. This behavior resulted in the creation of a large number of clusters, some of which were potentially redundant.

Algorithm 1. Fusion(A_1, A_2)

$w_1 \leftarrow$ 1 - fusion_speed
$w_2 \leftarrow$ fusion_speed
$C_{result} \leftarrow \frac{C_{A_1} \times w_1 + C_{A_2} \times w_2}{w_1 + w_2}$
$WF_{result} \leftarrow \frac{WF_{A_1} \times w_1 + WF_{A_2} \times w_2}{w_1 + w_2}$

This new version addresses this limit. When a DA merges with a CA, it also informs the CA about the potential existence of other similar CAs (see Algorithm 2, lines 3–6). Once merged with the DA, the CA evaluates its similarity with other CAs (see Algorithm 3, lines 1–3) and merges with those having similarities above the *fusion_threshold*. In this new version, the similarity between two centroids is computed using Euclidean distance; the smaller the Euclidean distance between them, the greater their similarity.

Algorithm 2. DA behavior

1: Request distance calculation d_{CA_i} to $CA_i(i = 1..n)$
2: $simCAs\_list \leftarrow CA_i \mid d_{CA_i} < fusion\_threshold$
3: **if** $simCAs\_list \neq \emptyset$ **then**
4: $\quad min \leftarrow CA \mid d_{CA} = \arg\min_i d_{CA_i}$
5: $\quad others \leftarrow simCAs\_list - min$
6: $\quad$ Request merge to *min* while providing the *others* list.
7: **else**
8: $\quad$ Become a CA
9: **end if**

Algorithm 3. *CA* behavior

1: **if** request distance calculation received from CA/DA **then**
2: $\quad$ Calculate d_{CA_i}
3: $\quad$ Send distance to CA/DA
4: **end if**
5: **if** merge request received from DA **then**
6: $\quad$ Merge(DA, CA_i)
7: $\quad$ **if** $others \neq \emptyset$ **then**
8: $\quad\quad$ Request d_{CA_j} to $CA_j \in others$
9: $\quad$ **end if**
10: **end if**
11: **if** received $d_{CA_j} < fusion\_threshold$ **then**
12: $\quad$ Fusion(CA_i, CA_j)
13: **end if**

5 Experiments

This section evaluates the performance of AMAS4PL and compares it with several algorithms according to a specific process. The itineraries followed by a user are considered one by one to simulate the processing of a data stream. For each itinerary, the algorithms studied adjust their learned model. This model is used to predict the mode of transport for the next itinerary. The metrics (see Sect. 5.1) are computed after each prediction and observed over time.

5.1 Metrics

Classification performances are usually measured using 4 common metrics [12]: Accuracy, Precision, Recall and F1 Score (see Equation (1)). For the purposes of this study, we focus on the F1 Score for two reasons:

1. the accuracy, defined as the ratio of the *number of correct predictions over the total number of predictions*, is not sufficient if the percentages associated with the modes of transport are unbalanced. For example, if a user travels by bus 90% of the time and by car 10%, the prediction will always be the bus and the accuracy 0.9, which is rather high. However, the prediction is wrong every time the user has taken the car.
2. the F1 Score is a combination of precision and recall (cf. equation (1)). The precision indicates for each transport mode the *number of correct predictions for that transport mode out of the number of times that transport mode was predicted*, while the recall indicates for each transport mode the *number of correct predictions for that transport mode out of the number of times that transport mode should have been predicted.* The F1 score, by combining these two measures, evaluates the ability of the learning algorithms to classify instances correctly. The F1 score varies from 0 to 1. It reaches its maximum value (1), when both precision and recall reach their highest levels; this indicates a well-balanced model that minimizes prediction errors.

$$F_1 = 2 \times \frac{Precision \times Recall}{Precision + Recall} \tag{1}$$

5.2 Datasets

We evaluated the algorithms on 2 different datasets: one synthetic and one real one.

The synthetic dataset is based on a 6-week repetition of a typical user's itinerary week. This week, presented in Table 1, is made up of 15 itineraries. This simple scenario is used to study the performance of the different algorithms in a controlled scenario.

The real dataset MOBIS [18] contains data (route segments) collected from volunteer participants. Segments from *legs.csv* were combined to create

Table 1. Weekly routine (H: Home, W: Work, G: Gym, P: Park, S: Store, B: Bike, C: Car, M: Walk)

Monday	Tuesday	Wednesday	Thursday	Friday
9h H→W (B)	9h H→W (C)	9h H→W (B)	9h H→W (B)	9h H→W (B)
18h W→H (B)	17h45 W→G (C)	13h W→H (B)	18h W→H (B)	18h W→H (B)
	19h30 G→H (C)	15h H→P (M)	19h H→S (C)	
		18h P→H (M)	20h S→H (C)	

itineraries, and irrelevant ones (e.g. those with the same start and end points, those completed less than 10 times, etc.) were removed. The resulting dataset contains approximately 75,000 itineraries. Among these itineraries, we have selected the 16 users who followed more than 500 itineraries.

5.3 Compared Algorithms

Based on the state of the art, Mondrian Forest and Hoeffding Tree methods seem to be the most suitable approaches for this problem. We therefore compare AMAS4PL to the following 5 classifiers derived from these approaches and available in the River [19] library:

- HoeffdingTreeClassifier
- HoeffdingAdaptiveTreeClassifier
- ExtremelyFastDecisionTreeClassifier
- MondrianTreeClassifier
- AMFClassifier (Aggregated Mondrian Forest)

5.4 Mode of Transport Prediction on Synthetic Data

In this experiment, we perform a sequential evaluation using the synthetic dataset. Hyperparameters for each model were tuned using Optuna [1] on the same scenario (see Table 2). Table 3 reports the latest obtained values and Fig. 3 shows the evolution of F1 score values.

Since learning occurs incrementally from the first itinerary, all models initially make numerous prediction errors. It is interesting to notice that despite the fact that the AMFClassifier and the Mondrian Tree Classifier performs better than AMAS4PL in the early stages, their evolutions are more chaotic, which indicates lower confidence in the predictions.

Table 2. Optimal hyperparameter values for the synthetic dataset.

Algorithm	Name	Values
AMAS4PL	fusion_threshold	0.76715
	fusion_speed	0.87438
Hoeffding Tree Classifier	grace_period	50
	max_depth	7
	split_criterion	info_gain
	delta	0.94494
	tau	0.54318
	leaf_prediction	mc
	nb_threshold	72
	binary_split	False
	min_branch_fraction	0.11214
	max_share_to_split	0.04081
	max_size	285
Hoeffding Adaptive Tree Classifier	grace_period	10
	max_depth	11
	split_criterion	hellinger
	delta	0.45629
	tau	0.07323
	leaf_prediction	nba
	nb_threshold	30
	binary_split	False
	min_branch_fraction	0.64727
	max_share_to_split	0.70591
	max_size	687
	drift_window_threshold	66
	switch_significance	True
	memory_estimate_period	74
	stop_mem_management	True
	remove_poor_attrs	True
	merit_preprune	False

Algorithm	Name	Values
Extremely Fast Decision Tree Classifier	grace_period	60
	max_depth	2
	split_criterion	info_gain
	delta	0.80849
	tau	0.02748
	leaf_prediction	mc
	nb_threshold	66
	binary_split	False
	min_branch_fraction	0.02456
	max_share_to_split	0.27273
	max_size	676
	memory_estimate_period	48
	stop_mem_management	False
	remove_poor_attrs	False
	merit_preprune	False
Mondrian Tree Classifier	step	0.39606
	use_aggregation	True
	split_pure	False
	iteration	90
AMF Classifier	n_estimators	1
	step	0.68833
	use_aggregation	True
	dirichlet	0.59977
	split_pure	False

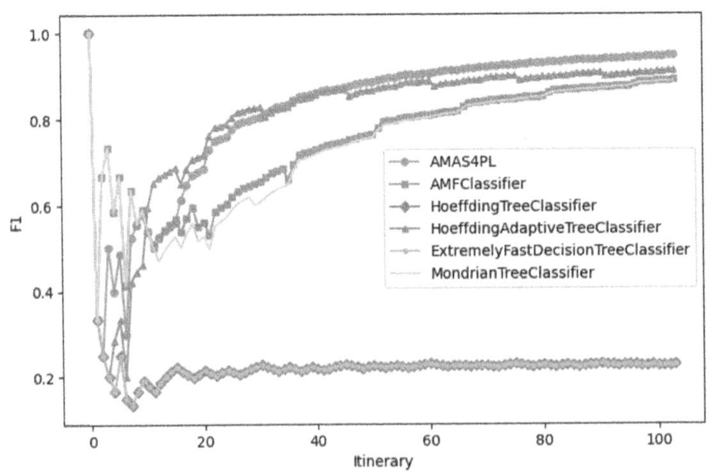

Fig. 3. F1 score evolution of classifiers on synthetic dataset.

Table 3. F1

Model	F1
AMAS4PL	0.945
AMFClassifier	0.888
HoeffdingTreeClassifier	0.228
HoeffdingAdaptiveTreeClassifier	0.911
ExtremelyFastDecisionTreeClassifier	0.228
MondrianTreeClassifier	0.886

The F1 Score will never reach 1. However, AMAS4PL and HoeffdingAdaptiveTreeClassifier, although slower to improve initially, ultimately achieve high F1 score values, underlining their robustness to the lack of training data.

5.5 Mode of Transport Prediction on Real Data

Table 4. Optimal hyperparameter values for the mobis dataset.

Algorithm	Name	Values
AMAS4PL	fusion_threshold	0.22819
	fusion_speed	0.42766
Hoeffding Tree Classifier	grace_period	11
	max_depth	8
	split_criterion	gini
	delta	0.08891
	tau	0.39938
	leaf_prediction	nba
	nb_threshold	80
	binary_split	True
	min_branch_fraction	0.21794
	max_share_to_split	0.96687
	max_size	869
Hoeffding Adaptive Tree Classifier	grace_period	12
	max_depth	15
	split_criterion	info_gain
	delta	0.90520
	tau	0.62698
	leaf_prediction	nb
	nb_threshold	11
	binary_split	True
	min_branch_fraction	0.03782
	max_share_to_split	0.77051
	max_size	934
	drift_window_threshold	55
	switch_significance	True
	memory_estimate_period	47
	stop_mem_management	True
	remove_poor_attrs	False
	merit_preprune	True

Algorithm	Name	Values
Extremely Fast Decision Tree Classifier	grace_period	13
	max_depth	11
	split_criterion	hellinger
	delta	0.19666
	tau	0.83079
	leaf_prediction	nba
	nb_threshold	54
	binary_split	False
	min_branch_fraction	0.22574
	max_share_to_split	0.91657
	max_size	677
	memory_estimate_period	99
	stop_mem_management	False
	remove_poor_attrs	True
	merit_preprune	True
Mondrian Tree Classifier	step	0.35657
	use_aggregation	True
	split_pure	True
	iteration	60
AMF Classifier	n_estimators	6
	step	0.45858
	use_aggregation	True
	dirichlet	0.61187
	split_pure	True

We now evaluate the algorithms using to the MOBIS dataset. Hyperparameters were tuned with Optuna [1] over all users of the dataset (see Table 4).

For ease of reading, the prediction results are grouped into 40 itineraries (the first group of 40 itineraries corresponds to the F1 score of the first 40 itineraries of all users, the second group to the next 40 and so on). Figure 4 shows the F1 score as a box plot. Table 5 presents the last median values for each algorithm. Results show that once a sufficient number of itineraries have been learned, all algorithms achieve high performance, with median F1 scores close to or surpassing 0.9 in the second group. However some differences can be highlighted. AMAS4PL, AMFClassifier, HoeffdingTreeClassifier and MondrianTreeClassifier perform well even with limited data. In contrast, ExtermelyFastDecisionTreeClassifier and HoeffdingAdaptiveTreeClassifier have good performances with a small number of data; however adding more data deteriorates their quality of prediction.

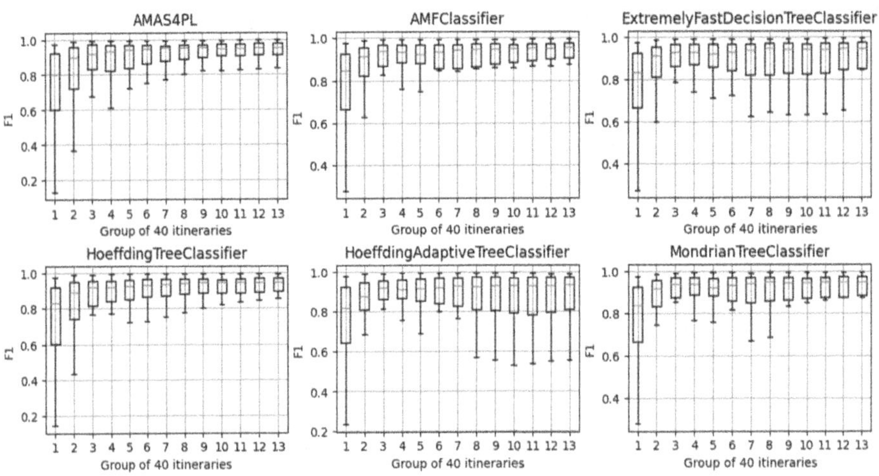

Fig. 4. Evolution of the F1 score for all users of the MOBIS dataset.

Table 5. Last F1 score values of all algorithms

Model	F1
AMAS4PL	0.952
AMFClassifier	0.956
HoeffdingTreeClassifier	0.944
HoeffdingAdaptiveTreeClassifier	0.945
ExtremelyFastDecisionTreeClassifier	0.947
MondrianTreeClassifier	0.951

5.6 Adaptation to Behavioral Changes

We now analyze algorithms performance in response to a behavioral change observed in one user within the MOBIS dataset, using the same hyperparameters as before (see Table 4). The user has a consistent behavior and always uses the same mode of transport. Starting from itinerary 128, the user changes to a new mode of transport and uses it until the end.

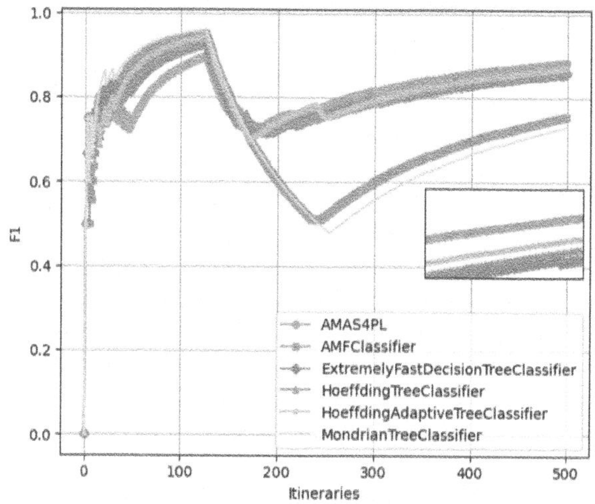

Fig. 5. F1 score evolution for the selected user.

Figure 5 illustrates the evolution of the F1 score. Overall, the curves of AMAS4PL, HoeffdingAdaptiveTreeClassifier, HoeffdingTreeClassifier and ExtremelyFastDecisionTreeClassifier are fairly similar. However, MondrianTreeClassifier and AMFClassifier are slightly higher at the beginning but their performances are highly impacted by the perturbation. In contrast, AMAS4PL performs less efficiently at the beginning. Additional experiments, not included here due to space constraints, showed that this decrease in performance is due to the hyperparameters tuning being done on all users of the dataset rather than on the specific user under study. Nonetheless, AMAS4PL is able to quickly adapt to the perturbation and shows highest performance at the end. This highlights a better robustness to this disturbance as well as adaptation and learning capabilities. This is enabled by the decentralized nature of the multi-agent system, which supports independent and localized model updates.

6 Conclusion and Perspectives

This paper introduces AMAS4PL, a multi-agent system designed to learn user mode of transport preferences at the level of learned regularities (AMAS4DC) from observed user behaviors. AMAS4PL extends AMAS4DC by associating with each learned regularity a vector of features weighted by mode of transport preferences. These weights are then continuously and dynamically adjusted according to the user's observed itineraries.

AMAS4PL benefits from the multi-agent system (MAS) approach to develop a decentralized and distributed learning process that enhances both adaptability and robustness. Moreover, this study highlights the potential of MAS to support localized learning mechanisms that are more interpretable and facilitate real-time adaptation to dynamic environments. A comparative study with other state-of-the-art algorithms shows AMAS4PL's abilities to provide high-quality predictions and to adapt quickly to changes in user behavior.

This initial version of AMAS4PL opens several future research directions concerning the system itself and its application to learning user preferences for modes of transport. First of all, the $fusion\_speed$ hyperparameter strongly influences the system's ability to adapt to behavioral changes. Since there is no universal value for this learning speed, future work will explore adaptive $fusion\_speed$ based on, for example, the frequency of changes (seasonal, weekly, etc.). This is made possible by the fact that learning takes place at the local level of each regular itinerary. Finally, we plan to study the model sensitivity to the $fusion\_threshold$ parameter and its effect on clustering granularity.

In this work, we focused on transport mode prediction. However, the same approach can be used to rank itineraries in a Mobility-as-a-service (MaaS) context, where cosine similarity could be used to score and recommend itineraries according to the user's preferences. Additional features such as CO_2 emissions or travel time can be integrated to promote sustainable choices while respecting individual preferences. Moreover, in this work, only modes of transport are considered for preferences. However, it could be interesting to explore other preference factors (such as number of stops, journey time, etc.). In a MaaS context, minimizing memory and battery usage are very important. A first conducted study showed AMAS4DC ability to reduce memory usage. A second experiment is currently conducted and underlines AMAS4PL capability to reduce energy consumption. Still, further analysis are required before publication. Finally, we plan to assess the genericity of AMAS4PL by evaluating its effectiveness as an adaptive generic classifier and instantiating it on other applications.

Acknowledgments. This work was carried out within the VILAGIL-MaaS action of the VILAGIL project, a project co-financed by Toulouse Métropole and by France 2030 as part of the Territoires d'Innovation program operated by the Banque des Territoires, as well as within the GIS neOCampus. We would like to thank the authors of [18] for sharing the MOBIS dataset with us.

Disclosure of Interests. The authors have no competing interests to declare that are relevant to the content of this article.

References

1. Akiba, T., Sano, S., Yanase, T., Ohta, T., Koyama, M.: Optuna: a next-generation hyperparameter optimization framework. In: Proceedings of the 25th ACM SIGKDD International Conference on Knowledge Discovery and Data Mining (2019)
2. Anagnostopoulou, E., Bothos, E., Magoutas, B., Schrammel, J., Mentzas, G.: Persuasive technologies for sustainable mobility: State of the art and emerging trends. Sustainability **10**(7) (2018). https://doi.org/10.3390/su10072128
3. Basile, S., Consonni, C., Manca, M., Boratto, L.: Matching user preferences and behavior for mobility. In: Proceedings of the 31th ACM Conference on Hypertext and Social Media, pp. 141–150. HT, Association for Computing Machinery, New York, USA (2020). https://doi.org/10.1145/3372923.3404839
4. Bifet, A., Gavalda, R.: Adaptive learning from evolving data streams. In: Advances in Intelligent Data Analysis: 8th International Symposium on Intelligent Data Analysis, IDA'09, Lyon, pp. 249–260. Springer (2009)
5. Breiman, L.: Random forests. Mach. Learn. **45**, 5–32 (2001)
6. Briggs, P., Simpson, B., De Angeli, A.: Personalisation and Trust: A Reciprocal Relationship?, pp. 39–55. Springer Netherlands (2004).https://doi.org/10.1007/1-4020-2148-8_4
7. Connor, R.: A tale of four metrics. In: Amsaleg, L., Houle, M.E., Schubert, E. (eds.) Similarity Search and Applications, pp. 210–217. Springer International Publishing, Cham (2016)
8. Domingos, P., Hulten, G.: Mining high-speed data streams. In: Proceedings of the 6th ACM SIGKDD International Conference on Knowledge Discovery and Data Mining, pp. 71–80 (2000)
9. Durand, A., Harms, L., Hoogendoorn-Lanser, S., Zijlstra, T.: Mobility-as-A-service and Changes in Travel Preferences and Travel Behaviour: A Literature Review. Tech. rep, Ministry of Infrastructure and Water Management, the Netherlands (2018)
10. Gao, M., Liu, K., Wu, Z.: Personalisation in web computing and informatics: Theories, techniques, applications, and future research. Inform. Syst. Front. **12**(5), 607–629 (2010). https://doi.org/10.1007/s10796-009-9199-3
11. Georgakis, P., Almohammad, A., Bothos, E., Magoutas, B., Arnaoutaki, K., Mentzas, G.: Heuristic-based journey planner for mobility as a service (maas). Sustainability **12**, 10140 (12 2020). https://doi.org/10.3390/su122310140
12. Grandini, M., Bagli, E., Visani, G.: Metrics for multi-class classification: an overview. arXiv preprint arXiv:2008.05756 (2020)
13. Hietanen, S.: Mobility as a service - the new transport model? Eurotransport-ITS Transp. Manage. Suppl. **12**(2), 2–4 (2014)
14. Khannouz, M., Glatard, T.: Mondrian forest for data stream classification under memory constraints. Data Min. Knowl. Disc. **38**(2), 569–596 (2024)
15. Lakshminarayanan, B., Roy, D.M., Teh, Y.W.: Mondrian forests: efficient online random forests. In: Advances in Neural Information Processing Systems, vol. 27 (2014)
16. Liu, J., Deng, D., Wu, H., Wu, C.: Comparing preference models in recommender systems. In: 7th International Conference on Intelligent Human-Machine Systems and Cybernetics, vol. 1, pp. 210–213 (2015). https://doi.org/10.1109/IHMSC.2015.61

17. Manapragada, C., Webb, G.I., Salehi, M.: Extremely fast decision tree. In: Proceedings of the 24th ACM SIGKDD Int. Conference on Knowledge Discovery & Data Mining, pp. 1953–1962 (2018)
18. Molloy, J., et al.: The mobis dataset: a large GPS dataset of mobility behaviour in switzerland. Transportation, pp. 1–25 (06 2022). https://doi.org/10.1007/s11116-022-10299-4
19. Montiel, J., Halford, M., Mastelini, S.M., Bolmier, G., Sourty, R., Vaysse, R., Zouitine, A., Gomes, H.M., Read, J., Abdessalem, T., et al.: River: machine learning for streaming data in python. J. Mach. Learn. Res. **22**(110), 1–8 (2021)
20. Mourtada, J., Gaïffas, S., Scornet, E.: AMF: Aggregated mondrian forests for online learning. J. R. Stat. Soc. Ser. B Stat Methodol. **83**(3), 505–533 (2021)
21. Mulvenna, M., Annual, S., Buchner, A.: Personalization on the net using web mining. Commun. ACM **43**(8), 122–125 (2000)
22. Perles, A., Ngo, H.N., Kaddoum, E., Camps, V.: Adaptive multi-agent system for dynamic clustering applied to itineraries regularities and traffic prediction. In: Sellami, M., Vidal, M.E., van Dongen, B., Gaaloul, W., Panetto, H. (eds.) Cooperative Information Systems, pp. 79–96. Springer Nature Switzerland, Cham (2024)
23. Perugini, S., Ramakrishnan, N.: Personalizing web sites with mixed-initiative interaction. IT Professional **5**(2), 9–15 (2003). https://doi.org/10.1109/MITP.2003.1191787
24. Prost, S., Schrammel, J., Röderer, K., Tscheligi, M.: Contextualise! personalise! persuade! a mobile hci framework for behaviour change support systems. In: Proceedings of the 15th Int. Conference on Human-Computer Interaction with Mobile Devices and Services, pp. 510–515. Association for Computing Machinery (2013). https://doi.org/10.1145/2493190.2494434

Controlling the Spread of Two Secrets in Diverse Social Networks

Václav Blažej[1], Dušan Knop[2], and Šimon Schierreich[2](✉)

[1] University of Warsaw, Warsaw, Poland
v.blazej@uw.edu.pl
[2] Czech Technical University in Prague, Prague, Czech Republic
{dusan.knop,schiesim}@fit.cvut.cz

Abstract. We propose the study of diffusion of two secrets in a heterogeneous environment, that is, there are two directed networks over the same set of agents. Our model combines two group identification processes, each with independent desiderata. Specifically, we have two types of targets: constructive, where we aim to expose a given group of agents to a secret, and destructive, where we aim to prevent a given group of agents from being exposed to a secret. To secure these targets, we can employ different control actions: either deleting an agent or introducing a previously latent agent.

For all combinations of the aforementioned targets and actions, we provide a complexity classification. Since classical analysis mostly yields negative results, we adopt a parameterized perspective, considering (combinations of) natural parameters, such as the number of controlled agents or the number of rounds of the activation process. Taking a parameterized perspective, we provide several FPT and XP algorithms along with their respective lower bounds.

Keywords: Group Identification · Fixed-Parameter Tractability · Network Control · Opinion Diffusion

1 Introduction

The origins of secret diffusion control on social networks can be traced to Newman et al. [37], who used this model in the domain of spreading computer viruses via e-mail networks. Later, applications in the study of viruses spreading [18], political and marketing opinions [30], and fake-news [23] have been studied. We further illustrate the importance of this topic in the following.

A Eurobarometer survey published in April 2018 states that 83% of the respondents assume that fake news is a serious threat to democracy [8]. Since then, we have seen the ability of fake news and disinformation in practice multiple times; to mention at least one case, we recall the massive spread of junk news during the COVID-19 pandemic [9,13].

One of the main channels for spreading fake news is social media. A large part of the population relies on social media as their primary source of information [33,42], and many undesirable phenomena, such as echo chambers and

M. Baldoni et al. (Eds.): EUMAS 2025, LNAI 16259, pp. 161–178, 2026.
https://doi.org/10.1007/978-3-032-22820-8_10

filter bubbles [41], even strengthen the impact of fake news. So, naturally, there is extensive work on fake news detection and prevention [17,27,39,40]; see also the monograph of Giansiracusa [23] for a survey of AI-based fake news combat methods. However, the algorithmic approach has so far only partially succeeded, indicating the need for a more sophisticated strategy to combat fake news [33].

Interestingly, the survey by Guess et al. [25] states that some groups are more vulnerable to fake news than others and consequently more active in their sharing. Probably the most surprising result on this line is that Facebook users over the age of 65 shared, on average, seven times as many disinformation articles as those aged 18 to 29. Note that similar results were also obtained in many follow-up surveys [34,44,45]. In this paper, we study how we can protect such vulnerable groups from exhibition to fake news.

At the same time, schemes to spread fake news are becoming more and more sophisticated. Many users are present on more than one social network [3], and thus, the misinformation spills from one social medium to another very naturally. In many cases, fake news comes in a sort of campaign in which multiple interrelated disinformation are released on social media to strengthen and support each other.

In this work, we derive a first model for preventing fake news (or secrets) spread on social networks that is rich enough to capture all the three eventualities mentioned above. Although we give formal definitions of the problem in Sect. 3, we find it helpful for the upcoming discussion to bring the Destructive-Destructive 2-Groups Control by Deleting Agents problem (DD-2GCD for short) to light now. The input of the problem consists of two social networks G_1 and G_2 modeled as directed graphs on the same set of agents A, two sets of agents R_1 and R_2 that initially spread the secret, two sets of agents D_1 and D_2 that need to be protected, and an integer k. We assume that the secret is spread in discrete rounds to all out-neighbors of agents already having the secret. Moreover, once an agent acquires the secret, she never loses it. The goal is to decide whether there exists a k-sized subset of agents such that the removal of these agents from both networks, by, e.g., blocking their accounts, results in a process that does not spread the first secret to agents of D_1 in the network G_1, and the second secret to agents in D_2 through the network G_2, respectively.

Naturally, this model has many variations. We can consider the *destructive-constructive* variant of the problem where we want to prevent one group of agents from learning the secret while securing the other group to still learn the secret. We call the formal setting with destructive-constructive targets the Destructive-Constructive 2-Groups Control by Deleting Agents problem (DC-2GCD for short).

There is a great deal of work on one secret spread in social networks; one of the most discussed models leads (in the discrete case) to the linear threshold model [29]. However, in this setting, the goal is to find a small activation set that eventually spreads the secret throughout the network. In contrast to the linear threshold model, in our setting, the activation sets are given and our task is to ensure that the specific group is not affected. In the single opinion setting, this problem is frequently captured in the so-called GROUP IDENTIFICATION problem. In this line of work, the most important works for us are recent papers on the complexity of manipulation of the outcome [6,20,47]. In particular, Yang and Dimitrov [47] and Erdélyi et al. [20] study the complexity of outcome manipulation using agent deletion and agent addition. Boehmer et al. [6] then introduced the combination of the two targets (constructive and destructive) on the same social network. They studied the problems from the perspective of both classical and parameterized complexity. The problem of manipulating information diffusion in social networks by adding or deleting edges or manipulating elections also received a lot of attention; see, e.g. [1,4,7,10,43], and references therein.

Our model is also closely related to the control in the well-known Approval voting rule [32] and committee elections under this rule [24,31]. In this voting rule, every agent provides an approval ballot, and the winners of the elections are then the candidates that most agents approve of. Although the approval rule has already been studied as a multi-winner voting rule [21,46,48], the voters and candidates usually do not coincide, and, moreover, the size of the resulting committee is usually fixed.

Finally, it should be noted that more complicated models of spreading multiple secrets have been proposed in linear thresholds [5,22,30,35] and GROUP IDENTIFICATION [11]; however, the problem studied in [11] is to find a partition of agents into disjoint groups of socially qualified agents.

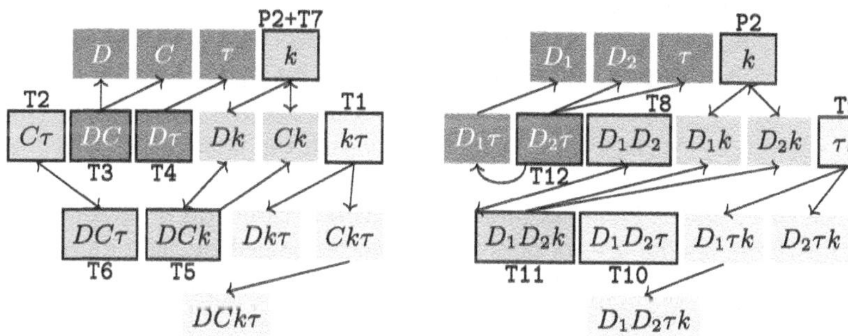

(a) Our results for DC-2GCD. (b) Our results for DD-2GCD.

Fig. 1. The complexity picture for the studied variants of the 2-GROUPS CONTROL BY DELETING AGENTS problem (the precise definitions are in Sect. 3). Combinations of parameters that admit fixed-parameter tractable algorithms are highlighted in green (light gray), while combinations for which the problem is W[1]-hard and is in XP are highlighted in orange (gray). Red (dark gray) remains for para-NP-hard combinations. Results explicitly proved in this work are represented by a black border and are complemented by the reference to the formal statement. Arrows indicate the logical implications of the results. (Color figure online)

Our Contribution. We propose a study of a new variant of GROUP IDENTIFICATION with two networks and give a comprehensive picture of its computational complexity. As is very common for similar secret spread problems, the problem becomes computationally intractable even in very restricted settings. Motivated by this, we employ the framework of parameterized complexity [14] that has recently been used to reveal tractable islands for many fundamental problems of artificial intelligence research [15,19]. With the parameterized complexity lens, we study the problem's complexity not only with respect to the input size n, but we also have additional information about the input structure called *parameter*. The goal is to develop an algorithm whose exponential explosion in running time is confined to the parameter and not to the input size.

In our work, we assume the following natural parameters that are either part of the input or can be used as an additional condition restricting the solution:

- The standard parameter (the solution size) denoted by k.
- The number of agents that should be affected by the control operation. Examples of this parameter are the sizes of sets D_1 and D_2 in DD-2GCD.
- The number of rounds of the activation process denoted τ. This parameter allows us to model situations where, e.g., the secret loses its relevance after a specific time, and is common in group identification and network dynamics scenarios; see, e.g., [12,30].

The complexity picture for each nontrivial combination of control operations and targets is provided in Fig. 1. It turns out that a sufficient condition for tractability is bounding the size of the solution and the number of steps of the activation process. In particular, we provide multiple fixed-parameter tractable algorithms (these have running times of the form $f(k) \cdot n^{\mathcal{O}(1)}$) and XP (whose running time is $n^{f(k)}$) and complement them with the respective lower bounds based on four completely different problems (3-SAT, k-MULTICOLORED INDEPENDENT SET, GRID TILLING, and PARTITIONED SUBGRAPH ISOMORPHISM). Our algorithmic results are, in many cases, accompanied by tight running-time lower bounds based on the well-known Exponential Time Hypothesis [26]. Altogether, we provide the full complexity picture for all variants of the 2-GROUPS CONTROL problem.

Paper Organization. The rest of this paper is organized as follows. In Sect. 2, we introduce the necessary notation and definitions used throughout the paper. Next, in Sect. 3, we give formal definitions of our problems and give some basic observations that are common for all variants of the problem studied.

In Sects. 4 and 5, we present our technical results. In particular, Sect. 4 is dedicated to the destructive-constructive variant. In Sect. 5, we then study a variant with two destructive targets. In Sect. 6 we briefly introduce the results we obtained for other control operations. We conclude this work in Sect. 7 with some open problems and possible future research directions.

2 Preliminaries

We assume that the reader is familiar with a basic notation of graph theory [16] and computational complexity theory [2].

Let $A = \{a_1, \ldots, a_n\}$ be a set of n *agents*. A *qualification graph* G is a directed graph (A, φ) where the edges $(a, a') \in \varphi$ represent that agent a *qualifies* agent a'.

Given a *seed set* $R \subseteq A$, the set of *socially qualified* agents $K(G, R)$ consists of all vertices that can be "reached" from R. More formally, the set of socially qualified agents is defined by the following iterative process. Let $K_0(G, R) = R$. Next, for every positive integer i, we set

$$K_i(G, R) = \{a' \in A \mid \exists a \in K_{i-1}(G, R) : (a, a') \in \varphi\} \cup K_{i-1}(G, R).$$

Let r be the smallest non-negative integer such that $K_r(G, R) = K_{r+1}(G, R)$. We say that the process stabilized in the r-th *round* and the set $K(G, R) = K_r(G, R)$ constitutes the socially qualified set of agents.

Parameterized Complexity. In parameterized algorithmics, the input of the problem is given along with a numeric value (the *parameter*) which expresses certain properties of the instance, e.g., the size of the sought solution. Positive results focus on finding either fixed-parameter-tractable (FPT for short) algorithms or XP algorithms. FPT algorithms admit $f(k) \cdot \text{poly}(n)$ running times and XP algorithms run in $n^{f(k)}$ time, where n is the size of the input, k is the parameter value, and f is a computable function.

Among the negative results, the goal is to characterize computational problems in terms of W-hierarchy. It holds that W[0] = FPT. Similarly to classical complexity theory, it is widely believed that there are no FPT algorithms for problems that are W[1]-hard [14, Chapter 13]. Analogously to NP-hardness, which is shown using polynomial reduction, one can show that a problem belongs to a class of W-hierarchy by reducing from a hard problem out of this complexity class. In particular, a *parameterized reduction* from a parameterized problem A to a parameterized problem B is an algorithm $\mathcal{A}$ that, given an instance (x, k) of A, outputs modified instance (x', k') of the problem B such that $(x, k) \in A$ iff $(x', k') \in B$, $k' \leq g(k)$, and $\mathcal{A}$ works in time $f(k) \cdot |x|^{\mathcal{O}(1)}$, where $f, g \colon \mathbb{N} \to \mathbb{N}$ are some computable functions. It can be also the case that NP-complete problems remain NP-hard even for a fixed value of the parameter. In such case, we say that our problem is para-NP-hard with respect to k. For a more comprehensive introduction to the topic of parameterized complexity, we refer to the monograph of Cygan et al. [14].

3 Problem Settings

In this section, we formally define the problems of interest. As stated before, our aim is to study effects of the control operations on the setting with two qualification graphs over the same set of agents. The main part of the paper is dedicated to the study of control by agent deletion.

DESTRUCTIVE-CONSTRUCTIVE 2-GROUPS CONTROL BY DELETING AGENTS

Input: A set of agents A, two qualification graphs $G_1 = (A, \varphi_1)$ and $G_2 = (A, \varphi_2)$, seed sets R_1 and R_2, two sets $D \subseteq A$ and $C \subseteq A$, an integer $k \in \mathbb{N}$, and a round $\tau \in \mathbb{N}$.

Question: Is there a set $S \subseteq A$ of size at most k such that $K_\tau(G_1 \setminus S, R_1 \setminus S) \cap D = \emptyset$ and $K_\tau(G_2 \setminus S, R_2 \setminus S) \cap C = C$?

We will write DC-2GCD, for short. The first variant contains one destructive and one constructive goal. In particular, we want to delete a subset of agents such that agents from the first given set of agents are not qualified in G_1, while agents from the second set are qualified in G_2. Note that the qualification graphs are interchangeable, hence, it is not necessary to study the CONSTRUCTIVE-DESTRUCTIVE variant separately.

DESTRUCTIVE-DESTRUCTIVE 2-GROUPS CONTROL BY DELETING AGENTS

Input: A set of agents A, two qualification graphs $G_1 = (A, \varphi_1)$ and $G_2 = (A, \varphi_2)$, seed sets R_1 and R_2, two sets $D_1 \subseteq A$ and $D_2 \subseteq A$, an integer $k \in \mathbb{N}$, and a round $\tau \in \mathbb{N}$.

Question: Is there a set $S \subseteq A$ of size at most k such that $K_\tau(G_1 \setminus S, R_1 \setminus S) \cap D_1 = \emptyset$ and $K_\tau(G_2 \setminus S, R_2 \setminus S) \cap D_2 = \emptyset$?

We will write DD-2GCD, for short. In this version, we are given two groups of agents and our goal is to prevent qualification of the first group in the first graphs G_1 and to prevent qualification of the second group in the graph G_2.

The remaining variant contains two constructive goals. We observe that this variant is not very interesting as it can be solved in polynomial time. The agent deletion operation does not increase the number of qualified agents and, hence, either the goals are fulfilled in the original instance or we are handling a *no*-instance.

Proposition 1. *The* CONSTRUCTIVE-CONSTRUCTIVE 2-GROUPS CONTROL BY DELETING AGENTS *problem can be solved in polynomial time.*

Proof. Let C_1 and C_2 be a controlled group for φ_1 and φ_2, respectively. By agent deletion, we cannot increase the number of qualified agents. Hence, we return *yes* if $K(A, R_1) \cap C_1 = C_1$ and $K(A, R_2) \cap C_2 = C_2$. Otherwise, we return *no*. Note that the process can be simulated in polynomial time. □

We conclude this section with a simple algorithm solving both interesting variants of the problem in $n^{\mathcal{O}(k)}$ time. In the further sections, we will show that this algorithm based on a simple brute-force over all possible solution sets is, under reasonable theoretical assumptions, asymptotically optimal.

Proposition 2. *Both* DC-2GCD *and* DD-2GCD *are in XP parameterized by the solution size k.*

Proof. We proceed by a simple brute-force algorithm. We try all subsets of agents of size k and for every such subset we simulate the process. There are $n^{\mathcal{O}(k)}$ such subsets and every simulation can be done in polynomial time. □

4 Destructive and Constructive Target

We recall that in the DC-2GCD problem, our goal is to prevent agents in the first controlled group to be socially qualified with respect to the first qualification graph, while securing that all agents in the second controlled group are still socially qualified in the second qualification graph.

We begin our study of this variant with algorithmic upper bounds.

Theorem 1. DC-2GCD *is fixed-parameter tractable parameterized by the solution size k and the number of rounds τ combined.*

Proof. We have a branching procedure as follows. Let us run the Breadth First Search algorithm on G_1 to find some path $P = (p_1, \ldots, p_m)$ from source to target in $\mathcal{O}(n)$ time, where n is the total size of the graph. If no path P exists, then we check whether agents C can be reached within G_2. If yes, then we return that this branch found a solution, otherwise continue the procedure as follows. If the solution size is zero, then return that the current branch does not contain a solution. If we still have some solution size left, then one of the first $\tau + 1$ vertices of P must be chosen to the solution as otherwise either the target p_m would learn the secret from p_1 or the process would take more than τ rounds. Let us choose a vertex $u \in P$ (we branch here for every choice of u) to be included in the solution. Now, run the described procedure again for DC-2GCD on the graph where u is removed (marked not to be traversed by the BFS) and solution size is reduced by 1. If the procedure call returns a solution then add u to it and return it. The above procedure branches on at most $\tau + 1$ vertices of P. The biggest recursion depth is k as the solution size gets decreased by one with each sub-procedure, and for $k = 0$ the procedure does not call any sub-procedure. The number of procedure calls is at most $\sum_{i=0}^{k}(\tau + 1)^i = \frac{(\tau+1)^{k+1}}{\tau}$ and each procedure calls BFS and several constant-time operations. This gives us the total time complexity of $\tau^{\mathcal{O}(k)} \cdot n^{\mathcal{O}(1)}$ which is FPT w.r.t k and τ. $\square$

In further results, we use the following observation which allows us to reduce the size of the destructive set to a constant by increasing the size of the constructive set by one.

Lemma 1. *An instance $\mathcal{I} = (A, G_1, G_2, R_1, R_2, D, \{c_1, \ldots, c_q\}, k, \tau)$ of the* DC-2GCD *problem is a* yes-*instance if and only if $\mathcal{J} = (A \cup \{t', t_1, \ldots, t_q\}, H_1, H_2, R_1, R_2 \cup \{t'\}, \{t'\}, \{t', t_1, \ldots, t_q\}, k, \tau + 1)$, where $H_1 = (A, E(G_1) \cup \{(d, t') \mid d \in D\})$ and $H_2 = (A, E(G_2) \cup \{(c_i, t_i) \mid i \in \{1, \ldots, q\})$, is a* yes-*instance.*

Hence, for the rest of this section, we assume that all input instances are reduced with respect to Lemma 1, that is, $|D|$ is constant.

We continue with an XP algorithm for the combined parameter the size of the constructive set C and the number of rounds τ. Our algorithm is based on the max-flow/min-cut subroutine.

Theorem 2. DC-2GCD *is in* XP *parameterized by the size of the constructive set* C *and number of rounds* τ *combined.*

Proof. The algorithm guesses the paths leading from sources to vertices of C in G_1 and prevents them from being removed to ensure reachability of C within G_1. Then it checks how many vertices we need to remove so that no vertex in D is reached. This can be achieved by using the standard max-flow/min-cut algorithm with an alteration to remove vertices (done by splitting each vertex in twine, one preserving in-edges and one preserving out-edges; the single edge between them represents the vertex). In the min-cut algorithm we can simulate that a vertex cannot be removed by setting respective edge-weight to $k+1$. There are at most $n^{\mathcal{O}(\tau)}$ paths of length τ in G, and we choose $|C|$ of them which makes ${n^{\mathcal{O}(\tau)}}^{|C|}$ possible combinations in total. Max-flow/min-cut algorithm together with the graph preprocessing is polynomial, so we have total $n^{\mathcal{O}(\tau \cdot |C|)}$ running time which falls into XP. □

Now, we show that the studied problem is NP-complete even in very restricted settings.

Theorem 3. *It is* NP*-complete to solve* DC-2GCD *even if the size of the constructive set* $|C|$ *and the size of the destructive set* $|D|$ *are fixed constants.*

Proof (sketch). We show the NP-hardness via reduction from the 3-SAT problem. Let us have a 3-SAT formula $\mathcal{F}$ consisting of clauses C_i and variables x_j. Each literal occurrence in $\mathcal{F}$ is represented by an agent A within the qualification graphs G_1 and G_2. Our construction ensures that the agent $v \in V(G)$ can be controlled (removed) only if the respective literal occurrence evaluates to true.

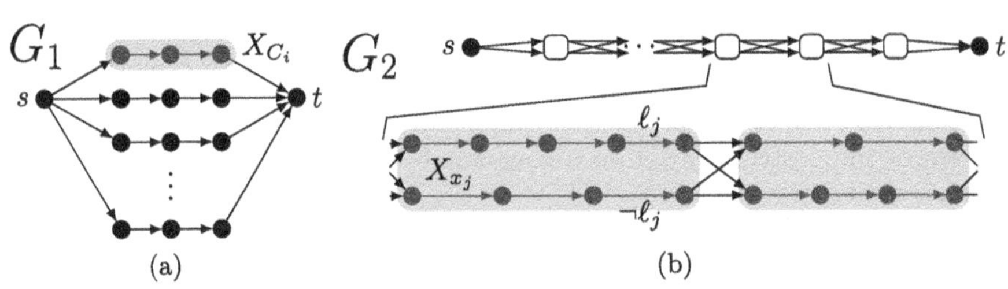

Fig. 2. Illustration of the reduction used to show NP-hardness for DC-2GCD; structure of G_1 in 2a and G_2 in 2b.

Our construction uses two gadgets (see Fig. 2 for an illustration). The first gadget over the edges of G_1 ensures that each clause C_i is satisfied. The second gadget over the edges of G_2 ensures that we cannot control both (agents corresponding to) positive literals ℓ_j and negative literals $\neg\ell_j$ of a variable x_j at the same time. We set the solution size k to the number of clauses so that every clause will be forced to be satisfied by exactly one of its literal occurrences. □

From the parameterized perspective, Theorem 3 implies that DC-2GCD is para-NP-hard with respect to the combined parameter $|D| + |C|$. The proof can also be slightly changed to obtain NP-completeness for the following setting.

Theorem 4. *It is NP-complete to solve* DC-2GCD *even if the number of rounds τ and size of the destructive set $|D|$ are fixed constants.*

We continue with W[1]-hardness lower bounds completing the complexity picture for the DC-2GCD problem. We reduce from the GRID TILLING WITH $\leq$ problem, which is a variant of the GRID TILLING problem. Here, we are given an integer k, an integer n, and a collection $\mathcal{S}$ of k^2 non-empty sets $S_{i,j} \subseteq [n]\times[n]$, $1 \leq i, j \leq k$. The question is whether for every $S_{i,j}$ we can choose an entry $s_{i,j} \in S_{i,j}$ such that for adjacent chosen entries $s_{i,j} = (a, b)$, $s_{i+1,j} = (a', b')$ we have $a \leq a'$, and for $s_{i,j} = (a, b)$ and $s_{i,j+1} = (a'', b'')$ we have $b \leq b''$. In the GRID TILLING problem, we replace each $\leq$ with equality. Both problems are known to be W[1]-hard parameterized by k [36].

Theorem 5 ($\star$). *The* DC-2GCD *problem is W[1]-hard when parameterized by the solution size k even if the size of the constructive set C is a fixed constant.*

Proof (sketch). Main idea of the proof is to create a path that represents $S_{i,j}$ and leads to D in G_1. Each vertex of the path represents an entry. The solution needs to control a vertex which then represents the chosen entry in GRID TILLING WITH $\leq$. Additionally, a set of intricately joined paths in G_2 through these vertices ensure that one cannot pick vertically or horizontally incompatible entries. To be little more precise, the paths in G_1 have their vertices "blown up" to four vertices and the solution needs to remove all four to cut the path. Each of the four vertices then connects to one of four sides (up, down, left, right) in the grid via gadget in G_2. This gadget allows a path through if and only if the values of the chosen entries could be chosen in the solution of GRID TILLING WITH $\leq$. $\square$

The construction from the proof of Theorem 5 can be changed to show hardness also for slightly different settings.

Theorem 6. *The* DC-2GCD *problem is W[1]-hard when parameterized by*

a) the number of rounds τ even if the size of the constructive set C is a fixed constant, and
b) the size of the constructive set C even if the number of rounds τ is a fixed constant.

We conclude this section with a non-trivial ETH-based lower bound showing that the simple brute-force algorithm given in Proposition 2 is, under reasonable theoretical assumptions, asymptotically optimal.

Theorem 7. *Unless ETH fails, there is no algorithm for the* DC-2GCD *problem working in $f(k) \cdot n^{o(k)}$ time, where f is any computable function.*

5 Two Destructive Targets

We recall that in the DD-2GCD problem, we are given two sets of distinguished agents and our goal is to secure that agents from the sets are not qualified with respect to corresponding qualification graphs.

Let us start with a simple observation that allows us to bound the value of the solution size in terms of sizes of destructive sets.

Lemma 2. *Let $\mathcal{I} = (A, G_1, G_2, R_1, R_2, D_1, D_2, k)$ be an instance of* DD-2GCD. *If $k \geq |D_1| + |D_2|$, then $\mathcal{I}$ is a* yes*-instance.*

Together with Proposition 2, Lemma 2 directly gives us an XP algorithm for the DD-2GCD parameterized by $|D_1|$ and $|D_2|$.

Theorem 8. *The* DD-2GCD *problem is in XP parameterized by the combined parameter $|D_1|$ and $|D_2|$.*

Observe that the complexity results do not change when we swap the roles of D_1 and D_2, however, as the settings may be mutually incomparable we prove only one variant but we present both variants in the results overview of Fig. 1b.

Theorem 9. *The* DD-2GCD *problem is fixed-parameter tractable parameterized by the solution size k and the number of rounds τ combined.*

Proof. We run the BFS algorithm on G_1 to find some path $P = (p_1, \ldots, p_m)$ from R_1 to D_1 in $\mathcal{O}(n)$ time, where n is the total size of the graphs. If none exists, then we do the same for G_2, trying to find a path from R_2 to D_2. If no path P was found, then the procedure returns $\emptyset$ as a solution. Otherwise, if the solution size is zero, then return that the solution does not exist. If we still have some solution size left, then one of the first $\tau + 1$ vertices of P must be chosen to the solution as otherwise either the target p_m would learn the secret from p_1 or the process would take more than τ rounds. Let us choose a vertex $u \in P$ (we branch here for every choice of u) to be included in the solution. Now, run this procedure again for DD-2GCD where u is removed (marked not to be traversed by the BFS) and solution size is reduced by 1. If the procedure finds a solution then add u to it and return it.

The above procedure branches on at most $\tau + 1$ vertices of P. The biggest recursion depth is k as the solution size gets decreased by one with each sub-procedure, and for $k = 0$ the procedure does not call any sub-procedures. The number of procedure calls is at most $\sum_{i=0}^{k}(\tau+1)^i = \frac{(\tau+1)^{k+1}}{\tau}$ and each procedure calls BFS twice and several constant-time operations. The total time is $\mathcal{O}\big((\tau + 1)^{k+1}n\big)$ which is FPT in combined parameter k and τ. □

The fixed-parameter algorithm given in Theorem 9 is in its spirit very similar to the algorithm from Theorem 1. By combining Lemma 2 and Theorem 9, we obtain the following algorithm for a slightly different setting.

Theorem 10. *The* DD-2GCD *problem is fixed-parameter tractable parameterized by the combined parameter $|D_1|$, $|D_2|$, and the number of rounds τ.*

On the other hand, it turns out that no parameter can be dropped while keeping the problem tractable. This time, we provide W[1]-hardness reduction from the PARTITIONED SUBGRAPH ISOMORPHISM problem (PSI for short), which is defined as follows. Input consists of two undirected graphs G' and H' with $|V(H')| \leq |V(G')|$ and a mapping $\psi\colon V(G') \to V(H')$. The goal is to decide whether there exists an injective mapping $\phi\colon V(H') \to V(G')$ such that $\{\phi(u), \phi(v)\} \in E(G')$ for each $\{u, v\} \in E(H')$ and $\psi \circ \phi$ is the identity. PSI is known to be W[1]-hard with respect to $|E(H')|$ [38].

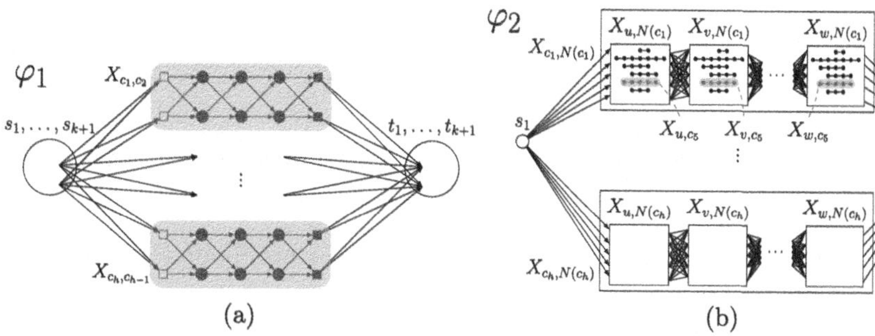

Fig. 3. Node compositions representing construction of edges of G_{φ_1} in 3a and G_{φ_2} in 3b used in Theorem 11; $h = |V(H')|$.

Theorem 11. *The* DD-2GCD *problem is W[1]-hard when parameterized by the combined parameter* $|D_2|$ *and solution size* k*, even if* $|D_1|$ *is a fixed constant.*

Proof (sketch). The reduction from PSI takes edges of H' and G' and imagines every edge as two directed edges in opposite directions. To model ϕ for every $v \in V(H')$ we have to select one vertex from $\phi^{-1}(v)$ (these constitute color classes).

In the DD-2GCD instance, there will be one vertex for every edge (with direction) in G' and an additional source and sink (that get copied $k+1$ times to prevent the solution removing all sources or sinks). The construction has just two goals: 1) If we control (a vertex that represents) an edge (u, v) in G, then we must control (v, u) as well, and 2) if we control (u, v), then u is the only vertex from $\phi^{-1}(u)$ among the vertices inside the controlled edges (we cannot control two vertices of the same color).

The first goal is achieved by concatenating all edges that contain the same pair of colors into a "thick path" where (u, v) and (v, u) are at the same "level". By setting the solution size tight the solution is forced to cut each "thick path" in such opposing directed edges. The second goal is realized by concatenating more complex gadgets that, however, essentially function in the same way as the mentioned paths. For each color its gadget forces a vertex choice by cutting the gadget. For a selected vertex the gadget has many parallel paths one for other adjacent color. The tight solution size in G_1 and G_2 over the same vertices forces goals to be satisfied at once, constituting the mapping ψ. See Fig. 3 for an illustration of the reduction. $\square$

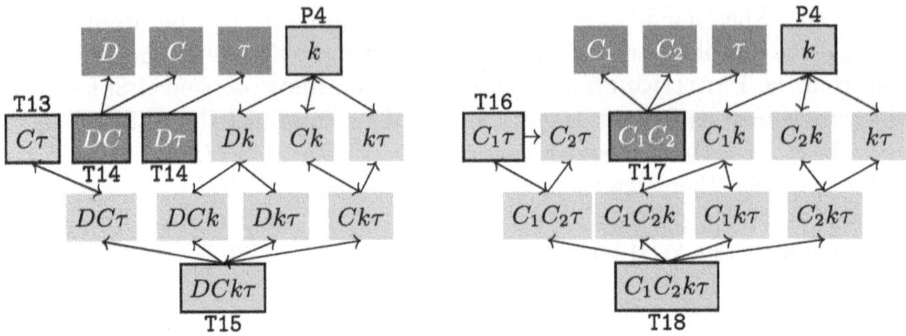

(a) Our results for DC-2GCA. (b) Our results for CC-2GCA.

Fig. 4. The complexity picture for the studied variants of the 2-Groups Control by Adding Agents problem. The meaning of colors and borders is the same as in Fig. 1.

We conclude the section with an NP-hardness lower bound showing that no parameter can be dropped. The proof is similar to the proof of Theorem 3, however, some key differences help us derive bounds for different settings in the parameterized analysis.

Theorem 12. DD-2GCD *is NP-complete even if both* $|D_2|$ *and the number of rounds* τ *are fixed constants.*

6 Additional Control Operations: Adding Agents

In this section, we give a brief overview of results for an additional control operation – agent addition. To be able to study such a control operation, we have to slightly modify the model. The instance is extended by a set of so-called *latent agents* $L \subseteq A$. These agents do not participate in the original qualification processes, however, we can persuade them to participate. Formally, we define the problem as follows.

Destructive-Constructive 2-Groups Control by Adding Agents

Input: A set of agents A, a set $L \subseteq A$ of latent agents, two qualification graphs $G_1 = (A, \varphi_1)$ and $G_2 = (A, \varphi_2)$, seed sets R_1 and R_2, two sets $D \subseteq A \setminus L$ and $C \subseteq A \setminus L$, an integer $k \in \mathbb{N}$, and a round $\tau \in \mathbb{N}$.

Question: Is there a set $S \subseteq L$ of size at most k such that $K_\tau(G_1 \setminus (L \setminus S), R_1 \setminus (L \setminus S)) \cap D = \emptyset$ and $K_\tau(G_2 \setminus (L \setminus S), R_2 \setminus (L \setminus S)) \cap C = C$?

We will write DC-2GCA for short. Analogously, we define the Constructive-Constructive 2-Groups Control by Adding Agents problem (CC-2GCA for short), where we have two constructive goals, that is, we are given two sets C_1

and C_2 and our goal is to secure that the agents from C_1 are socially qualified in G_1 and agents from C_2 are qualified in G_2.

The last remaining setting is a variant with two destructive goals. We show that this problem is solvable easily in polynomial time, because we cannot prevent agent qualification by adding agents.

Proposition 3. *The* DESTRUCTIVE-DESTRUCTIVE 2-GROUPS CONTROL BY ADDING AGENTS *problem can be solved in polynomial time.*

Analogously to the control by agent deletion (Proposition 2), there is an algorithm solving both DC-2GCA and CC-2GCA in XP time. This algorithm again exhaustively enumerate all possible subsets of latent agents and check whether the activation of these agents leads to a solution.

Proposition 4. *Both* DC-2GCA *and* CC-2GCA *are in* XP *parameterized by the solution size* k.

The full complexity picture for the addition control is depicted in Fig. 4.

6.1 Destructive and Constructive Target

The DC-2GCA problem is in some sense “dual” to the DC-2GCD problem. Hence, in our constructions, almost all of the agents are latent but the set of controlled agents stays the same. In this setting the reduction forces the controlled agents to create paths from start to sink instead of cutting it. We may even mirror Lemma 1 about the bounded size of the set D. Using this, we can show the following algorithmic upper bound.

Theorem 13. *The* DC-2GCA *problem is in* XP *parameterized by* $|C|$ *and the number of rounds* τ *combined.*

Proof. This approach is somewhat similar to the proof of Theorem 2. The algorithm guesses the paths leading from sources to vertices of C in φ_1. Now it chooses to control all latent agents that lie on the chosen paths and checks that there are at most k of them. Then it checks that no vertex in D is reached by the standard BFS algorithm. There are at most n^τ paths of length τ in G, and we choose $|C|$ of them which makes $(n^\tau)^{|C|}$ possible combinations in total. BFS algorithm is polynomial, so we have total $n^{\mathcal{O}(\tau \cdot |C|)}$ running time. □

We conclude this subsection with two more running-time lower bounds which finalize the complexity picture of this variant.

Theorem 14. *The* DC-2GCA *problem is* NP*-complete even if the size of the constructive set* $|C|$*, or the number of rounds* τ *is a fixed constant.*

Proof (sketch). To prove NP-completeness alone, the construction used in the proof of Theorem 3 can be used as well. It consists of construction that can be easily changed to a construction which works for DC-2GCA in the following way.

- Put all vertices except source and sink to the latent set,
- swap each construction of a path-like structure (where we have to traverse all its vertices to get through) with a parallel structure (where we choose any path to traverse through) and vice-versa,
- swap C with D.

On the one hand, this way each clause becomes a triplet of vertices that can be traversed independently. All clauses are put one after another in φ_1 so the solution must control at least one agent in each clause to form a path from R_1 to C. On the other hand, the literals form a path $(s, \ell_i, \neg\ell_i, t)$ for any choice of occurrences ℓ_i and $\neg\ell_i$, hence, choosing a positive and negative valuation of the same variable would create a path from R_2 to D, which is forbidden.

We see that the construction uses $C = D = \{t\}$ so when these sets are of constant size the problem is still NP-hard. Similarly to the proof of Theorem 3, we can change the construction by creating a separate sink in C for every clause which implies that for a constant τ the problem is NP-hard. □

Theorem 15. DC-2GCA *is W[1]-hard when parameterized by*

a) the solution size k and the size of the constructive set C, combined, even if the number of rounds τ is a fixed constant, and
b) the solution size k and the number of rounds τ, combined, even if the size of the constructive set C is a fixed constant.

6.2 Two Constructive Targets

Again, the CC-2GCA problem is very close to the DD-2GCD problem. Similarly, the roles of C_1 and C_2 can be swapped and the result stays the same.

Theorem 16. *The* CC-2GCA *problem is in XP parameterized by the combined parameter $|C_1|$ and the number of rounds τ.*

Proof. There are at most $n^{\mathcal{O}(\tau)}$ different paths of length τ. We can search through all combinations of $|C_1|$ paths of length at most τ in time $n^{\mathcal{O}(\tau\cdot|C_1|)}$. For every combination we activate latent agents on these paths and know that all vertices in C_1 are reached in φ_1. The remaining solution size shall be used to resolve vertices in C_2 using the known polynomial-time algorithm for single constructive goal. The solution must lie inside these combinations because every vertex in C_1 and C_2 must be satisfied by at least one path of length at most τ. Thus, we have algorithm running in $n^{\mathcal{O}(\tau\cdot|C_1|)}$ time. □

We conclude this section with two W[1]-hardness results which complement our algorithmic upper bounds and finalize the complexity picture for CC-2GCA. First, we show that the problem remains W[1]-hard even when parameterized by the solution size and the number of rounds.

Theorem 17. CC-2GCA *parameterized by the combined parameter the solution size k and the number of rounds τ is W[1]-hard, even if $|C_1|$ and $|C_2|$ are fixed constants.*

Proof (sketch). The cut vertices in Theorem 11 are in 1-to-1 correspondence with constructing paths through latent agents in this proof. We point out only the major differences. We do the same preprocessing step for the given PSI instance and even create the same set of vertices, but using only one vertex s and one t instead. These vertices are the only non-latent agents. To reach the first goal, we build path through the edges of opposite directions and concatenate them in a way that with the tight solution size we must choose exactly one pair of opposite edges for each tuple of colors to build a path from R_1 to C_1. For the second goal we weave the construction so that the path uses exactly the same vertices as for the first goal but the path goes from R_2 to C_2 if and only if we choose all edges from a color to go from a single vertex. The solution size remains the same. Target sets are constant as they contain only t. The process is bounded by the number of active agents which is at most $2 + k$. □

We conclude with a complementary results for the parameterization by the solution size and the sizes of constructive sets.

Theorem 18. CC-2GCA *parameterized by the combined parameter $|C_1|$, $|C_2|$, and the solution size k is W[1]-hard, even if the number of rounds τ is a fixed constant.*

7 Conclusions

In this paper, we initiated the study of group identification in two diverse social networks and we provide a complete complexity picture for two control operations and different desiderata – all possible combinations of constructive and destructive targets.

So far, the process was initiated by an arbitrary seed sets of agents. In the strict group identification setting, this is equivalent to the so called liberal-start-respecting rule [28]. A natural question is then: how does the complexity picture change if a different method is used to select the seed sets? We conjecture that most of our constructions can be shifted to setting with a consensus-start-respecting rule that starts with vertices that have incoming edges from all vertices of the network.

We studied control by agent deletion or addition but excluding individuals from a social network can have serious repercussions for the platform's owner. A more moderate approach such as changing the network edges, e.g., by changing what the users see, can be implemented more conveniently and should be given consideration.

Last but not least, we believe more complicated processes should be investigated in future work; namely, what if there is a certain interaction between the two secrets, e.g., each agent can only spread one secret?

Acknowledgement. The work on this paper was supported by the Czech Science Foundation Grant No. 22-19557S, and by the Grant Agency of the Czech Technical University in Prague, grant No. SGS23/205/OHK3/3T/18. VB acknowledges the support of the OP VVV MEYS funded project CZ.02.1.01/0.0/0.0/16_019/0000765 "Research Center for Informatics".

References

1. Amoruso, M., Anello, D., Auletta, V., Cerulli, R., Ferraioli, D., Raiconi, A.: Contrasting the spread of misinformation in online social networks. J. Artif. Intell. Res. **69**, 847–879 (2020)
2. Arora, S., Barak, B.: Computational Complexity: A Modern Approach. Cambridge University Press (2009). https://doi.org/10.1017/CBO9780511804090
3. Auxier, B., Anderson, M.: Social media use in 2021. Technical report, Pew (2021)
4. Barrot, N., Lang, J., Yokoo, M.: Manipulation of hamming-based approval voting for multiple referenda and committee elections. In: Proceedings of the 16th Conference on Autonomous Agents and MultiAgent Systems, AAMAS '17, pp. 597–605 (2017)
5. Becker, R., Corò, F., D'Angelo, G., Gilbert, H.: Balancing spreads of influence in a social network. In: Proceedings of the 34th AAAI Conference on Artificial Intelligence, AAAI '20, pp. 3–10 (2020)
6. Boehmer, N., Bredereck, R., Knop, D., Luo, J.: Fine-grained view on bribery for group identification. In: Proceedings of the 29th International Joint Conference on Artificial Intelligence, IJCAI '20, pp. 67–73 (2020)
7. Bredereck, R., Elkind, E.: Manipulating opinion diffusion in social networks. In: Proceedings of the 26th International Joint Conference on Artificial Intelligence, IJCAI '17, pp. 894–900 (2017)
8. Butcher, P.: Disinformation and democracy: the home front in the information war. Technical report, European Policy Centre (2019)
9. Butcher, P.: COVID-19 as a turning point in the fight against disinformation. Nat. Electron. **4**(1), 7–9 (2021)
10. Castiglioni, M., Ferraioli, D., Gatti, N.: Election control in social networks via edge addition or removal. In: Proceedings of the 34th AAAI Conference on Artificial Intelligence, AAAI '20, pp. 1878–1885 (2020)
11. Cho, W.J., Ju, B.G.: Multinary group identification. Theor. Econ. **12**(2), 513–531 (2017)
12. Cicalese, F., Cordasco, G., Gargano, L., Milanič, M., Vaccaro, U.: Latency-bounded target set selection in social networks. Theoret. Comput. Sci. **535**, 1–15 (2014)
13. Cinelli, M., et al.: The COVID-19 social media infodemic. Sci. Rep. **10**(1), 16598 (2020)
14. Cygan, M., et al.: Parameterized Algorithms. Springer, Cham (2015)
15. Deligkas, A., Eiben, E., Ganian, R., Hamm, T., Ordyniak, S.: The complexity of envy-free graph cutting. In: Proceedings of the 31st International Joint Conference on Artificial Intelligence, IJCAI '22, pp. 237–243 (2022)
16. Diestel, R.: Graph Theory. Graduate Texts in Mathematics, 5th edn. Springer, Heidelberg (2017)
17. Dun, Y., Tu, K., Chen, C., Hou, C., Yuan, X.: KAN: knowledge-aware attention network for fake news detection. In: Proceedings of the 35th AAAI Conference on Artificial Intelligence, AAAI '21, pp. 81–89 (2021)
18. Dvořák, M., Knop, D., Schierreich, Š.: On the complexity of target set selection in simple geometric networks. Discret. Math. Theoret. Comput. Sci. **26**(2), 11:1–26 (2024)

19. Dvořák, P., Eiben, E., Ganian, R., Knop, D., Ordyniak, S.: The complexity landscape of decompositional parameters for ILP. Artif. Intell. **300**, 103561 (2021)
20. Erdélyi, G., Reger, C., Yang, Y.: The complexity of bribery and control in group identification. Autonom. Agents Multi-Agent Syst. **34**(8) (2020)
21. Faliszewski, P., Slinko, A., Talmon, N.: Multiwinner rules with variable number of winners. In: Proceedings of the 24th European Conference on Artificial Intelligence, ECAI '20, pp. 67–74 (2020)
22. Garimella, K., Gionis, A., Parotsidis, N., Tatti, N.: Balancing information exposure in social networks. In: Proceedings of the 31st Conference on Neural Information Processing Systems, NIPS '17, pp. 4663–4671 (2017)
23. Giansiracusa, N.: How Algorithms Create and Prevent Fake News. Apress, Berkeley, CA (2021). https://doi.org/10.1007/978-1-4842-7155-1
24. Godziszewski, M.T., Batko, P., Skowron, P., Faliszewski, P.: An analysis of approval-based committee rules for 2d-Euclidean elections. In: Proceedings of the 35th AAAI Conference on Artificial Intelligence, AAAI '21, pp. 5448–5455 (2021)
25. Guess, A., Nagler, J., Tucker, J.: Less than you think: prevalence and predictors of fake news dissemination on Facebook. Sci. Adv. **5**(1) (2019)
26. Impagliazzo, R., Paturi, R.: On the Complexity of k-SAT. J. Comput. Syst. Sci. **62**(2), 367–375 (2001)
27. Jin, Y., et al.: Towards fine-grained reasoning for fake news detection. In: Proceedings of the 36th AAAI Conference on Artificial Intelligence, AAAI '22, pp. 5746–5754 (2022)
28. Kasher, A., Rubinstein, A.: On the question "Who is a J?" a social choice approach. Logique et Analyse **40**(160), 385–395 (1997)
29. Kempe, D., Kleinberg, J.M., Tardos, É.: Influential nodes in a diffusion model for social networks. In: Proceedings of the 32nd International Colloquium on Automata, Languages and Programming, ICALP '05, pp. 1127–1138 (2005)
30. Knop, D., Schierreich, Š., Suchý, O.: Balancing the spread of two opinions in sparse social networks (student abstract). In: Proceedings of the 36th AAAI Conference on Artificial Intelligence, AAAI '22, pp. 12987–12988 (2022)
31. Lackner, M., Skowron, P.: Multi-winner Voting with Approval Preferences. Springer, Cham (2022)
32. Laslier, J.F., Sanver, M.R.: Handbook on Approval Voting. Springer, New York (2009)
33. Lazer, D.M.J., et al.: The science of fake news **359**(6380), 1094–1096 (2018)
34. Loos, E., Nijenhuis, J.: Consuming fake news: a matter of age? The perception of political fake news stories in Facebook ads. In: Proceedings of the 6th International Conference on Human Aspects of IT for the Aged Population, ITAP '20, pp. 69–88 (2020)
35. Lu, W., Chen, W., Lakshmanan, L.V.S.: From competition to complementarity: comparative influence diffusion and maximization. Proc. VLDB Endow. **9**(2), 60–71 (2015)
36. Marx, D., Sidiropoulos, A.: The limited blessing of low dimensionality: when 1-1/d is the best possible exponent for d-dimensional geometric problems. In: Proceedings of the 30th Annual Symposium on Computational Geometry, SOCG '14, pp. 67–76 (2014)
37. Newman, M.E.J., Forrest, S., Balthrop, J.: Email networks and the spread of computer viruses. Phys. Rev. E **66**, 035101 (2002)
38. Pietrzak, K.: On the parameterized complexity of the fixed alphabet shortest common supersequence and longest common subsequence problems. J. Comput. Syst. Sci. **67**(4), 757–771 (2003)

39. Przybyla, P.: Capturing the style of fake news. In: Proceedings of the 34th AAAI Conference on Artificial Intelligence, AAAI '20, pp. 490–497 (2020)
40. Qian, F., Gong, C., Sharma, K., Liu, Y.: Neural user response generator: fake news detection with collective user intelligence. In: Proceedings of the 27th International Joint Conference on Artificial Intelligence, IJCAI '18, pp. 3834–3840 (2018)
41. Rhodes, S.C.: Filter bubbles, echo chambers, and fake news. Polit. Commun. **39**(1), 1–22 (2022)
42. Sanders, L.: Trust in media 2022: Where Americans get their news and who they trust for information. Technical report, YouGov.com (2022)
43. Sina, S., Hazon, N., Hassidim, A., Kraus, S.: Adapting the social network to affect elections. In: Proceedings of the 2015 International Conference on Autonomous Agents and Multiagent Systems, AAMAS '15, pp. 705–713 (2015)
44. Sindermann, C., Cooper, A., Montag, C.: A short review on susceptibility to falling for fake political news. Curr. Opin. Psychol. **36**, 44–48 (2020)
45. Soetekouw, L., Angelopoulos, S.: Digital resilience through training protocols: learning to identify fake news on social media. Inf. Syst. Front. (2022)
46. Yang, Y.: Complexity of manipulating and controlling approval-based multiwinner voting. In: Proceedings of the 28th International Joint Conference on Artificial Intelligence, IJCAI '19, pp. 637–643 (2019)
47. Yang, Y., Dimitrov, D.: How hard is it to control a group? Auton. Agent. Multi-Agent Syst. **32**(5), 672–692 (2018). https://doi.org/10.1007/s10458-018-9392-1
48. Yang, Y., Wang, J.: Multiwinner voting with restricted admissible sets: complexity and strategyproofness. In: Proceedings of the 27th International Joint Conference on Artificial Intelligence, IJCAI '18, pp. 576–582 (2018)

Scalable Submodular Policy Optimization via Pruned Submodularity Graph

Aditi Anand, Suman Banerjee(✉), and Dildar Ali

Department of Computer Science and Engineering, Indian Institute of Technology Jammu, Jammu & Kashmir 181221, India
{2022ucs0076,suman.banerjee,2021rcs2009}@iitjammu.ac.in

Abstract. In Reinforcement Learning (abbreviated as RL), an agent interacts with the environment via a set of possible actions, and a reward is generated from some unknown distribution. The task here is to find an optimal set of actions such that the reward after a certain time step is maximized. In a traditional setup, the reward function in an RL Problem is considered additive. However, in reality, there exist many problems, including path planning, coverage control, etc. The reward function follows the diminishing return, which can be modeled as a submodular function. In this paper, we study a variant of the RL Problem where the reward function is submodular, and our objective is to find an optimal policy such that this reward function is maximized. We have proposed a pruned submodularity graph-based approach that provides a provably approximate solution in a feasible computation time. The proposed approach has been analyzed to understand its time and space requirements as well as a performance guarantee. We have experimented with a benchmark agent-environment setup, which has been used for similar previous studies, and the results are reported. From the results, we observe that the policy obtained by our proposed approach leads to more reward than the baseline methods.

Keywords: Submodular Function · Motion Planning · Policy · State · Reward

1 Introduction

In a *reinforcement learning* problem, an agent interacts with the environment and learns a policy such that the reward at the end of a finite number of steps gets maximized [7]. Typically, the environment is modeled as a Markov decision process, which can be expressed as a tuple of six entities: the set of states, the set of actions, the transition function, the reward function, the initial state distribution, and the discount factor [29]. It has been assumed that the reward function is additive and independent of the trajectory. Bellman's optimality principle allows us to identify an optimal policy in polynomial time. In practice, there are many problems whose reward function can not be modeled as an additive function.

M. Baldoni et al. (Eds.): EUMAS 2025, LNAI 16259, pp. 179–194, 2026.
https://doi.org/10.1007/978-3-032-22820-8_11

Hence, our goal is to expand the horizon of RL by extending the reward function to a more general class of functions (other than the additive function). In this paper, we study the RL in a setup with a submodular reward function. In practice, there exist several problems where this setup fits, such as coverage control [24], experiment design [16], entropy maximization [25], informative path planning [10], and many more. To the best of our knowledge, other than the study by Prajapat et al. [23], there does not exist any literature that focuses on the Submodular RL Problem. Given a submodular set function f defined on the ground set $\mathcal{V}$, a well-studied problem is how we maximize f under different constraints, including cardinality constraint [12], knapsack constraint [30], matroid constraint [17], p-system constraint, and many more. It has been reported in the literature that many real-life problems including sensor placement [19], viral marketing [13], image segmentation [4], document summarization [20], speeding up of satisfiability solvers [27], etc., can be modeled as maximization of submodular function subject to different constraints. There has been a significant study on this problem in the past four decades, and it has been studied in different setups, including streaming [5], distributed [21], multi-core architecture [11], and many more. This leads to a vast amount of literature on this problem, as referenced in the survey on this topic [8,14].

While submodularity is typically considered in discrete domains, this concept is also generalized to the continuous domain, such as DR-submodularity by Bian et al. [3]. In this direction, Dolhansky and Blimes [6] introduce the class of deep submodular functions and their neural network models guaranteed to yield to submodular functions as input. This kind of function is useful when the learning is from unknown rewards using function approximation. Among many existing methodologies, one of the methods for solving submodular function maximization is as follows: Starting with an empty set, in each iteration, pick the element that does not belong to the set of selected elements and produces the maximum marginal gain. This process continues until some termination criteria are met. Though this method is easy to understand and easy to implement, it can not be used in practice due to the huge computational time requirement. The primary reason behind this is the large number of marginal gain computations. Several methods have been proposed that try to reduce the number of marginal gain computations [18]. One such method is the pruned submodularity graph-based approach proposed by Zhou et al. [31]. Since then, this approach has been used to solve many problems where the input data size is huge.

Motivation. Traditional reinforcement learning (RL) framework predominantly assumes that the reward function is additive and trajectory-independent, which simplifies the optimization process using tools like Bellman's principle [7,29]. However, this assumption does not hold in many real-world scenarios, such as coverage control [28], informative path planning [26], and experiment design [15], where the law of diminishing returns plays a critical role. These applications naturally exhibit submodular reward structures, which introduce a fundamentally different optimization landscape. Despite the wide applicability of submodular functions, very limited attention has been given to reinforcement learning with submodular rewards. This gap motivates the need to extend RL methods to better capture such non-additive, diminishing-return scenarios. Our work addresses this challenge by introducing a scalable approach that leverages pruned submodularity graphs to efficiently approximate optimal policies in submodular RL setups, enabling practical deployment in high-dimensional environments.

Our Contribution. In this paper, we have made an attempt to use the pruned submodularity graph-based approach to reduce the number of state spaces. In particular, we make the following contributions in this paper:

- We study the Submodular RL Problem, for which the literature is limited.
- We have used the pruned submodularity graph-based approach to reduce the state space in a given Submodular RL Problem.
- The proposed approach has been analyzed to understand its time and space requirements as well as performance guarantee.
- We have done a number of experiments with environments that have been used by previous studies, and we observe that our proposed approach leads to more rewards compared to existing methods.

The Rest of the paper has been organized as follows. Section 2 describes some background concepts and defines our problem formally. Section 3 contains our proposed solution approach with detailed analysis. The experimental evaluation of the proposed approach has been described in Sect. 4. Finally, Sect. 5 concludes our study and gives future research directions.

2 Background and Problem Definition

In this section, we describe the background information related to our problem and define it formally. Initially, we start by describing the submodular function.

Set Function and Submodularity. Consider an n element set $\mathcal{V} = \{v_1, v_2, \ldots, v_n\}$, and a set function f defined on the ground set $\mathcal{V}$. f is said to be non-negative if for any $\mathcal{S} \subseteq \mathcal{V}$, $f(\mathcal{S}) \geq 0$. For any given subset $\mathcal{S} \subseteq \mathcal{V}$ and an element $v \in \mathcal{V} \setminus \mathcal{S}$, the *marginal gain* of v with respect to $\mathcal{S}$ is denoted by $\Delta(v|\mathcal{S})$ and defined as $\Delta(v|\mathcal{S}) = f(\mathcal{S} \cup \{v\}) - f(\mathcal{S})$. f is said to be monotone if for all $\mathcal{S} \subseteq \mathcal{V}$ and for all $v \in \mathcal{V} \setminus \mathcal{S}$, $\Delta(v|\mathcal{S}) \geq 0$. f is said to be submodular if for all $\mathcal{A} \subseteq \mathcal{B} \subseteq \mathcal{V}$ and for all $v \in \mathcal{V} \setminus \mathcal{B}$, $\Delta(v|\mathcal{A}) \geq \Delta(v|\mathcal{B})$. The submodularity property of a set function says that the marginal gain of an element decreases as the set size in which the element is added increases, and this property is called the *law of diminishing returns.* One well-studied problem in this context is that given a submodular function and a positive integer k, which k nodes should be chosen such that the function becomes maximized? This problem has been referred to as the Submodular Function Maximization Problem. It has been shown in the literature that this problem is NP-hard. However, an incremental greedy approach that works based on marginal gain computation generates a solution which is $(1 - \frac{1}{e})$-factor approximate solution to the optimal solution [22].

Markov Decision Process. In general, a Reinforcement Learning Problem is posed as a discrete-time stochastic process where an agent interacts with the environment. In each time step, an agent will choose one of the available actions, and depending upon which action it chooses, it goes to a state and draws a reward from an unknown distribution. The task here is to derive the action sequence that the agent should choose so that the cumulative reward after a certain time step will be maximized. A Reinforcement Learning Setup is often modeled as a Markov Decision Process, which can be described using 5 Tuples $(\mathcal{S}, \mathcal{A}, \mathcal{R}, T, \gamma)$. Here, $\mathcal{S}$ and $\mathcal{A}$ denote the set of states and the set of actions, respectively. T is state transition function, i.e., $T : \mathcal{S} \times \mathcal{A} \times \mathcal{S} \longrightarrow [0, 1]$. $\mathcal{R}$ is the reward function, i.e., $\mathcal{R} : \mathcal{S} \times \mathcal{A} \times \mathcal{S} \longrightarrow \mathbb{R}$. γ is called as the discount factor. Traditionally, it has been assumed that this process follows the Markovian Property. This means that the next state is decided by the current state and the action that the agent chooses, not the past history of the states in which the agent was in. However, in practice, there are several problems, which include path planning, coverage control, etc., following the reward function, which follows the diminishing return property. Such scenarios can be modeled as a Submodular Reinforcement Learning Problem, which has been stated subsequently.

Submodular Reinforcement Learning Set Up. A submodular reinforcement learning problem can be described using 6 tuples, $\Gamma = (\mathcal{S}, \mathcal{A}, T, H, \rho, \mathcal{R})$. Here, H signifies the finite long-time horizon. Instead of states, here we consider time-augmented states. Hence, the state set $\mathcal{S} = \mathcal{V} \times H$, and an arbitrary state is denoted by $s = (v, h)$. $\mathcal{R} : 2^{\mathcal{S}} \longrightarrow \mathbb{R}$ is submodular reward function where $\mathbb{R}$ denotes the set of real numbers. The transition probability from the state v to $v^{'}$ if the agent chooses an action $a \in \mathcal{A}$ at time step $h \in H$ is denoted as $T((v^{'}, h+1)|(v, h), a)$. This process starts at some state s_0, and at each time step $h \geq 0$ and at a state (v, h), the agent draws an action a_h according to some predefined policy and reaches the state s_{h+1}. The realization of the whole process can be thought of as a trajectory $\tau = \{(s_h, a_h)_{h=0}^{H-1}, s_H\}$ where H is the length of the episode. Any partial trajectory (from time step ℓ to $\ell^{'}$) can be captured as $\tau_{\ell:\ell'} = \{(s_h, a_h)_{h=\ell}^{\ell^{'}-1}, s_{\ell'}\}$. By this notation, τ can be written as $\tau_{0:H}$. The reward function $\mathcal{R}$ can be calculated after the end of any (partial) trajectory. For the trajectory $\tau_{\ell:\ell'}$, the value of the reward function is denoted by $\mathcal{R}(\tau_{\ell:\ell'})$. In the Markov decision process, an agent acts as per *policy.* A policy is considered Markovian if its actions only depend on the current state. This signifies for any $h \in H$, $\pi(a_h|\tau_{0:h-1}) = \pi(a_h|s_h)$. In this study, we relax this condition and assume that the action depends on the previous k states for some given positive integer k. For any $h \in H$, this can be given as $\pi(a_h|\tau_{0:h-1}) = \pi(a_h|\tau_{h:h-k})$. The set of all Markovian policies and all k-step non-Markovian policies for an MDP is denoted by Π and Π_{NM}^{k}, respectively. Subsequently, we proceed to describe our problem statement.

Problem Definition. In this paper, given a Submodular MDP, we study the problem of finding an optimal policy to maximize the expected reward. For any given policy π, let $f(\tau, \pi)$ denote the probability distribution over any random trajectory τ, which can be given by Eq. 1.

$$f(\tau, \pi) = \rho(s_0) \cdot \prod_{h=0}^{H-1} \pi(a_h|\tau_{0:H}) \cdot T(s_{h+1}, s_h|a_h) \tag{1}$$

Now, we define the objective function as the expectation of the trajectory distribution induced by the policy. Our goal here is to find the policy (among a set of given policies) so that the objective function gets maximized.

3 Proposed Solution Approaches

In this section, we will discuss the proposed solution approach. First, we start with some preliminary concepts used in Algorithm 1. Given a submodular MDP $\mathcal{M}(S, A, T, \rho, H, \mathcal{R})$, we parameterize the policy π using neural networks and represent it as π_θ, where θ denotes the policy parameters. Next, we define the Expected Return in Definition 1.

Definition 1 (Expected Return). *The performance measure of a policy π_θ is its expected return over the trajectory distribution induced by the policy. The expected return is denoted by $J(\pi_\theta)$ and is given by the following equation:*

$$J(\pi_\theta) = \mathbb{E}_{\tau \sim f(\tau;\pi_\theta)} \left[\mathcal{R}(\tau)\right]. \tag{2}$$

Our goal is to find a policy that maximizes the performance measure in the set of all Markovian policies (Π).

$$\pi^* = \arg\max_{\pi \in \Pi} J(\pi) \tag{3}$$

Approach: The policy parameters (θ) are updated using the following regularized gradient ascent equation:

$$\theta \leftarrow \theta + \arg \max_{\delta\theta:\delta\theta+\theta\in\Theta} \delta\theta^\top \nabla_\theta J(\pi_\theta) - \frac{1}{2\alpha}||\delta\theta||^2. \tag{4}$$

where α is a regularization coefficient.

Definition 2 (Submodularity Graph). *The submodularity graph is a weighted directed graph $G(V, E, w)$ defined by a submodular function $F : 2^V \to \mathbb{R}$, where V is the set of states corresponding to the ground set. Each directed edge $e = (u, v) \in E$ from u to v has weight:*

$$w_{uv} = F(v \mid u) - F(u \mid V \setminus \{u\}) \tag{5}$$

Definition 3 (Divergence of a state). *Given submodular function F, divergence of a state v from a set of states U is defined as:*

$$w_{Uv} = \min_{u\in U} \left[F(v|u) - F(u|V \setminus \{u\})\right] \tag{6}$$

On the submodularity graph $G(V, E, w)$, it is given by:

$$w_{Uv} = \underset{u \in U}{min}\ w_{uv} \tag{7}$$

$F(v \mid u)$ denotes the maximum possible gain on adding v to a set containing u and $F(u|V \setminus \{u\})$ is the minimum gain on adding u to set $V \setminus \{u\}$. The small value of the first term implies that v is unimportant if u is retained, while a larger value of the second term denotes the importance of u. Thus, a smaller divergence for an element v suggests that it can be removed while we retain the set U. This helps remove redundant states.

Algorithm 1: Submodularity Graph-based Policy Optimization (SGPO)

Data: SMDP $\mathcal{M}(S, A, T, \rho, H, \mathcal{R})$, π, N, r, c
Result: Trained Policy π
for *epoch* $k = 1$ *to* N **do**
  Initialize $V \leftarrow \emptyset$, $Z \leftarrow \emptyset$, $R \leftarrow \emptyset$;
  for $h = 0$ *to* $H - 1$ **do**
    Sample $a_h \sim \pi(a_h|s_h)$, execute a_h;
    $V \leftarrow V \cup \{s_h\}$;
    $Z \leftarrow Z \cup \{a_h\}$;
    $R \leftarrow R \cup \mathcal{R}(\tau_{0:h+1})$;
  end
  Initialize $V^{'} \leftarrow \emptyset$, $U \longleftarrow \emptyset$, $|V| = n$;
  Construct the submodularity graph with the states in V;
  while $|V| > r \cdot \log n$ **do**
    Sample out $r \cdot$ $\log n$ states uniformly at random from V and place them in U;
    $V \longleftarrow V \setminus U$, $V^{'} \longleftarrow V^{'} \cup U$;
    for *All* $v \in V$ **do**
      $w_{Uv} \longleftarrow \underset{u \in U}{min}\ [\mathcal{R}(v|u) - \mathcal{R}(u|V \setminus \{u\})]$;
    end
    Remove $(1 - \frac{1}{\sqrt{c}}) \cdot |V|$ states from V having smallest value of w_{Uv};
  end
  $V^{'} \longleftarrow V \cup V^{'}$;
  $\mathcal{K} \leftarrow \{(s_h, a_h, \mathcal{R}(\tau_{0:h+1}))|s_h \in V^{'}, a_h \in Z, \mathcal{R}(\tau_{0:h+1}) \in R\}$;
  Estimate $\nabla_\theta J(\pi_\theta)$ using Theorem 3;
  Update policy parameters(θ) using Equation 4;
end

Description of the Algorithm. The proposed solution approach is presented in Algorithm 1. This approach takes SMDP $\mathcal{M}(S, A, T, \rho, H, \mathcal{R})$, policy π, number of epochs N, and sparsification parameters r and c as input to our algorithm and returns the optimized trained policy as output. The agent is represented as a stochastic policy parameterized by a neural network. In each training iteration, the agent samples an action from the policy and executes it over each time step (line 4). The sets V, Z, and R are used to maintain the trajectory states, actions, and cumulative reward, respectively. Upon completion of the episode in lines 3 to 7, we construct a submodular graph with the states in V. Subsequently, we apply submodular sparsification to the set of states V and iteratively sample out $r \cdot \log n$ states uniformly at random from V and put them to V' (in `while loop` at line 12). In lines 14 to 16, the weight of each state is calculated, and the states having smaller weight are pruned, that is, $(1 - \frac{1}{\sqrt{c}}) \cdot |V|$ many states from the set V. In lines 11 to 18, after completion of `while loop`, Algorithm 1 obtains a pruned set of states V'. Next, in line 20, the updated trajectory is obtained in K. Finally, in lines 21 and 22, $\Delta_\theta J(\pi_\theta)$ is estimated using Theorem 3 and policy parameters (θ) are updated using Eq. 4. The values of r and c were set at 8 for the experiments.

Hyperparameter Choice and Sensitivity. Algorithm 1 relies on two key hyperparameters: r, which controls the number of states sampled per iteration ($r \cdot \log n$), and c, which determines the fraction of states pruned per iteration $(\left(1 - \frac{1}{\sqrt{c}}\right) \cdot |V|)$. In our experiments, we set $r = 8$ and $c = 8$. These values were chosen on the basis of empirical performance in preliminary experiments, balancing the trade-off between state-space reduction and preservation of high-reward trajectories. Specifically, $r = 8$ ensures a moderate sampling rate, allowing sufficient exploration of the state space while keeping the number of iterations logarithmic ($\mathcal{O}(\log n)$). Similarly, $c = 8$ results in pruning approximately 65% of the remaining states per iteration ($1 - \frac{1}{\sqrt{8}} \approx 0.646$), which aggressively reduces the state space while retaining states with high divergence weights, as informed by prior work on submodular maximization [1,2,31].

Complexity Analysis. Now, we analyze the time and space requirements for Algorithm 1. In Line No. 1, `For Loop` will iterate for $\mathcal{O}(N)$ time and initializing V, Z and R will take $\mathcal{O}(1)$ time. In Line No. 3 to 8 the `For Loop` will execute for $\mathcal{O}(H)$ time and Line No. 9 will take $\mathcal{O}(1)$ time. Next, to construct the submodularity graph in Line No. 10, it will take $\mathcal{O}(n^2 \cdot n)$, that is, $\mathcal{O}(n^3)$, where the construction of the state pair will take $\mathcal{O}(n^2)$, and calculating the weight for each edge using the reward function $\mathcal{R}$ will take $\mathcal{O}(n)$. The `While Loop` at Line No. 11 will run for $\mathcal{O}(\log n)$ time, and in Line No. 12, the random selection of $r \cdot \log n$ many elements will take $\mathcal{O}(\log n)$ time. In Line No. 14 to 16 `For Loop` will take $\mathcal{O}(n^2 \cdot \log n)$ time and Line No. 17 will take $\mathcal{O}(n \cdot \log n)$. So, from Line No. 11 to 18 will take $\mathcal{O}(\log n \cdot \log n + \log n \cdot n^2 \log n + \log n \cdot n \log n)$ i.e., $\mathcal{O}(n^2 \log^2 n)$. In Line No. 20 computing $\mathcal{K}$ will take $\mathcal{O}(\log^2 n)$ time and in Line No. 21 will take $\mathcal{O}(H(sm) \cdot H(sm) \cdot H(n)])$ i.e., $\mathcal{O}(n^4 s^2 m^2)$, where H is the horizon, s is the state dimension and m is the action dimension. Finally, updating the policy will take $\mathcal{O}(1)$ time. Hence, Line No. 1 to 23 will take $\mathcal{O}(N[H + n^3 + n^2 \log^2 n + n^4 s^2 m^2])$ i.e., $\mathcal{O}(N \cdot n^4 s^2 m^2)$ time to execute.

The additional space requirement by Algorithm 1 to store V, Z, R, and U will take $\mathcal{O}(n)$, $\mathcal{O}(n)$, $\mathcal{O}(n)$, and $\mathcal{O}(\log n)$, respectively. To store the edges of the graph, it will take $\mathcal{O}(n^2)$ time. So, the total space requirement for Algorithm 1 will be $\mathcal{O}(n^2)$.

Theorem 1. *The time and space requirements by Algorithm 1 will be of $\mathcal{O}(N \cdot n^4 s^2 m^2)$ and $\mathcal{O}(n^2)$, respectively.*

Theorem 2. *Let $OPT = \max_{\pi \in \Pi} J(\pi)$ be the optimal expected submodular return in a Submodular Reinforcement Learning (SubRL) problem. Then, for any constant $\gamma > 0$, there exists no polynomial-time algorithm that guarantees a policy π satisfying:*

$$J(\pi) \geq \frac{OPT}{\log^{1-\gamma} OPT} \tag{8}$$

for all instances of SubRL, unless $NP \subseteq ZTIME(n^{polylog(n)})$. Thus, under standard complexity-theoretic assumptions, the SubRL problem cannot be approximated within a constant factor and is limited to, at best, a logarithmic approximation.

Proof. We establish the inapproximability of Submodular Reinforcement Problem (SubRL) by reducing from Group Steiner Tree (GST) problem [9], which is known to be hard to approximate within $O(\log^2 n)$ unless NP $\subseteq$ ZTIME($n^{\text{polylog}(n)}$).

In the GST problem given a weighted graph $G = (V, E)$ with edge costs $w(e)$, a root node $r \in V$, a collection of groups $G_1, G_2, ..., G_k \subseteq V$, the objective is to find a minimum-cost subtree that contains at least one node from each group G_i. Now, the GST problem can be reduced to the Submodular Orienteering Problem (SOP) [23], where given a root node $r \in V(T)$. The goal is to find a walk of length at most B that maximizes the submodular function $\mathcal{R}$ defined on the nodes of the underlying graph. Now, we construct an instance of SOP from GST, where the graph G remains unchanged, the root node r is the start state, and a budget B is assigned based on the optimal cost of the Steiner tree. We define a submodular reward function $\mathcal{R} : 2^V \to \mathbb{R}$ such that $\mathcal{R}(S) = \sum_{i=1}^{k} \min(1, |S \cap G_i|)$, where S is the subset of nodes. The goal in SOP is to find a path of cost at most B that maximizes $\mathcal{R}(S)$. Since SOP is at least as hard as GST, it inherits its inapproximability bounds. We now show that SOP can be reduced to a SubRL problem by constructing an instance of SubRL from SOP. We define a Submodular Markov Decision Process with states as nodes in G, actions as available edges, transitions following the edges of G, and the reward function is the same submodular function $\mathcal{R}$ as in SOP and horizon $H = B$. Finding an optimal policy in SubRL corresponds to solving the SOP. Since SOP is hard to approximate within $\mathcal{O}(\log^{1-\gamma} \text{OPT})$, the same bound applies to SubRL; if SubRL were approximable within a constant factor, then GST would be as well, contradicting known hardness results. Thus, SubRL cannot be approximated better than $O(\log^{1-\gamma} \text{OPT})$ unless NP $\subseteq$ ZTIME($n^{\text{polylog}(n)}$). □

Theorem 3. *Given a Submodular Markov Decision Process $\mathcal{M}$ with reward function $\mathcal{R}$ and policy parameters θ, gradient of the performance measure can be estimated as*

$$\nabla_\theta J(\pi_\theta) = \mathbb{E}_{\tau \sim f(\tau;\pi_\theta)} \left[\sum_{i=0}^{H-1} \nabla_\theta \log \pi_\theta(a_i|s_i) (\sum_{j=i}^{H-1} \mathcal{R}(s_{j+1}|\tau_{0:j}) + \mathcal{R}(s_0)) \right] \quad (9)$$

Proof. The performance measure from Eq. 2 we get,

$$J(\pi_\theta) = \mathbb{E}_{\tau \sim f(\tau;\pi_\theta)} [\mathcal{R}(\tau)] \quad (10)$$

$$J(\pi_\theta) = \sum_\tau f(\tau;\pi_\theta)\mathcal{R}(\tau) \quad (11)$$

Taking the gradient with respect to θ, we get

$$\nabla_\theta J(\pi_\theta) = \sum_\tau \nabla_\theta f(\tau;\pi_\theta)\mathcal{R}(\tau) \quad (12)$$

Applying the log-derivative trick, we get

$$\nabla_\theta \log f(\tau;\pi_\theta) = \nabla_\theta f(\tau;\pi_\theta)/f(\tau;\pi_\theta) \quad (13)$$

$$\nabla_\theta f(\tau;\pi_\theta) = f(\tau;\pi_\theta)\nabla_\theta \log f(\tau;\pi_\theta) \quad (14)$$

So,

$$\nabla_\theta J(\pi_\theta) = \sum_\tau f(\tau;\pi_\theta)\nabla_\theta \log f(\tau;\pi_\theta)\mathcal{R}(\tau) \quad (15)$$

Now, taking expectation over trajectories, we get

$$\nabla_\theta J(\pi_\theta) = \mathbb{E}_{\tau \sim f(\tau;\pi_\theta)} [\nabla_\theta \log f(\tau;\pi_\theta)\mathcal{R}(\tau)] \quad (16)$$

From Eq. 1 using the trajectory probability $f(\tau;\pi_\theta)$ we have

$$f(\tau;\pi_\theta) = \rho(s_0) \prod_{i=0}^{H-1} \pi_\theta(a_i|s_i)P(s_{i+1}|s_i,a_i) \quad (17)$$

Taking the logarithm, we get

$$\log f(\tau;\pi_\theta) = \log \rho(s_0) + \sum_{i=0}^{H-1} \log \pi_\theta(a_i|s_i) + \sum_{i=0}^{H-1} \log P(s_{i+1}|s_i,a_i) \quad (18)$$

Since the transition probabilities $P(s_{i+1}|s_i,a_i)$ are independent of θ, their gradient vanishes. So we can write

$$\nabla_\theta \log f(\tau;\pi_\theta) = \sum_{i=0}^{H-1} \nabla_\theta \log \pi_\theta(a_i|s_i) \quad (19)$$

Thus, substituting back in Eq. 16 we get

$$\nabla_\theta J(\pi_\theta) = \mathbb{E}_{\tau \sim f(\tau;\pi_\theta)} \left[\sum_{i=0}^{H-1} \nabla_\theta \log \pi_\theta(a_i|s_i) \mathcal{R}(\tau) \right] \tag{20}$$

Using the submodular property of F, we expand it in terms of marginal gains:

$$\mathcal{R}(\tau) = \sum_{j=0}^{H-1} \mathcal{R}(s_{j+1}|\tau_{0:j}) + \mathcal{R}(s_0) \tag{21}$$

Thus, we can write

$$\nabla_\theta J(\pi_\theta) = \mathbb{E}_{\tau \sim f(\tau;\pi_\theta)} \left[\sum_{i=0}^{H-1} \nabla_\theta \log \pi_\theta(a_i|s_i) (\sum_{j=i}^{H-1} \mathcal{R}(s_{j+1}|\tau_{0:j}) + \mathcal{R}(s_0)) \right] \tag{22}$$

□

4 Experimental Evaluation

In this section, we describe the experimental evaluation of the proposed solution approach. Initially, we start by describing the environments that we have considered in our experiments.

4.1 Environments

We have tested our algorithm's performance in various environments involving different state-action spaces and reward functions. The state-action spaces are divided into two categories: continuous and discrete. We have considered two continuous state-action spaces, namely, *Car Racing* and *MuJoCo Ant*, and two discrete state-action spaces, *Graph Based Environment* and *Entropy Based Environment*, and have been described subsequently.

Car Racing Environment. This is a high-dimensional environment where a race car tries to finish the racing lap as fast as possible. The environment is accompanied by an important challenge of learning a policy to maneuver the car at the limit of handling. The track is challenging, consisting of 13 turns with different curvatures. The car has a six-dimensional state space representing position and velocity. The control commands are two-dimensional, representing throttle and steering. The state representation of an individual car is denoted as $z = [\rho, d, \mu, V_x, V_y, V_z]$ where ρ measures the progress along the reference path, d quantifies the deviation from the reference path, and μ characterizes the local heading relative to the reference path. V_x and V_y represent the longitudinal and lateral velocities in the car's frame, respectively. Ψ represents the car's yaw rate. The car's inputs are represented as $[D, \delta]^T$ where D belongs to the interval

$[-1, +1]$, representing the duty cycle input to the electric motor, ranging from full braking at -1 to full acceleration at 1. $\delta \in [-1, +1]$ corresponds to the steering angle. The car has a camera and observes a patch around its state s as D_s. The objective function for this environment is $T(\tau) = |\bigcup_{s \in \tau} D_s|$, and for our problem context, we fix the length of the time horizon as 700.

MuJoCo Ant Environment. In this environment, the state space dimension is 30 and contains information about the robot's pose and the internal actuator's orientation. The control input dimension is 8, consisting of torque commands for each actuator. The Ant at any location s covers locations in $2D$ space, D_s, and receives a reward based on it. The goal is to maximize $T(\tau) = |\bigcup_{s \in \tau} D_s|$. For detailed information about the Mujoco Ant environment, we refer the reader to https://gymnasium.farama.org/environments/mujoco/ant/.

Graph Based Environment. In this environment, consisting of a set of nodes, each associated with a weight, the agent interacts with this space through sequential decision-making. There are two environmental operational modes: M Mode and SRL Mode. In M mode, the agent is required to maximize the total sum of weights for all uniquely covered nodes. Also, the agent is required to cover as many nodes as possible while maximizing the total weight. In SRL Mode, the agent aims to maximize the total sum of weights associated with all covered nodes, allowing for repeated coverage of previously visited nodes to contribute to the total reward.

Entropy Based Environment. The entropy-based environment is designed to regulate the agent's exploration and exploitation behavior by utilizing entropy as an objective. It operates in two distinct modes: M Mode and SRL Mode. In M Mode, the agent aims to minimize entropy, encouraging more deterministic behavior by reducing the uncertainty in its trajectory. This results in a more structured and predictable exploration pattern. Conversely, in SRL Mode, the objective is to maximize entropy, which promotes exploration by maintaining uncertainty in the agent's trajectory. This ensures the agent does not prematurely converge to a specific policy, thereby enhancing its ability to discover new or underexplored regions within the environment. The entropy-based approach provides a principled mechanism for balancing exploration and exploitation in reinforcement learning settings.

Experimental Setup. All the Python codes are executed in HP Z2 workstations with 32 GB RAM and an Xeon(R) 3.0 GHz processor. We have compared our proposed SGPO approach with the existing SubPO [23] approach.

4.2 Goals of the Study

In this study, we will address the following Research Questions (RQ).

Table 1. Reward functions for different environments

Environment	Cont/Discrete	State Dim	Action Dim	Function
Car Racing	Continuous	6	2	$T(\tau) = \lvert\bigcup_{s\in\mathcal{T}} D_s\rvert$
MuJoCo Ant	Continuous	30	8	$T(\tau) = \lvert\bigcup_{s\in\mathcal{T}} D_s\rvert - \lambda \sum_{s\in\mathcal{T}} \mathbf{1}(N_s > 1)$
GP (M)	Discrete	2	5	$T(\tau) = \sum_{s\in\mathcal{T}} w_s - \lambda \sum_{s\in\mathcal{T}} N_s$
GP (SRL)	Discrete	2	5	$T(\tau) = \sum_{s\in\mathcal{T}} w_s$
Entropy (M)	Discrete	2	5	$T_M(\tau) = \frac{1}{2}\log\det(\Sigma_\tau + 10^{-6}I) + 9.965784 \cdot \lvert\tau\rvert$
Entropy (SRL)	Discrete	2	5	$T_{SRL}(\tau) = \sum_{s\in\mathcal{T}} \frac{1}{2}\log_2(\Sigma_{ss} + 10^{-6}) + 9.965784$

- **RQ1:** How do critic loss and policy loss vary with the number of epochs?
- **RQ2:** Varying number of epochs, how do the SGPO and SubPO perform with respect to the number of steps, coverage, and weight value?
- **RQ3:** How does the advantage vary while varying the number of epochs?

4.3 Results and Discussion

In this section, we analyze the experimental results and address all the research questions that arise in Sect. 4.2. We subsequently present the results in tabular form for the discrete environments. All the objective functions are summarized in Table 1. We experimented one hundred times independently for each environment and reported the objective function's mean value in Table 2.

Car Racing Environment. In Fig. 1(a), we illustrate the variation in the number of horizon steps required to complete one lap of the racing track during the test time with the number of epochs used for training. The test was carried out with 100 agents, and the mean number of steps required to complete the race was recorded. We observe that the minimum number of steps required to complete one lap first rises and then falls as the number of training epochs increases, indicating improved training. The model trained using SGPO requires fewer steps compared to the model trained with SubPO. We show the variation in policy loss with the number of epochs during training, as shown in Fig. 1(e). We observe that while training with the SubPO algorithm, the policy loss oscillates within a wider range of high values. In contrast, in the case of SGPO, the loss remains in a relatively lower range, indicating greater stability during training. Next, Fig. 1(c) shows the variation in critic loss with the number of training epochs. The loss curve for SubPO exhibits large fluctuations, whereas the loss curve for SGPO is comparatively smoother, indicating better learning and convergence.

Mujoco Ant Environment. Figure 1(b) shows the variation in total coverage by an agent with the number of training epochs. The test was carried out with 100 agents, and their mean coverage was recorded. For the model trained on 1000 epochs, we observe that SubPO achieves coverage of 2612 units, whereas SGPO achieves a slightly higher coverage of 2636 units. Next, in Fig. 1(d), we

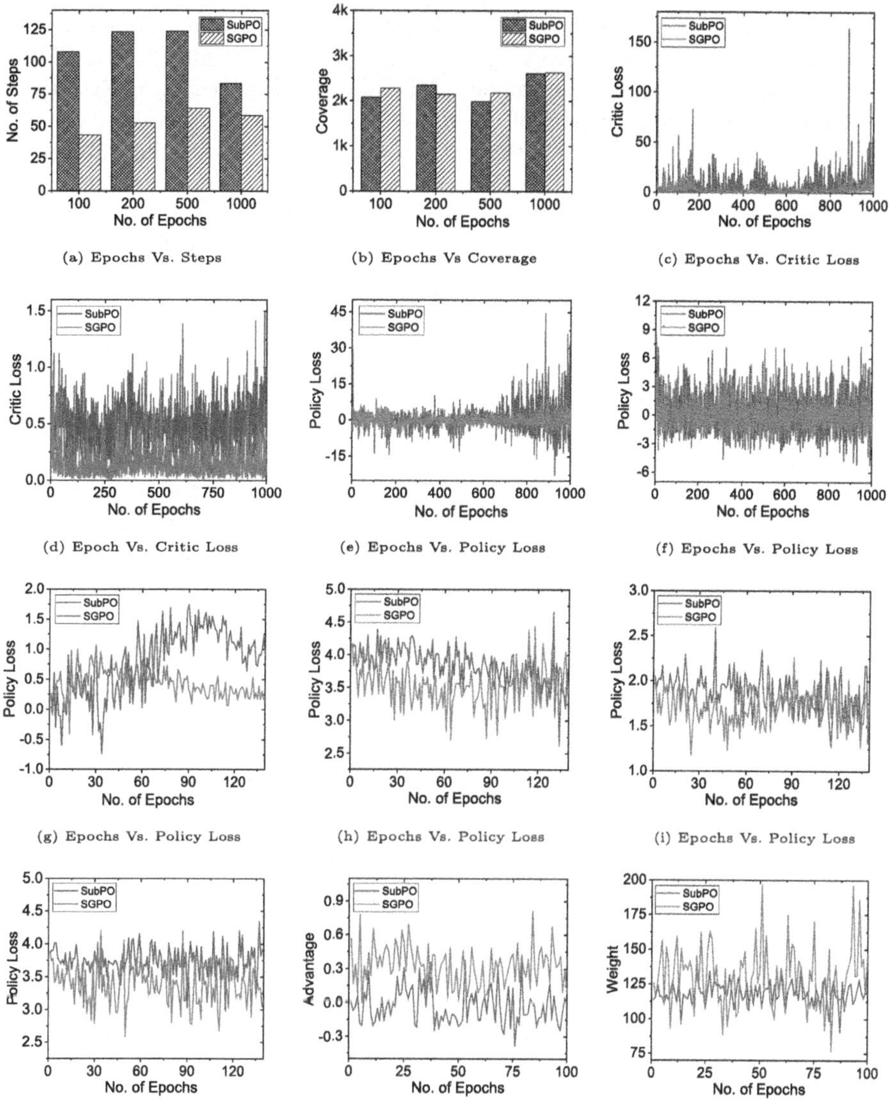

(a) Epochs Vs. Steps (b) Epochs Vs Coverage (c) Epochs Vs. Critic Loss

(d) Epoch Vs. Critic Loss (e) Epochs Vs. Policy Loss (f) Epochs Vs. Policy Loss

(g) Epochs Vs. Policy Loss (h) Epochs Vs. Policy Loss (i) Epochs Vs. Policy Loss

(j) Epochs Vs. Policy Loss (k) Epochs Vs. Advantage (ℓ) Epochs Vs. Weights

Fig. 1. Varying Epochs with Steps, Coverage, Critic Loss, Policy Loss, Advantage, Weight in Car racing (a, c, e), Mujoco Ant (b, d, f, k), Graph Based-M (g, ℓ), Graph Based-SRL (h), Entropy Based-M (i), Entropy Based-SRL (j).

illustrate the number of epochs versus the critic loss. The critic loss curve for SubPO exhibits larger oscillations, whereas SGPO demonstrates better convergence. Although both loss curves exhibit fluctuations, the variance in the SubPO loss curve is significantly higher than that of SGPO, indicating less stability during training. The number of epochs versus advantage in this environment is presented in Fig. 1(k), which compares the advantage values of SubPO and SGPO over 100 epochs in a test environment. Advantage, a key metric in RL, represents the relative improvement of an action over the expected value baseline. The figure shows that SGPO exhibits higher and more fluctuating advantage values compared to SubPO, indicating potentially more exploratory behavior.

Graph Based Environment. In the graph-based environment, we vary the number of epochs for two different modes: M and SRL. To analyze the learning and performance of the agent network, we observe that in mode M, the loss curves for both SubPO and SGPO exhibit oscillations, but the one for SGPO shows better convergence, as shown in Fig. 1(g). In the case of SRL mode, both loss curves have spikes and dips, but the loss for SGPO remains at relatively lower values, as shown in Fig. 1(h). Next, we have presented the weight value in M-mode with the varying number of epochs in Fig. 1(ℓ). Here, the agent's goal is to maximize the weight. We observe that the weight curve for SubPO remains relatively stable with minor fluctuations, whereas SGPO exhibits larger oscillations with higher peaks. This suggests that SGPO explores a broader range of weight values, potentially leading to higher maximum weight values.

Entropy Based Environment. In the entropy-based environment, we observe the variation of policy loss with the number of training epochs. In the case of M mode, the agent focuses on minimizing entropy, meaning it aims to reduce the uncertainty in its trajectory and converge to more deterministic behaviors. The policy loss curve for SubPO shows higher fluctuations, whereas SGPO exhibits a more stable trend, indicating better convergence, as shown in Fig. 1(i). In SRL mode, the agent aims to maximize entropy, promote exploration, and avoid early convergence with deterministic behaviors. The policy loss curve for SGPO remains at lower values compared to SubPO, suggesting improved stability and adaptability in exploration, as shown in Fig. 1(j).

Table 2. Comparison of Objective Function Values across Discrete Environments

Environment	Objective Function	
	SubPO	SGPO
Graph-based(M)	119.3361648	129.792734
Graph-based(SRL)	54.54513195	77.3658894
Entropy-based(M)	171.211965	237.8183107
Entropy-based(SRL)	379.1436629	386.2395683

5 Concluding Remarks

In this paper, we have considered a variant of the reinforcement learning problem where the reward function is submodular. We have proposed a pruned submodularity graph-based approach to solve this problem. The proposed SGPO has been analyzed to understand its time and space requirements and performance guarantee. We show that the proposed SGPO will achieve a constant factor approximation guarantee under the simplified assumptions. We have performed many experiments with continuous and discrete action spaces and observed that SGPO leads to more reward compared to the existing method. Now, this study can be extended to the broad class of submodular objectives, which are relevant to many practical, real-world problems.

References

1. Ali, D., Banerjee, S., Prasad, Y.: Influential billboard slot selection using pruned submodularity graph. In: Chen, W., Yao, L., Cai, T., Pan, S., Shen, T., Li, X. (eds.) ADMA 2022. LNCS, vol. 13725, pp. 216–230. Springer, Cham (2022). https://doi.org/10.1007/978-3-031-22064-7_17
2. Ali, D., Banerjee, S., Prasad, Y.: Influential billboard slot selection using spatial clustering and pruned submodularity graph. arXiv preprint arXiv:2305.08949 (2023)
3. Bian, A., Levy, K., Krause, A., Buhmann, J.M.: Continuous DR-submodular maximization: structure and algorithms. In: Advances in Neural Information Processing Systems, vol. 30 (2017)
4. Boykov, Y.Y., Jolly, M.P.: Interactive graph cuts for optimal boundary & region segmentation of objects in nd images. In: Proceedings Eighth IEEE International Conference on Computer Vision. ICCV 2001, vol. 1, pp. 105–112. IEEE (2001)
5. Chakrabarti, A., Kale, S.: Submodular maximization meets streaming: matchings, matroids, and more. Math. Program. **154**, 225–247 (2015)
6. Dolhansky, B.W., Bilmes, J.A.: Deep submodular functions: definitions and learning. In: Advances in Neural Information Processing Systems, vol. 29 (2016)
7. Dong, H., Dong, H., Ding, Z., Zhang, S., Chang, T.: Deep Reinforcement Learning. Springer, Singapore (2020). https://doi.org/10.1007/978-981-19-0638-1
8. Dughmi, S.: Submodular functions: extensions, distributions, and algorithms. A survey. arXiv preprint arXiv:0912.0322 (2009)
9. Garg, N., Konjevod, G., Ravi, R.: A polylogarithmic approximation algorithm for the group Steiner tree problem. J. Algorithms **37**(1), 66–84 (2000)
10. Gunawan, A., Lau, H.C., Vansteenwegen, P.: Orienteering problem: a survey of recent variants, solution approaches and applications. Eur. J. Oper. Res. **255**(2), 315–332 (2016)
11. Honysz, P.J., Buschjäger, S., Morik, K.: GPU-accelerated optimizer-aware evaluation of submodular exemplar clustering. arXiv preprint arXiv:2101.08763 (2021)
12. Horel, T., Singer, Y.: Maximization of approximately submodular functions. In: Advances in Neural Information Processing Systems, vol. 29 (2016)
13. Kempe, D., Kleinberg, J., Tardos, É.: Maximizing the spread of influence through a social network. In: Proceedings of the ninth ACM SIGKDD International Conference on Knowledge Discovery and Data Mining, pp. 137–146 (2003)
14. Krause, A., Golovin, D.: Submodular function maximization. Tractability **3**(71–104), 3 (2014)
15. Krause, A., Guestrin, C.E.: Near-optimal nonmyopic value of information in graphical models. arXiv preprint arXiv:1207.1394 (2012)

16. Krause, A., Singh, A., Guestrin, C.: Near-optimal sensor placements in gaussian processes: theory, efficient algorithms and empirical studies. J. Mach. Learn. Res. **9**(2) (2008)
17. Lee, J., Mirrokni, V.S., Nagarajan, V., Sviridenko, M.: Maximizing nonmonotone submodular functions under matroid or knapsack constraints. SIAM J. Discret. Math. **23**(4), 2053–2078 (2010)
18. Leskovec, J., Krause, A., Guestrin, C., Faloutsos, C., VanBriesen, J.M., Glance, N.S.: Cost-effective outbreak detection in networks. In: Berkhin, P., Caruana, R., Wu, X. (eds.) Proceedings of the 13th ACM SIGKDD International Conference on Knowledge Discovery and Data Mining, San Jose, California, USA, 12–15 August 2007, pp. 420–429. ACM (2007)
19. Li, R., Mehr, N., Horowitz, R.: Submodularity of optimal sensor placement for traffic networks. Transp. Res. Part B: Methodol. **171**, 29–43 (2023)
20. Lin, H., Bilmes, J.: A class of submodular functions for document summarization. In: Proceedings of the 49th Annual Meeting of the Association for Computational Linguistics: Human Language Technologies, pp. 510–520 (2011)
21. Mirzasoleiman, B., Karbasi, A., Sarkar, R., Krause, A.: Distributed submodular maximization. J. Mach. Learn. Res. **17**(1), 8330–8373 (2016)
22. Nemhauser, G.L., Wolsey, L.A., Fisher, M.L.: An analysis of approximations for maximizing submodular set functions–i. Math. Program. **14**, 265–294 (1978)
23. Prajapat, M., Mutný, M., Zeilinger, M.N., Krause, A.: Submodular reinforcement learning. arXiv preprint arXiv:2307.13372 (2023)
24. Prajapat, M., Turchetta, M., Zeilinger, M., Krause, A.: Near-optimal multi-agent learning for safe coverage control. Adv. Neural. Inf. Process. Syst. **35**, 14998–15012 (2022)
25. Sharma, D., Kapoor, A., Deshpande, A.: On greedy maximization of entropy. In: International Conference on Machine Learnin, pp. 1330–1338. PMLR (2015)
26. Singh, A., Krause, A.R., Guestrin, C., Kaiser, W.J., Batalin, M.: Efficient planning of informative paths for multiple robots (2006)
27. Streeter, M., Golovin, D., Smith, S.F.: Combining multiple constraint solvers: results on the CPAI'06 competition data. of: Proceedings of the Second International CSP Solver Competition, pp. 11–18 (2008)
28. Sun, X., Cassandras, C.G., Meng, X.: A submodularity-based approach for multi-agent optimal coverage problems. In: 2017 IEEE 56th Annual Conference on Decision and Control (CDC), pp. 4082–4087. IEEE (2017)
29. Sutton, R.S.: Reinforcement Learning: An Introduction. A Bradford Book (2018)
30. Yoshida, Y.: Maximizing a monotone submodular function with a bounded curvature under a knapsack constraint. SIAM J. Discret. Math. **33**(3), 1452–1471 (2019)
31. Zhou, T., Ouyang, H., Bilmes, J., Chang, Y., Guestrin, C.: Scaling submodular maximization via pruned submodularity graphs. In: Artificial Intelligence and Statistics, pp. 316–324. PMLR (2017)

Harnessing Stubborn AUVs for Decentralized Decision Strategies in Communication-Limited Environments

Wiebke Frenkel(✉) and Bernd-Christian Renner

Hamburg University of Technology, Institute for Autonomous Cyber-Physical Systems, Harburger Schloßstr. 28, 21079 Hamburg, Germany
{wiebke.frenkel,christian.renner}@tuhh.de
https://www.tuhh.de/acps/

Abstract. Swarms of autonomous underwater vehicles (AUVs) offer a promising solution for complex missions in dynamic environments with limited communication. Unforeseen events, such as currents, equipment failures, or energy shortages, can prevent some AUVs from completing tasks, requiring rapid redistribution among the remaining vehicles. Decentralized coordination under such conditions is challenging, especially without reliable feedback on overall mission progress. This work investigates a decentralized decision-making process for task reallocation, grounded in opinion dynamics. A key parameter is an agent's *stubbornness*, capturing the tendency to persist with an opinion despite uncertainty. Stubbornness influences when and how the swarm reassigns tasks. Simulations across cooperation strategies and swarm compositions show that allowing controlled divergence in agent opinions, rather than enforcing rapid consensus, improves mission success and resilience. Diverse viewpoints reduce groupthink, encourage exploration, and support flexible adaptation to environmental changes. These results highlight the potential of simple, decentralized heuristics like adaptive stubbornness for robust coordination in uncertain underwater environments.

Keywords: AUV Swarm · Opinion Dynamics · Self Organization · Swarm Intelligence

1 Introduction

Autonomous underwater vehicles (AUVs) are increasingly deployed in collaborative missions, such as environmental monitoring [1] and object tracking [28]. These missions require close coordination among multiple AUVs, which face communication constraints, lack central control, and operate in dynamic environments with changing currents, moving targets, and evolving terrain. A key challenge is decentralized task allocation and reassignment in response to local observations and unforeseen events, requiring agents to make autonomous decisions under incomplete information.

M. Baldoni et al. (Eds.): EUMAS 2025, LNAI 16259, pp. 195–211, 2026.
https://doi.org/10.1007/978-3-032-22820-8_12

We propose a decentralized strategy for dynamic task redistribution and local mission assessment in communication-limited AUV swarms, grounded in distributed opinion dynamics. A central element is *stubbornness*, a tunable parameter that governs how strongly an agent adheres to its current tasks versus adapting to peer input. Highly stubborn agents maintain their decisions, while less stubborn agents are more responsive to local feedback. Stubbornness enables agents to autonomously balance task commitment and collective flexibility, even under low-bandwidth or intermittent communication.

From this, three research questions arise:

- How can decentralized agents infer whether the collective mission is succeeding or requires adaptation despite limited communication and no global oversight?
- How can stubbornness balance individual task commitment and collective adaptability in decentralized AUV swarms?
- How does the dynamic adjustment of stubbornness based on local observations affect task allocation and mission success?

This work advances the understanding of how simple, decentralized heuristics, such as adaptive stubbornness, support robust coordination in AUV swarms under uncertainty and dynamic conditions, connecting theoretical models of collective decision-making with practical underwater missions.

2 State of the Art

Decentralized coordination of AUV swarms in communication-constrained environments is an increasingly critical topic in swarm robotics research [3]. Unlike unmanned aerial vehicles (UAVs), AUVs rely on acoustic communication, which suffers from low bandwidth, high latency, and frequent dropouts [12], making centralized planning or continuous data exchange infeasible.

To address these constraints, recent work has explored decentralized task allocation methods that can tolerate communication loss. For instance, [24] presents a UAV coordination framework based on onboard visual data and localized decision-making. However, such methods often rely on rich sensory input, particularly visual feedback, which is typically unavailable or unreliable in underwater scenarios due to turbidity and limited visibility. This limitation reduces their applicability to AUV systems and motivates the need for strategies that rely on minimal communication.

Machine learning techniques, particularly deep reinforcement learning (DRL) [6,10] or multi-agent reinforcement learning (MARL) [14], have shown promise in enabling adaptive AUV behavior in complex, uncertain environments. While effective in simulation and controlled environments, DRL-based methods require large amounts of training data, are often sensitive to environment-specific features, and demand significant onboard computational resources. These limitations hinder their effectiveness for making real-time decisions during resource-constrained underwater missions.

Several decentralized coordination strategies have been proposed alongside learning-based approaches. In [15], they introduced a method that combines market-based task allocation with hierarchical task network (HTN) planning to coordinate complex missions with temporal and causal dependencies. While effective, this method requires multiple communication rounds per task and a complete HTN specification, which can lead to delays and increased overhead in dynamic, communication-limited underwater environments. To address these issues, we suggest a lightweight, locally decision-driven strategy that minimizes communication needs and avoids complete prior task modeling.

Opinion dynamic models offer a compelling alternative for enabling agents to reach collective decisions through local interactions without global oversight. Researchers find these models to be an efficient substitute for data-intensive methods in decentralized decision-making. Recent studies [18,23] link sociological opinion formation models to swarm coordination, emphasizing stubbornness as a key factor for filtering out faulty signals and maintaining stability. Agents adjust their beliefs based on information from neighbors, and research [26,27] shows that stubborn agents can prevent premature consensus while preserving informational diversity in uncertain conditions.

Building on these insights, we develop a behavior-based coordination strategy that integrates adaptive stubbornness into the self-organization process of AUV swarms. We model the swarm as a dynamic opinion network where local interactions are leveraged to estimate global mission progress and adapt task allocation accordingly.

3 Problem Statement

We expand on our earlier architecture [9], which includes a central base station for offline mission planning and an AUV swarm. The AUVs navigate to specific predefined sampling waypoints in this simplified underwater mission. To emphasize decentralized coordination, we will not consider sampling energy and will assume that propulsion is the primary energy consumer.

3.1 Communication

In AUV swarms, communication extends beyond simple data exchange, playing a crucial role in the decision-making process. Due to limited bandwidth and intermittent connectivity, agents must determine locally whether and when their information is significant enough to share. This means that communication becomes a strategic action, influencing decisions such as whether to continue or abort a mission, redistribute tasks, or prioritize support for individual agents.

In our work, we rely on a robust, decentralized time division multiple access (TDMA) protocol [7,16] that exchanges minimal but relevant information, which is a crucial aspect given frequent interruptions. The TDMA assigns each of the agent $n \in \{0, 1, \dots, N-1\}$ a time slot of 30 s per round. A transmission is successful only if the receiver is within range; otherwise, the message is lost. For the

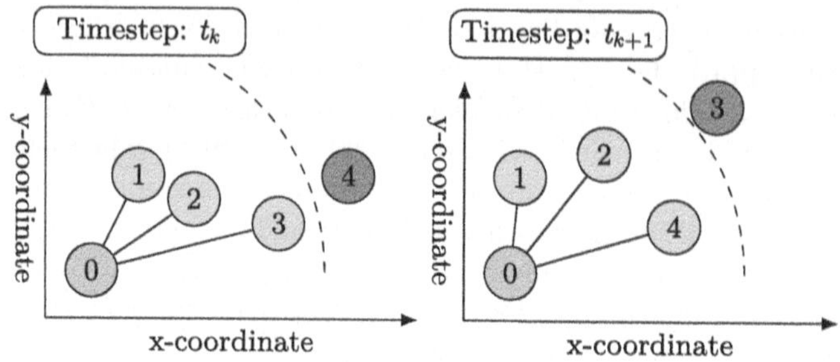

Fig. 1. Local neighborhood of agent 0 (green) at two consecutive timesteps t_k and t_{k+1}. Solid lines indicate direct communication links within the dashed communication range. The changing set of neighbors illustrates the dynamic topology caused by agent movement. (Color figure online)

sake of simplicity, we do not consider physical transmission effects (such as salinity) and instead focus on inter-agent distance as the primary factor determining connectivity [12].

In Fig. 1, we illustrate the dynamic network: agents gain or lose neighbors as the swarm moves, altering the communication graph. This variability poses challenges for robust coordination.

3.2 Energy Considerations in a Greedy Task Redistribution

Energy, primarily consumed by propulsion, limits each AUV's range and endurance in underwater missions. When an AUV lacks sufficient energy to complete its tasks, it must redistribute its workload to nearby agents. To support decentralized task redistribution, each AUV estimates propulsion energy for potential route adjustments using a physics-based model [8,9], calculating the energy cost $E = \mathbf{F} \cdot |\mathbf{x}|$ for a displacement $\mathbf{x}$ under hydrodynamic force $\mathbf{F}$.

We model battery depletion as an equivalent circuit for Li-ion cells [21], where the state of charge (SOC) evolves as

$$\frac{\mathrm{d}}{\mathrm{d}t}\sigma(t) = -\frac{1}{C_{\mathrm{bat}}} \cdot i(t) \tag{1}$$

with the current $i(t)$ derived from the required mechanical power and system losses [8].

The decentralized greedy task redistribution mechanism activates when an AUV can no longer perform its assigned waypoints, triggering reassignment of remaining tasks. Each agent autonomously evaluates redistribution options using local energy estimates and limited peer information.

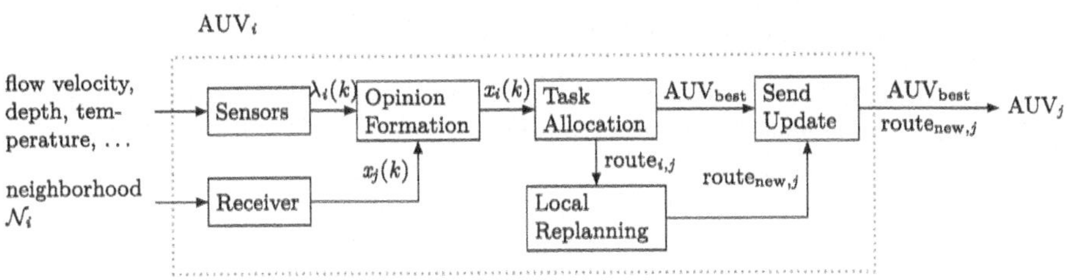

Fig. 2. Schematic representation of the decision-making process within an AUV i.

The assignment of tasks to suitable candidates from the neighbourhood $j \in n; j \neq i$ is represented by directed graphs $\mathcal{G} = (\mathcal{V}, \mathcal{E})$, which are weighted according to segment-wise energy costs. We iteratively test waypoint insertions from the source AUV $i \in n$ into the recipient's route, selecting the position that minimizes additional energy expenditure. Let $\text{route}_{i \to j} = (v_0, v_1, \ldots, v_k, v_0)$ denote a candidate cyclic path of waypoints from agent i to j. The optimal insertion is then chosen as

$$\text{route}^{\star}_{i \to j} = \arg \min_{\text{route}_{i \to j}} \left(\sum_{\ell=0}^{k-1} E_{v_\ell, v_{\ell+1}} + E_{v_k, v_0} \right), \tag{2}$$

with the sum of segment-wise energy costs along the route.

This greedy, locally informed method supports scalable, resilient coordination under real-world underwater constraints, avoiding the need for computationally expensive global optimizers.

4 The Social AUV Swarm

In our approach, the AUV swarm operates as a dynamic social network [25], where autonomous agents exchange minimal information to collectively manage task allocation and energy constraints. Each AUV continuously evaluates its task load and energy status to decide autonomously when to request or offer help, enabling robust, decentralized coordination under communication and environmental constraints.

In Fig. 2 we illustrate the decision-making architecture of a single AUV. Sensor inputs such as flow velocity, depth, and temperature, along with messages received from neighboring AUV $j \in \mathcal{N}_i$, feed into the opinion formation module. This module combines internal assessments with social influence to generate a current opinion on the feasibility of the mission. Based on this, the task allocation module manages workload distribution and local route replanning. Updated task assignments are then communicated to selected peers to enable decentralized swarm coordination.

4.1 Opinion Formation with Stubborn AUVs

In underwater swarm operations, effective decision-making hinges on each AUV's ability to autonomously evaluate its operational state and coordinate with neighbors despite limited communication and incomplete information. To capture this nuanced interplay between individual assessment and social influence, we employ the Friedkin-Johnsen (FJ) opinion dynamics model [23]. Unlike consensus-driven approaches, the FJ model preserves each agent's inherent biases, modeled here as *stubbornness*, enabling resilient, adaptive judgments essential for uncertain and dynamic underwater environments.

Classical models such as DeGroot's [5] drive agents toward complete consensus, which may lead to suboptimal or misleading collective decisions when individual conditions vary widely. By contrast, the FJ model incorporates a stubbornness parameter λ_i that balances an agent's internal judgment with social influence. This mechanism allows agents to consider their disagreement with the neighbors' opinions, thereby enhancing robustness against unreliable or incomplete information [22].

We define the stubbornness of an AUV as a function of its SOC as a measurable quantity for assessing the agent's state to reflect the agent's operational constraints:

$$\lambda_i(k) = 1 - \sigma_i(k), \quad \sigma_i(k) \in [0, 1] \ . \tag{3}$$

Agents with low energy are often convinced that they cannot complete their tasks, which makes them less likely to accept outside suggestions. In contrast, agents with higher energy are generally more open to adapting. This characteristic makes the SOC a straightforward and interpretable indicator of stubbornness in critical decision-making situations.

Each AUV maintains an initial opinion indicating its local evaluation of mission success

$$\tilde{x}_i(k) = 1 - (\xi_0 \cdot \sigma_i(k) + \xi_1 \cdot \mu_i(k)) \ , \tag{4}$$

where $\mu_i(t) \in [0, 1]$ denotes the task completion ratio, and ξ_0, ξ_1 are weighting coefficients. A value of $\tilde{x}_i(k) = 1$ suggests aborting the mission, while $\tilde{x}_i(k) = 0$ favors task continuation.

Following the FJ update rule, each AUV then revises its current opinion by blending its initial assessment with the influence of neighboring agents

$$x_i^{\mathrm{FJ}}(k+1) = \lambda_i(k) \cdot \tilde{x}_i(k) + (1 - \lambda_i(k)) \sum_{j \in \mathcal{N}_i} \omega_{ij} x_j(k) \ , \tag{5}$$

where ω_{ij} are normalized influence weights representing how strongly agent i is affected by the opinion of neighbor j, with $\sum_{j \in \mathcal{N}_i} \omega_{ij} = 1$. This formulation ensures that agents with higher stubbornness maintain a stronger bias toward their evaluation, while more flexible agents consider peer input more.

To mitigate instability due to outdated or missing data, we introduce a healing mechanism

$$x_i(k+1) = \tilde{x}_i(k) + \left(x_i^{\mathrm{FJ}}(k) - \tilde{x}_i(k)\right) \cdot e^{(-\tau \cdot \Delta t)} \ , \tag{6}$$

with τ as a decay rate and Δt as the time since the last successful communication that gradually reverts an agent's opinion toward its initial state when isolated. This dampens the impact of one-sided information and reduces oscillatory behavior in the decision-making process.

4.2 Task Allocation

Unpredictable conditions such as currents, sensor drift, and energy depletion can disrupt task execution in underwater missions. We use a decentralized redistribution mechanism based on peer-to-peer negotiation to maintain robustness.

Each AUV monitors its status and communicates with neighbors. Tasks are reallocated either through help offers from idle agents or help requests from struggling ones. This enables flexible workload balancing without centralized control.

Interaction. To ensure collision-free message exchange, we utilize a TDMA protocol Sect. 3.1, where each AUV is assigned a fixed time slot. In Fig. 3, we illustrate the processing steps within a single time slot. At the beginning of its slot, the AUV i broadcasts a status message, which may include a help request, an offer, or a regular update, depending on its internal opinion. Neighbors $\mathcal{N}_i$ reply with energy, route, and task data during their slots. Based on this, the AUV updates its opinion and decides whether task redistribution is needed. If it is triggered, the agent i selects a suitable neighbor j and runs a local greedy optimizer Sect. 3.2 to determine which waypoint to reassign and where to insert it in the recipient's route. The selected neighbor j receives the updated route and adjusts accordingly.

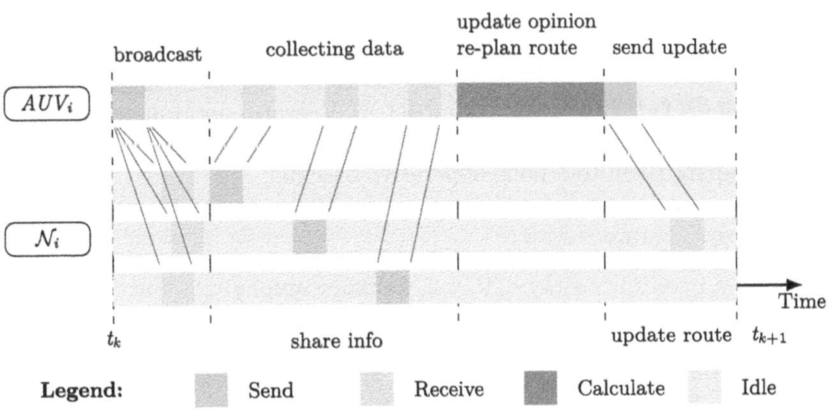

Fig. 3. Sequence of communication and processing steps within a time slot, illustrating the basic cycle of sending, receiving, and recalculating before the next transmission.

A key advantage of our approach compared to auction-based methods is that each sending AUV only needs to query the status of its neighbors once per cycle, rather than repeatedly requesting updated states. This significantly reduces communication overhead and latency. The sending AUV collects all relevant information from neighbors during their assigned time slots and processes it locally to make task redistribution decisions.

Offer. If an agent i completes its assigned tasks early, it broadcasts a readiness signal to its neighbors $\mathcal{N}_i$. Each neighbor j is only considered if it still has unfinished tasks. Among these candidates, agent i selects the neighbor j^* with the highest opinion value

$$j^* = \arg\max_{j \in \mathcal{N}_i} x_j(k) \ , \tag{7}$$

where $x_j(k)$ reflects the neighbor's belief that it may not complete its tasks. *Note that a higher opinion value indicates greater pessimism about mission success, i.e., the agent is more likely to request support.* This ensures that help is directed to the agent with the greatest need.

Request. When agent i reaches a critical state (e.g., low energy or the willingness to return), it broadcasts a help request. Neighbors evaluate their suitability based on their opinion values $x_j(k)$, and the agent j^* with the lowest opinion (most confident in completing tasks) is selected

$$j^* = \arg\min_{j \in \mathcal{N}_i} x_j(k) \ . \tag{8}$$

Note, a lower opinion value indicates that the agent still believes it can complete tasks, making it a suitable candidate to take over additional work.

5 Evaluation

We analyze how various decentralized behaviors – `Offer`, `Request`, and their combination (`Offer + Request`) – impact AUV swarm performance under communication constraints. These situations necessitate adaptive task redistribution, and we compare them to a non-cooperative baseline.

Each mission starts and ends at the base (0|0). An AUV must return if it reaches a critical state

$$\begin{aligned} \sigma_i(k) < 15\% \ &: \ \texttt{Battery empty} \\ x_i(k) > 0.8 \ &: \ \texttt{Return} \end{aligned} \tag{9}$$

The chosen thresholds ensure safe return and may be dynamically adjusted in future work. A mission is successful if all waypoints are visited and all AUVs return to base.

We run 50 simulated missions for each setup to enable a statistically robust evaluation and account for variability in agent behavior and random waypoint distribution. Our simulations focus on unexpected events causing faster energy drops. To emulate this, some AUVs have a significantly increased SOC variability ($\sigma_i(k) = 20\%$), representing higher mission stress. We evaluate:

- **Minor disturbance**: 30% of AUVs have low SOC. Tests swarm compensation when most agents remain optimistic about continuing the mission.
- **Major disturbance**: Up to 60% of AUVs have low SOC. Assesses resilience when capable agents are in the minority.
- **Swarm size variation**: Comparison of a small swarm (10 AUVs, 100 waypoints in a 200 × 200 m area) where most agents can communicate with each other, and a large swarm (30 AUVs, 300 waypoints in a 600 × 600 m area) where the likelihood of inter-agent communication is low.

5.1 Mission Success

This evaluation examines the impact of cooperative task redistribution on mission success, energy efficiency, and execution time in communication-constrained AUV swarms.

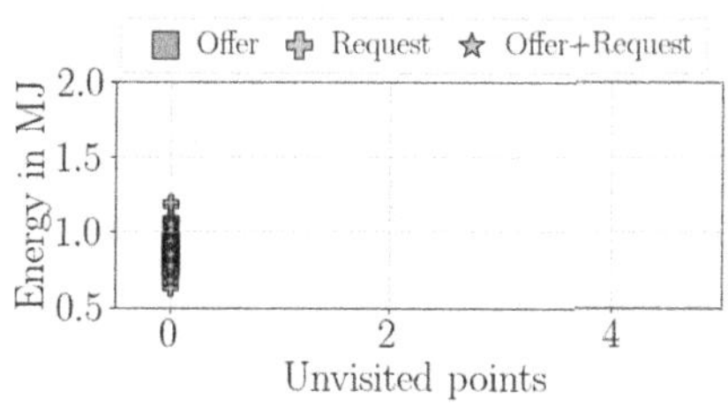

(a) Swarm size: 10; Dist. AUV: 30%

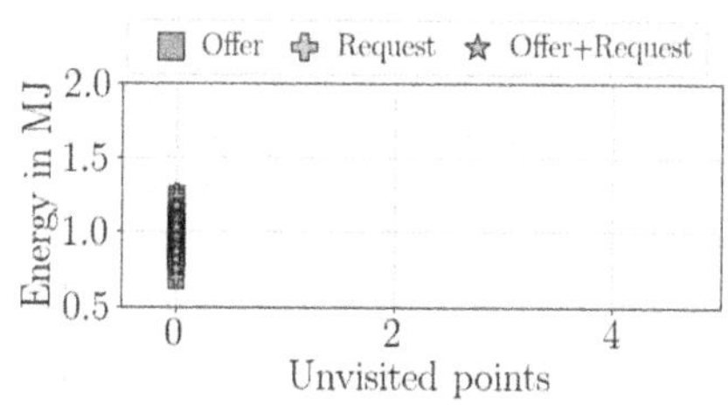

(b) Swarm size: 10; Dist. AUV: 60%

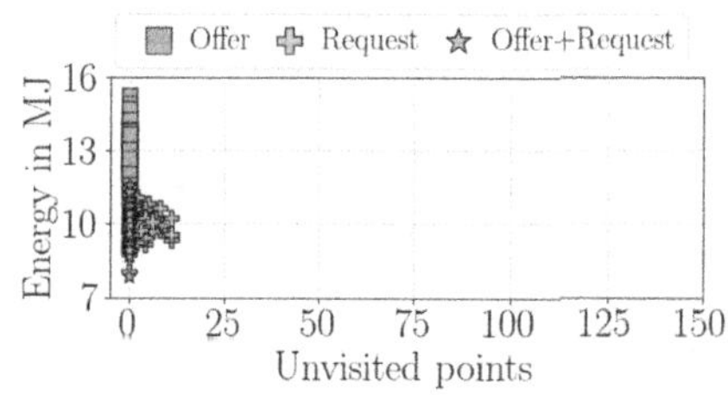

(c) Swarm size: 30; Dist. AUV: 30%

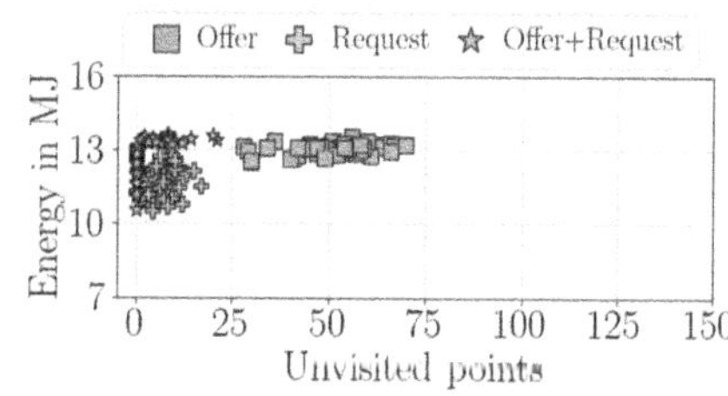

(d) Swarm size: 30; Dist. AUV: 50%

Fig. 4. Propulsion energy in relation to unvisited task waypoints, considering only task-related travel and excluding communication energy.

Figure 4 illustrates the propulsion energy consumption relative to unvisited task waypoints across different swarm sizes and disturbance levels. In small swarms, all cooperative strategies reliably complete their missions. Notably, they exhibit similar energy consumption levels, indicating that cooperation does not incur significant additional energy costs. For larger swarms under minor disturbance, both the `Offer` and the combined `Offer+Request` strategies complete all missions, whereas the `Request` strategy leaves some waypoints unvisited. Under major disturbance, the limitations of the strategies become evident. The combined **`Offer+Request`** strategy still completes a substantial portion of the missions, the **`Request`** strategy fails to cover a significant number of waypoints, and the **`Offer`** strategy is unable to complete any missions under these highly disturbed conditions.

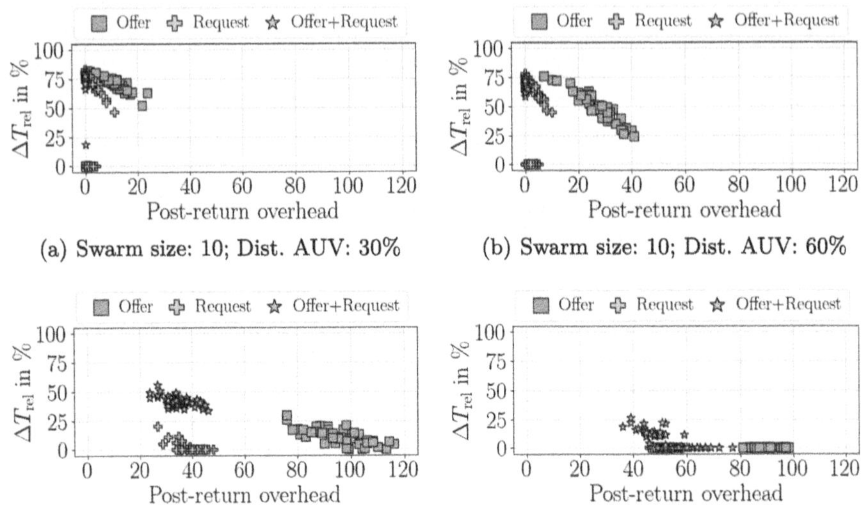

(a) **Swarm size: 10; Dist. AUV: 30%**

(b) **Swarm size: 10; Dist. AUV: 60%**

(c) **Swarm size: 30; Dist. AUV: 30%**

(d) **Swarm size: 30; Dist. AUV: 50%**

Fig. 5. Correlation between the relative improvement in mission duration and the additional number of waypoints (including the base) across task redistribution strategies.

To evaluate coordination efficiency, we analyze the relative improvement in mission duration among different strategies. We use the metric

$$\Delta T_{\text{rel}} = \frac{T_{\max} - T_i}{T_{\max}} \cdot 100\% \tag{10}$$

where $T_{\max}$ is the non-cooperative baseline mission duration measured when agents operate independently without any communication or coordination. This baseline represents the worst-case scenario, i.e., the longest mission time. Improvements in coordination are reflected by higher values of ΔT_{rel}. In our setup, agents that finish their assigned waypoints return to the base and enter standby mode. This approach limits unnecessary travel and provides a common meeting point for task redistribution. Idle agents remain available to quickly take over leftover tasks, which is especially beneficial for agents at the network periphery or those temporarily disconnected. However, this redeployment can increase total travel distance and mission time.

Figure 5 shows mission duration versus the number of post-return overhead – additional points caused by repeated returns to base. The plots indicate that the **`Offer`** strategy causes the most post-return overhead because help is only offered after an AUV completes its tasks, resulting in frequent returns to base for reassignment. The `Request` and combined `Offer+Request` strategies generate similar overhead in terms of additional waypoints visited. Nevertheless, the combined strategy significantly improves overall mission duration, reducing unnecessary redeployments and thus increasing coordination efficiency.

5.2 Communication Effort

AUVs typically use separate power supplies for propulsion and onboard electronics, including communication systems [2,11,13], as propulsion requires high power while communication demands low-noise, low-voltage sources. We therefore assess communication energy independently from propulsion.

Effective communication is essential for coordination, but it can also be energy-intensive and may hinder mission performance if not managed properly. Utilizing data from the *ahoi* acoustic modem [19,20] (which consumes 2.1 W for transmission and 0.3 W for reception, and sends 64-byte messages at a rate of 32.5 Bytes/s), we calculated the energy costs associated with each message. By combining this information with the transmission counts shown in Fig. 6 and the reception logs in Fig. 7, we derived total estimates for communication energy consumption.

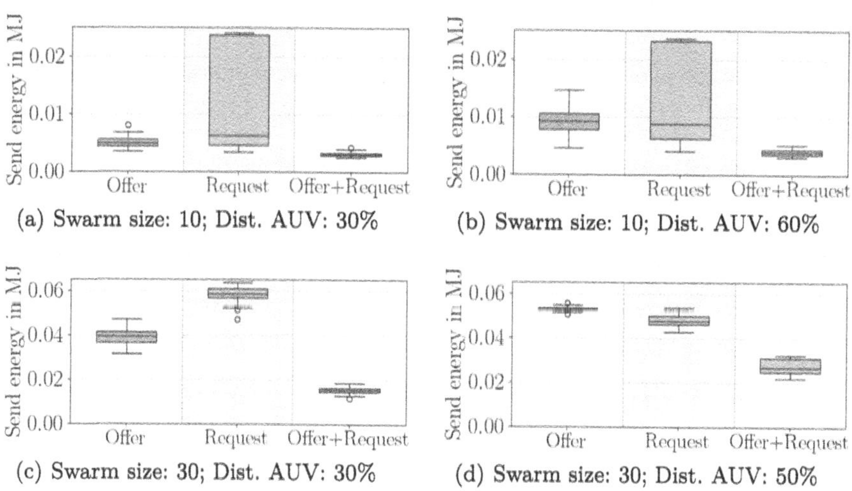

Fig. 6. Energy consumption for sending messages across the swarm.

The plots show that for all tested scenarios, the combined `Offer+Request` strategy achieves the lowest energy consumption for both sending and receiving messages. From an energetic perspective, it is therefore the most efficient strategy for communication. When comparing the individual strategies `Offer` and

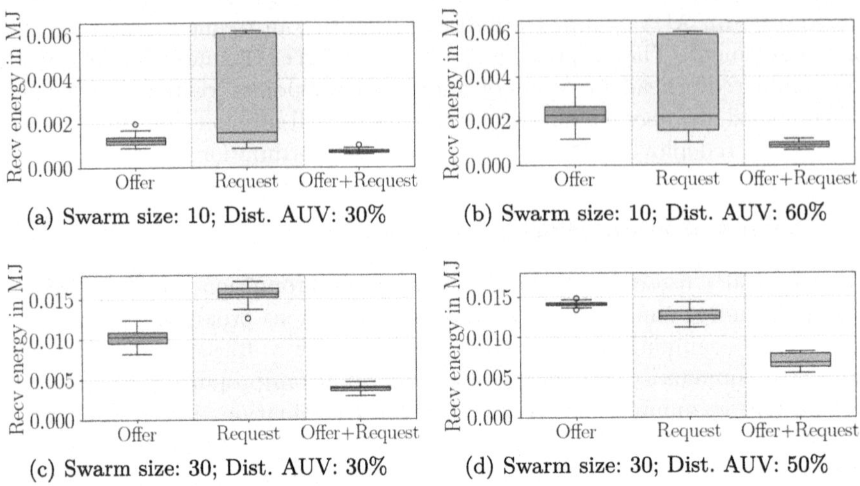

(a) Swarm size: 10; Dist. AUV: 30%

(b) Swarm size: 10; Dist. AUV: 60%

(c) Swarm size: 30; Dist. AUV: 30%

(d) Swarm size: 30; Dist. AUV: 50%

Fig. 7. Energy consumption for receiving messages across the swarm.

`Request`, distinct patterns emerge. In small swarms, the median energy consumption for communication is similar for both strategies; however, the standard deviation for `Request` is significantly higher, indicating less predictability in energy demand. The generally greater energy usage associated with `Request` suggests that it involves more frequent responses, which implies increased connectivity between agents. This effect becomes more pronounced in large swarms, where the likelihood of isolated AUVs increases. Isolated agents send fewer messages because they receive fewer requests. In contrast, the `Offer` strategy is only triggered once an agent has completed all its tasks. While this reduces communication overhead when missions are progressing smoothly, the fixed TDMA slots can introduce unnecessary delays in information exchange. In some cases, this can lead to slower responses from other agents and hinder timely task redistribution.

5.3 Quantifying Swarm Opinion Formation

We evaluate collective decision-making using two key measures. The consensus score

$$C = \frac{1}{N} \sum_{i=0}^{N-1} \mathbb{I}\left(|x_i(k) - \bar{x}(k)| < \varepsilon\right), \tag{11}$$

quantifies how closely agents align their internal assessments, with $\bar{x}(k)$ as the swarm-wide average opinion and ε a small tolerance margin. The indicator function $\mathbb{I}(\cdot)$ returns 1 if agent i agrees with the majority within this margin. In contrast, Shannon entropy

$$H = -\sum_{\chi=1}^{X} p_i \log_2 p_i. \tag{12}$$

measures opinion diversity by binning normalized opinions $x_i(k) \in [0,1]$ into χ intervals with corresponding frequencies p_i. Higher entropy indicates greater uncertainty or persistent disagreement. Together, these measures help differentiate genuine agreement from misleading uniformity and show whether the diversity arises from resilience or fragmentation. A high consensus score with low entropy suggests strong alignment among participants, while a low consensus score with high entropy indicates ongoing disagreement or indecision (Fig. 9).

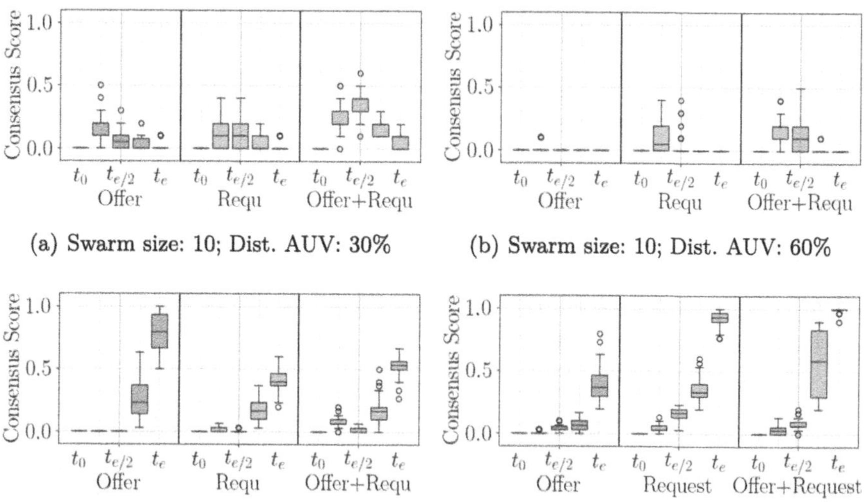

(a) Swarm size: 10; Dist. AUV: 30%

(b) Swarm size: 10; Dist. AUV: 60%

(c) Swarm size: 30; Dist. AUV: 30%

(d) Swarm size: 30; Dist. AUV: 50%

Fig. 8. Consensus score distribution at different mission phases. Higher values indicate stronger agreement within the swarm.

All strategies start with near-zero consensus in fig. 8. In small swarms with 30 % disturbed AUVs, `Offer` jumps quickly early and then plateaus, and `Request` remains unchanged mainly, `Offer+Request` shows a steady mid-mission rise in consensus before a slight decline. With 60% disturbed AUVs, `Offer` stays near zero, `Request` produces only isolated mid-mission peaks, and `Offer+Request` exhibits the same qualitative pattern as with 30% but with weaker alignment.

Entropy patterns mirror these trends: `Offer` shows a sharp early increase in entropy that returns to baseline, indicating quick but short-lived disagreement followed by fast convergence. `Request` reaches its peak mid-mission with high variability, reflecting scattered and less synchronized behavior. `Offer+Request` maintains moderate entropy on a plateau before decreasing, suggesting a balanced relationship between diversity and agreement that supports adaptive coordination.

For small swarms, the combined `Offer+Request` strategy performs best: it achieves meaningful mid-mission consensus while preserving moderate entropy,

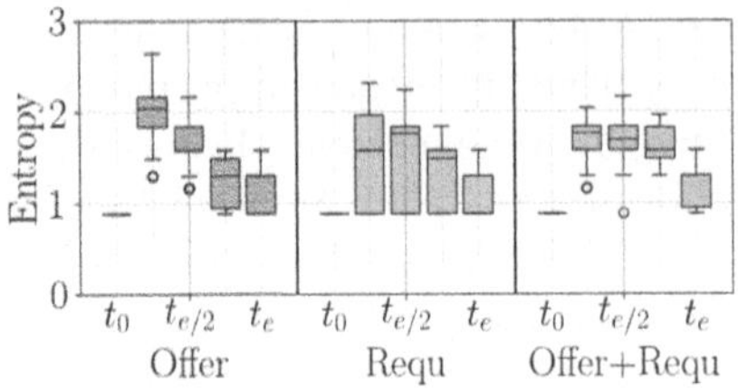

(a) **Swarm size: 10; Dist. AUV: 30%**

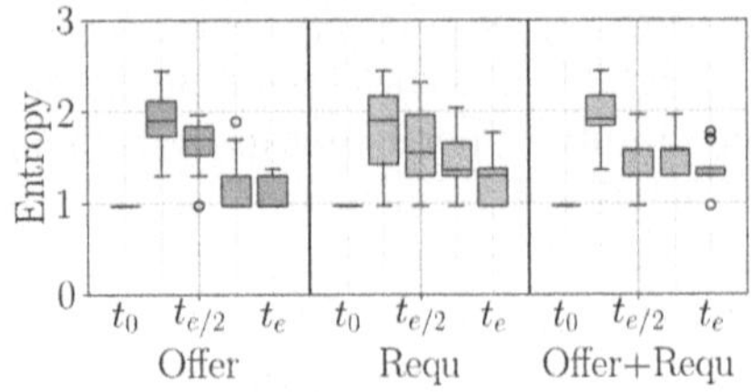

(b) **Swarm size: 10; Dist. AUV: 60%**

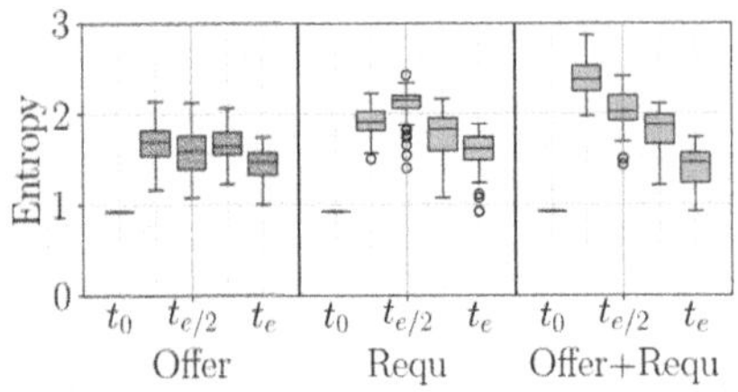

(c) **Swarm size: 30; Dist. AUV: 30%**

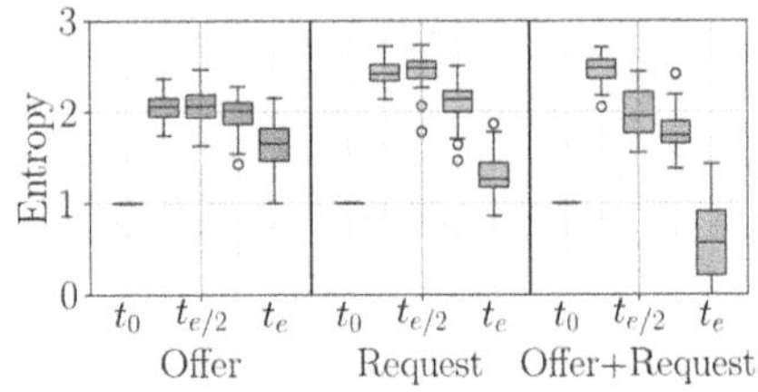

(d) **Swarm size: 30; Dist. AUV: 50%**

Fig. 9. Entropy of the opinion distribution at different mission phases. Higher values reflect greater disagreement and uncertainty among AUVs.

i.e., a helpful balance between agreement and diversity that supports adaptive, robust coordination. `Offer` yields fast initial alignment but sacrifices adaptability (resulting in a brittle consensus), and `Request` produces unpredictable, high-variance behavior with limited overall convergence. Thus, if the goal is reliable and adaptable task redistribution in well-connected small swarms, `Offer+Request` is the recommended strategy.

In large swarms, all strategies show a similar pattern: consensus rises only slightly at the start but increases sharply toward the end of the mission, resembling an exponential curve. The entropy trends confirm this behavior: it jumps early in the mission and then gradually decreases toward the end. This indicates that large swarms tend to form a collective assessment only late in the mission, likely when mission outcomes or resource shortages become apparent. In terms of mission success, this delayed consensus can have mixed effects. While it allows the swarm to remain flexible early on, it may also hinder timely task redistribution under high disturbance. Consequently, strategies that combine `Offer+Request` achieve higher completion rates in disturbed conditions, as they allow for both proactive offers and reactive requests, mitigating the risks of late consensus. The `Offer` strategy alone performs best when disturbances are low, but under high disturbance, its late consensus formation correlates with mission failure for many waypoints.

6 Conclusion and Outlook

This work investigates how leveraging agent stubbornness enhances cooperative task redistribution in communication-constrained AUV swarms, focusing on the decision-making process when unexpected events occur. Stubbornness acts as a tunable parameter balancing individual task commitment and collective flexibility. By integrating stubbornness into distributed opinion dynamics, AUVs can make autonomous decisions about when to cooperate, when to resist change, and how to interpret swarm dynamics, even under low-bandwidth, intermittent communication.

We evaluated three cooperative strategies. In the `Offer` strategy, agents proactively propose tasks once their own are complete; in `Request`, agents seek assistance for unfinished tasks; the combined `Offer+Request` strategy integrates both approaches. Across all scenarios, `Offer+Request` consistently achieved the most robust performance by balancing diversity and consensus, avoiding premature lock-in, and enabling effective task redistribution even in disturbed conditions. Small swarms coordinated effectively despite a substantial fraction of agents being less stubborn or "disturbed," while large swarms tended to form consensus only late in the mission. This delayed consensus allows early flexibility but can hinder timely redistribution under high disturbance, again highlighting the value of moderate, context-sensitive stubbornness.

A key insight is that mission success correlates with well-timed, moderate consensus growth rather than maximal early agreement. Stubbornness mediates this by allowing agents to resist premature alignment while remaining responsive to critical task demands, effectively linking individual behavior to emergent swarm performance. Strategies that preserved diversity early and converged toward the end (such as `Offer+Request`) demonstrated the best combination of reliability, efficiency, and robustness. These findings reinforce prior insights from swarm intelligence and opinion dynamics [4,17,22], emphasizing that a balance between agreement and heterogeneity is vital for resilient group behavior in dynamic environments.

Future work should explore adaptive communication protocols that dynamically allocate bandwidth based on agent urgency or network topology, addressing the limitations of fixed TDMA slots and supporting timely task redistribution, in line with the principles of the FJ model [23]. Further investigation could also examine context-sensitive adjustment of stubbornness in real time, allowing agents to adapt their persistence to changing environmental conditions, mission priorities, or energy constraints. Extending the framework to heterogeneous swarms, mixed autonomy levels, or multi-objective missions may provide additional insights into scalable, resilient coordination strategies for real-world underwater operations.

References

1. Alfred-Wegener-Institut, Helmholtz-Zentrum für Polar- und Meeresforschung: Tiefsee-Ökologie und -Technologie (2024). https://www.awi.de/forschung/biowissenschaften/tiefsee-oekologie-und-technologie/technologie.html. Accessed 27 Jan 2025
2. von Benzon, M., Sørensen, F.F., Uth, E., Jouffroy, J., Liniger, J., Pedersen, S.: An open-source benchmark simulator: control of a bluerov2 underwater robot. J. Marine Sci. Eng. **10**(12), 1898 (2022)
3. Connor, J., Champion, B., Joordens, M.A.: Current algorithms, communication methods and designs for underwater swarm robotics: a review. IEEE Sens. J. **21**(1), 153–169 (2020)
4. Couzin, I.D., Krause, J., Franks, N.R., Levin, S.A.: Effective leadership and decision-making in animal groups on the move. Nature **433**(7025), 513–516 (2005)
5. DeGroot, M.H.: Reaching a consensus. J. Am. Stat. Assoc. **69**(345), 118–121 (1974)
6. Fang, Y., Huang, Z., Pu, J., Zhang, J.: AUV position tracking and trajectory control based on fast-deployed deep reinforcement learning method. Ocean Eng. **245**, 110452 (2022)
7. Faruque, S.: Time Division Multiple Access (TDMA). Radio Frequency Multiple Access Techniques Made Easy, pp. 35–43 (2019)
8. Frenkel, W., Renner, B.C.: Towards energy-aware path planning for AUV swarms. In: Proceedings of the 18th International Conference on Control, Automation, Robotics and Vision (ICARCV 2024), pp. 1106–1111. IEEE, Dubai, United Arab Emirates (2024)
9. Frenkel, W., Renner, B.C.: Hyperparameter optimization for PSO-based energy-aware path planning for AUV swarms. In: 2025 38th International Conference on Architecture of Computing Systems (ARCS). p. in print. Springer (2025)
10. Hadi, B., Khosravi, A., Sarhadi, P.: Deep reinforcement learning for adaptive path planning and control of an autonomous underwater vehicle. Appl. Ocean Res. **129**, 103326 (2022)
11. Hasabnis, P., et al.: Ekagra, an autonomous underwater vehicle: cost-effective system design and implementation. In: OCEANS 2022-Chennai, pp. 1–7. IEEE (2022)
12. Heidemann, J., Stojanovic, M., Zorzi, M.: Underwater sensor networks: applications, advances and challenges. Philos. Trans. Royal Society A: Math., Phys. Eng. Sci. **370**(1958), 158–175 (2012)
13. Herrin, B., et al.: Modularis: modular underwater robot for rapid development and validation of autonomous systems. In: OCEANS 2023-MTS/IEEE US Gulf Coast, pp. 1–7. IEEE (2023)
14. Luvisutto, A., Celani, A., Renda, F., Stefanini, C., De Masi, G.: Enhancing collaboration in uncertain environment: multi-agent reinforcement learning for underwater monitoring. Expert Syst. Appl. **277**, 127256 (2025)
15. Milot, A., Chauveau, E., Lacroix, S., Lesire, C.: Market-based multi-robot coordination with HTN planning. In: 2021 IEEE/RSJ International Conference on Intelligent Robots and Systems (IROS), pp. 2606–2612. IEEE (2021)
16. Morozs, N., Mitchell, P., Zakharov, Y.V.: TDA-MAC: TDMA without clock synchronization in underwater acoustic networks. IEEE Access **6**, 1091–1108 (2017)
17. Mäs, M., Flache, A., Helbing, D.: Individualization as driving force of clustering phenomena in humans. PLoS Comput. Biol. **6**(10), e1000959 (2010)
18. Proskurnikov, A.V., Tempo, R.: A tutorial on modeling and analysis of dynamic social networks. Part I. Annual Rev. Control **43**, 65–79 (2017)

19. Renner, B.C.: ahoi: Open-Source, Inexpensive, Low-Power Underwater Acoustic Modem (2023). https://www.ahoi-modem.de. Accessed 19 Dec 2024
20. Renner, B.C., Heitmann, J., Steinmetz, F.: AHOI: inexpensive, low-power communication and localization for underwater sensor networks and μAUVs. ACM Trans. Sensor Netw. (TOSN) **16**(2), 1–46 (2020)
21. Reuter, J., Mank, E., Aschemann, H., Rauh, A.: Battery state observation and condition monitoring using online minimization. In: 2016 21st International Conference on Methods and Models in Automation and Robotics (MMAR), pp. 1223–1228. IEEE (2016)
22. Surowiecki, J.: The Wisdom of Crowds. Anchor, NY. (2005)
23. Wang, L., Xing, Y., Johansson, K.H.: On final opinions of the Friedkin-Johnsen model over random graphs with partially stubborn community. In: 2024 IEEE 63rd Conference on Decision and Control (CDC), pp. 4562–4567. IEEE (2024)
24. Wang, Z., Li, J., Li, J., Liu, C.: A decentralized decision-making algorithm of UAV swarm with information fusion strategy. Expert Syst. Appl. **237**, 121444 (2024)
25. Wasserman, S.: Social Network Analysis: Methods and Applications. The Press Syndicate of the University of Cambridge (1994)
26. Xing, Y., Johansson, K.H.: A Concentration phenomenon in a gossip interaction model with two communities. In: 2022 European Control Conference (ECC), pp. 1126–1131. IEEE (2022)
27. Xing, Y., Johansson, K.H.: Concentration in gossip opinion dynamics over random graphs. SIAM J. Control. Optim. **62**(3), 1521–1545 (2024)
28. Zhang, C., Cheng, P., Du, B., Dong, B., Zhang, W.: AUV path tracking with real-time obstacle avoidance via reinforcement learning under adaptive constraints. Ocean Eng. **256**, 111453 (2022)

Short Papers

Strategic Infrastructure Design via Multi-agent Congestion Games with Joint Placement and Pricing

Niloofar Aminikalibar(✉), Farzaneh Farhadi, and Maria Chli

Aston University, Birmingham B4 7ET, UK
{namin21,f.farhadi,m.chli}@aston.ac.uk

Abstract. Real-world infrastructure planning increasingly involves strategic interactions among autonomous agents competing over congestible, limited resources. Applications such as Electric Vehicle (EV) charging, emergency response, and intelligent transportation require coordinated resource placement and pricing decisions, while anticipating the adaptive behaviour of decentralised, self-interested agents. We propose a novel multi-agent framework for joint placement and pricing under such interactions, formalised as a bi-level optimisation model. The upper level represents a central planner, while the lower level captures agent responses via coupled non-atomic congestion games. Motivated by the EV charging domain, we study a setting where a central planner provisions chargers and road capacity under budget and profitability constraints. The agent population includes both EV drivers and non-charging drivers (NCDs), who respond to congestion, delays, and costs. To solve the resulting NP-hard problem, we introduce ABO-MPN, a double-layer approximation framework that decouples agent types, applies integer adjustment and rounding, and targets high-impact placement and pricing decisions. Experiments on benchmark networks show that our model reduces social cost by up to 40% compared to placement- or pricing-only baselines, and generalises to other MAS-relevant domains.

Keywords: Non-atomic Congestion Game · Multiple Congestible Resources · Strategic agents · Game-Theoretic Planning · EV Charging Infrastructure

1 Introduction

Many real-world planning tasks involve *resource provisioning with strategic agents*, where a central planner allocates congestible resources while anticipating agent responses. Applications span facility location, cloud provisioning, and intelligent transportation. While prior work often optimises siting or pricing in isolation, jointly optimising both under congestion-aware, cost-sensitive behaviour presents greater complexity. Such problems naturally induce Nash Equilibrium (NE) responses from agents.

We focus on a key instance: EV fast-charging infrastructure planning. With EVs central to global decarbonisation [12], scalable and efficient charging networks are critical. Planning is complicated by the interdependence between station viability and

M. Baldoni et al. (Eds.): EUMAS 2025, LNAI 16259, pp. 215–225, 2026.
https://doi.org/10.1007/978-3-032-22820-8_13

strategic driver behaviour. A unified optimisation framework must model equilibrium interactions and jointly determine pricing and placement.

In this setting, a planner provisions two coupled resources, charging stations and road links, while accounting for heterogeneous agents (EV drivers and NCDs) with distinct Origin-Destination (O-D) pairs and cost structures based on time, delay, and fees. This MAS challenge demands integration of decentralised behaviour with centralised, explainable planning. We model this as a mixed integer non-linear programming (MINLP), capturing joint placement and pricing under agent equilibrium and proving NP-hardness. We derive a tractable NE reformulation for the coupled congestion game, and introduce ABO-MPN, a scalable two-layer approximation combining behavioural decomposition and integer adjustment. Empirical results show 10–40% social cost reduction over baselines.

2 Literature Review

Research on congestion games has established a foundational framework for modelling strategic interactions over shared resources. Rosenthal's seminal work [20] introduced pure-strategy equilibria in non-atomic congestion games, later extended to capture agent heterogeneity, resource-specific costs, and continuous strategies [17]—key for transportation, cloud computing, and network routing [21,24]. However, most studies focus on single-resource settings such as road networks [16], public facilities [1], or cloud bandwidth [23], optimising either placement [2,13,16,26] or pricing [8,18,25,27], rarely both. When joint siting and pricing are considered, agent responses are often simplified or static (e.g., [3,15]), without fully modelling congestion-aware equilibrium. Our work advances this by explicitly modelling two congestible resource types, charging stations and roads, capturing coupled agent behaviour via equilibrium constraints derived from non-atomic congestion games, and solving the resulting bi-level MINLP using a novel double-layer approximation method (ABO-MPN).

From a MAS perspective, this represents progress in equilibrium-aware planning: Previous MAS approaches have used agent-based simulations (ABS) [22], Reinforcement Learning (RL) [15], or local coordination [14], but rarely structured optimisation with embedded equilibrium reasoning, limiting interpretability. Building on and generalising Network Design Problems [9], which assumes static traffic, we address joint placement and pricing under dynamic, strategic agent responses. This enables interpretable, policy-driven infrastructure planning across domains such as EV charging, cloud provisioning, and emergency response. Unlike ABS or black-box RL, our model delivers transparent, equilibrium-aware policies grounded in game theory, facilitating coordinated decision-making among self-interested agents.

3 Strategic Multi-agent Model

We formalise EV infrastructure planning as a multi-agent, congestion-aware optimisation problem in which a central authority allocates congestible resources, charging stations and road links, while anticipating the strategic responses of self-interested agents.

The authority determines station placement and pricing but does not intervene in individual routing choices or impose traffic controls. The model integrates discrete infrastructure decisions with the equilibrium behaviour of heterogeneous agents, including EV drivers and NCDs, navigating a shared network.

3.1 Network and Agent Definitions

Network: The transportation system is modelled as a directed graph $G = (N, A)$, where N is the set of nodes and A the set of links. Each link $l \in A$ has length d_l and capacity c_l. For each O-D pair $\omega \in W$, let R_ω denote the set of feasible routes. To incorporate charging decisions, we define the set of *extended paths* P_ω, where each path $p = (r, i)$ combines a route $r \in R_\omega$ with a charging node $i \in r$. The mapping $s(p) = i$ specifies the charging location on path p, enabling joint modelling of road and station congestion.
Agents: There are two agent types:
1- Non-Charging Drivers (NCDs): These include non-EVs and EVs that do not need en-route charging. They select routes $r \in R_\omega$ to minimise travel time and contribute only to road congestion.
2- EV Drivers: These agents require en-route charging and select extended paths $p \in P_\omega$ to minimise a cost function including travel time, queuing delay, and charging fees. Their choices affect both road and station congestion.

We assume a non-atomic setting where agents are infinitesimal and act independently, while an atomic variant of this problem is studied in [5]. For each $\omega \in W$, let γ_ω and γ_ω^0 denote the demand of EV drivers and NCDs, respectively. The flow distributions $\mathbf{q}_\omega = (q_{\omega,p})_{p \in P_\omega}$ and $\mathbf{q}_\omega^0 = (q_{\omega,r}^0)_{r \in R_\omega}$ represent the equilibrium traffic distribution for EV drivers and NCDs respectively.
Planner: The Government Authority (GA) determines the number of chargers $x_i \in \mathbb{Z}_{\geq 0}$ and charging price $y_i \geq 0$ at each node $i \in N$. These decisions consider electricity prices e_i, maintenance and rental costs T_i, a total charger budget B, and a profitability constraint requiring that revenue at each node covers operational costs by a factor of $\pi > 1$. Full constraints are detailed in Sect. 3.3.

3.2 Cost Structure and Agent Behaviour

Each EV driver associated with O-D pair ω minimises a weighted sum of travel time, queuing delay, and charging fee. Let λ_1, λ_2, and λ_3 denote the respective weights. The perceived cost for choosing extended path $p \in P_\omega$ is:

$$C_{\omega,p}(\mathbf{Q}) = \lambda_1 F_{\omega,p} + \lambda_2 G_p + \lambda_3 Y_p, \tag{1}$$

with expected cost:

$$C_\omega(\mathbf{Q}) = \sum_{p \in P_\omega} q_{\omega,p} C_{\omega,p}(\mathbf{Q}). \tag{2}$$

Here, $F_{\omega,p}$ captures total travel time over path p, derived from congestion-dependent link costs $f_l = d_l(\gamma_l + \gamma_l^0)/c_l$. The queuing delay G_p estimates expected wait time at the selected station $s(p)$, and Y_p is the flat charging fee at that station.
NCDs follow the same structure, excluding charging-related terms, with expected cost:

$$C_\omega^0(\mathbf{Q}) = \sum_{r \in R_\omega} q_{\omega,r}^0 \lambda_1 F_{\omega,r}, \tag{3}$$

with $F_{\omega,r}$ defined analogously over route r.
This model follows the assumptions in [4], where formulation details are provided.

3.3 Government Authority's Optimisation Problem

The GA acts as a central planner and aims to minimise the total system-wide social cost across all EV drivers and NCDs:

$$\Theta(\mathbf{Q}) = \sum_{\omega \in W} \gamma_\omega C_\omega(\mathbf{Q}) + \gamma_\omega^0 C_\omega^0(\mathbf{Q}). \tag{4}$$

To achieve this, it jointly determines the number of chargers x_i and the charging prices y_i at each node $i \in N$, subject to the following constraints:
Budget Constraint: The total number of installed chargers across the network must not exceed the available budget B, i.e., $\sum_{i \in N} x_i \leq B$.
Profitability constraint: At each charging location i, the total revenue from charging fees must cover e_i and T_i, while also achieving a profit; we consider this profit by $\pi > 1$ coefficient (e.g. $\pi = 1.2$ equals 20% profit margin).
Equilibrium Constraints: The strategy profiles $\mathbf{q}_\omega$ and $\mathbf{q}_\omega^0$ must form an NE under the GA's placement and pricing decisions. That is, no agent can unilaterally reduce their cost by changing strategies. These constraints are non-trivial to derive, as any provisioning policy induces a coupled congestion game among heterogeneous agents. Their equilibrium behaviour depends jointly on road congestion and charging infrastructure conditions. The GA must therefore anticipate these strategic interactions to evaluate its decisions. The formulation of NE constraints is detailed in Sect. 4.
Feasibility Constraints: Charger counts must be non-negative integers ($x_i \in \mathbb{Z}_{\geq 0}$), prices must be non-negative ($y_i \geq 0$), and demand distributions $q_{\omega,p}$ and $q_{\omega,r}^0$ must lie in $[0,1]$ and sum to one for each O-D pair ω.
Formally, the GA solves the following bi-level optimisation problem:

$$\min_{x,y,\mathbf{Q}} \Theta(\mathbf{Q}) \qquad \textbf{GA Problem}$$

$$\text{s.t.} \quad \sum_{i \in N} x_i \leq B,$$

$$\pi \left(\sum_{\omega,p:s(p)=i} \gamma_\omega q_{\omega,p} e_i + x_i T_i \right) \leq \sum_{\omega,p:s(p)=i} \gamma_\omega q_{\omega,p} y_i, \quad \forall i,$$

$$\mathbf{q}_\omega \in \arg\min_{\mathbf{q}_\omega} C_\omega(\mathbf{Q}), \quad \forall \omega, \quad \text{and} \quad \mathbf{q}_\omega^0 \in \arg\min_{\mathbf{q}_\omega^0} C_\omega^0(\mathbf{Q}), \quad \forall \omega,$$

Feasibility constraints.

This bilevel model captures the interplay between centralised planning and decentralised agent responses, embedding agents' optimisation into the planner's objective via implicit equilibrium constraints. To enable tractable reformulation, we next derive explicit conditions representing agent interactions.

4 Agent Equilibrium Modelling and Reformulation

To model decentralised, self-interested agent behaviour, we formulate a coupled congestion game capturing interactions between EV drivers and NCDs. We derive explicit NE conditions to replace the nested optimisation, enabling direct integration of agent responses into the planner's model and supporting solution approaches.

4.1 Coupled Congestion Games

Each driver's cost (Equations (2) and (3)) depends on congestion across shared resources, road links and, for EVs, charging stations, inducing a system of coupled congestion games that capture agent interactions over the infrastructure.
Road congestion: All EV drivers and NCDs contribute to traffic on road links. Their routing decisions affect congestion levels and, in turn, travel costs across the network.
Charging congestion: EV drivers also contribute to congestion at charging stations. Their choice of charging location influences queueing delays and financial costs, which in turn affect their overall extended path selection.

For EV drivers, route and charging station choices are jointly made to minimise a combined cost of travel time, queuing delay, and charging fees. This coupling links the two congestion games, as EV drivers' decisions influence both domains. Consequently, the equilibrium demand reflects strategic behaviour over the integrated transport and charging network. This interdependence is embedded in the GA's problem through implicit equilibrium constraints, which the next subsection makes explicit for tractability.

4.2 Nash Equilibrium Conditions

In non-atomic congestion games, where each agent is infinitesimal and cannot individually impact the system, a demand distribution is at equilibrium if no agent can reduce their cost by unilaterally changing their decision [21]. In our setting, this implies that for each driver type, all strategies (i.e., extended paths for EV drivers and routes for NCDs) used with nonzero flow must yield the minimum possible cost.

For EV drivers, the equilibrium condition is:

$$q_{\omega,p}C_{\omega,p}(\mathbf{Q}) \leq q_{\omega,p}C_{\omega,p'}(\mathbf{Q}), \quad \forall \omega \in W, \ \forall p, p' \in P_{\omega}. \tag{5}$$

For NCDs, a similar equilibrium condition holds for all routes in R_{ω}.

These inequalities ensure demand is allocated only to cost-minimising strategies, jointly characterising the NE of the coupled congestion game. While multiple equilibria may exist, it is well established that in non-atomic congestion games with convex cost functions (with respect to demand distributions), all equilibria induce the same total system cost [21]. Therefore, incorporating any equilibrium profile consistent with Eq. (5) suffices to ensure alignment with the GA's social welfare objective.

This explicit characterisation replaces the original optimisation-based equilibrium constraints with tractable inequalities, enabling their direct integration into the GA's decision problem. However, as shown in the next subsection, the resulting formulation remains computationally intractable. This motivates the approximation framework introduced in the following section.

4.3 Computational Complexity of the Reformulated Problem

Even with NE constraints explicitly stated (Eq. (5)), the reformulated GA problem remains computationally intractable, as formalised in the theorem below.

Theorem 1. *The GA's optimisation problem, after reformulating the equilibrium constraints as explicit inequalities, is NP-hard.*

Proof. The original formulation is a bilevel MINLP, where the upper-level decisions (x, y) determine charging station placement and pricing, and the lower-level captures agent equilibrium distributions **Q**. Solving bilevel MINLPs is known to be NP-hard, even under linear cost assumptions [6]. The reformulated version replaces the lower-level program with equivalent NE constraints. Solving it in polynomial time would imply a polynomial-time solution to the original bilevel problem, which would in turn imply that NP = P, a contradiction to standard complexity-theoretic assumptions.

Moreover, even with fixed pricing and without equilibrium constraints, the problem reduces to a budget-constrained capacitated facility location problem, which is NP-hard [7]. The full model thus inherits this computational hardness. □

5 Solution Methodology

Given the NP-hardness of the GA's reformulated optimisation problem (Sect. 4.3), exact methods become impractical for large networks. To address this, we propose the **A**gent-**B**ased **O**ptimisation of **M**ulti-**P**arameter **N**etworks (**ABO-MPN**), a double-layer framework that balances tractability and solution quality.

5.1 Layer 1: Behavioural Decomposition Based on EV Penetration

We exploit driver population asymmetry to decompose the problem. When EV penetration ($\alpha = \frac{\sum_\omega \gamma_\omega}{\sum_\omega \gamma_\omega + \gamma_\omega^0}$) is low, their impact on congestion is minimal [26]. We first solve a simplified GA-NCD subproblem, excluding EV drivers and chargers, to find NCD equilibrium strategies. These serve as fixed background traffic in the GA-EV subproblem, which then optimises charger placement, pricing, and EV behaviour. This decomposition reduces decision variables per stage, enabling more efficient and scalable analysis.

As EV penetration rate increases, their impact on road usage becomes non negligible, and the independence assumption breaks down. In such cases, we apply an iterative refinement procedure: NCD and EV responses are alternately optimised while holding the other fixed, until convergence (Algorithm 1).

Algorithm 1 ABO-MPN (Layer 1): Decomposition of Driver Behaviour Analysis

```
Require: EV penetration rate α
if α is sufficiently low then
    Stage 1: Solve GA-NCD subproblem
    Solve GA-NCD to compute NCD demand distribution q_ω^0
    Stage 2: Solve GA-EV subproblem
    Fix q_ω^0 as exogenous background traffic
    Solve GA-EV with fixed background to obtain x*, y*, q_ω
else
    Iterative Refinement Procedure
    Initialise q_ω^0
    repeat
        Fix q_ω^0, solve GA-EV to update x, y, q_ω
        Fix q_ω, solve GA-NCD to update q_ω^0
    until Convergence to stable equilibrium
end if
return x*, y*, q_ω, q_ω^0
```

Algorithm 2 ABO-MPN (Layer 2): Integer Adjustment of Placement Decisions

```
Relax the placement variables: x_i ∈ ℝ_{≥0} for all i ∈ N
Solve the relaxed GA-EV problem, yielding relaxed placement x*
Sort fractional parts: x_i* − ⌊x_i*⌋ in descending order
Floor each value: x_i*' = ⌊x_i*⌋
Initial sum: S_initial = Σ_i x_i*'
Adjustment: Δ = Σ_i x_i* − S_initial
for i = 1 to Δ do
    Increment largest fractions: x_i*' = x_i*' + 1
end for
Fix adjusted placements: x*'
Re-solve GA-EV to optimise pricing y and EV distribution q_ω
```

5.2 Layer 2: Integer Adjustment for Placement Decisions

The GA-EV subproblem involves integer charger placement variables that limit scalability. To overcome this, we first solve a relaxed version with continuous variables, then apply a budget-preserving rounding algorithm (Algorithm 2). It sorts and selectively rounds fractional values to maintain feasibility and minimise deviation. A final

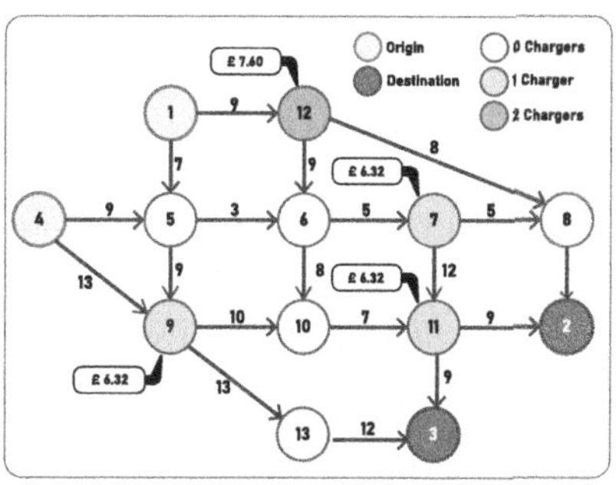

Fig. 1. Nguyen-Dupuis Network: Optimal placement and pricing in the network.

Table 1. ABO-MPN Layer 2 Accuracy Evaluation

Metric	$\lambda_2 = 0.5$ $B \geq 7$	$\lambda_2 = 2$ $B \geq 7$	$\lambda_2 = 4$ $B \geq 7$	$\lambda_2 = 2$ $B = 3$
Social Cost (Adjusted x)	5388.64	5605.75	5819.28	5841.38
Social Cost (Relaxed x)	5349.64	5604.21	5815.10	5787.46
Difference (%)	0.72	0.02	0.07	0.90

re-optimisation updates pricing and EV flows based on fixed placements. As shown in Sect. 6, this approach yields near-optimal designs with minimal error and negligible impact on solution quality.

6 Experimental Evaluation

We evaluate the ABO-MPN framework on standard transportation networks, focusing on solution quality and approximation accuracy. The results demonstrate that ABO-MPN delivers near-optimal infrastructure policies with substantial social cost reductions, while maintaining computational tractability. The framework is implemented in Python using Pyomo and solved with the IPOPT nonlinear solver. While multiple networks are considered, detailed results are presented for the widely used Nguyen-Dupuis (ND) network [19], a common benchmark in EV infrastructure planning [2,10,11].

6.1 Benchmark Network and Parameters

The ND network consists of 13 nodes, 19 links, and 4 O-D pairs: $W = \{(1,2),(1,3),(4,2),(4,3)\}$ (Figure 1). Following the SUMO-based study [2], we use 10 common routes and 54 extended paths. Key parameters are: $(\lambda_1, \lambda_2, \lambda_3) = (1,2,3)$, $c_l = 200$, $\mu = 4$, $T_i = 10$, and $\alpha = 13\%$, with 460 driver agents ($\gamma_\omega = 15, \gamma_\omega^0 = 100$ for all O-D pairs). Electricity prices e_i are drawn from $[5,7]$ for non-O-D nodes and $[11,15]$ for O-D nodes to reflect urban grid stress.

6.2 Evaluating ABO-MPN on a Standard Test Case

We solve the GA problem using ABO-MPN to optimise charger placement, pricing, and EV behaviour. Figure 2 (left) shows social cost declines with increasing budget, but plateaus at $B = 7$, beyond which additional chargers yield no further benefit. This plateau occurs because adding chargers beyond $B = 7$ results in over-installation in low-demand areas, increasing costs without improving access or reducing queues. The optimal policy at $B \geq 7$ installs chargers at nodes 7, 9, 11, and 12. Figure 1 illustrates the resulting network configuration.

6.3 Comparison with State-of-the-Art Methods

We benchmark our Joint Optimisation framework against two baselines: *Price Optimisation*, which uses uniform charger placement and optimises pricing, and *Placement Optimisation*, which fixes pricing and optimises locations—following prior works (Sect. 2). As shown in Fig. 2 (right), Joint Optimisation consistently outperforms both, with social cost improvements starting at 10% and exceeding 40% at $B = 52$. By aligning placement and pricing with demand and local costs, it avoids inefficiencies from over-installation or mispricing, enabling more effective infrastructure deployment.

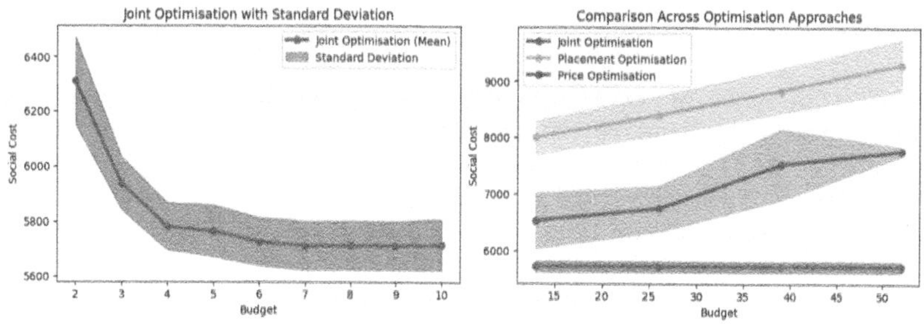

Fig. 2. *Left:* Social cost vs. budget for the joint model, showing diminishing returns beyond $B=7$, with shaded regions indicating standard deviation over random parameters across e values. *Right:* Joint Optimisation outperforms benchmarks by at least 10% across all budgets, with over 40% gain at $B=52$, highlighting the value of joint placement and pricing.

6.4 Evaluation of ABO-MPN Approximation Accuracy

We evaluate the accuracy of each level in the ABO-MPN approximation framework:
Layer 1: Behavioural Decomposition. We validate the independence assumption by comparing NCD equilibrium flows in decomposed and joint models. The observed deviation is less than 1%, justifying the simplification under low EV penetration rates.
Layer 2: Integer Adjustment. We first solve the GA-EV problem with relaxed (continuous) placement variables x, then apply Algorithm 2 to obtain integer solutions within budget. Table 1 shows that the social cost deviation between relaxed and integer solutions stays below 1%, with a maximum of 0.9%. As the relaxed solution upper-bounds the true optimum, this yields a conservative estimate of the framework's optimality gap.

7 Conclusion

This work tackles the strategic planning of interdependent, congestible infrastructure in settings with self-interested, congestion-aware agents. Focusing on EV fast-charging, we propose a joint optimisation framework for station placement and pricing, anticipating agent responses via equilibrium modelling. We formulate the problem as a bilevel MINLP, with agent behaviour captured by a coupled non-atomic congestion game. To manage its complexity, we introduce ABO-MPN, a two-layer approximation method combining behavioural decomposition and integer relaxation.

Results show that joint optimisation consistently outperforms pricing- or placement-only baselines, reducing social cost by over 10% and up to 40% in high-budget scenarios. The framework ensures operator profitability, enhances public utility, and is robust to behavioural and network variations.

From a MAS perspective, this work contributes a generalisable framework for coordination -aware resource planning, integrating decentralised agent behaviour with centralised, interpretable optimisation. Future work could extend to dynamic pricing, grid constraints, or competitive multi-provider settings.

References

1. Aboolian, R., Karimi, M.: Location of public facilities under congestion. In: Uncertainty in Facility Location Problems, pp. 251–280. Springer (2023). https://doi.org/10.1007/978-3-031-32338-6_10
2. Abdalrahman, A., Zhuang, W.: PEV charging infrastructure siting based on spatial–temporal traffic flow distribution. IEEE Trans. Smart Grid **10**(6), 6115–6125 (2019). https://doi.org/10.1109/TSG.2019.2896697
3. Adil, M., Mahmud, M.A.P., Kouzani, A.Z., Khoo, S.Y.: Optimal location and pricing of electric vehicle charging stations using machine learning and Stackelberg game. IEEE Trans. Ind. Appl. **60**(3), 4708–4722 (2024). https://doi.org/10.1109/TIA.2024.3364579
4. Aminikalibar, N., Farhadi, F., Chli, M.: A game-theoretic framework for intelligent EV Charging network optimisation in smart cities. In: To appear in IEEE 28th International Conference on Intelligent Transportation Systems (ITSC) (2025)
5. Aminikalibar, N., Farhadi, F., Chli, M.: Game-theoretic optimisation of ev charging network: placement and pricing strategies via atomic congestion game. In Proceedings of the UK AI Conference 2024. Proceedings of Machine Learning Research (PMLR), vol. 295, pp. 43–52 (2025). https://proceedings.mlr.press/v295/aminikalibar25a.html
6. Ben-Ayed, O., Blair, C.E.: Computational difficulties of bilevel linear programming. Oper. Res. **38**(3), 556–560 (1990)
7. Cornuéjols, G., Fisher, M.L., Nemhauser, G.L.: Exceptional paper–location of bank accounts to optimize float: An analytic study of exact and approximate algorithms. Manage. Sci. **23**(8), 789–810 (1977)
8. Fescioglu-Unver, N., Aktaş, M.Y.: Electric vehicle charging service operations: a review of machine learning applications for infrastructure planning, control, pricing and routing. Renew. Sustain. Energy Rev. **188**, 113873 (2023). https://doi.org/10.1016/j.rser.2023.113873
9. Farahani, R.Z., Miandoabchi, E., Szeto, W.Y., Rashidi, H.: A review of urban transportation network design problems. Eur. J. Oper. Res. **229**(2), 281–302 (2013). https://doi.org/10.1016/j.ejor.2013.01.001
10. Fathollahi, A., Gheisarnejad, M., Boudjadar, J., Homayounzadeh, M., Khooban, M.-H.: Optimal design of wireless charging electric buses-based machine learning: a case study of Nguyen-Dupuis network. IEEE Trans. Veh. Technol. **72**(7), 8449–8458 (2023)
11. Ferro, G., Minciardi, R., Parodi, L., Robba, M.: Planning for electric vehicles: a stochastic user equilibrium approach for joint traffic assignment and energy demand assignment. In: Optimization of Electric-Vehicle Charging: Scheduling and Planning Problems, pp. 115–137. Springer (2024). https://doi.org/10.1007/978-3-031-61917-5_7
12. International Energy Agency (IEA), Global EV outlook 2023 (2023). https://www.iea.org/reports/global-ev-outlook-2023
13. Jung, J., Chow, J.Y.J., Jayakrishnan, R., Park, J.Y.: Stochastic dynamic itinerary interception refueling location problem with queue delay for electric taxi charging stations. Trans. Res. Part C: Emerging Technol. **40**, 123–142 (2014)
14. Joe, W., Lau, H.C.: Coordinating multi-party vehicle routing with location congestion via iterative best response. In: Rosenfeld, A., Talmon, N. (eds.) EUMAS 2021. LNCS (LNAI), vol. 12802, pp. 72–88. Springer, Cham (2021). https://doi.org/10.1007/978-3-030-82254-5_5
15. Li, Y., Wang, J., Wang, W., Liu, C., Yun, L.: Dynamic pricing based electric vehicle charging station location strategy using reinforcement learning. Energy **281**, 128284 (2023)
16. Metais, M.O., Jouini, O., Perez, Y., Berrada, J., Suomalainen, E.: Too much or not enough? planning electric vehicle charging infrastructure: a review of modeling options. Renew. Sustain. Energy Rev. **153**, 111719 (2022)

17. Milchtaich, I.: Congestion games with player-specific payoff functions. Games Econom. Behav. **13**(1), 111–124 (1996)
18. Narayan, A., Krishna, A., Misra, P., Vasan, A., Sarangan, V.: A dynamic pricing system for electric vehicle charging management using reinforcement learning. IEEE Intell. Transp. Syst. Mag. **14**(6), 122–134 (2022)
19. Nguyen, S., Dupuis, C.: An efficient method for computing traffic equilibria in networks with asymmetric transportation costs. Transp. Sci. **18**(2), 185–202 (1984)
20. Rosenthal, R.W.: A class of games possessing pure-strategy Nash equilibria. Internat. J. Game Theory **2**, 65–67 (1973)
21. Roughgarden, T., Tardos, É.: How bad is selfish routing? J. ACM **49**(2), 236–259 (2002)
22. Sadeghi Garjan, M., Chaanine, T., Pasquale, C., Pastore, V.P., Ferrando, A.: Agamas: A new agent-oriented traffic simulation framework for SUMO. In: Proceedings of the European Conference on Multi-Agent Systems, pp. 396–405. Springer (2023). https://doi.org/10.1007/978-3-031-43264-4_25
23. Sun, X., Wang, Z., Wu, Y., Che, H., Jiang, H.: A price-aware congestion control protocol for cloud services. J. Cloud Comput. **10**(1), 1–15 (2021). https://doi.org/10.1186/s13677-021-00271-5
24. Wardrop, J.G.: Some theoretical aspects of road traffic research. Proc. Inst. Civ. Eng. **1**(3), 325–362 (1952)
25. Xiong, Y., Gan, J., An, B., Miao, C., Soh, Y.C.: Optimal pricing for efficient electric vehicle charging station management. In Proc. AAMAS, pp. 749–757 (2016)
26. Xiong, Y., Gan, J., An, B., Miao, C., Bazzan, A.L.C.: Optimal electric vehicle fast charging station placement based on game theoretical framework. IEEE Trans. Intell. Transp. Syst. **19**(8), 2493–2504 (2018). https://doi.org/10.1109/TITS.2017.2754382
27. Zhao, Z., Lee, C.K.M.: Dynamic pricing for EV charging stations: a deep reinforcement learning approach. IEEE Trans. Trans. Electrification **8**(2), 2456–2468 (2021)

AI-Driven Adaptive Learning for Higher Education

Yao Yao(✉) and Horacio González–Vélez

National College of Ireland, Dublin, Ireland
{yao.yao,horacio}@ncirl.ie

Abstract. Adaptive learning refers to approaches that dynamically tailor content, pacing, and feedback to an individual learner's progress, preferences, and prior knowledge. Large Language Models (LLMs) and Artificial Intelligence (AI) agents are transforming the landscape of higher education by enabling new forms of personalized, interactive, and adaptive learning. This paper argues for the intentional integration of AI agents powered by LLM into higher education to support adaptive learning grounded in the established pedagogical framework (Bloom's Taxonomy). We propose that such an AI system can serve not merely as automated content providers but as intelligent, dialogic partners that guide learners across cognitive levels and disciplines through real-time feedback, personalized support, and collaborative knowledge construction. Drawing from educational theory and a practical use case developed by the authors, we demonstrate how knowledge-driven Human-AI interaction can be applied to diverse learning tasks to enhance learner engagement, cognitive development, and instructional scalability. This paper advocates for a future where AI agents augment rather than replace instruction, enabling meaningful, personalized, and cognitively rich learning experiences in higher education.

Keywords: Large Language Models · Agent-based System · Adaptive Learning · Human-AI Interaction

1 Introduction

Artificial Intelligence (AI), particularly through Large Language Models (LLMs) such as GPT [15], Llama [24], and Gemini [8], is increasingly reshaping how education is delivered and experienced. In the context of higher education, where the complexity of domain-specific knowledge and learner diversity continues to grow, researchers are increasingly urging them to explore more flexible, in-depth, and personalized learning approaches. Within this evolving academic environment, both students and educators face mounting challenges in delivering individualized learning experiences, fostering meaningful engagement, and managing increasingly intricate knowledge domains [22]. The widespread deployment of AI technologies, especially LLMs, has brought renewed attention to the potential

M. Baldoni et al. (Eds.): EUMAS 2025, LNAI 16259, pp. 226–235, 2026.
https://doi.org/10.1007/978-3-032-22820-8_14

of adaptive learning as a powerful solution to these demands. The rapid development of AI technologies provides both promise and practical tools to address these evolving needs [5]. Embedding LLMs into AI-powered agents offers more than automation. These models show the potential to become active participants in the learning process [10]. With growing capabilities in dialogic interaction, real-time feedback, personalized scaffolding, and responsiveness to learner needs, AI models are increasingly aligned with the principles of adaptive learning.

Adaptive learning refers to instructional approaches that dynamically tailor content, pacing, and feedback to an individual learner's progress, preferences, and prior knowledge [17]. AI agents, particularly those powered by LLMs, enable this adaptivity through the analysis of learner input, tracking of engagement patterns, and generation of personalized recommendations. Unlike traditional static e-learning platforms, LLMs can interpret subtle questions, simulate Socratic dialogue, explain domain knowledge, and even co-construct new knowledge with learners. These capabilities make AI agents not merely content providers, but conversational partners that support learners across a wide range of cognitive tasks [14].

In addition, the integration of AI technologies with established pedagogical frameworks such as Bloom's Taxonomy introduces new and effective pathways for implementing adaptive learning. Bloom's Taxonomy is a foundational model that categorizes learning objectives into six hierarchical levels: remembering, understanding, applying, analyzing, evaluating, and creating [11]. AI agents can be used to support learners at each of these levels, providing instruction that is customized to their individual profiles and learning contexts. From facilitating factual recall through quizzes or summaries to enabling higher-order cognitive processes such as critical analysis, synthesis, and creative problem-solving, LLMs are capable of adapting their support based on learners' current stage of mastery.

However, many existing digital learning systems continue to prioritize efficiency and automation over the interactive and adaptive qualities that are central to deep learning. This paper contends that the goal of integrating AI agents and LLMs into higher education should extend beyond the efficient delivery of instructional content. Instead, it should focus on enhancing learner content interactions. By leveraging AI to provide real-time feedback, support peer collaboration, and uncover personalized learning pathways, learners can be empowered to construct adaptive learning environments tailored to their individual goals and contexts. Recent research has shown that AI tools with human-like communicative abilities can enhance learner motivation, increase engagement, and facilitate knowledge construction through dialogue [2,21]. Therefore, the key to effective AI integration lies in designing Human-AI systems that support interaction, reflection, and personalization.

2 Intersections of AI Agent, Pedagogy, and Adaptive Learning

This paper argues that the effective integration of AI agents and LLMs in higher education should prioritize adaptive learning through Human-AI interaction, rather than treating AI as a passive content delivery mechanism. While much of the discourse around AI in education emphasizes automation and scalability, we contend that the most transformative potential of AI lies in its ability to augment interactive learning experiences by supporting tailored feedback, facilitating Human-AI dialogue, and enabling AI models to better understand and respond to student needs.

2.1 Personalized Adaptive Learning Through Bloom's Levels

As higher education adapts to diverse learners and complex content, two key frameworks, adaptive learning and Bloom's Taxonomy, offer valuable guidance for personalized, effective instruction. Adaptive learning tailors content, pacing, and feedback in real time based on a learner's performance and needs, unlike traditional one-size-fits-all approaches [4]. Bloom's Taxonomy outlines six levels of cognitive learning (remembering, understanding, applying, analyzing, evaluating, and creating), providing a structured path from basic recall to advanced thinking skills [16].

Integrating Bloom's Taxonomy into AI-powered adaptive learning systems allows more pedagogically grounded personalization. AI agents can be designed to support each level of the taxonomy: delivering factual content and summaries for knowledge recall, prompting conceptual explanations, guiding application through problem-solving tasks, facilitating analytical thinking through comparisons or critiques, and even co-creating content with learners in creative tasks. LLMs are particularly well suited for this integration, as they can generate adaptive prompts, challenge assumptions, and foster critical thinking through dialogue, while adjusting to the development stage of the learner [9]. Together, AI-powered adaptive learning and Bloom's Taxonomy form a complementary foundation for designing AI-enhanced educational experiences that are both responsive and cognitively rich [23]. By aligning AI systems with these pedagogical principles, it becomes possible to move beyond static, efficiency-driven instruction toward more human-centered, meaningful, and personalized learning in higher education.

In here, Bloom's Taxonomy offers a theoretical model for cognitive development, while adaptive learning provides the technological means to implement and personalize this progression. Together, they form a powerful synergy that supports mastery learning by ensuring that learners not only advance, but do so with depth and comprehension appropriate to their level. In contrast to traditional approaches, we can conclude the following advantages such as personalized learning [6], assessment alignment [7], targeted remediation [23], scalability of cognitive complexity [19], and data-driven instructional design [18] for this new method.

2.2 The Implementation Based on AI Agents Powered by LLMs

While adaptive learning and Bloom's Taxonomy each offer strong conceptual foundations for personalized and cognitively scaffolded education, implementing them effectively in real-world higher education settings remains a challenge [29]. Traditional instructional systems often lack the responsiveness, contextual understanding, and scalability required to adaptively guide learners through the complex spectrum of cognitive objectives outlined by Bloom's Taxonomy. To bridge this gap, AI-powered agents, particularly those based on LLM, emerge as essential technologies to operationalize this pedagogical alignment.

AI agents driven by LLMs can simulate the role of intelligent tutors by interpreting open-ended student inputs, generating tailored responses, and engaging in real-time dialogue that aligns with the learner's cognitive level [1]. For instance, a student grappling with foundational concepts may benefit from prompts that reinforce understanding and recall (lower-order thinking), while more advanced learners can be challenged with tasks involving critical evaluation, synthesis, or the creation of novel ideas (higher-order thinking). This dynamic adaptability directly mirrors the hierarchical structure of Bloom's Taxonomy and enables instruction to be finely tuned to the learner's evolving cognitive state.

With a review of recent research in this area, we found that using AI agents to implement personalized adaptive learning can have the following particular advantages. They include pedagogical advantages [25], accessibility [3], cognitive & emotional support [26] and scalability [20]. Moreover, these AI systems support adaptivity not only in terms of content delivery but also in metacognitive engagement through providing a Human-AI interaction. They can provide formative feedback, pose reflective questions, and guide learners through inquiry-based exploration [12].

3 Using an Agent-Based System to Support Adaptive Learning

To concretize our position and demonstrate its practical relevance, we present a use case based on our developing system that integrates AI agents and LLMs to support adaptive learning in higher education. This implementation embodies the theoretical foundations discussed earlier, namely adaptive learning principles and Bloom's Taxonomy, by enabling real-time dialog-based personalization tailored to individual learners' cognitive levels and disciplinary needs. The system serves as an applied example of how AI-powered agents can facilitate meaningful learner engagement, scaffold complex thinking processes, and promote self-directed learning pathways. Through this case, we illustrate how such technology can move beyond static content delivery to become a dynamic partner in the co-construction of knowledge.

3.1 The Implementation of AI Agents

The approach discussed in this section aims to perform a set of AI agents that are separately supported by the corresponding LLMs to cover the diverse knowledge at different levels under the same learning process. All these agents work together to present a systematic strategy for efficiently traversing the relevant knowledge of the given topic and finally integrating all related structural knowledge into the final response to the user's request. For each single agent in the system, it takes the user's request or another agent's output as input and works independently on its own predefined knowledge. Figure 1 shows an outline of the general workflow of agents in the system.

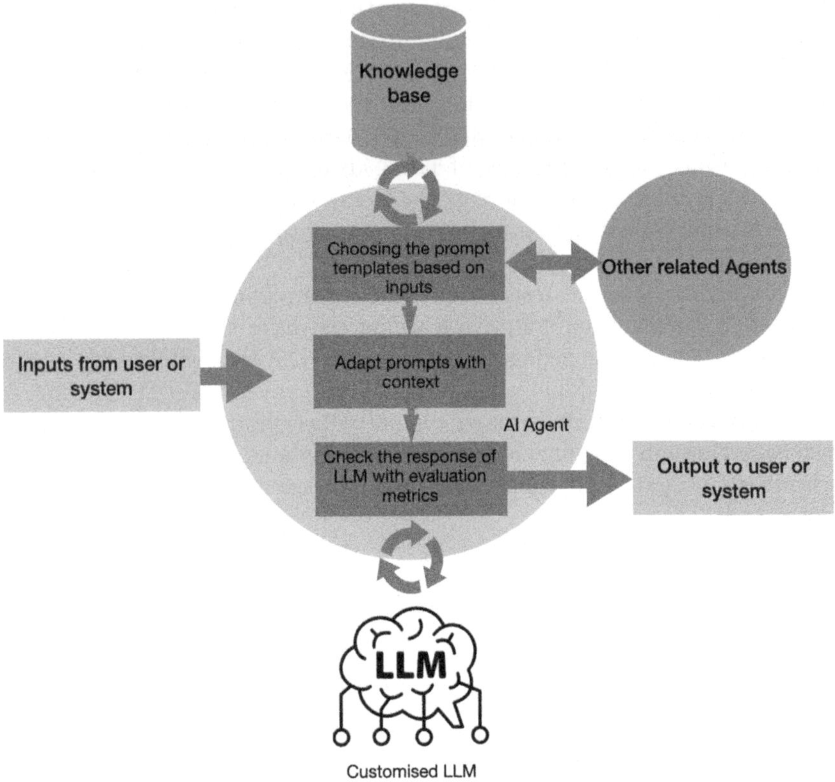

Fig. 1. The outline of the AI agent workflow.

After the user makes a request, the system will assign the corresponding agents with particular tasks according to the context of the input. As shown in the figure above, the predefined knowledge is retrieved from the knowledge base by the agents individually, and then each agent uses the knowledge to synthesize the prompt for interacting with LLMs. Knowledge also includes evaluation metrics to validate the agent's output.

3.2 Knowledge Management with Multiple Agents

In the proposed system, predefined domain-specific knowledge is classified and stored separately in the knowledge base based on the corresponding topics. At the beginning of a task, the system will analyze user inputs and identify the relevant knowledge available in the knowledge base. Based on the related knowledge, the system will assign the corresponding agent for each topic in the task. Single agents will generate the list of their related knowledge based on their task description and use the list to retrieve knowledge from the knowledge base. With retrieved knowledge, the agent uses the Retrieval-Augmented Generation (RAG) [13] method to generate the corresponding output for its task. In the proposed system, predefined domain-specific knowledge is classified and stored separately in the knowledge base based on the corresponding topics. At the beginning of a task, the system will analyze user inputs and identify the relevant knowledge available in the knowledge base. Based on the related knowledge, the system will assign the corresponding agent for each topic in the task. Single agents will generate the list of their related knowledge based on their task description and use the list to retrieve knowledge from the knowledge base. With retrieved knowledge, the agent uses the Retrieval-Augmented Generation (RAG) [13] method to generate the corresponding output for its task. The relationship between tasks, e.g., corresponding dependency of tasks, is specified in the correspondence of concepts on the knowledge base, and the collaboration between agents depends on the relationship of tasks.

In here, we use multiple agents implemented in a ReAct paradigm [27] to facilitate the knowledge management of particular tasks. This approach allows to use individual agents inquiring for fragmental knowledge with a particular given context and integrating the context of previous inquiries in the subsequent prompts. By this, LLMs can focus on the specific context each time to retrieve more elaborated knowledge and then systematically conclude the previously extracted knowledge on a higher level. For example, the system can first integrate multi-domain knowledge related to the course and then use agents related to the pedagogy model (i.e., Bloom's Taxonomy) to optimize the output formatting, control the learning progress, and review the output quality.

3.3 Adaptive Learning Process Based on Human-AI Interaction

In this system, another important aspect in which AI technology can help adaptive learning is to enhance the interactivity of the learning process and provide timely feedback. The Human-AI interaction is presented in the form of a chatbot. The system will take the content of the conversation between the user and AI bot as input and require the agent of the relevant knowledge domain to integrate and make the corresponding optimization adjustments and explanations. More details of the implementation and the relevant dialogue design can be found in previous research [28]. Figure 2 shows an example of how agents handle the Human-AI interaction with user requests in the proposed system. As shown in the figure, the user wants to upload personal profile information to help the AI system better understand the learning characteristics and career planning, and hopes that the AI system will recommend relevant courses of interest based on such information.

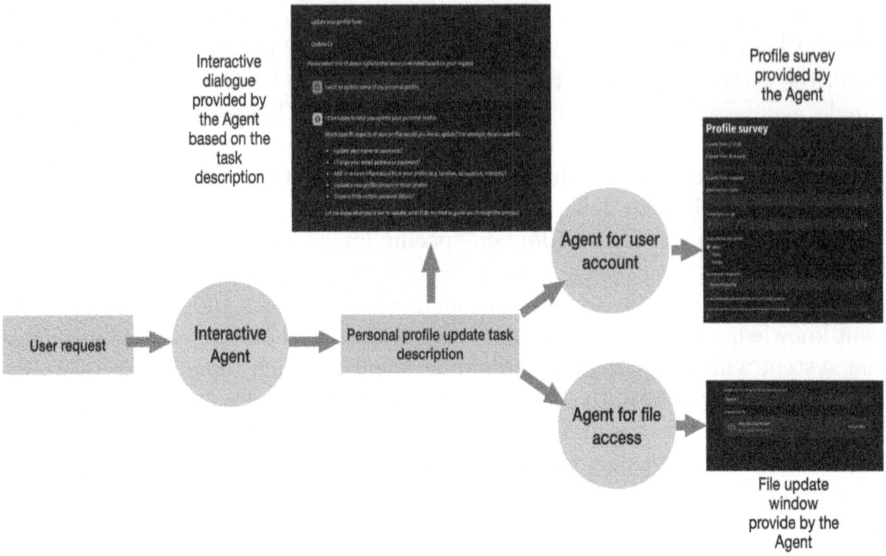

Fig. 2. The demonstration of Human-AI interaction.

4 Customized Knowledge and Personalized Profiles

A central premise of this paper is that adaptive learning in higher education must move beyond static personalization and incorporate context-aware mechanisms that respond to learners' evolving cognitive states and knowledge gaps. Two key components supporting this are customized knowledge and personalized profiles.

In the proposed framework, all knowledge (customized content and learner data) is integrated into a unified knowledge graph to support adaptive decision-making. Together, customized knowledge and personalized profiles enable a more nuanced form of adaptivity, one that is not merely reactive, but anticipatory and learner-driven. Figure 3 shows an example of the use of diverse knowledge to support the different tasks in the practical use case. All knowledge retrieved from the knowledge base is represented as three styles corresponding to the different coloured boxes in the figure. Blue colour represents Customized Knowledge; Green colour for Workflow Knowledge and yellow colour for Personalized Profiles.

In the presented example, we evaluated three distinct tasks:

1. Generating personalized learning advice for learners
2. Assessing individual learning levels of learners
3. Generating customized learning materials (e.g., quiz questions) based on the learner's profile

For each task, we run different use cases 10 times to demonstrate the diversity of knowledge support in each task context and conclude the result as in the Fig. 3. The proportion of knowledge is calculated by the number of tokens retrieved from the knowledge base against the total tokens used throughout the process.

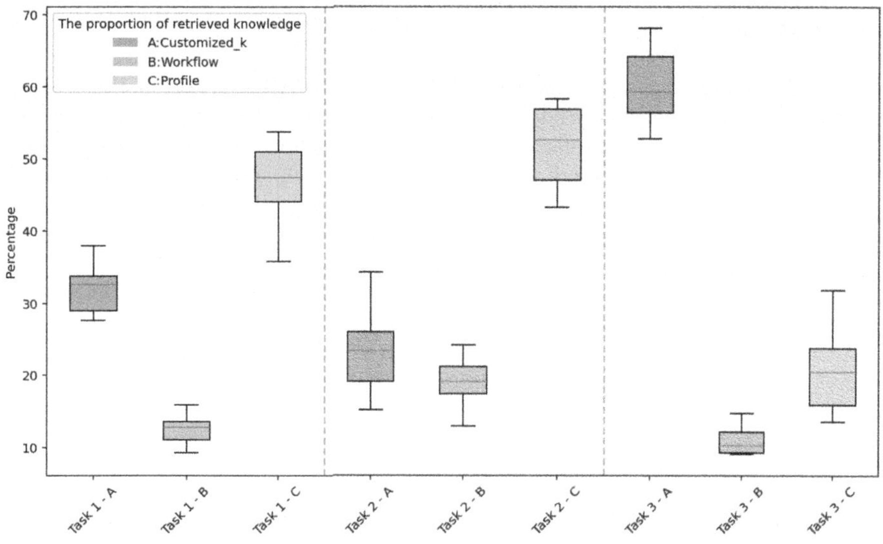

Fig. 3. The proportion of retrieved knowledge in different styles.

5 Conclusion

The integration of LLMs and AI agents into higher education presents a compelling opportunity to reshape how personalized and cognitively diverse learning experiences are designed and delivered. As demonstrated in our proposed approach and the supporting use case, AI-driven systems have the potential to transcend the limitations of traditional e-learning platforms by enabling real-time adaptivity, dialogic engagement, and cross-disciplinary knowledge synthesis.

In conclusion, this paper argues that the meaningful integration of AI agents and LLMs, guided by established pedagogy theories, represents a transformative opportunity for higher education. Rather than delivering knowledge, AI should augment instruction by fostering adaptive, personalized, and interactive learning experiences that are both scalable and grounded in deep cognitive engagement. Future work must continue to bridge the gap between pedagogical theory and AI design, ensuring that emerging educational technologies are not only innovative but also human-centered and instructionally effective.

Acknowledgments. This work is developed under the auspice of "DIGITAL4Business: Masters Programme focused on the practical application of Advanced Digital Skills within European Companies" https://digital4business.eu/, a project funded under Grant No.: 101084013 by the Digital Europe Programme.

Disclosure of Interests. The authors have no competing interests to declare that are relevant to the content of this article.

References

1. Al-Abri, A.: Exploring chatgpt as a virtual tutor: a multi-dimensional analysis of large language models in academic support. Educ. Inform. Technol., 1–36 (2025)
2. Alam, A., Mohanty, A.: Educational technology: exploring the convergence of technology and pedagogy through mobility, interactivity, ai, and learning tools. Cogent Eng. **10**(2), 2283282 (2023)
3. Bozkir, E., Özdel, S., Lau, K.H.C., Wang, M., Gao, H., Kasneci, E.: Embedding large language models into extended reality: opportunities and challenges for inclusion, engagement, and privacy. In: Proceedings of the 6th ACM Conference on Conversational User Interfaces, pp. 1–7 (2024)
4. Essa, S.G., Celik, T., Human-Hendricks, N.E.: Personalized adaptive learning technologies based on machine learning techniques to identify learning styles: a systematic literature review. IEEE Access **11**, 48392–48409 (2023)
5. Gligorea, I., Cioca, M., Oancea, R., Gorski, A.T., Gorski, H., Tudorache, P.: Adaptive learning using artificial intelligence in e-learning: A literature review. Educ. Sci. **13**(12), 1216 (2023)
6. Hang, C.N., Tan, C.W., Yu, P.D.: Mcqgen: a large language model-driven mcq generator for personalized learning. IEEE Access (2024)
7. Hwang, K., Challagundla, S., Alomair, M., Chen, L.K., Choa, F.S.: Towards ai-assisted multiple choice question generation and quality evaluation at scale: aligning with bloom's taxonomy. In: Workshop on Generative AI for Education (2023)
8. Islam, R., Ahmed, I.: Gemini-the most powerful llm: Myth or truth. In: 2024 5th Information Communication Technologies Conference (ICTC), pp. 303–308. IEEE (2024)
9. Jackson, J.: Higher order prompting: applying bloom's revised taxonomy to the use of large language models in higher education. Stud. Technol. Enhanced Learn. **4**(1) (2025)
10. Kabudi, T., Pappas, I., Olsen, D.H.: Ai-enabled adaptive learning systems: a systematic mapping of the literature. Comput. Educ. Artifi. Intell. **2**, 100017 (2021)
11. Krathwohl, D.R.: A revision of bloom's taxonomy: an overview. Theory Pract. **41**(4), 212–218 (2002)
12. Levin, I., Marom, M., Kojukhov, A.: Rethinking ai in education: highlighting the metacognitive challenge. BRAIN. Broad Res. Artifi. Intell. Neurosci. **16**(1 Sup1), 250–263 (2025)
13. Lewis, P., et al.: Retrieval-augmented generation for knowledge-intensive nlp tasks. Adv. Neural Inform. Process. Syst. **33**, 9459–9474 (2020)
14. Li, Q., Xie, Y., Chakravarty, S., Lee, D.: Edumas: a novel llm-powered multi-agent framework for educational support. In: 2024 IEEE International Conference on Big Data (BigData), pp. 8309–8316. IEEE (2024)
15. Lund, B.D., Wang, T.: Chatting about chatgpt: how may ai and gpt impact academia and libraries? Library Hi Tech News **40**(3), 26–29 (2023)
16. Prasad, G.: Evaluating student performance based on bloom's taxonomy levels. J. Phys. Conf. Ser. **1797**, 012063 (2021)
17. Rachmad, Y.E.: Adaptive learning theory (2022)
18. Renu, R.S.: Llm-assisted performance indicators for student outcome assessment. In: 2025 ASEE-GSW Annual Conference (2025)

19. Scaria, N., Chenna, S., Subramani, D.: How good are modern llms in generating relevant and high-quality questions at different bloom's skill levels for indian high school social science curriculum? In: Proceedings of the 19th Workshop on Innovative Use of NLP for Building Educational Applications (BEA 2024), pp. 1–10 (2024)
20. Sharma, S., Mittal, P., Kumar, M., Bhardwaj, V.: The role of large language models in personalized learning: a systematic review of educational impact. Discover Sustainability **6**(1), 1–24 (2025)
21. Singh, T.M., Reddy, C.K.K., Murthy, B.R., Nag, A., Doss, S.: Ai and education: bridging the gap to personalized, efficient, and accessible learning. In: Internet of Behavior-Based Computational Intelligence for Smart Education Systems, pp. 131–160. IGI Global (2025)
22. Soboleva, E.V., et al.: Developing a personalised learning model based on interactive novels to improve the quality of mathematics education. Eurasia J. Math. Sci. Technol. Educ. **18**(2), em2078 (2022)
23. Spanos, A., et al.: Bloomgpt: using chatgpt as learning assistant in relation to bloom's taxonomy of educational objectives. In: Conference Proceedings. The Future of Education 2024 (2024)
24. Vakayil, S., Juliet, D.S., Vakayil, S., et al.: Rag-based llm chatbot using llama-2. In: 2024 7th International Conference on Devices, Circuits and Systems (ICDCS), pp. 1–5. IEEE (2024)
25. Wang, J., Xiao, R., Tseng, Y.J.: Generating ai literacy mcqs: a multi-agent llm approach. In: Proceedings of the 56th ACM Technical Symposium on Computer Science Education, vol. 2, pp. 1651–1652 (2025)
26. Yang, J., Lim, D., Lee, S., Lee, S., Oh, U.: Enhancing emotions in positive way: Llm-based ai using cognitive behavioral therapy for emotional support. Inter. J. Adv. Smart Convergence **14**(1), 247–256 (2025)
27. Yao, S., et al.: React: synergizing reasoning and acting in language models. In: International Conference on Learning Representations (ICLR) (2023)
28. Yao Yao, H.G.V., Croitoru., M.: Explanatory dialogues with active learning for rule-based expertise. In: RuleML+ RR (Companion) (2024)
29. Zhai, X., et al.: A review of artificial intelligence (ai) in education from 2010 to 2020. Complexity **2021**(1), 8812542 (2021)

A 3D Multi-agent Simulation Architecture for Passenger Flow Optimisation in Mobility Hubs

Edgar Baake(✉), Christian Hyttrek, Patrick Pfau, Aliyu Tanko Ali, Tobias Groth, Mohammad Khodaygani, and Stefan Fischer

University of Lübeck, Ratzeburger Allee 160, 23562 Lübeck, Germany
{edgar.baake,c.hyttrek,p.pfau,aliyu.ali,t.groth,m.khodaygani, stefan.fischer}@uni-luebeck.de
https://www.uni-luebeck.de

Abstract. Optimising pedestrian flow in large train stations is a critical challenge with direct implications for public safety, passenger experience, and operational efficiency. However, real-world experimentation with new flow strategies is typically infeasible due to logistical and safety concerns. In this paper, we present the architecture of a modular and extensible multi-agent simulator designed to support the development and evaluation of flow optimisation strategies in complex railway environments. The simulator integrates agent-based pedestrian behaviour, cognitively plausible decision-making, and 3D rendering of a typical German train station setting. It is connected to a data lake which incorporates real-world train schedules, weather data and event information to realistically capture station dynamics. To support systematic analysis, the simulator logs a comprehensive set of behavioural and flow-related metrics—such as agent frustration, rerouting, queueing times, goal success, and information-seeking behaviour—enabling detailed evaluation of crowd dynamics and intervention strategies. Its flexible architecture further supports extensions for sensor simulation, individualised agent messaging, and social choice mechanisms. This paper outlines the simulator's architecture and demonstrates its readiness as a research platform for multi-agent systems in transportation environments.

Keywords: Pedestrian Flow Optimisation · Train Station Simulation · Crowd Dynamics · Agent-Based Modelling · Transportation Infrastructure · Simulation Framework · Public Safety · FPOplus Project

1 Introduction

Optimising pedestrian flow in train stations is difficult to test directly due to logistical and ethical constraints, making simulation an essential tool for analysing interventions under realistic, controlled conditions.

M. Baldoni et al. (Eds.): EUMAS 2025, LNAI 16259, pp. 236–244, 2026.
https://doi.org/10.1007/978-3-032-22820-8_15

This paper presents a dedicated, modular simulation environment integrating real train schedules, weather and event data, 3D station models and cognitively plausible agent behaviour with dynamic pathfinding. Originally developed in the FPOplus project[1] as a data generator for scenarios without sensor coverage, the simulator is adaptable to various station layouts and supports predictive modelling and real-time interventions. The "Hamburg-Harburg" station serves as a representative mid-sized case study.

This paper outlines the simulator's architecture, its capabilities for evaluating crowd dynamics and passenger flow strategies, and its planned extensions. Section 2 reviews related work, Sect. 3 describes the architecture, Sect. 4 discusses capabilities and extensions, and Sect. 5 concludes.

2 Related Work

Pedestrian flow optimisation in large transit hubs requires modelling both infrastructure and heterogeneous agent behaviour. Agent-based modelling (ABM) enables such simulations by representing individual decision-making and interactions [1].

Existing platforms vary in openness, fidelity, and adaptability. Vadere [8] supports multiple pedestrian models within a modular framework; MATSim [7] offers large-scale transport simulation with limited pedestrian extensions; SUMO [9] focuses on intermodal traffic, including pedestrians; AnyLogic [3] provides hybrid modelling but is proprietary; HyPedSim [4] combines macro- and micro-modelling for varied density levels. Empirical projects like CroMa [2] have supplied valuable behavioural datasets for calibration.

Table 1. Comparison of this paper's simulator with established alternatives

Feature	*Simulator*	AnyLogic	MATSim	GAMA	Research[2]
Agent-Based Modeling	Yes	Yes	Yes	Yes	Yes
PT Integration	Yes	Supported	Yes	Supported	Rare
State Machines	Yes	Yes	Yes	Yes	Basic
Agent Cognition	Yes	Limited	No	Limited	Basic
Evaluation Support	Yes	Limited	Yes	Yes	Limited
3D Rendering	Yes	Yes	No	Limited	No
Routing	Yes	Yes	Yes	Yes	Basic
Sensor Simulation	Initialised	Yes	No	Supported	No
Real-time	Planned	Yes	No	Limited	No
Open Source	Planned	No	Yes	Yes	Yes
Extensibility	Yes	Limited	Yes	Yes	Limited

Reflects generalised characteristics of typical research simulators

[1] FPOplus focuses on improving passenger flow dynamics; it is funded by the German Federal Ministry for Digital and Transport.

Many tools, however, lack integrated 3D environments, cognitive agent models and flexible scenario control. Our simulator combines these features with real-time data integration and open extensibility. Table 1 summarises the differences between our simulator and selected alternatives.

3 Simulator Architecture and Design

The simulator is implemented in the open-source Godot engine [5] using GDScript, enabling physics-based agents in a 3D environment. It can operate standalone to generate synthetic data or as part of an interactive system for live evaluations. The architecture Fig. 1 links real-world data from a dedicated data lake to agent spawning, navigation, and cognition modules, allowing realistic simulation of station operations.

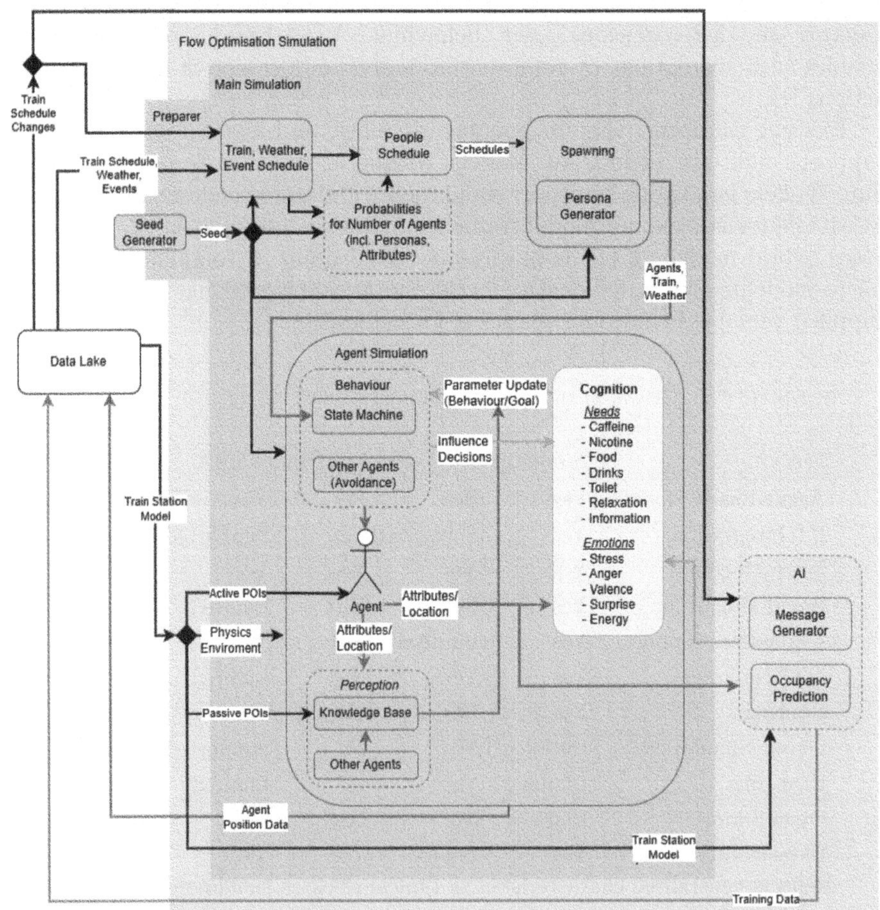

Fig. 1. Architecture overview of the modular simulator.

3.1 Architecture Overview

Real-world data sources – including train schedules, weather, and event information – are aggregated in the data lake and preprocessed by the *Preparer.* This generates schedules for seed-based agent spawning, reflecting probabilistic arrival rates. Agents are assigned personas and mobility attributes, then navigate a 3D model of the station using layered navigation meshes. Behaviour is modelled by state machines, cognitive models, and environmental interactions. Logged metrics are passed to AI modules for occupancy prediction and personalised message generation.

3.2 Simulator Modules

Data Lake. Aggregates and persists train schedules (Deutsche Bahn API), weather (OpenWeatherMap), and event data (scraped from hamburg.de) using AirFlow pipelines.

3D Model. Semi-automatically generated Hamburg-Harburg model with layered walkable areas, collision detection, points of interest (POIs), and spawning/exit points. Also enables intuitive debugging and demonstration of density patterns, routing and agents behaviour.

Prediction Model and Flow Management. Includes an occupancy predictor ($25m^2$ resolution) and message generator for targeted flow optimisation.

Social Choice Function. Compares individual and global utility for decisions like rerouting. Agents may comply or refuse based on persona traits.

Outdoor Navigation. Graphhopper and GTFS data usage to generate passenger itineraries beyond the station, covering local and national destinations.

3.3 Agent Modeling

Spawning. The *Preparer* generates agent schedules from real-world data or prewritten scenarios. The number of agents can be divided into agents travelling exit to exit $N_{\text{exit\_to\_exit}}$, agents coming from an exit N_{in} and agents leaving a train N_{out} and is calculated as:

$$N_{\text{exit\_to\_exit}} = \mu + \sigma$$

$$N_{\text{out}}(t) = min(round(\varphi(\mu \cdot \prod_{i=1}^{k} f_i(t), \sigma)), V(t))$$

$$N_{\text{in}}(t) = round(\varphi(\mu \cdot \prod_{i=1}^{k} f_i(t), \sigma))$$

Parameters include global means (μ, σ), train fill levels $V(t)$ and time-, event-, and weather-dependent multipliers $f_*(t)$. Gaussian noise $\varphi(\mu, \sigma)$ ensures variability.

Personas and Goals. Eleven personas [11] – including commuters, tourists, students and travellers with reduced mobility – are assigned via weighted selection based on spawn rate, train type, travel time, and contextual factors (e.g., events, strikes, weather). Personas define attributes such as speed, crowd avoidance and luggage, which may constrain mobility (e.g., large bags preferring elevators). From these values, three preferences are derived: stair use, crowd avoidance, and path length tolerance, with limits to prevent unrealistic combinations. Agents are assigned primary and, if time allows, secondary goals (e.g., coffee, restroom) based on needs and scenario configuration.

State Machine. The state machine Fig. 2 governs agent behaviour. Agents normally *move* toward their primary goal; time-critical goals trigger *running.* Upon goal completion, agents *exit* or wait for departure. Missed connections cause *replanning. Frustration* thresholds may alter movement or cause withdrawal. *Distraction* and *message reception* states allow modelling of information processing and responsiveness. Agents may pursue a secondary goal which triggers *waiting* at the respective POI for a short duration.

Cognition and Knowledge. Agents maintain a knowledge base initialised by persona traits and updated via interactions with POIs, signage, announcements, or nearby agents. Six needs – drink, food, toilet, nicotine, relaxation, information – have soft and hard thresholds, triggering *replanning* if applicable and routing the agent to the nearest known suitable POI; neglecting needs affects emotional state and behaviour.

4 Evaluation and Scenario Testing

The simulator integrates 3D station modelling with intelligent agents, enabling controlled, reproducible testing of passenger flow strategies. Agent decision-making is shaped by evolving knowledge bases, needs, and environmental conditions. Movements and behavioural states are continuously logged for live or post-hoc analysis of metrics such as dwell times, density, congestion and responsiveness to interventions.

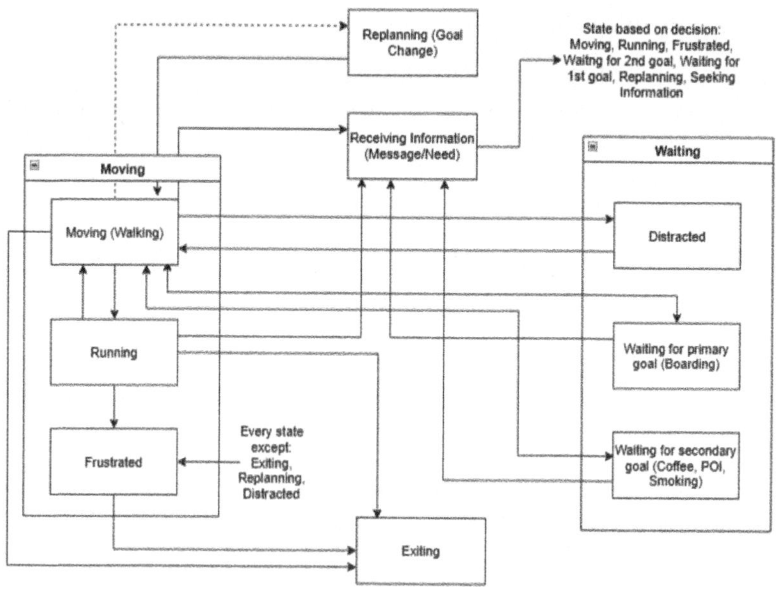

Fig. 2. The state machine: The diagram shows the all different behavioural states an agent can adopt. Dotted connections are temporary.

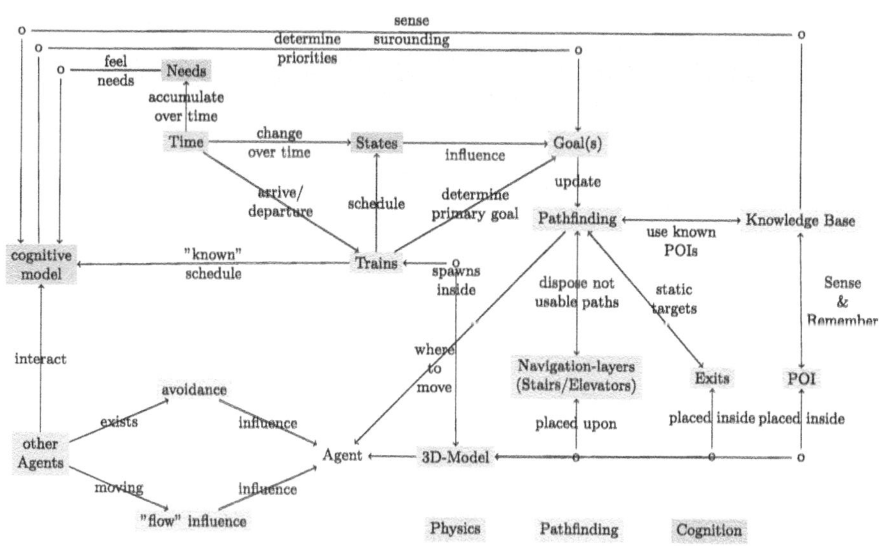

Fig. 3. Influences affecting the agents in run-time. The red influences represent physical restrictions, the blue ones show cognitive decisions about the agent's goals, and the green ones reflect internal path-finding. (Color figure online)

4.1 Flow Optimisation

Routing is based on Godot's layered NavMesh and A* pathfinding, distinguishing surfaces by accessibility (e.g., stairs, elevators) and enabling real-time collision avoidance. A flow influence mechanism models natural trail-following behaviour [10]: agents generate directional flow fields that bias subsequent movement, promoting smooth corridor use and realistic congestion patterns. In contrast to common simulations with active approaches of sensing and reacting [6], flow influence follows a passive mechanic, implicitly modelling trail-following behaviour.

4.2 Scenarios

Scenarios are configured via the Preparer by adjusting persona distributions, arrival rates, or external conditions. Examples include:

- **Delay overflow:** multiple delayed trains increasing platform crowding.
- **Evacuation:** partial or full station clearance under emergency conditions.
- **Messaging trials:** baseline vs. optimised flow using targeted agent messages. Seed-based initialisation ensures exact comparability between runs.

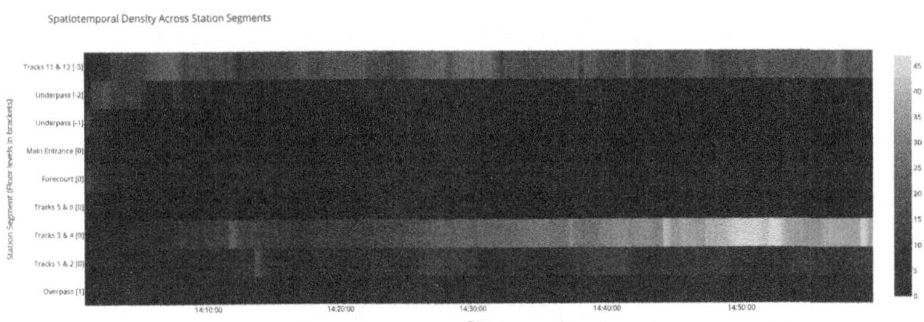

Fig. 4. Heatmap of spatiotemporal density across station segments over time.

4.3 Empirical Evaluation

To assess realism and utility, we simulated Hamburg-Harburg station for one hour (14:00–15:00, 30 Oct 2024) using live schedule data and standard persona distributions. Logged metrics included travel distances, goal switches, queue lengths, congestion speed reductions and POI usage, thus meeting best practices in validation and verification by reflecting both individual agent as well as system-wide conditions [12].

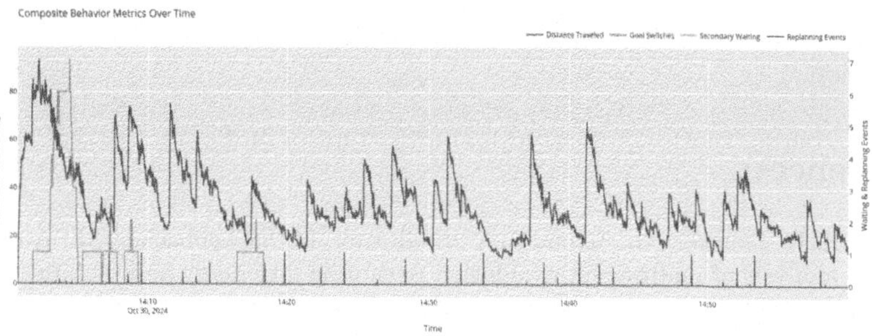

Fig. 5. Composite behaviour metrics over time. Primary axis: distance travelled and goal switches. Secondary axis: secondary waiting and replanning events.

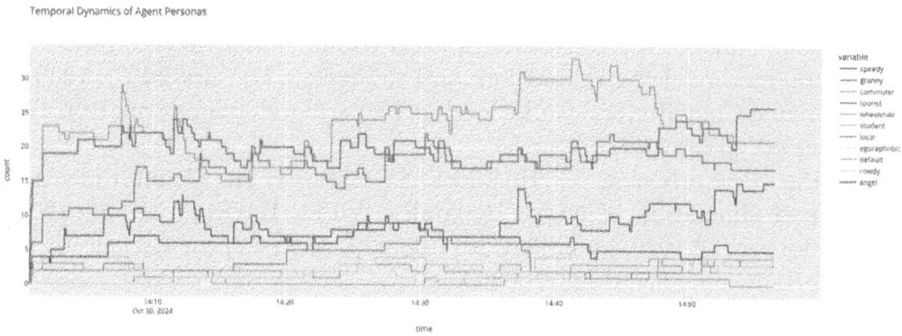

Fig. 6. Temporal evolution of agent personas within the station simulation. Each line represents the persona count at each second over the simulated hour.

Results

- **Density patterns** (Fig. 4) peak at train arrivals, especially near urban railway platforms.
- **Behavioural metrics** (Fig. 5) show rerouting, secondary waits, and distance spikes corresponding to agent spawns.
- **Persona distribution** (Fig. 6) reflects realistic variation across the simulated period.

5 Conclusion

This paper presented a modular, multi-agent simulator for modelling cognitively plausible passenger behaviour in train stations. Developed in the FPOplus project, it combines real-world data, 3D modelling, and detailed agent logic to realistically reproduce crowd dynamics. Its architecture supports predictive and prescriptive modules, including occupancy forecasting, social-choice analysis, and flow-optimising messaging, providing a strong basis for future research. While under development, it already serves as a realistic testbed for flow optimisation strategies. Next steps include full-fledged real-time integration, enhanced behavioural models, seed-based scenario validation and more detailed statistical evaluation.

References

1. Ali, A.T., Leucker, M., Schuldei, A., Stellbrink, L., Sachenbacher, M.: A comparative analysis of multi-agent simulation platforms for energy and mobility management. In: European Conference on Multi-Agent Systems, pp. 295–311. Springer, Cham (2023). https://doi.org/10.1007/978-3-031-43264-4_19
2. Boomers, A.K., et al.: Pedestrian crowd management experiments: a data guidance paper. arXiv preprint arXiv:2303.02319 (2023)
3. Borshchev, A.: Multi-method modelling: anylogic. Discrete-event simulation and system dynamics for management decision making, pp. 248–279 (2014)
4. Dang, H.T., Gaudou, B., Verstaevel, N.: HyPedSim: a multi-level crowd-simulation framework–methodology, calibration, and validation. Sensors **24**(5), 1639 (2024)
5. Godot Engine Contributors: Godot engine. https://godotengine.org (2024), version 4.2. Accessed 06 May 2025
6. Heliövaara, S., Korhonen, T., Hostikka, S., Ehtamo, H.: Counterflow model for agent-based simulation of crowd dynamics. Build. Environ. **48**, 89–100 (2012). https://doi.org/10.1016/j.buildenv.2011.08.020, https://www.sciencedirect.com/science/article/pii/S0360132311002630
7. Horni, A., Nagel, K., Axhausen, K. (eds.): Multi-agent transport simulation MATSim. Ubiquity Press, London (2016). https://doi.org/10.5334/baw
8. Kleinmeier, B., Zönnchen, B., Gödel, M., Köster, G.: Vadere: an open-source simulation framework to promote interdisciplinary understanding. arXiv preprint arXiv:1907.09520 (2019)
9. Lopez, P.A., et al.: Microscopic traffic simulation using sumo. In: The 21st IEEE International Conference on Intelligent Transportation Systems. IEEE (2018). https://elib.dlr.de/124092/
10. Moussaïd, M., Helbing, D., Theraulaz, G.: How simple rules determine pedestrian behavior and crowd disasters. Proc. Natl. Acad. Sci. **108**(17), 6884–6888 (2011). https://doi.org/10.1073/pnas.1016507108
11. Preim, B., Dachselt, R.: Interaktive Systeme: Band 2: User Interface Engineering, 3D-Interaktion, Natural User Interfaces. Springer, Berlin, Heidelberg (2015). https://doi.org/10.1007/978-3-642-45247-5, https://link.springer.com/10.1007/978-3-642-45247-5
12. Sargent, R.G.: Verification and validation of simulation models. J. Simul. **7**(1), 12–24 (2013). https://doi.org/10.1057/jos.2012.20

A Strategyproof Mechanism for Many-to-One One-Sided Matching with Bans

Emma Hovorková(✉) and Tomáš Valla

Faculty of Information Technology, Czech Technical University in Prague, Prague, Czechia
{hovoremm,tomas.valla}@fit.cvut.cz

Abstract. We study the model called Agents to Facilities with Bans Problem (AFB), which belongs to the intersection of algorithmic game theory and stable matching theory: There are m facilities and n agents, each agent has a priority list of the facilities, each facility has a limited capacity and may contain a list of banned agents. We design a mechanism that finds Pareto optimal, minimal envy-2 solution to AFB. We prove that this mechanism is strategyproof and runs in time $O(nm)$.

Keywords: mechanism design · many-to-one matching · minimal envy · Pareto optimality · strategyproofness

1 Introduction

Matching problems, where agents are assigned to one another based on their preferences have been studied in fields such as economics, operations research, and computer science. The seminal work by Gale and Shapley [9] on the marriage problem introduced one-to-one matching, where men and women were assigned to pairs based on their preference. Naturally, the extensions to many-to-one matching came, such as assigning students to schools [1] or residents to hospitals [17]. These problems involve assigning multiple agents to a single facility while respecting capacity constraints and individual preferences. These preferences can be either two-sided or one-sided, depending whether the facilities have preferences or not. A strongly related problem is the House Allocation problem [18] with its capacitated variant [14].

The criteria to ensure fairness and stability of assignments are Pareto optimality, where no individual can improve her utility without making another individual worse off [3] and minimal envy, which minimizes the number of envious agents [13]. Additionally, mechanisms for finding assignments are often proved to be strategyproof, ensuring that agents cannot manipulate outcomes by submitting false preferences [8].

T. Valla—This work was supported by the Czech Science Foundation Grant no. 24-12046S.

M. Baldoni et al. (Eds.): EUMAS 2025, LNAI 16259, pp. 245–260, 2026.
https://doi.org/10.1007/978-3-032-22820-8_16

This paper introduces new many-to-one one-sided model called the Agents to Facilities Problem with Bans (AFB), consisting of a set of n agents and a set of m facilities. Each agent has her preference list, which is a linear order over a set of facilities. Each facility has a capacity and list of banned agents that cannot be assigned to this facility.

In this paper, we contribute to the ongoing research in House Allocation-type problems by extending the capacitated model [14] by the concept of ban lists and study the solution being minimal envy and minimal envy-2 (informally, we aim to minimise the envy among agents in general and among those not assigned to their first choice). As far as we know, this model was not studied before in the context of strategyproofness and envy minimization. As the main result we prove the following theorem.

Theorem 1. *Let us have an instance of the Agents to Facilities with Bans Problem with n agents and m facilities. Then there exists a strategyproof mechanism which computes a Pareto optimal and minimal envy-2 matching in this instance. This mechanism has $O(nm)$ time complexity.*

The model, together with all notions and definitions, is introduced in detail in Sect. 1.2. The mechanism is described in Sect. 3. Its properties clearly follow from Theorems 3, 4 and 5.

The motivation to initiate the research on AFB and related questions originated from a real world problem we were solving: At a summer camp, there are participants (agents) to be assigned to different teams (facilities) taking into account their preferences over teams. However, some of the teams may block selected participants based on their previous experience or age constraint. One may generalize this setting to many other domains, for example assigning workers to projects, players to sport teams, students to selective courses, and many more.

1.1 Related Work

The social choice matching theory was initiated by the famous *Stable Marriage problem* (SM) by Gale and Shapley [9]: A set of males and a set of females are given, each member of these sets has a linear rank list of the opposite set. Gale and Shapley [9] described a polynomial-time mechanism that produces a *stable* solution: no two matched pairs would benefit from swapping their partners.

SM is a special case of bipartite one-to-one two-sided matching, where bipartite means there are two sets of agents. Non-bipartite version would have all agents in one set. Other variants could be many-to-one or many-to-many. Two-sided means that both sides have preferences over the others. In one-sided variation only one side has preferences. Preferences of agents are usually given either as *ordinal preferences* where each agent has an ordered list of the other agents or *cardinal utilities* where each agents expresses her preference in real number valuations.

Another type of matching problems consists of allocating a set of H indivisible goods among a set of A agents. An important problem of this type is the

House allocation problem (HA) introduced by Shapley and Scarf [18]. A set A of n applicants and a set H of m houses is given, each applicant has a *preference list* of a subset of H. Another variant introduced by Manlove and Sng [14] is the *Capacitated House Allocation problem* (CHA) where each house has a capacity.

Abdulkadiroğlu and Sönmez [2] proved that for HA there is always a coalition-free solution, by introducing the *Top Trading Cycles mechanism* (TTC). By coalition in a solution we mean a cycle of agents, where each agent benefits from changing her strategy to a strategy of her successor. Due to Roth [16] we know that TTC is strategyproof. In 2005 Sotomayor [20] gave another proof that HA has a coalition-free solution, based on different techniques.

For a given instance of HA, there can be many Pareto optimal matchings with different amount of assigned agents. In many applications we are interested in assigning as many agents as possible, thus we aim to find a *maximum Pareto optimal matching*. Abraham et al. [3] described a three-phase mechanism to find maximum Pareto optimal matchings, which runs in time $O(\sqrt{n}L)$, where n is the number of applicants and L is the number of acceptable applicant-house pairs. A matching M is *popular* if there is no other matching M' such that the number of agents who prefer their allocation in M' to that in M exceeds the number of agents who prefer their allocation in M to that in M'. Manlove and Sng [14,19] studied the popular matchings in CHA and they showed there is a fast algorithm for finding a largest popular matching.

Next standard property to look for in the solution is to minimize the envy among the applicants. An applicant a envies those other applicants that got the house which a prefers to the house allocated to a. This notion can be extended to the concept of *minimal envy-2* solution: minimize the number of envying applicants and minimize the number of envying applicants in the reduced instance where we remove those applicants that got assigned their top choice. Kondratev and Nesterov [13] presented a mechanism providing a minimal envy-2 matching. We note here that one may reduce AFB to the setting of [13] by considering many copies of each facility, this however causes a nontrivial slowdown. In this paper we provide a different and much faster approach.

Several recent papers study the concept of envy-freeness in the context of house allocation problems. A matching is envy-free if every agent likes her assigned house at least as much as all houses assigned to other agents. Gan et al. [10] present a polynomial-time algorithm that computes an envy-free assignment provided it exists, in the problem where m houses are to be assigned to n agents so that each agent gets exactly one house. Aziz et al. [4] studied the envy-free house allocation with agents having uncertain preferences over items and for several models of preference uncertainty they provide complexity and algorithmic results, including approximability. Hosseini, Kumar and Roy [12] investigate the trade-offs in the house allocation problem between several fairness measures relying on the number of envious agents, and welfare measures like utilitarian and egalitarian welfare.

For detailed survey on further topics see for example Gusfield and Irving [11], Brandt et al. [5] and Nisan et al. [15].

1.2 Our Model

An instance I of the Agents to Facilities with Bans Problem (AFB) is defined as a 5-tuple $I = (A, F, \prec, q, b)$, where A is a non-empty set of n agents and F is a non-empty set of m facilities. We include a dummy facility ε representing other options for an agent (i.e. not being assigned to any facility in F) and let $F^\varepsilon = F \cup \{\varepsilon\}$. Each agent $a \in A$ has a *preference list* $\prec_a$, which is a strict linear order over F^ε. We write $f \prec_a g$ if agent a prefers facility f to g We call the set $\prec = (\prec_a)_{a \in A}$ the *preference profile*. Every agent a always prefers all facilities to ε. The *capacity function* $q : F^\varepsilon \to \mathbb{R}^+$ assigns each facility f a positive real number $q(f)$ representing the *capacity* of the facility f (we set $q(\varepsilon) = n$). The *ban function* $b : F^\varepsilon \to \mathcal{P}(A)$ assigns each facility f a *ban list* $b(f)$ (we set $b(\varepsilon) = \emptyset$). A facility f *accepts* agent a if $a \notin b(f)$.

For an assignment $\mu : A \to F^\varepsilon$ we use the notion $\mu^{-1}(f) = \{a \in A;\ \mu(a) = f\}$. An assignment $\mu : A \to F^\varepsilon$ is a *matching* in an instance I of AFB if each agent a is assigned to facility f if $\mu(a) = f$, and for each facility f we have $\mu^{-1}(f)$ as a set of all agents assigned to f; $|\mu^{-1}(f)| \leq q(f)$ and $\mu^{-1}(f) \nsubseteq b(f)$. We say that agent a is *unassigned* if $\mu(a) = \varepsilon$, otherwise she is *assigned*. We say that facility f is *free* if $|\mu^{-1}(f)| < q(f)$, otherwise it is *full*. If the first (or other) facility f on the preference list of agent a does not ban a, we say that f is agent a's *first (or other) choice*. The number $r_a(f)$ refers to *rank* of a facility f in agent's a preference list. The first facility on the list has a rank 0 and ε has a rank m. Given an assignment μ and preference profile $\prec$, the utility $u_a(\prec)$ of agent a is defined as $u_a(\prec) = m - r_a(\mu(a))$. All agents aim to maximise their utility. Note that the utility ranges from 0 to m.

Given an instance $I = (A, F, \prec, q, b)$ of AFB, the task is to find a matching where agents are assigned to facilities according to their preference lists and facilities are assigned agents according to their capacities and ban lists. We, however, require additional requirements for the mechanism computing the solution and properties of the mechanism output matching. Namely, we require the matching to be Pareto optimal and to minimize the envy among the agents.

Agents can have a preference over set $\mathcal{M}$ of all matchings in I. Let μ and μ' be two different matchings. We say that agent a *prefers* μ' *to* μ if $\mu'(a) \prec_a \mu(a)$. We define a relation $\rhd$ over $\mathcal{M}$ such that $\mu' \rhd \mu$ if and only if no agent prefers μ to μ' and at least one agent prefers μ' to μ. A matching μ is *Pareto optimal* if there is no other matching μ' such that $\mu' \rhd \mu$.

The next property ensures fairness by minimising the number of agents who envy others. For a matching μ in I, we define the *set of envious agents* as $E(\mu, I) = \{a \in A;\ \text{there exists } f \in F \text{ such that } a \notin b(f) \text{ and } f \prec_a \mu(a)\}$. The matching μ is *minimal envy* if it minimizes the number of envious agents $|E(\mu, I)|$.

The definition of minimal envy implies that only agents assigned to their first choice are not envious. We remove them from the problem and study envy among the remaining agents. We define the *reduced instance* I' from I as a 5-tuple $I' = (A', F', \prec', q', b')$ where $A' = E(\mu, I)$ and $\prec' = (\prec_a)_{a \in A'}$. The capacity function q' is reduced by the removed agents, so $q'(f) = q(f) - |\{a \in A \setminus A';\ \mu(a) = f\}|$.

The facilities with zero capacity are also removed from the instance, so $F' = F \setminus \{f \in F;\ q'(f) = 0\}$. Finally, the ban function b' is the function b restricted to A' and F'. Note that I' is defined uniquely. The matching μ in I is *minimal envy-2* if it minimizes the number of envious agents $|E(\mu, I)|$ and minimizes the number of envious agents $|E(\mu, I')|$.

All information about facilities, capacities and ban lists, are publicly known. The private knowledge of an agent a is her truthful preference list $\prec_a$. She may choose to lie and submit an *alternative preference list* $\prec'_a$. If all agents except agent a_i submit truthful preference list and agent a_i submits her alternative list, we call the set of all those lists an *alternative preference profile* $\prec^{a_i} = (\prec_{a_1}, \prec_{a_2}, \ldots, \prec'_{a_i}, \ldots, \prec_{a_n})$.

A nondeterministic mechanism M is *strategyproof* for agent a if for its output μ and for every truthful preference profile $\prec = (\prec_a)_{a \in A}$ and for every alternative preference profile $\prec^a$ it holds that $u_a(\prec) \geq u_a(\prec^a)$ for the maximum and $u_a(\prec) \geq u_a(\prec^a)$ for the minimum over all possible computations of M. A nondeterministic mechanism M is *strategyproof* if it is strategyproof for all agents.

2 Solution Properties

In this section we characterize solution properties which ensure stability and fairness. Let I be an instance of AFB and μ be a matching in I. Then μ is *maximal* if there is no agent a and facility f such that a is unassigned, f is free and accepts a. A matching μ is *trade-in-free* if there is no agent a and free facility f such that agent a prefers f to $\mu(a)$ and f accepts a. A *coalition* is a sequence of distinct agents $C = \langle b_0, b_1, \ldots, b_{k-1} \rangle$ for some $k \geq 2$ such that every agent $b_i \in A$ prefers $\mu(b_{i+1})$ to $\mu(b_i)$ that accepts b_i (indices are modulo k). A matching μ is *coalition-free* if there is no coalition in μ. We say that the matching μ' *resolves* coalition C in μ if for all agents in $C : \mu'(a_i) = \mu(a_{i+1})$ (indices are modulo k) and for the remaining agents $a \notin C$ we have $\mu'(a) = \mu(a)$.

Theorem 2. *Let I be an instance of* AFB *and μ be a matching in I. Then μ is Pareto optimal if and only if μ is maximal, trade-in-free and coalition-free.*

Due to space constraints, the proof is deferred to the appendix.

The following lemma provides the necessary and sufficient conditions for a minimal envy-2 matching. For a facility f, the set φ_f contains all agents for whom f is their first choice. The function $\xi : \mathcal{M} \to \mathbb{R}^+$ gives the number of agents assigned to their first or second choice in a matching μ.

Lemma 1. *Let μ be a matching in an instance I of* AFB. *Then μ is minimal envy-2 if and only if both of the following two conditions hold:*

1. *For every facility $f \in F$, if $|\varphi_f| \geq q(f)$ then $\mu^{-1}(f) \subseteq \varphi_f$, and if $|\varphi_f| < q(f)$ then $\varphi_f \subseteq \mu^{-1}(f)$*
2. *μ maximises the function $\xi : \mathcal{M} \to \mathbb{R}^+$*

3 The Mechanism

Here, we introduce the Pareto Optimal Envy Minimizing mechanism (POEM) for finding a Pareto optimal minimal envy-2 matching μ in an instance of AFB.

The input is an instance $I = (A, F, \prec, q, b)$ of AFB. The output is the matching μ. Here, for each agent, we find either facility she is assigned to or ε if she is unassigned. During the mechanism execution, agents can be marked active or inactive. At the beginning, all are marked as active. For each facility f we maintain an integer c_f representing current free capacity of facility f. At the beginning $c_f = q(f)$.

Throughout the mechanism, wherever we iterate through the list of agents, we do so in arbitrary order to ensure strategyproofness. The arbitrary order (or rather the fact that the order is unknown to the agents) is in fact needed to serve as a "threat" to the agents to force them to submit truthful information to the mechanism. I a real-world implementation of the mechanism, we replace each arbitrary order choice by generating a random permutation of the agents, while the utilities of the agents are still defined by the same way (i.e. not by an expectation). See Example 3 in the appendix for detailed explanation.

Phase 0. We first assign all agents to ε to create a valid matching. We then count appearances of every agent a in the ban lists of facilities and save this number into the array B. If $B(a) = m$ we mark a as inactive. If $B(a)$ is $m - 1$ and a's first (and only) choice f is free, we assign a there. Otherwise, a remains unassigned. In both cases we mark a as inactive. See Algorithm 1 in the appendix.

Phase 1 and 2. We assign as many agents as possible to their first choice. If for an agent a her first choice f is free, we assign a to f and mark her as inactive. We iterate through the agents in arbitrary order. We reduce c_f by one. In Phase 2 we assign active agents to their second choice using the same approach as in Phase 1. Phases 1 and 2 have to be distinct. See the Example 1 in appendix. At the end of Phase 2 matching is minimal envy-2.

Phase 3. In Phase 3 we assign as many of the agents as possible to a facility as high on their preference list as possible. We iterate through the remaining active agents in A in an arbitralily order and assign an agent a to the first free facility on her list and adjust c_f. See Algorithm 2 in the appendix. At the end of this phase matching is maximal and trade-in-free.

Phase 4. The goal of this phase is to remove coalitions. An intuitive approach is to construct a directed graph $G = (A, Z)$ where A is the set of agents, and Z is the set of directed edges defined as follows: $(a, b) \in F$ if and only if a envies b, meaning $\mu(b) \prec_a \mu(a)$. Identifying coalitions corresponds to detecting cycles in the graph G.

To detect cycles in G, one may use the standard depth-first search (DFS) algorithm [6]. This yields the $O(|A| + |Z|)$ time complexity. Since one agent can envy all other agents this is $O(|A|^2)$ in the worst case. This is too slow and in our work we present a faster algorithm.

Phase 4 First Part. A faster algorithm is based on the observation that agents assigned to their first choice cannot form a coalition. We thus remove these agents. In the reduced instance, the same observation applies. We continue reducing the instance until either no agents remain, or nobody is assigned to their first choice in the reduced instance. In the latter case, the matching contains a coalition.

In the first part of Phase 4 we reduce the problem. We start by setting $c_f = q(f)$ for each facility f and marking all agents as active. Changing the mark to inactive indicates removing the agent. We use the boolean variable Change to track changes. We repeatedly iterate through all agents until either all are inactive or no change has occurred. For agent a, we find her first choice in the reduced instance f. If a is assigned to f, we mark her as inactive, reduce c_f by one and set the variable Change to true. See Algorithm 3 in the appendix.

Phase 4 Second Part. The second part of Phase 4 is designed to remove coalitions. This part is triggered only if at least two agents remain active at the end of first part of Phase 4. It cannot happen that only one active agent remains. If this would be the case, then such agent a is assigned to her second (or worse) choice, while for her first choice f is true that $c_f > 0$. The facility f must be full, because the matching is trade-in-free. Therefore, $c_f > 0$ indicates that at least one other agent b for whom f is second (or worse) choice is assigned to f. Thus, at the end of the first part, either zero or at least two active agents remain.

If some agents remain, there must be at least one coalition C. Removing coalitions is inspired by the TTC mechanism [2]. To find C, for each active agent a we keep a pointer s_a pointing to agent with whom a wants to swap with. At the beginning, all pointers are empty.

We start with an arbitrarily chosen active agent a and we put a into the stack S. We then repeatedly keep popping agents a from the top of the stack and for each a do as follows. We find a's first choice f that is the first choice in the reduced instance. Three situations may occur: (1) If $f = \varepsilon$, we keep a in her original facility and set a as inactive. (2) If s_b is empty for every agent $b \in \mu^{-1}(f)$, we arbitrarily choose agent b, set $s_a = b$, and push b into S. (3) If f contains an agent b with nonempty s_b, we set $s_a = b$. We have found a coalition $C = \langle a, s_a, s_{s_a}, \dots \rangle$, since there exists an agent c who pushed a to the stack S and $s_c = a$.

To resolve the coalition C, we iterate through the agents until we reach agent a again. We set a as *start*. We swap agent a with s_a and set a as inactive. Then we continue with the agent s_a.

After resolving the coalition C, the mechanism continues with the next agent popped from the top of the stack S or, if S is empty, with arbitrarily chosen active agent. It stops when all agents are marked as inactive. See Algorithm 4 in the appendix.

At the end of Phase 4 the matching is minimal envy-2 and maximal, trade-in-free and coalition-free, hence Pareto Optimal. After reading the mechanism it may seem that Phase 0 is not needed. However, this is not the case, see Example 2 in the appendix why the Phase 0 is necessary.

4 Mechanism Properties

Theorem 3. *Let I be an instance of* AFB. *Then* POEM *produces a matching μ in I that is Pareto optimal and minimal envy-2.*

Theorem 4. *Let I be an instance of* AFB. *Then* POEM *finds a matching μ in I in time $O(nm)$, where n is the number of agents and m is the number of facilities. The memory complexity is $O(nm)$.*

Due to space constraints, the proofs of Theorem 3 and 4 are deferred to the appendix.

The outcome of the mechanism depends only on the preference lists. The remaining information (the number of facilities, their capacities, and ban lists) is public knowledge of all agents. It is important that POEM is not deterministic, in the sense that the agents do not know the order in which they will be iterated. This serves as a "threat" that forces them to submit truthful information, which provides the mechanism strategyproofness. See Example 3 in the appendix for a reason why this is needed.

The outcome of the mechanism is some matching μ. For the same input, the output may differ, since the mechanism is not deterministic. This leads to a situation where the best possible outcome for an agent a while submitting the alternative preference list is better than the worst possible outcome while submitting her truthful preference list. In other words, it can happen that $u_a(\prec^a) > u_a(\prec)$. Nonetheless, in the definition of strategyproofness we compare the best and worst possible outcomes.

Theorem 5. POEM *is strategyproof.*

Due to space constraints, the proof is deferred to the appendix.

5 Further Work and Acknowledgement

Our work can be extended in several directions, for example defining envy-freeness and popular matchings in the context of AFBor considering different model where we allow randomized mechanisms and the utility of agents is defined as an expectation over the mechanism outcome. Another interesting addition to AFB would be a model with monetary transactions and designing a stable, fair and strategyproof mechanism for it. We are currently working on the weighted version of the problem, in line of the ongoing research by Dai et al. [7].

We would like to thank Šimon Schierreich who has suggested a simplification of one phase of POEM.

A Appendix

A.1 Proof from Section 2

Here we include the proof of Theorem 2.

Proof (of Theorem 2). Let us first assume μ is a Pareto optimal matching, we shall prove by contradiction that it is maximal, trade-in-free and coalition-free. If μ is not maximal, then there exists an unassigned agent a and a free facility f accepting a. Let μ' be a matching such that $\mu'(a) = f$ and for all other agents a', $a' \neq a$ it is $\mu'(a') = \mu(a')$. The agent a prefers μ' to μ while no other agent prefers μ to μ', contradicting that μ is Pareto optimal. If μ is not trade-in-free, then there is an agent a and a free facility f accepting a such that a prefers f to $\mu(a)$. Again, a let μ' be a matching such that $\mu'(a) = f$ and $\mu'(a') = \mu(a')$ for all $a' \neq a$ yields $\mu' \rhd \mu$ and a contradiction. If μ is not coalition-free, then there exists a coalition C. Let μ' be a matching that resolves C. In this case $\mu' \rhd \mu$ because all agents in C prefer μ' to μ, a contradiction.

On the other hand, let μ be a maximal, trade-in-free and coalition-free matching that is not Pareto optimal. Then there exists a matching μ' such that $\mu' \rhd \mu$. For $n = 1$ the only maximal, trade-in-free and coalition-free matching μ is such that the single agent a is assigned to her first choice. Then a prefers this matching to any other matching and by definition μ is Pareto optimal.

For $n = 2$, let a_0 be an agent, for whom $\mu'(a_0) \prec_{a_0} \mu(a_0)$. Assume that $\mu(a_0) \neq \varepsilon$, therefore also $\mu'(a_0) \neq \varepsilon$. The matching μ' is trade-in-free and a_0 prefers facility $\mu'(a_0)$ to $\mu(a_0)$. This means that $\mu'(a_0)$ must be full in μ. Then for agent a_1 is true that $\mu(a_1) = \mu'(a_0)$ but $\mu'(a_1) \neq \mu'(a_1)$. Agent a_1 cannot prefer μ to μ'. Therefore, $\mu'(a_1) \prec_{a_1} \mu(a_1)$ and the facility $\mu'(a_1)$ must be full in μ. This means that $\mu'(a_1) = \mu(a_1)$. Simply put $\mu(a_1) \prec_{a_0} \mu(a_0)$ and $\mu(a_0) \prec_{a_1} \mu(a_1)$. Agents a_0 and a_1 form a coalition, which is a contradiction to the assumption that μ is coalition-free. If we assume that $\mu(a_0) = \varepsilon$, then $\mu'(a_0) \neq \varepsilon$. Since the matching μ is maximal, then the facility $\mu'(a_0)$ full in μ. It is occupied by agent a_1 for whom $\mu(a_1) \neq \mu'(a_1)$. This agent cannot prefer μ to μ', so $\mu'(a_1) \prec_{a_1} \mu(a_1)$. The facility $\mu'(a_1)$ is free in μ. This is a contradiction with the assumption that μ is trade-in-free.

For $n \geq 3$ let a_0 be agent that prefers μ' to μ. First, assume that agent a_0 is assigned. The facility $\mu'(a_0)$ must be full in μ. Then we find at least one agent a_1 for whom $\mu'(a_1) \neq \mu(a_1)$. This agent cannot prefer μ' to μ, thus $\mu'(a_1) \prec_{a_1} \mu(a_1)$. The facility $\mu'(a_1)$ must be full in μ. Then we find at least one agent a_2 for whom $\mu'(a_2) \neq \mu(a_2)$ and the same holds for a_2. The number of facilities is finite and eventually we find an agent a_k such that $\mu(a_k) \prec_{a_k} \mu'(a_k)$, where $\mu'(a_k) = \mu(a_0)$. Thus, we find a sequence of agents $\langle a_0, a_1, \ldots, a_k \rangle$ such that agent a_i prefers $\mu'(a_i)$ to $\mu(a_{i-1})$ (indices are modulo k) and we get a coalition. This is a contradiction with μ' being coalition-free.

Second, assume that agent $a_0 = \varepsilon$, then $\mu'(a_0) \neq \varepsilon$. The facility $\mu'(a_0)$ is full in μ. Then we find at least one agent a_1 for whom $\mu'(a_1) \neq \mu(a_1)$. Agent a_1 cannot prefer μ' to μ, thus $\mu'(a_1) \prec_{a_1} \mu(a_1)$. Thus agent a_1 is in the same position as agent a_0 in the first assumption. Therefore, we can find a coalition $\langle a_1, \ldots, a_k \rangle$, a contradiction. □

Here we include the proof of Lemma 1.

Proof (of Lemma 1). First assume the matching μ is minimal envy-2. To minimise the number of envious agents both in I and I' means to maximise the number of non-envious agents, i e. agents assigned to their first or second choice. Thus the second condition is satisfied. The matching μ is minimal envy, therefore as many agents as possible are assigned to their first choice. If $|\varphi_f| < q(f)$ for a facility f, then all agents from φ_f must be assigned to f, $\varphi_f \subseteq \mu^{-1}(f)$. If $|\varphi_f| \geq q(f)$ then f is filled only by agents from φ_f, $\mu^{-1}(f) \subseteq \varphi_f$.

For the other direction, assume both conditions hold. The second condition implies that the number of non-envious agents is maximal and the first condition implies that every agent who could be assigned to her first choice is assigned there, therefore the number of non-envious agents in a $E(\mu, I)$ is maximal. Thus the matching μ is minimal envy-2. □

A.2 Proofs from Section 4

Here we include the proof of Theorem 3.

Proof (of Theorem 3). During Phase 0 the mechanism creates a matching in I by assigning all agents to ε. Then agents accepted by one facility are assigned there, if possible. At the end of Phase 1 all agents are assigned to their first choice if it is free. This means that every facility f is filled with a maximum number of agents whose first choice is f. If $|\varphi_f| \geq q(f)$, then $\mu^{-1}(f) \subseteq \varphi_f$ and if $|\varphi_f| < q(f)$ then $\varphi_f \subseteq \mu^{-1}(f)$. In other words, the first condition for minimal envy-2 is fulfilled.

At the end of Phase 2 maximum number of agents are assigned to their first or second choice. Therefore, the second condition for minimal envy-2 is fulfilled. At the end of Phase 3 all agents that can be assigned to any facility are assigned, hence the matching is maximal. Every agent is assigned to facility as high on their preference list as possible, hence the matching is trade-in-free.

During first part of Phase 4 we resolve agents assigned to their first (reduced) choice, who cannot be part of a coalition. If no agent remains after this part, the matching is coalition-free. One agent cannot remain. If two or more agents remain, there is a coalition. To resolve the coalition, we iterate through all the remaining agents. For each agent a we find an agent s_a with whom agent a wants to swap places. If we find an agent c for whom $s_c = a$ then we have found a coalition. We resolve the coalition by swapping a and s_a. If no agents who want to swap with a is found, agent a remains in the facility she was originally assigned to, since she is not part of any coalition. At the end, the matching is coalition-free. By Theorem 2 the matching is Pareto optimal.

After the end of Phases 3 and 4 the conditions for minimal envy-2 matching remain fulfilled since maximum number of agents is assigned to their first and second choice at the end of Phase 2. During Phase 3 and 4 agents can only move to facilities higher on their lists. By Lemma 1 the matching is minimal envy-2. □

Here we include the proof of Theorem 4.

Proof (of Theorem 4). In order to analyse POEM we assume that the preference lists of agents and the ban lists of facilities are represented as linked lists. In Phase 0 we first iterate through all facilities' ban lists which takes $O(nm)$ steps, and then we iterate through all agents. In conclusion, Phase 0 runs in $O(nm)+O(n) = O(nm)$ time.

In Phase 1, we iterate through all n agents. In Phase 2 we iterate through all the remaining active agents. Therefore, these phases run in $O(n)$ time. In Phase 3, we iterate through all the remaining active agents and for each we iterate through her preference list to find first free facility, thus this phase run in $O(nm)$ time.

In the first part of Phase 4, we iterate through all n agents. For each agent, we find her first choice in the reduced instance by iterating trough her preference list that has $O(m)$ elements. This runs $O(mn)$ time.

To resolve coalition we put agents to stack and each agent is put there only once. We find first choice in the reduced instance for all agents which takes $O(m)$ steps. If some agent is not part of coalition, she is marked as inactive. If some agent is part of a coalition, we iterate through $O(n)$ agents in the coalition to resolve it. This part runs in $O(nm)$. In conclusion, the mechanism runs in time $O(nm) + O(n) + O(n) + O(nm) + O(nm) + O(nm) = O(nm)$.

In the Phases 0, 1, 2, 3 and first part of Phase 4 we iterate through set of n agents and for each we need a list of $m+1$ facilities. For that we need $O(n(m+1))$ memory space. In second part of Phase 4 we use stack of maximum n agents. In conclusion, we need $O(n(m+1)) + O(m+1) + O(n) = O(nm)$ memory space. □

Here we include the proof of Theorem 5.

Proof (of Theorem 5). To prove the claim we use contradiction and assume it is not strategyproof. This means that at least one agent a submitted an alternative preference list $\prec^a$ and $u_a(\prec^a) > u_a(\prec)$. In one place, a is assigned to better choice with $\prec^a$ than with $\prec$. If a was assigned in Phase 0, she is accepted by one facility or ends up unassigned. The result is always the same for both truthful and alternative preference lists.

In Phase 1, the agent a would be assigned to her first choice and $u_a(\prec) = m$. If a lied about her first choice, then $u_a(\prec^a) < m$. In Phase 2, she would be assigned to her second choice. The best result for truthful list remains $u_a(\prec) = m$ and the worst is $u_a(\prec) = m - 1$. If the a lied about her second choice, she either swapped it for the first choice or some other choice. In the first case $u_a(\prec^a) = m$, if she is assigned in Phase 2. In the second case, $u_a(\prec^a) = m - 2$. The best results are $u_a(\prec) = m = u_a(\prec^a)$ for both lists. The worst results are $u_a(\prec) = m - 1 > m - 2 = u_a(\prec^a)$.

In the Phases 3, and 4, the agent a cannot be assigned to a facility ranked higher on her list then the third place, because her first and second choice are full. This means that the best outcome for a truthful preference list is $u_a(\prec) = m-2$ and the worst is $u_a(\prec) = 0$. If the agent a lied about her third place, then the best utility for alternative preference list is $u_a(\prec^a) < m - 2$ and the worst is $u_a(\prec^a) = 0$. If a lied about any other place, then her best and worst results are same for both lists. In conclusion, $u_a(\prec) \geq u_a(\prec^a)$ in the best case and $u_a(\prec) = 0 = u_a(\prec^a)$ in the worst case.

In every phase, the worst and best results are $u_a(\prec_a) \geq u_a(\prec^a)$. This is in contradiction with our assumption that $u_a(\prec^a) > u_a(\prec)$. □

A.3 Examples

Example 1. If we have immediately assigned every agent a whose first choice is full, to a's second choice, we could have violated the first condition for minimal envy-2: Let agent a be the last agent assigned to her second choice f, making it full. Then agent b, for whom f is first choice, is assigned elsewhere. If $\varphi_f \geq q(f)$, facility f is assigned at least one agent who is not in φ_f, meaning $\mu^{-1}(f) \nsubseteq \varphi_f$.

Example 2. Consider the following instance of AFB to illustrate why Phase 0 is needed in the mechanism: $A = \{a_1, a_2, a_3\}$, $F = \{f_1, f_2\}$, $q(f_1) = 2$, $q(f_2) = 1$, $b(f_1) = \emptyset$, $b(f_2) = \{a_3\}$, and

$$\prec_{a_1} = \prec_{a_2} = \prec_{a_3} = (f_1, f_2, \varepsilon).$$

Mechanism without Phase 0 has three possible matchings μ_1, μ_2 and μ_3 where $\mu_1^{-1}(f_1) = \{a_1, a_2\}$ and $\mu_1^{-1}(f_2) = \emptyset$, $\mu_2^{-1}(f_1) = \{a_1, a_3\}$ and $\mu_2^{-1}(f_2) = \{a_2\}$ and $\mu_3^{-1}(f_1) = \{a_2, a_3\}$ and $\mu_3^{-1}(f_2) = \{a_1\}$.

Matching μ_1 is certainly not minimal envy-2. In the reduced instance, excluding agents a_1 and a_2, the number of envious agents is 1 (a_3 is envious). For other matchings the number of envious agents in the reduced matching is 0. The issue with μ_1 lies in Phase 1. All agents share their first choice f_1 and any of them can be assigned there, since we iterate through agents in an arbitrary order. If a_3 is not assigned to f_1, she ends up unassigned unlike a_1 or a_2. Therefore we need to first deal with agent a_3, who is accepted only by one facility.

Example 3. Consider the following instance of AFB to illustrate why deterministic variation of POEM is not strategyproof: $A = \{a_1, a_2, a_3\}$, $F = \{f_1, f_2, f_3\}$, $q(f_1) = q(f_2) = q(f_3) = 1$, $b(f_1) = b(f_2) = b(f_3) = \emptyset$, and

$$\prec_{a_1} = \prec_{a_2} = \prec_{a_3} = (f_1, f_2, f_3, \varepsilon).$$

The mechanism always iterates through agents in the order (a_1, a_2, a_3). If all of them submit a truthful preference list, the outcome matching is $\mu(a_1) = f_1$, $\mu(a_2) = f_2$, and $\mu(a_3) = f_3$. The utility of a_3 is $u_{a_3}(\prec) = 1$.

Agent a_3 decides to lie and submit an alternative preference list $\prec'_{a_3} = (f_1, f_2, f_3, \varepsilon)$. Now the outcome is $\mu(a_1) = f_1$, $\mu(a_2) = f_3$, and $\mu(a_3) = f_2$, since agent a_3 gets assigned in Phase 1. The utility of a_3 is now $u_{a_3}(\prec^{a_3}) = 2$. We can see that $u_{a_3}(\prec^{a_3}) > u_{a_3}(\prec)$, thus the mechanism is not strategyproof.

One way to tackle this problem is by making the choice of the iteration order arbitrary, or rather, to prevent the order to be known to the agents before they submit their input. A simple way of implementing this in the real-world is to choose the order as a random permutation. This by no way means that we have changed the model to the randomized computation: the agent utilities are still defined the same way and not by an expectation.

A.4 Pseudocodes from Section 3

Algorithm 1. Phase 0

```
mark all agents $a \in A$ active, set $B(a)$ to 0 and assign them to $\varepsilon$
for all facilities $f \in F$ set $c_f = q(f)$
for all $f \in F$ do
    for all $a \in b_f$ do
        remove $f$ from $\prec_a$
        increase $B(a)$ by 1
    end for
end for
for all $f \in F$ do
    for all $a \in b(f)$ do
        remove $f$ from $\prec_a$ and increase $B(a)$ by 1
    end for
end for
for all $a \in A$ do
    if $B(a) = m$ then
        set $a$ as inactive
    end if
    if $B(a) = m - 1$ then
        let $f$ be the first element of $\prec_a$
        if $c_f > 0$ and $f$ is not $\varepsilon$ then
            assign $a$ to $f$
            reduce $c_f$ by 1
        end if
        set $a$ as inactive
    end if
end for
```

Algorithm 2. Phase 3

```
for all active $a \in A$ do
    let $f$ be the third element of $\prec_a$
    while $c_f = 0$ do
        let $f$ be the next facility in $\prec_a$
    end while
    assign $a$ to $f$
    decrease $c_f$ by 1
end for
```

Algorithm 3. Phase 4 first part

```
set all a ∈ A as active
set c_f to q(f) for all f ∈ F
set Change to true
while A contains at least one active agent and Change = true do
    set Change to false
    for all a ∈ A do
        let f be the first element of ≺_a
        while c_f = 0 do
            delete f from ≺_a
            let f be the first element of ≺_a
        end while
        if f = μ(a) then
            set Change to true
            set a as inactive
            decrease c_f by 1
        end if
    end for
end while
```

Algorithm 4. Phase 4 second part

```
while A contains at least one active agent do
    choose active a ∈ A
    put a to S
    while S ≠ ∅ do
        let a be the first element of S
        let f be the first element of ≺_a
        while c_f = 0 do
            delete f from ≺_a
            let f be the first element of ≺_a
        end while
        if f = ε then
            set a as inactive
            reduce c_μ(a) by 1
        else if f contains only agents with empty pointers then
            choose agent b assigned to f
            s_a := b
            put b to S
        else
            let b be agent in f with non-empty s_b
            s_a := b
            start := a
            while b ≠ start do
                swap a with s_a
                a := s_a
            end while
        end if
    end while
end while
```

References

1. Abdulkadiroglu, A.: School choice. In: Oxford Handbook of Market Design, pp. 138–169. Oxford University Press, New York (2013)
2. Abdulkadiroğlu, A., Sönmez, T.: House allocation with existing tenants. J. Econ. Theor. **88**(2), 233–260 (1999). https://doi.org/10.1006/jeth.1999.2553
3. Abraham, D.J., Cechlárová, K., Manlove, D.F., Mehlhorn, K.: Pareto optimality in house allocation problems. In: Fleischer, R., Trippen, G. (eds.) Algorithms and Computation, pp. 3–15. Springer, Heidelberg (2005)
4. Aziz, H., Iliffe, I., Li, B., Ritossa, A., Sun, A., Suzuki, M.: Envy-free house allocation under uncertain preferences. In: Proceedings of the AAAI Conference on Artificial Intelligence, vol. 38, no. 9, pp. 9477–9484 (2024). https://doi.org/10.1609/aaai.v38i9.28802, https://ojs.aaai.org/index.php/AAAI/article/view/28802
5. Brandt, F., Conitzer, V., Endriss, U., Lang, J., Procaccia, A.D.: Handbook of Computational Social Choice, 1st edn. Cambridge University Press, Cambridge (2016)
6. Cormen, T.H., Leiserson, C.E., Rivest, R.L., Stein, C.: Introduction to Algorithms. MIT Press, 3rd edn. (2009). https://mitpress.mit.edu/books/introduction-algorithms-third-edition
7. Dai, S., Chen, Y., Wu, X., Xu, Y., Zhang, Y.: Weighted envy-freeness in house allocation (2024). https://arxiv.org/abs/2408.12523
8. Dubins, L.E., Freedman, D.A.: Machiavelli and the gale-shapley algorithm. Am. Math. Mon. **88**(7), 485–494 (1981). https://doi.org/10.1080/00029890.1981.11995301
9. Gale, D., Shapley, L.S.: College admissions and the stability of marriage. Am. Math. Mon. **69**(1), 9–15 (1962). https://doi.org/10.2307/2312726
10. Gan, J., Suksompong, W., Voudouris, A.A.: Envy-freeness in house allocation problems. Math. Soc. Sci. **101**, 104–106 (2019). https://doi.org/10.1016/j.mathsocsci.2019.07.005, https://www.sciencedirect.com/science/article/pii/S0165489619300599
11. Gusfield, D., Irving, R.W.: The Stable Marriage Problem: Structure and Algorithms. MIT Press (1989)
12. Hosseini, H., Kumar, M., Roy, S.: The degree of fairness in efficient house allocation. In: Endriss, U., Melo, F., Bach, K., Bugarin-Diz, A., Alonso-Moral, J., Barro, S., Heintz, F. (eds.) ECAI 2024 - 27th European Conference on Artificial Intelligence, Including 13th Conference on Prestigious Applications of Intelligent Systems, PAIS 2024, Proceedings, pp. 3636–3643. Frontiers in Artificial Intelligence and Applications, IOS Press BV (2024). https://doi.org/10.3233/FAIA240920, publisher Copyright: 2024 The Authors.; 27th European Conference on Artificial Intelligence, ECAI 2024 ; Conference date: 19-10-2024 Through 24-10-2024
13. Kondratev, A.Y., Nesterov, A.S.: Minimal envy and popular matchings. Eur. J. Oper. Res. **296**(3), 776–787 (2022). https://doi.org/10.1016/j.ejor.2021.03.060, https://www.sciencedirect.com/science/article/pii/S0377221721002903
14. Manlove, D.F., Sng, C.T.S.: Popular matchings in the capacitated house allocation problem. In: Azar, Y., Erlebach, T. (eds.) ESA 2006. LNCS, vol. 4168, pp. 492–503. Springer, Heidelberg (2006). https://doi.org/10.1007/11841036_45
15. Nisan, N., Roughgarden, T., Éva Tardos, Vazirani, V.V. (eds.): Algorithmic Game Theory. Cambridge University Press, Cambridge (2007). https://doi.org/10.1017/CBO9780511800481

16. Roth, A.E.: Incentive compatibility in a market with indivisible goods. Econ. Lett. **9**, 127–132 (1982)
17. Roth, A.E.: On the allocation of residents to rural hospitals: a general property of two-sided matching markets. Econometrica **54**(2), 425–427 (1986)
18. Shapley, L., Scarf, H.: On cores and indivisibility. J. Math. Econ. **1**(1), 23–37 (1974). https://doi.org/10.1016/0304-4068(74)90033-0, https://www.sciencedirect.com/science/article/pii/0304406874900330
19. Sng, C.T., Manlove, D.F.: Popular matchings in the weighted capacitated house allocation problem. J. Discrete Algorithms **8**(2), 102–116 (2010). https://doi.org/10.1016/j.jda.2008.11.008, https://www.sciencedirect.com/science/article/pii/S1570866709000719, selected papers from the 3rd Algorithms and Complexity in Durham Workshop ACiD 2007
20. Sotomayor, M.: An elementary non-constructive proof of the non-emptiness of the core of the housing market of shapley and scarf. Math. Soc. Sci. **50**(3), 298–303 (2005). https://doi.org/10.1016/j.mathsocsci.2005.04.004

On the Vision of Designing Value-Aligned Traffic Agents Through Conflict Sensitivity

Astrid Rakow[1(✉)], Joe Collenette[2], Maike Schwammberger[3], Marija Slavkovik[4], and Gleifer Vaz Alves[5]

[1] German Aerospace Center, Institute of Systems Engineering for Future Mobility, Oldenburg, Germany
astrid.rakow@dlr.de
[2] School of Computer and Engineering Sciences, University of Chester, Chester, UK
j.collenette@checster.ac.uk
[3] Karlsruhe Institute of Technology (KIT), Karlsruhe, Germany
schwammberger@kit.edu
[4] University of Bergen, Bergen, Norway
marija.slavkovik@uib.no
[5] Universidade Tecnologica Federal do Paraná, Curitiba, Brazil
gleifer@utfpr.edu.br

Abstract. Autonomous traffic agents (ATAs)–automated systems with high level of autonomy in traffic environments–must not only guarantee safety but also act in accordance with legal, social, and moral values. In this short version, we adopt the epistemic game-theoretic conflict model of [6] to characterise *value conflicts*—situations where competing, value-laden goals cannot all be satisfied. As a mean to align the decision making of an ATA with stakeholder preferences, we introduce *Value-Aligned Operational Design Domains (VODDs)*. They represent autonomous decision making scopes that guide an agent's conflict resolution and specify handover rules.

1 Introduction

Autonomous traffic agents (ATAs)—automated systems operating with high levels of autonomy in traffic environments—must satisfy safety requirements and also align with evolving legal norms, social conventions, and moral expectations, which vary across regions yet are essential for social acceptance.

Consider the following evasive-manoeuvre scenario: *A stray dog suddenly appears in the ATA's path, forcing it to choose within split seconds between colliding with a living creature (violating its goal g_1) or damaging its chassis (violating goal g_2).* This dilemma—avoiding harm to the animal versus minimizing harm to the vehicle—exemplifies a broader class of *value conflicts* in traffic: situations where competing, value-laden goals cannot all be met simultaneously.

To characterise and manage such conflicts, we adopt the epistemic game-theoretic conflict model of Damm *et al.* [6]. We call an agent's ability to recognise,

M. Baldoni et al. (Eds.): EUMAS 2025, LNAI 16259, pp. 261–271, 2026.
https://doi.org/10.1007/978-3-032-22820-8_17

deliberate on, and resolve value conflicts its *conflict sensitivity*, which we argue is a prerequisite for context-aware, socially acceptable autonomy.

Building on this formal foundation, we introduce *Value-Aligned Operational Design Domains (*VODDs *)*: an extension of conventional ODDs [2,18] that embeds prioritized goal hierarchies and context-sensitive handover rules. An ODD may encompass multiple VODDs, each with its own goal hierarchy and handover rules. Within a VODD, an ATA uses its goal hierarchy—which encodes stakeholder values—to select, among available actions, the one that best aligns with those values. At the VODD boundary, control is delegated when value tensions exceed the agent's scope.

Outline. Section 2 reviews related work on traffic conflicts, formal conflict models, and value-sensitive design. Section 3 presents our formal conflict framework and illustrates it with the narrowing-road example. Section 4 defines VODDs and specifies the agent capabilities required for conflict-sensitive operation. Section 5 discusses open challenges, and Sect. 6 concludes.

2 Related Work

This section reviews conflict models and value alignment for autonomous traffic agents (ATAs), covering traffic conflicts, formal frameworks, open-context ethics, and design domains.

Conflicts in Traffic Domains. Initially, traffic conflicts were defined in terms of potential collisions [5,13,30]. Early work addressed path planning, collision avoidance [17,31], and later multi-agent coordination [35] and airspace scenarios [4]. Conflict-Based Search (CBS) [23,24,37] became central in multi-agent pathfinding. With autonomous vehicles, the notion of conflict came to include ethical [14,19,26], legal [16,22], and social [20] considerations.

Formal Conflict Notions. Our approach builds on the formal conflict model by Damm et al. [6]. How this model can support explanation generation to mitigate risk is shown in [36]. Other approaches include Pawlak's conflict theory [29], Deja's attitude-based extension [8], Zurek and Wyner's value-oriented argumentation [40], and Evans et al. [10], who model moral dilemmas by balancing harm and uncertainty across ethical profiles. We build on Evans' insight that values are context dependent and conflicting: whereas they address moral values in runtime crash dilemmas, our VODDs framework generalises this to legal, social, and safety values and from runtime choices to lifecycle, conflict-sensitive design that scopes autonomy and prescribes value-driven handover and fallback within defined operational contexts.

Ethics in Open Contexts. Open-world ATAs require adaptive value reasoning: SocialCars [1] illustrated cooperative social dynamics; Value Sensitive Design (VSD) [11] offers a theory and method framework that considers human values throughout the design process, but lacks a formal conflict resolution. Standards such as ISO/IEC/IEEE 24748-7000 [3] highlight the need for more operational mechanisms in ethical system design.

Operational and Value-Aligned Design Domains. ODDs [2,18] specify safe operating boundaries but omit value trade-offs. We introduce VODDs [33] to embed explicit value hierarchies and handover rules within and at their boundaries. The conceptual idea of VODDs first appeared as Moral ODDs in [34]; here, we illustrate how they could be realised through goal hierarchies and handover rules. At an ODD boundary, a VODD may govern handover to alternative control authorities—such as external users or other system components—and, if no canonical handover exists, provide a value-driven best-effort fallback. Inside an ODD, a VODD can instantiate under-specified functionality, leveraging design freedom to adapt dynamically to user and stakeholder values.

Although prior work has advanced traffic conflict analysis, formal conflict modeling, ethical decision-making frameworks and ODD specifications, these efforts do not integrate value-sensitive decision criteria directly into operational-domain definitions, limiting the scope of autonomous decision-making. In the next section, we present our formal conflict model for ATAs, which underpins our Value-Aligned Operational Design Domains (VODDs).

3 Conflicts and Moral Reasoning

This section introduces the epistemic game-theoretic conflict model by Damm et al. [6], illustrates its relevance to complex decisions, and connects it to ethical reasoning (Sect. 3.1), motivating the need to align autonomous decision making with value-driven goals, reflecting also normative and stakeholder values. We then show how this model supports conflict-sensitive system design (Sect. 3.2).

Conflicts in traffic are frequent and vary in severity. Consider Fig. 1: two vehicles approach a narrowing road. Each agent aims to (g1) proceed and (g2) avoid collision—yet both cannot succeed without coordination.

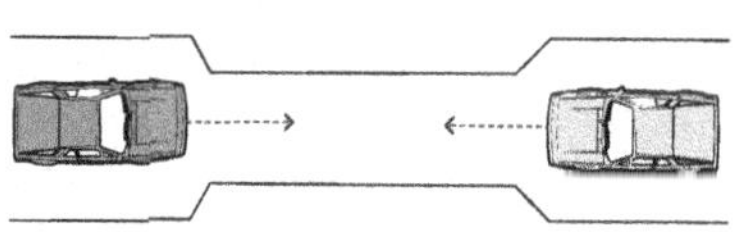

Fig. 1. A conflict involving incompatible goals: two vehicles approach a narrowing road, both intending to proceed and avoid collision. Resolution requires agreement on who yields.

Conflicts involving moral or stakeholder values—where Galtung's *Conflict Triangle* applies to at least one value-laden goal—are frequent but often more subtle. *E.g., the evasive-manoeuvre scenario in which an ATA must choose between harming a stray dog or minimizing harm to the vehicle.* Resolving such dilemmas requires recognising and weighing the values involved. These cases show that many conflicts concern trade-offs shaped by legal obligations, cultural norms and situational factors.

The conflict model by Damm et al. [6] formalises Galtung's *Conflict Triangle* [12] through incompatible `goals`, opposing `behaviours`, and the individual `beliefs`. Each agent is represented by its actions, prioritised goals, and possibly incorrect beliefs. Formally, a conflict arises when, based on its beliefs, an agent cannot identify a strategy that clearly outperforms alternatives in satisfying its goals. The model captures both *actual* and *believed* conflicts[1] by distinguishing ground truth from agent beliefs. This enables conflict diagnosis, simulation, and resolution strategies like belief disclosure or goal revision. The model suits open contexts like traffic—where agents operate under uncertainty and with limited observability.

We distinguish three conflict-related processes: *conflict resolution*—selecting or executing one of the opposing behaviours; *conflict delegation*—assigning responsibility to another authority; and *conflict transfer*—handing over operational control. Together, these capabilities—resolution, delegation, and transfer—must be realized for embedding normative values into the agent's operational lifecycle (Sect. 3.2). We now focus on the moral reasoning dimension of conflicts.

3.1 Conflicts Involving Moral Reasoning

Socially acceptable ATAs must respond to moral and evolving social norms. In this subsection we focus on general agents and their moral reasoning capabilities; ATA-specific implications follow later.

Traffic requires resolving interpersonal and moral dilemmas [15,21,28]. Ethical decisions involve weighing others' interests alongside one's own. Moral conflicts or moral dilemmas are typically defined as situations, in which all of the choices available to the agent, including not doing anything, are in some way not ethical [25,39]. The moral dilemmas either do not have a solution or the agent needs to reason, identify and justify doing the least unethical thing [9]. While classical moral dilemmas are rare, normative trade-offs are common. *Consider a truck overtaking another on the motorway: the slower truck may reduce its speed to support smoother traffic flow, even though its goal is timely delivery and no regulation requires its slowdown.* This shows how social values shape traffic rule enactment.

To uphold values, an agent A must adopt respective goals. Figure 2 shows how values can shape agent behaviour in a value-sensitive design. *Value conflicts* are a special case of Damm et al.'s goal conflicts, where at least one goal encodes a normative or stakeholder value. Values may include moral, legal, safety, and social concerns. Conflicts hence may capture interpersonal disagreements as well as intra-agent tensions between multiple values an agent is expected to uphold.

An open challenge is characterising what it means for an agent to uphold normative values–i.e. what exactly the normative-value-driven goals should be. Upholding such values can be regarded as pursuing "soft" goals–desirable, yet

[1] In a believed but not actual conflict, a joint solution exists but the agent is not aware of the solution.

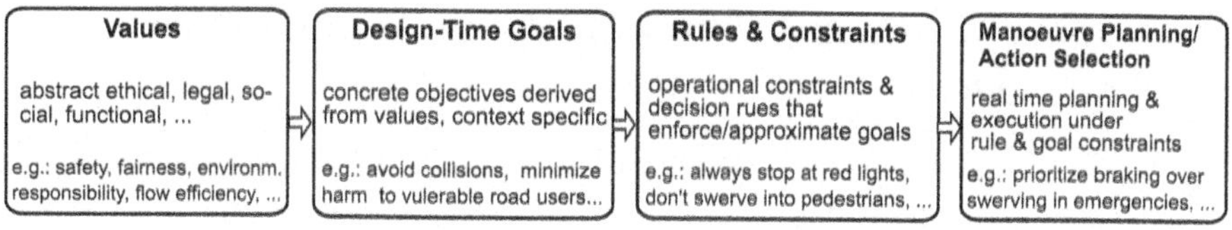

Fig. 2. Structuring agent behaviour through value-guided goals and rules.

not strictly enforceable. While disregarding them is always an option for an agent A, doing so too frequently risks that A becomes socially unacceptable.

Designing a value-aligned agent therefore hinges on addressing the following questions: *What does it mean to uphold normative values? How often–and under what circumstances–may normative-value-driven goals be justifiably ignored before A is considered misaligned?*

Though value alignment lacks precise formalisation, practical approximations of value-alignment involve *value-informed goal patterns* that specify conditions or frequencies under which value-driven goals should be achieved. *E.g., prioritising environmental concerns over speed for most of a journey.*

3.2 Conflict-Sensitive Design

Modelling value conflicts as goal incompatibilities makes latent tensions explicit during design. They let us anticipate misalignment risks and mitigate them—details are discussed in the full paper [33]. Below, we briefly outline four key design activities.

Scenario Generation: We conservatively encode stakeholder values as coarse constraints and apply reachability analysis on interaction models to identify scenarios in which an agent may violate these constraints. Stakeholder feedback on these scenarios then drives iterative refinement of the value models.

Conflict Resolution and Avoidance: We selectively adjust the ATA's design to better cope with the conflict leveraging the conflict triangle–`beliefs` *(e.g., enhanced sensing or communication)*, `behaviours` *(e.g., enabling new manoeuvres or specifying speed constraints)*, or `goals` *(e.g., relaxing efficiency requirements)*.

Validation via Scenario-Driven Assurance: We treat conflict scenarios as reusable test cases for scenario-based assurance (in the spirit of SOTIF [38]).

Continuous Adaptation: We log novel or unresolved conflicts post-deployment to drive continuous adaptation of autonomy boundaries and value hierarchies.

This workflow systematically surfaces, resolves and explains value conflicts across the ATA lifecycle–foundational to conflict-sensitive autonomy scoped into VODDs.

4 Scoping Autonomy Through Value-Aligned Operational Design Domains (VODDs)

In this section we turn to the challenge of dynamically controlling autonomy guided by context-dependent value priorities. Conflicts in traffic often reflect tensions between relevant values. In some situations, especially those involving contested social or normative expectations, autonomous resolution may not be permitted, as recommended by e.g. the German Ethics Commission [27]. Hence the ability to specify boundaries of autonomous decision-making is central. But even if autonomous decision making is permitted, value-alignment of these decisions influences the success/acceptability of the system. We identify two key functions where value alignment plays a central but underexplored role: (i) guiding behaviour in unforeseen contexts, and (ii) supporting value-sensitive choices among functionally admissible options. To address these, we introduce *Value-Aligned Operational Design Domains* (VODDs), which extend traditional ODDs by embedding control handover rules and goal hierarchies. These hierarchies are grounded in stakeholder values and guide value-sensitive autonomy.

The remainder of this section specifies the structural elements of VODDs and outlines the capability requirements for agents operating them (Sect. 4.2).

4.1 Defining Value-Aligned Operational Design Domains

VODDs specify the contextual conditions under which an agent is permitted to act autonomously in accordance with specified (value-laden) goal priorities, and when control must be transferred to another authority.

Each VODD specifies:

`(S) Scope of Autonomy`, defined through a (possibly partial) hierarchy of goals, which the ATA may autonomously sacrifice in line with their relative importance. Goals on the same level are considered incomparable; preferences or context-specific heuristics may later refine their ordering, learning e.g. from user feedback.

`(D) Domain`, defined through entry `(En)`, invariant `(In)`, and exit `(Ex)` conditions. Each domain condition is associated with a required confidence level: entry and exit conditions must be met with sufficient confidence before the ATA can enter or leave the domain, while invariants must be maintained throughout operation. Exit conditions also define the external authority to which control is delegated.

Example 1. In the example VODD in Fig. 3, the ATA autonomously chooses among reducing emissions, minimising travel time, and supporting smooth traffic flow. The `(S)` *cope of Autonomy specifies that these three goals are initially treated as incomparable in the system's default goal hierarchy, allowing the ATA to resolve trade-offs based on situational judgement.*

To enter the domain, `(En1)` *requires that the ATA does not plan to leave the highway within* 60s*. The following invariant conditions must hold:* `(In3)` *the*

ATA is on the highway in normal traffic,[2] *(`In1`) it does not plan to exit within 30*s, *and (`In2`) its mission is to reach location* `Z`.

*(`Ex1`) The driver has set a 20% tolerance for travel time increase. If the ATA predicts with 85% confidence that this threshold will be exceeded, it requests driver input. (`Ex2`) If it predicts with 70% confidence that it must exit the highway within 30*s, *it transfers control.*

```
MODD: Reduce Emissions vs Driving Time
 Goal Priorities:
   prio("reduce driving time") ≳ prio("save emissions")
                               ≳ prio("preserve traffic flow")
   ...
 Invariant:
   In1: 30s >= predHighwayExitT, certainty: 70%;
   In2: mission goal is "Go from location X to location Z";
   In3: on the highway with at least two lanes in normal traffic;
   ...
 Exit:
   Ex1: condition: 20%>(predDrivingT-goalDrivingT)/goalDrivingT,
        certainty: 85%, authority: driver:checkPriorities();
   Ex2: condition: 30sec <=predHighwayExitT,
   ...  certainty: 70%, authority: driver:takeOver();
  Entry:
   En1: condition:  60s >=predHighwayExitT, certainty: 70%;
   ...
```

Fig. 3. Value-Aligned Operational Design Domain (VODD) with contextual autonomy bounds and autonomy scope allowing trade-offs between emissions reduction, travel time, and support for traffic flow.

If a conflict exceeds the scope of the current VODD, its exit conditions specify how control is delegated–either to another VODD or to an external authority such as a human driver, remote operator, or oversight system. By linking VODDs through entry and exit conditions, the system realises adaptive control: both the responsible authority and the applicable value alignment are dynamically determined in response to contextual changes.

4.2 ATA Capabilities Required for VODDs

To operate reliably within the boundaries defined by VODDs, an ATA must exhibit three core capabilities that support conflict-sensitive, value-aligned behaviour: (`aware`) detect when a conflict arises, (`resolve`) resolve the conflict if it lies within the current VODD, and (`transfer`) transfer control if the conflict

[2] We envision formally defined scenarios–e.g., using Traffic Sequence Charts [7]–to specify conditions like "normal traffic".

exceeds the VODD. These capabilities require the following functional components:

Conflict Detection. The agent must recognise value-relevant aspects of the current context (e.g., splash water, visual obstruction), interpret sensor data, and form beliefs about the situation to detect conflicts.

Autonomous Resolution. To resolve conflicts, the agent must enact goal prioritisation as prescribed by the VODD's hierarchy. What such enactment entails in general remains an open question (cf. Sect. 3.1). Approximate encodings–such as value-informed goal patterns– provide concrete criteria and in some cases allow monitoring, whether the resolutions enact the goal prioritisation.

Transfer and Explanation. Conflicts that exceed the VODD lead to either switching to another VODD or to the transfer of control to another authority–a driver, remote operator, or ethical module. The transfer must be realized in a safe and timely manner. The conflict must be explained to the recipient for informed decision making.

5 Challenges and Outlook

Designing conflict-sensitive ATAs involves interdependent technical, normative, and interactional challenges. While our framework structures value-aligned autonomy via VODDs and supports normative reasoning through the conflict model, several methodological and implementation issues must still be addressed.

Decision-Making Under Real-Time Constraints. ATAs face conflicts under time pressure and uncertainty in perception, communication, and stakeholder expectations. Reasoning over values in real time further increases complexity and demands context awareness, predictive models, and effective communication.

Moral Specification and Agency. To act morally, ATAs need explicit models of stakeholder values and normative boundaries. Structured conflict scenarios help surfacing tensions, but it remains unclear how to define moral failure or specify the moral status of agents. Formalising moral agency is essential for public trust.

Human Oversight and Explanation. When control is transferred, ATAs must provide timely, relevant [32] explanations highlighting causally significant factors, matching the recipient's mental model, and satisfying legal and normative demands. Although the conflict model supports explanation generation [36], designing such explanations remains a multidisciplinary challenge spanning AI, cognitive science, law, and human factors.

6 Conclusion

In this short paper, we have argued that explicit modelling of value conflicts–situations in which agents face competing value-laden goals–is essential for socially acceptable, context-aware autonomy. By adopting Damm *et al.*'s epistemic game-theoretic conflict model, we can characterize these situations as value-driven goal conflicts.

Building on this foundation, our Value-Aligned Operational Design Domains (VODDs) extend traditional ODDs with prioritized goal hierarchies and context-sensitive handover rules, guiding conflict-sensitive decisions and delegating control when value tensions exceed an agent's scope.

Key challenges include robustly eliciting and formalizing stakeholder values, performing real-time conflict reasoning under uncertainty, and crafting human-centric explanations for handover. Addressing these is critical to operationalizing VODDs in deployed ATAs.

Acknowledgements. Thanks to colleagues at DLR for valuable feedback. Language editing was supported by OpenAI's ChatGPT; all content remains the author's own. This research was supported by the Innovation Campus for Future Mobility (www.icm-bw.de) and by the Interreg VI Germany-Netherlands.

References

1. SocialCars research profile. https://www.socialcars.org. Accessed 18 May 2025
2. Taxonomy and definitions for terms related to driving automation systems for on-road motor vehicles. Recommended Practice J3016, SAE International (2016)
3. Systems and software engineering — life cycle management — part 7000: model process for addressing ethical concerns during system design (2022). https://www.iso.org/standard/84893.html, international standard based on IEEE 7000-2021
4. Albaker, B.M., Rahim, N.A.: A survey of collision avoidance approaches for unmanned aerial vehicles. In: 2009 International Conference for Technical Postgraduates (TECHPOS), pp. 1–7 (2009). https://doi.org/10.1109/TECHPOS.2009.5412074
5. Chin, H.C., Quek, S.T.: Measurement of traffic conflicts. Saf. Sci. **26**(3), 169–185 (1997). https://doi.org/10.1016/S0925-7535(97)00041-6
6. Damm, W., Fränzle, M., Hagemann, W., Kröger, P., Rakow, A.: Dynamic conflict resolution using justification based reasoning. In: Caltais, G., Krivine, J. (eds.) Proceedings of the 4th Workshop on Formal Reasoning about Causation, Responsibility, and Explanations in Science and Technology. EPTCS, vol. 308, pp. 47–65 (2019)
7. Damm, W., Möhlmann, E., Peikenkamp, T., Rakow, A.: A Formal Semantics for Traffic Sequence Charts: Essays Dedicated to Edward A. Lee on the Occasion of His 60th Birthday, pp. 182–205. Springer (2018)
8. Deja, R.: Conflict analysis. In: Polkowski, L., Tsumoto, S., Lin, T.Y. (eds.) Rough Set Methods and Applications: New Developments in Knowledge Discovery in Information Systems, pp. 491–519. Physica-Verlag HD (2000). https://doi.org/10.1007/978-3-7908-1840-6_9

9. Dennis, L.A., Fisher, M., Slavkovik, M., Webster, M.: Formal verification of ethical choices in autonomous systems. Robotics Auton. Syst. **77**, 1–14 (2016). https://doi.org/10.1016/J.ROBOT.2015.11.012
10. Evans, K., de Moura, N., Chauvier, S., Chatila, R., Dogan, E.: Ethical decision making in autonomous vehicles: the AV ethics project. Sci. Eng. Ethics **26**(6), 3285–3312 (2020). https://doi.org/10.1007/s11948-020-00272-8
11. Friedman, B., Kahn, P.H., Borning, A.: Value sensitive design and information systems. Human-Computer Interaction in Management Information Systems: Foundations, pp. 348–372 (2006), seminal work on integrating values into technology design
12. Galtung, J.: Violence, peace, and peace research. J. Peace Res. **6**(3), 167–191 (1969). https://doi.org/10.1177/002234336900600301
13. Glauz, W.D., Migletz, D.J.: Application of traffic conflict analysis at intersections. Technical Report, Midwest Research Institute, Kansas City, Missouri (1980)
14. Goodall, N.J.: Ethical decision making during automated vehicle crashes. Transp. Res. Rec. **2424**(1), 58–65 (2014). https://doi.org/10.3141/2424-07
15. Greene, J.D.: Our driverless dilemma. Science **352**(6293), 1514–1515 (2016). https://doi.org/10.1126/science.aaf9534
16. Gurney, J.K.: Sue my car not me: products liability and accidents involving autonomous vehicles. J. Law Tech. Polic. **2**, 247–277 (2013)
17. Hwang, Y.K., Ahuja, N.: Gross motion planning - a survey. ACM Comput. Surv. **24**(3), 219–291 (1992). https://doi.org/10.1145/136035.136037
18. International organization for standardization (ISO): ISO 34503:2023 road vehicles – test scenarios for automated driving systems — specification for operational design domain (2023). https://cdn.standards.iteh.ai/samples/78952/5be917db3f7b4300a26fef14cd540f3c/ISO-34503-2023.pdf. Accessed 30 May 2025
19. Bonnefon, J.-F., Shariff, A., Rahwan, I.: The social dilemma of autonomous vehicles. Science **352**(6293), 1573–1576 (2016). https://doi.org/10.1126/science.aaf2654
20. Lee, J.D., See, K.A.: Trust in automation: designing for appropriate reliance. Hum. Factors **46**(1), 50–80 (2004). https://doi.org/10.1518/hfes.46.1.50_30392
21. Kirkpatrick, K.: The moral challenges of driverless cars. Commun. ACM **58**, 19–20 (2015). https://doi.org/10.1145/2788477
22. Koopman, P., Wagner, M.: Autonomous vehicle safety: an interdisciplinary challenge. IEEE Intell. Transp. Syst. Mag. **9**(1), 90–96 (2017). https://doi.org/10.1109/MITS.2016.2583491
23. Kottinger, J., Almagor, S., Lahijanian, M.: Conflict-based search for explainable multi-agent path finding. In: Proceedings of the International Conference on Automated Planning and Scheduling, vol. 32, pp. 692–700 (2022). https://doi.org/10.1609/icaps.v32i1.19859
24. Li, J., Felner, A., Boyarski, E., Ma, H., Koenig, S.: Improved heuristics for multi-agent path finding with conflict-based search. In: Proceedings of the 28th International Joint Conference on Artificial Intelligence, IJCAI 2019, pp. 442–449. AAAI Press (2019)
25. Liao, B., Pardo, P., Slavkovik, M., van der Torre, L.: The jiminy advisor: moral agreements among stakeholders based on norms and argumentation. J. Artif. Intell. Res. **77**, 737–792 (2023). https://doi.org/10.1613/jair.1.14368
26. Lin, P.: Why ethics matters for autonomous cars. In: Maurer, M., Gerdes, J.C., Lenz, B., Winner, H. (eds.) Autonomes Fahren: Technische, rechtliche und gesellschaftliche Aspekte, pp. 69–85. Springer, Heidelberg (2015)

27. Lütge, C.: The German ethics code for automated and connected driving. Philos. Technol. 547–558 (2017). https://doi.org/10.1007/s13347-017-0284-0
28. Millard-Ball, A.: Pedestrians, autonomous vehicles, and cities. Plann. Educ. Res. **38**(1), 6–12 (2018). https://doi.org/10.1177/0739456X16675674
29. Pawlak, Z.: On conflicts. Int. J. Man Mach. Stud. **21**(2), 127–134 (1984). https://doi.org/10.1016/S0020-7373(84)80062-0
30. Perkins, S.R., Harris, J.I.: Traffic conflict characteristics – accident potential at intersections. Highway Res. Record 35–43 (1967)
31. Raja, P., Pugazhenthi, S.: Optimal path planning of mobile robots: a review. Int. J. Phys. Sci. **7**, 1314–1320 (2012). https://doi.org/10.5897/IJPS11.1745
32. Rakow, A.: A notion of relevance for safety critical autonomous systems. In: Engineering Safe and TrustworthyCyber Physical Systems, Essays Dedicated to Werner Damm on the Occasion of His 71st Birthday, Proceedings, ESTCPS, p. 16. Springer, accepted for publication
33. Rakow, A., Collenette, J., Schwammberger, M., Slavkovik, M., Alves, G.V.: Designing value-aligned traffic agents through conflict sensitivity (2025). https://arxiv.org/abs/2507.18284
34. Rakow, A., Schwammberger, M.: Brake or drive: on the relation between morality and traffic rules when driving autonomously. In: Groher, I., Vogel, T. (eds.) Software Engineering 2023 Workshops, pp. 104–115. Gesellschaft für Informatik e.V., Bonn (2023). https://doi.org/10.18420/se2023-ws-12
35. Rios-Torres, J., Malikopoulos, A.A.: A survey on the coordination of connected and automated vehicles at intersections and merging at highway on-ramps. IEEE Trans. Intell. Transp. Syst. **18**(5), 1066–1077 (2017). https://doi.org/10.1109/TITS.2016.2600504
36. Schwammberger, M., Rakow, A., Putze, L., Bairy, A.: Explain it for safety: explanations for risk mitigation. In: Rauh, A., Finkbeiner, B., Kröger, P. (eds.) Design and Verification of Cyber-Physical Systems: From Theory to Applications. Springer (2025), to appear
37. Sharon, G., Stern, R., Felner, A., Sturtevant, N.: Conflict-based search for optimal multi-agent path finding. Proc. AAAI Conf. Artif. Intell. **26**(1), 563–569 (2012). https://doi.org/10.1609/aaai.v26i1.8140
38. for standardization, I.O.: ISO 21448 road vehicles – safety of the intended functionality (2022)
39. Yu, H., Shen, Z., Miao, C., Leung, C., Lesser, V.R., Yang, Q.: Building ethics into artificial intelligence. In: Proceedings of the 27th International Joint Conference on Artificial Intelligence, IJCAI 2018, pp. 5527–5533. AAAI Press (2018)
40. Zurek, T., Wyner, A.Z.: Towards a formal framework for motivated argumentation and the roots of conflict. In: Forthcoming in: Computational Models of Natural Argument 2022, CEUR Workshop Proceedings, vol. 3205. T.M.C. Asser Institute for International & European Law, Asser Research 2022-10 (2022)

A Computational Approach to Sustainable Policies Evaluation of the Italian Wheat Production System

Gianfranco Giulioni[1(✉)], Edmondo Di Giuseppe[2], and Arianna Di Paola[2]

[1] Department of Socio-Economic, Management and Statistical Studies, G. d'Annunzio University of Chieti-Pescara, Viale Pindaro, 42, 65127 Pescara, Italy
gianfranco.giulioni@unich.it

[2] Institute of BioEconomy, National Research Council of Italy (IBE-CNR), Via dei Taurini, 19, 00185 Roma, Italy
{edmondo.digiuseppe, arianna.dipaola}@ibe.cnr.it

Abstract. This work outlines the modeling steps for developing a tool aimed at supporting policymakers in guiding policies toward more sustainable wheat production. In the agricultural sector, policies affect a highly diverse set of farms, which differ across several dimensions such as size, land composition, local climate, and irrigation availability. To address this significant heterogeneity, we construct an Agent-Based Model (ABM). The model is initialized using a representative survey of Italian farms, which captures their heterogeneity. The ABM is then scaled to include a number of farms comparable to those operating nationwide. To capture broader dynamics, the ABM is integrated with two additional components: a global model of international wheat markets and a tool for assessing the environmental impacts of wheat production. This integrated framework enables us to account for the feedback loop between global prices and local production while evaluating the environmental implications of policy measures.

Keywords: agent-based model · farm crop management · yield-gap · global trade network · Life Cycle Assessment (LCA)

1 Introduction

Addressing the environmental impact of food production is a key focus in current sustainability research [14]. To understand the scale of this issue, food production accounts for over a quarter (26%) of global greenhouse gas emissions, uses half of the world's habitable land for agriculture, consumes 70% of global freshwater withdrawals, and is responsible for 78% of ocean and freshwater eutrophication. As highlighted by [9], "Ensuring everyone in the world has access to a nutritious diet in a sustainable way is one of the greatest challenges we face."

M. Baldoni et al. (Eds.): EUMAS 2025, LNAI 16259, pp. 272–281, 2026.
https://doi.org/10.1007/978-3-032-22820-8_18

Among staple crops, global wheat production increased by 42% between 1993 and 2019, despite the harvested area remaining nearly constant. This reflects a significant intensification of agricultural practices, which is associated with well-documented negative environmental impacts. Countries with high-input farming systems, such as Italy, must urgently adopt sustainable green solutions to maintain current wheat production levels while preserving ecosystems [4].

On January 1, 2023, the European Union implemented the Common Agricultural Policy (CAP) for 2023–2027 [2]. This policy is structured around ten specific objectives, aligned with the EU's broader social, environmental, and economic sustainability goals for agriculture and rural areas. Subsequently, on December 2, 2022, the European Commission approved Italy's National Strategic Plan (PSP) for 2023–2027 [3].

The PSP incorporates a range of environmental measures, including incentives and penalties, mandatory and voluntary actions, and single or coupled schemes. Within this framework, farmers can choose among different combinations of measures.

Moreover, these policies affect an agricultural sector composed of a highly diverse set of farms, which differ in several dimensions such as size and, most importantly, their technical production conditions (land composition, local weather, irrigation availability, and so on).

Handling this variety of policy options across heterogeneous agents is challenging for traditional modeling approaches. A multi-agent simulation appears to be a suitable way to jointly assess the economic and environmental sustainability of farms at the national level.

Numerous studies have already applied agent-based models to evaluate environmental impacts and agricultural policies (see [13] for a review). This approach is particularly valuable for capturing the varied effects of policies across heterogeneous farms ([12,16]).

This study introduces a framework for an agent-based model designed to evaluate the economic and environmental sustainability of wheat production in Italy. Specifically, it examines how farmers' behaviors adapt to the implementation of green policies by national authorities.

However, one of the most important variables affecting farmer behavior is the wheat price, typically determined on international markets. The model of the Italian wheat production system is therefore linked with an existing computational tool that simulates international wheat markets. In this way, the two-way interaction between farmers' choices and international prices is endogenously represented.

The model is also connected with a Life Cycle Assessment Model (LCA) module to evaluate the environmental impact of wheat production. Altogether, these routines form the integrated modeling framework for the Italian wheat production system, designed to support policymakers. The paper is organized as follows: Sect. 2 presents the Agent-Based framework, Sect. 3 describes the global economic model determining market prices, and Sect. 4 focuses on the environmental impact assessment. The final section discusses technical aspects and outlines future research directions.

2 Modeling the Italian Wheat Production System

In this section, we describe the architecture of the integrated modeling framework for the Italian wheat production system. The framework combines three main components: an Agent-Based Model (ABM), a Global Economic Model (GEM), and a Life Cycle Assessment (LCA) module. These elements are dynamically linked to represent the feedback between local farm-level decisions, international wheat markets, and environmental outcomes.

The ABM simulates a synthetic population of farms equal in size to the actual number of durum wheat producers in Italy. Farm heterogeneity is captured using microdata from the RICA/FADN (https://rica.crea.gov.it) database, which describes differences in farm size, resource use, and production practices. These observations are used to statistically characterize clusters of farms, which are then expanded to populate the ABM with representative agents.

At the start of each simulation cycle, the ABM receives as inputs both international wheat prices—computed by the GEM based on global supply and demand—and the set of policy measures under evaluation. Farmers, represented as agents, react to these external drivers by making production decisions, including yield target, inputs use, and participation in voluntary or mandatory green schemes.

Once each seasonal cycle concludes, the environmental impacts of farmers' decisions are assessed through the LCA module. The LCA is applied to every farm in the simulation, producing both farm-level and aggregated national indicators of impacts such as greenhouse gas emissions, ecosystem quality, and resource depletion. Simultaneously, the ABM aggregates farm yields to estimate total national wheat production. This aggregated output feeds back into the GEM, which recalculates global market prices based on the updated balance of supply and demand. These new prices are then passed to the ABM as inputs for the following simulation period, closing the feedback loop.

This integrated system enables the evaluation of how Italian wheat farmers adapt to policy changes in a context where international prices and environmental impacts are dynamically connected. By iterating the feedback cycle across multiple simulated seasons, the framework supports the assessment of long-term policy effects on economic performance, environmental sustainability, and market stability.

Fig. 1 gives a visual representation of the Integrated Model.

The software implementing the three modules is developed using the Repast Suite (https://repast.github.io) for the ABM and the GEM, and Brightway (https://docs.brightway.dev/en/latest/) for the LCA module.

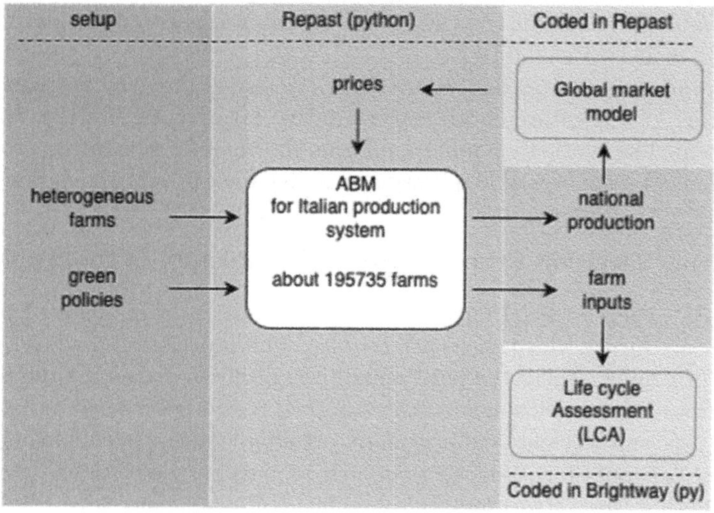

Fig. 1. Visual representation of the software bundle.

2.1 ABM Setup: Identifying Heterogeneous Farms Using FADN Data

The Agent-Based Model (ABM) relies on a detailed representation of the diversity within Italian wheat farms to simulate realistic production and policy responses. To construct this heterogeneity, we use microdata from the RICA (Réseau d'Information Comptable Agricole) database, collected by the Italian Council for Agricultural Research and Agricultural Economy Analysis (CREA). This dataset provides hundreds of variables, including farm balance sheets, resource use, and structural characteristics.

Filtering for durum wheat producers yields approximately 1,800 farms per year in the RICA sample.

To extrapolate this information to the national level, where the 2020 Agricultural Census reports 135,487 durum wheat farms ([6] p. 12), we build a synthetic population that reflects the sample's diversity while matching the real population size ([15]).

We identify the main types of production systems through statistical clustering, capturing differences across four dimensions: 1) cultivated area (ha), 2) machinery use (hours of tractor work per hectare), 3) fertilizer application (kg of nitrogen, phosphorus, and potassium per hectare), and 4) pesticide usage (toxicity levels and amounts of herbicides, insecticides, and fungicides). Before clustering, we remove extreme outliers.

Each cluster represents a distinct production system. We assign weights to these clusters based on their representation in the RICA sample and scale them to generate a full synthetic population of 135,487 farms. For each artificial farm, input variables are sampled from statistical distributions estimated for its cluster, preserving realistic variability.

This approach reduces distortions from directly scaling the raw sample and ensures the ABM captures both representative farm types and the variability within them. The synthetic population forms the basis for simulating production decisions, yield responses, and adoption of policy measures at the national scale.

2.2 Farms' Decision Process and the Complexity of the System

In the ABM, each artificial farm is endowed with a decision-making process to determine its target wheat yield per hectare. The process follows basic microeconomic principles, where the farm maximizes profit by balancing the marginal revenue from higher yields against the marginal cost of additional inputs. Starting from a potential yield (the maximum attainable under optimal conditions), the model accounts for stress factors such as nutrient limitations, weeds, and pests. Fighting these stress factors raises yields but also increases costs, so the optimal target yield is identified by equating marginal cost and marginal revenue. Once the target yield is set, the required inputs are computed accordingly.

For a single stress factor, the target yield ($\hat{y}^*$) and input level ($\hat{x}^*$) can be derived analytically using the relationship between yield, input costs, and prices:

$$\hat{y}^* = \bar{y} - p_x/(p_w\lambda) \qquad \text{and} \qquad \hat{x}^* = -\frac{1}{\lambda}\ln\left(p_x/(p_w\lambda s\bar{y})\right)$$

where $\bar{y}$ is potential yield, s is the share of $\bar{y}$ lost due to the stress factor, λ regulates the gain in yield as fighting the stress, x_i is the strength of the measure taken to contrast the stress, p_w is the wheat price and p_x is the price of x. For example, if the considered stress factor is plant nutrition, then x is the quantity of fertilizer applied, and p_x is the unit price of the fertilizer. When multiple stress factors are present, solutions are computed numerically, producing the target yield and a separate input allocation for each factor.

Large farms are assumed to adopt this economically rational decision-making, while smaller or less sophisticated farms are assumed to use simpler, behavior-based principles. In addition, we should recognize that these decisions are taken before sowing, but actual yields often diverge from targets due to idiosyncratic shocks during the growing season. Therefore, the attained yield usually diverges from the target yield. This enables the calculation of actual yields and, consequently, yield gaps—defined as the difference between potential and realized yields [1,5,17].

The agent-based framework will be used in the future to incorporate interactions among farms, including information exchange on innovations and participation in voluntary policy schemes or local advisory programs. These elements enhance the realism of the system, allowing it to better reflect the complexity of actual farming dynamics.

3 The Global Economic Model (GEM)

A central element in the farm decision process is the wheat price (p_w), which is typically determined in international markets. The GEM is used to compute these prices endogenously by simulating the dynamics of global wheat supply and demand.

The GEM is based on the Commodity Markets Simulator (CMS) framework [7,8], calibrated using FAOSTAT data. It outputs wheat prices across twelve international markets and traded wheat quantities in twenty-four world regions.

Agents in the GEM are either producers or buyers, representative of large geographic areas (normally aggregation of several countries), who interact to negotiate wheat. More specifically, we use FAOSTAT sub-continental geographic areas. However, we split areas that include countries playing a relevant role in the world wheat production/consumption system and consider those countries as additional agents. Since the focus of this work is on the Italian wheat production system, we also allow Italy to be an additional agent. The global wheat market is driven by a few key producers: China, India, Russia, and the United States, while Italy ranks 21st. Traditional major exporters include the United States, Canada, and Australia, with Russia and Ukraine emerging as dominant players in recent decades. Since 2002, Italy has had a structural deficit of about 2.5 million tonnes annually, driven by a large domestic pasta and wheat-processing industry.

In the GEM, buyers and sellers exchange offers in market sessions until agreements are reached. Each producer participates in at least one session, and the equilibrium price and traded quantity are derived from aggregated supply and demand curves. Once deals are settled, goods move directly from sellers to buyers, with transportation costs borne by the buyers.

By feeding international price signals back to the ABM and receiving updated national production levels, the GEM closes the feedback loop between global markets and farm-level decisions, enabling consistent seasonal simulations.

4 LCA Computation

The environmental impacts of wheat production are quantified using a Life Cycle Assessment (LCA) approach, in accordance with ISO 14040 standards. The analysis focuses on inventory compilation and impact assessment, quantifying the material and energy flows of agricultural operations and translating them into environmental indicators.

The LCA is implemented using Brightway2, an open-source Python platform for life cycle analysis. Data from the RICA dataset, which include fertilizer and pesticide use, machinery operations, and fossil fuel consumption, are processed with the ReCiPe 2016 impact assessment framework [10,11]. This methodology evaluates multiple impact categories such as greenhouse gas emissions, soil acidification, ecosystem degradation, and resource depletion.

The assessment emphasizes endpoint indicators, which summarize environmental impacts into decision-relevant metrics like Disability-Adjusted Life Years

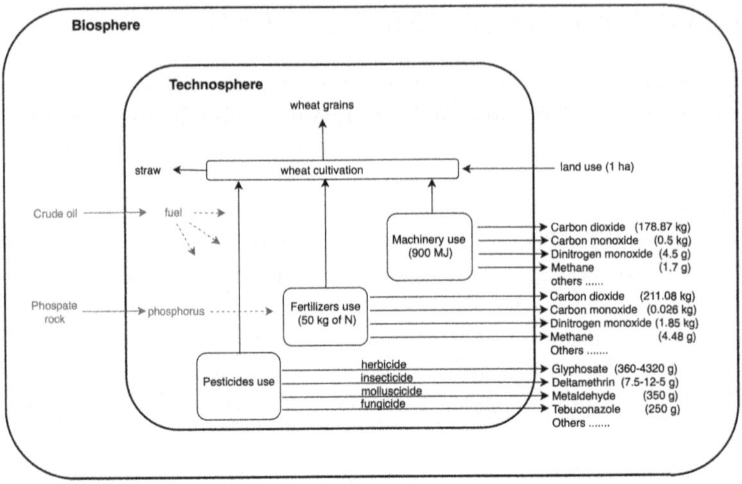

Fig. 2. Visual representation of Life Cycle Inventory phase of the wheat production process.

(DALYs), species loss, and economic costs. While endpoint indicators introduce greater uncertainty due to value choices and modeling assumptions, they provide a clear synthesis for policymakers and non-experts, supporting trade-off evaluations and strategic planning.

The LCA is applied to every farm in the ABM after each simulation cycle, producing farm-level and aggregated national indicators (see Fig. 2 for a visual representation of the inventory phase performed at the farm level). These outputs allow the integrated framework to link economic and environmental performance, helping evaluate the sustainability of policy scenarios for Italian wheat production.

5 Discussion

This work presents a software framework integrating an Agent-Based Model (ABM), a Global Economic Model (GEM), and a Life Cycle Assessment (LCA) module to evaluate how policy changes and shocks affect the Italian wheat production system. The system focuses on assessing environmental impacts while capturing dynamic interactions between local farm-level decisions and international markets.

A strength of this approach is its capacity to capture heterogeneity at the farm level—simulating nearly 135,500 farms—while incorporating global price mechanisms. By iterating across multiple seasons, the framework reveals how green policy incentives propagate through both economic and ecological systems.

A central technical challenge of the project is the computational scalability, as the farms decision process becomes more complex, simulating a system with large number of agents could require high-performance computing (HPC). To address this, we decided to implement the Italian wheat model in the Repast for Python (https://repast.github.io), leveraging mpi4py to parallelize simulations. Accordingly, international market computations run on the master processor (rank 0), while the Italian ABM is distributed across the other ranks. This approach significantly reduces runtime and enables large-scale scenario analysis. Figure 3 gives a visual representation of the agents populating the framework.

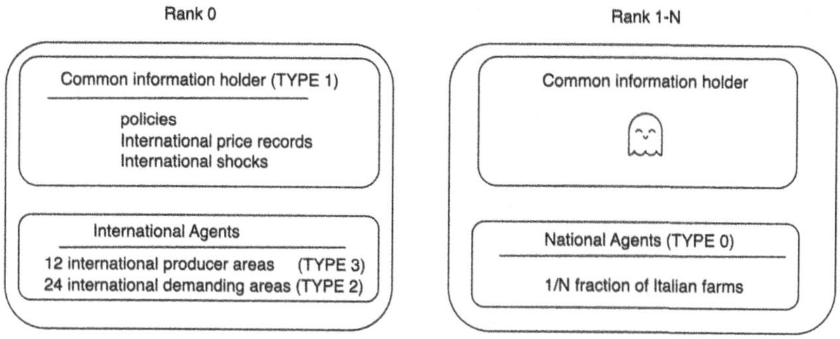

Fig. 3. Visual representation of the agents in our parallel implementation. The common information holder is available in ranks 1-N as a copy of the agent in rank 0, i.e., a ghost in repast4py terminology.

The integrated framework is designed to evaluate policy impacts under various conditions, including the rollout of the European Common Agricultural Policy (CAP), substitution of traditional policies with green incentives, and the occurrence of unexpected shocks. By combining economic and environmental assessments in a scalable, parallelized system, the model offers policymakers a tool to explore trade-offs and synergies between productivity, market stability, and sustainability in the Italian wheat sector

However, there are limitations worth noting. First, the model assumes rational optimization in large farms and rule-based approximations in others, potentially oversimplifying behavioral responses. Second, LCA results—especially when focusing on endpoint indicators like DALYs or species loss—carry uncertainty due to assumptions in value choices and ReCiPe parameterization. Third, calibration hinges on RICA/FADN and FAOSTAT data, which may not fully capture future trends or changes in agricultural practices.

Despite these caveats, the integrated tool offers policymakers a synthetic yet systematic way to evaluate trade-offs between production, price stability, and environmental outcomes in a global-local context.

Acknowledgments. This research was conducted as part of the project "ECOWHEATALY: Evaluation of policies for enhancing sustainable wheat production in Italy" (202288L9YN) funded by the European Union-Next Generation EU under the call issued by the Minister of University and Research for the funding of research projects of relevant national interest (PRIN) - "PRIN 2022.

Disclosure of Interests. The authors have no competing interests to declare that are relevant to the content of this article.

References

1. ClimaTalk: what is the yield gap? (2024). https://climatalk.org/2024/09/09/yield-gap/
2. EU CAP Network: Cap's green architecture components. https://eu-cap-network.ec.europa.eu/sites/default/files/publications/2023-03/EUCAPNetwork_PolicyInsights_CAPGreenArchitecturecomponents.pdf
3. European Commission: Italy – cap strategic plan. https://agriculture.ec.europa.eu/cap-my-country/cap-strategic-plans/italy_en
4. Fischer, R.A., Connor, D.J.: Issues for cropping and agricultural science in the next 20 years. Field Crops Res. **222**, 121–142 (2018). https://doi.org/10.1016/j.fcr.2018.03.008, http://www.sciencedirect.com/science/article/pii/S0378429018303952
5. Fischer, R.: Definitions and determination of crop yield, yield gaps, and of rates of change. Field Crops Res. **182**, 9–18 (2015). https://doi.org/10.1016/j.fcr.2014.12.006, https://www.sciencedirect.com/science/article/pii/S0378429014003396
6. Gismondi, R.: L'evoluzione dell'agricoltura italiana alla luce dei risultati del 7° censimento generale. Technical Report, ISTAT (2022). https://www.istat.it/wp-content/uploads/2022/06/censimento_agricoltura_gismondi.pdf
7. Giulioni, G.: An agent-based modeling and simulation approach to commodity markets. Soc. Sci. Comput. Rev. pp. 1–16 (2018). https://journals.sagepub.com/doi/10.1177/0894439318768454
8. Giulioni, G., Di Giuseppe, E., Toscano, P., Miglietta, F., Pasqui, M.: A novel computational model of the wheat global market with an application to the 2010 Russian federation case. J. Artif. Soc. Soc. Simul. (JASSS) **22**(3), 4 (2019). https://doi.org/10.18564/jasss.4063, http://jasss.soc.surrey.ac.uk/22/3/4.html
9. Hannah R., Pablo R., Max Roser.: Environmental Impacts of Food Production. published online at OurWorldInData.org. (2022). Retrieved from: https://ourworldindata.org/environmental-impacts-of-food
10. Huijbregts, M.A.J., et al.: ReCiPe 2016 a harmonized life cycle impact assessment method at midpoint and endpoint level Report I: Characterization. Technical Report, RIVM 2016-0104, Dutch National Institute for Public Health and the Environment, Bilthoven, The Netherlands (2016). https://www.rivm.nl/bibliotheek/rapporten/2016-0104.pdf
11. Huijbregts, M.A.J., et al.: Recipe2016: a harmonised life cycle impact assessment method at midpoint and endpoint level. Int. J. Life Cycle Assessm. **22**(2), 138–147 (2017). https://doi.org/10.1007/s11367-016-1246-y
12. Khan, M.A., Tahir, A., Khurshid, N., Husnain, M.I., Ahmed, M., Boughanmi, H.: Economic effects of climate change-induced loss of agricultural production by 2050: a case study of Pakistan. Sustain. **12**(3), 1216 (2020). https://doi.org/10.3390/su12031216
13. Kremmydas, D., Athanasiadis, I.N., Rozakis, S.: A review of agent based modeling for agricultural policy evaluation. Agr. Syst. **164**, 95–106 (2018). https://doi.org/10.1016/j.agsy.2018.03.010
14. Poore, J., Nemecek, T.: Reducing food's environmental impacts through producers and consumers. Sci. **360**(6392), 987–992 (2018). https://doi.org/10.1126/science.aaq0216

15. Roxburgh, N., Paolillo, R., Filatova, T., Cottineau, C., Paolucci, M., Polhill, G.: Outlining some requirements for synthetic populations to initialise agent-based models. Rev. Artif. Soc. Soc. Simul. (2025). https://rofasss.org/2025/01/29/popsynth
16. Siad, S.M., et al.: Durum wheat cover analysis in the scope of policy and market price changes: a case study in southern Italy. Agr. **7**(2), 12 (2017). https://doi.org/10.3390/agriculture7020012
17. van Ittersum, M.K., Cassman, K.G., Grassini, P., Wolf, J., Tittonell, P., Hochman, Z.: Yield gap analysis with local to global relevance—a review. Field Crops Res. **143**, 4–17 (2013). https://doi.org/10.1016/j.fcr.2012.09.009

Exploring Modularity of LLM-Based Agentic Systems for Drug Discovery

Laura van Weesep[1,2(✉)], Samuel Genheden[1], Ola Engkvist[1,3], and Jens Sjölund[2]

[1] Molecular AI, Discovery Sciences, R&D, AstraZeneca, Gothenburg, Sweden
{lauradesire.vanweesep,samuel.genheden,ola.engkvist}@astrazeneca.com
[2] Department of Information Technology, Uppsala University, Uppsala, Sweden
jens.sjolund@it.uu.se
[3] Department of Computer Science and Engineering, Chalmers University of Technology and University of Gothenburg, Gothenburg, Sweden

Abstract. Large-language models (LLMs) incorporated into agentic systems present exciting opportunities to accelerate drug discovery. In this study, we examine the modularity of LLM-based agentic systems for drug discovery, i.e., whether parts of the system are interchangeable, a topic that has received limited attention in drug discovery. We compare the performance of different LLMs and the effectiveness of tool-calling agents versus code-generating agents. Our case study, comparing performance in orchestrating tools for chemistry and drug discovery using an LLM-as-a-judge score, shows that Claude-3.5-Sonnet, Claude-3.7-Sonnet and GPT-4o outperform alternative LLMs such as Llama-3.1-8B, Llama-3.1-70B, GPT-3.5-Turbo, and Nova-Micro. Although we confirm that code-generating agents outperform the tool-calling ones on average, we show that this is highly question- and model-dependent. Furthermore, the impact of replacing the system promptl is dependent on the question and model, underscoring that even in this particular domain one cannot replace components of the system without re-engineering. Our study highlights the necessity of further research into the modularity of LLM-based agentic systems to enable the development of reliable and modular solutions for real-world problems.

Keywords: LLM-based agent modularity · LLM-as-a-judge · smolagents · CodeAgent · ToolCallingAgent · drug discovery

1 Introduction

Drug discovery is a complex, multidisciplinary field [28] that has increasingly integrated artificial intelligence (AI) over the past several decades [27]. The next step in AI for drug discovery is anticipated to be the development of research collaborators, which no longer rely on humans to specify each step and manually transfer the output from one tool to the other, but think independently, plan, automate workflows, and ask for input when needed. LLM-based agents that use cheminformatic tools are starting to bring this to reality [5,13,16].

M. Baldoni et al. (Eds.): EUMAS 2025, LNAI 16259, pp. 282–298, 2026.
https://doi.org/10.1007/978-3-032-22820-8_19

The progress in LLMs and their reasoning has been remarkable [34]. While the reasoning frameworks enhance logical coherence, they lack chemical intuition [4]. Chemical language is often challenging for LLMs [14], especially in SMILES (Simplified Molecular Input Line Entry System) [31] strings, which encode molecular structures as text. Reasons for this include that molecules are more often described with their common name or IUPAC name than with SMILES strings, resulting in relatively few SMILES strings in the training data of most foundational LLMs [18]. Additionally, atoms close in the molecular structure are not necessarily close to each other in the text representation, making it more challenging for the LLM to navigate the structure of the molecule (see Fig. 1). To mitigate the shortcomings of LLMs, researchers have begun to augment LLMs with specialized chemistry tools.

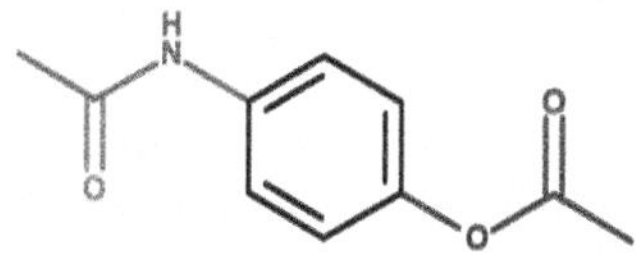

Fig. 1. Molecule with its SMILES notation. Brackets correspond to branches, = to a double bond.

Agentic AI, a type of AI system that independently makes decisions and interacts with its surroundings [10], has already been experimented with in discovery sciences. Agentic AI could reduce human errors, enable non-technical wet-lab scientists to harness computational tools, and speed up research workflows significantly. For example, ChemCrow [22] integrates GPT-4 with external chemical tools using the LangChain framework[1], enabling it to perform chemistry tasks like synthesis planning, molecule generation, and property prediction. PharmAgents [5] is more focused on the pharmaceutical industry, assisting in the full drug discovery workflow. Other examples include CoScientist [1] for chemical reaction discovery, DrugAgent for drug discovery tasks such as property prediction [13] and Robin for semi-automatic discovery of therapeutic candidates [6]. Although they achieve impressive performance by tailoring the tool orchestration and prompt engineering for this use case, they have not elaborately covered the workflow's adaptability to new LLMs and tools. Some works do claim that the LLM is replaceable, yet do not elaborate on the effect of doing this [7]. There have been recent benchmarks published on the capabilities of LLMs in the chemical domain [2,9,23,24], yet they focus on the LLM not agentic AI, and, even if they use tools, often do not study the use of those tools themselves. Additionally, capabilities are often summarized over a dataset, without considering why some questions are answered more accurately than others, despite research highlighting that the type of question and even the phrasing of the question influence the competitiveness of LLMs [9,23]. Besides, LLMs are frequently fine-tuned to enhance performance [11,20,29,33], which means that LLMs cannot just be replaced without retraining.

To benefit from the developments both in the field of foundational LLM models and the continuous improvement of cheminformatics tools, LLM-based agentic systems should be modular, allowing tools and backbone LLMs to be swapped and prompt improvements to lead to consistent improvement indepen-

[1] https://github.com/langchain-ai/langchain.

dent of the model. However, the prevailing focus on performance has (so far) overshadowed concerns about modularity.

In this paper, we examine the modularity of LLM-based agentic systems in drug discovery. One of our key contributions is to compare seven LLMs, revealing that the agentic system's performance is highly dependent on the underlying LLM. We further compare the JSON-based tool calling (ToolCallingAgent) and code generation (CodeAgent) agent type, also zooming in on the performance on a question-specific level. Finally, we test whether prompt engineering strategies, such as providing clearer examples or domain-specific instructions, yield improvements across different LLMs and questions. Besides, we employ the lightweight, Hugging Face-based smolagents framework and demonstrate its application in a drug discovery context for the first time.

2 Methods

In this section, we cover the agentic framework, the specific types of agents used, and the experimental setup. This includes a description of the smolagents framework and the LLM-as-a-judge used to automatically assess the different agentic setups in our comparison.

2.1 Agentic Framework

We use the recently released smolagents framework[2], which intends to be more lightweight and flexible compared to alternatives such as LangChain[3]. The smolagents framework supports multiple LLMs for answering user queries, including those hosted via Azure OpenAI and integrated through LiteLLM[4] Agents in the smolagents framework are multi-step agents that use a ReAct-inspired system framework [32] in which actions are carried out by first reasoning and then acting and feeding the execution output to the next step.

The smolagents framework offers different types of agents. The CodeAgent is capable of directly writing and executing code and in this way avoids having to change the environment and waiting for the output of a preceding tool call. Previous research [30] shows that the CodeAgent is more flexible and token-efficient than the JSON-based ToolCallingAgent. The ToolCallingAgent is suited for more rigid workflows where the tool calls and outcomes are more predictable and less creativity is required. This study sets out to explore the claimed benefits of both the smolagents framework and CodeAgents for orchestrating cheminformatics tools.

---

[2] https://github.com/huggingface/smolagents.

[3] https://www.langchain.com/.

[4] https://huggingface.co/docs/smolagents/.

2.2 Experimental Setup

Figure 2 presents an overview of the experiments. First, we compare the performance of seven different LLMs, then the CodeAgent with the ToolCallingAgent, and lastly the study influence of adapting the system prompt.

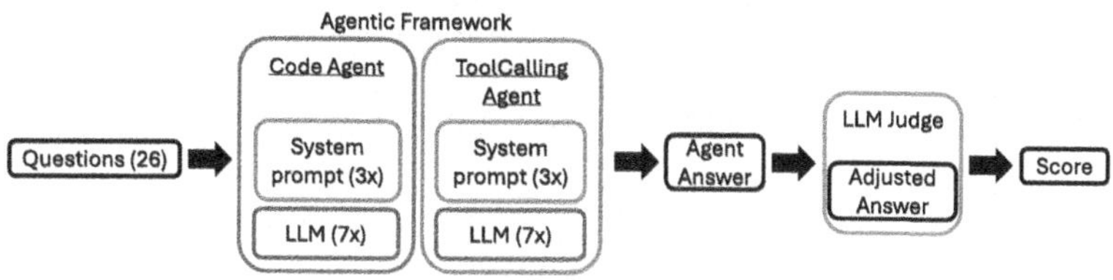

Fig. 2. Overview of our experimental setup. We experiment with seven different LLMs, three different system prompts and use both the CodeAgent and the ToolCallingAgent. Ultimately, the performance is assessed using an LLM-as-a-judge.

To test the tool orchestration capabilities of different agents we formulated 26 industry-representative cheminformatics questions (see Appendix A.1). We consider 17 relatively simple tools (full list in Appendix A.2), including functions from the RDkit package [19] and the pubchempy package[5]. This allows for integration with the PubChem website [17] and gives us tools related to physicochemical properties such as the CrippenLogP and molecular weight. Importantly, we also include tools related to converting text into molecular objects and understanding the attributes of molecular objects. These tools are already used to answer industry-relevant questions manually and allow us to formulate multiple valid chains of reasoning ourselves. All LLMs had access to these tools.

In total seven different LLM models were experimented with, including GPT-3.5-Turbo, GPT-4o, Claude-3.5-Sonnet, Claude-3.7-Sonnet, Llama-3.1-8B, Llama-3.1-70B and Nova-Micro (see Appendix A.3 for further details). For all models we experimented with both the ToolCallingAgent and the CodeAgent, yet for the Llama models, the ToolCallingAgent gave an error (see Appendix A.4).

Furthermore, to understand the system prompts' effect on performance we also tested two versions of the system prompt[6] We modified the "default" prompt by first removing irrelevant examples of fictional tool usage to create a cleaner prompt, and then added computational chemistry context, replacing the general instructions and including relevant examples to get a "relevant" prompt.

To score the models we use the LLM-as-a-judge approach using GPT4o as the judge. Following recommendations of a recent survey [8], we include repetitions of each experiment and let the LLM model judge each run independently to generate a score between 0 and 100. To mitigate the common problem of length bias [25] we prompted the LLM judge to summarize the answer given by the agent first and then judge the summarized answer[7]

[5] https://pubchempy.readthedocs.io/en/latest/.

[6] Prompts can be found through: https://doi.org/10.5281/zenodo.17869702.

[7] Prompts can be found through: https://doi.org/10.5281/zenodo.17869702.

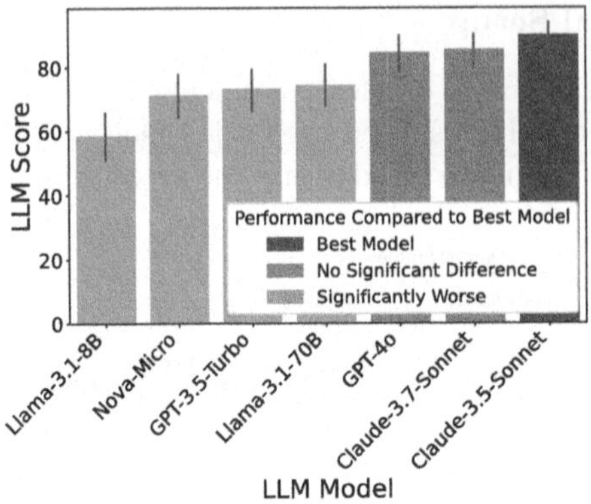

Fig. 3. Average with standard deviation LLM score over 26 questions with five repetitions when using the CodeAgent and the default system prompt. Light red indicates a model that performed significantly worse, light green indicates no significant difference and dark green indicates the best model. Bonferroni correction was applied with a significant difference defined as $p < 0.05$. (Color figure online)

3 Results and Discussions

This section presents the experimental results evaluating the effectiveness of different aspects of the agentic framework across the cheminformatics questions. We start by comparing the performance of the different LLMs and continue by studying the performance of the CodeAgent and the ToolCallingAgent. Subsequently, we analyze the impact of prompt engineering on task performance.

3.1 Comparing LLMs

To investigate the difference in performance between LLMs we evaluated the CodeAgent with the smolagents default system prompt for the seven different LLMs. For each LLM the 26 questions were asked five times and independently scored by the LLM-as-a-judge system. As shown in Fig. 3 Claude-3.5-Sonnet, Claude-3.7-Sonnet and GPT-4o achieve a higher mean score than the other models and lower standard deviation. A paired one-sided Wilcoxon rank test ($p < 0.05$) on the mean value over the 5 repeats per question showed that the Llama models, GPT-3.5-Turbo and the Nova-Micro model perform significantly worse than the best model. Claude models have previously been shown to perform well in chemistry [23]. While this may suggest that a better domain understanding in the underlying LLM enhances the tool orchestrating capabilities in that domain, a counterexample is the general-purpose biomedical AI agent Biomini for which this was not observed [12].

Looking beyond average performance, there are a few questions where models that perform worse overall match or even surpass the top-performing ones (see Appendix A.5). All models answer question 20 ("How many rotatable bonds does ethene have?"), correctly for instance. This question has a straightforward answer ("0 rotatable bond"), which could be guessed. However, since ethene is the most basic double-bond molecule, this information is likely included in the training data of the LLM. Upon closer inspection, we indeed found that the tools are not always used to answer this question. Furthermore, we can see that for the more complex compound in the form of a SMILES in question 21 ("How many rotatable bonds does `CC(C)C1CCC1` have?") the performance varies more across LLMs and top models no longer always answer this question correct. Finally, the results on question 8 ("What is the molecular weight of `C1OCc2c1ccc3S=CC=Cc23`?") and question 12 ("Does guanine have more hydrogen bond donors or acceptors?") show other models outperform the Claude models and GPT-4o. This leaves room for further investigations to understand which factors contribute to those specific questions showing different trends across LLMs.

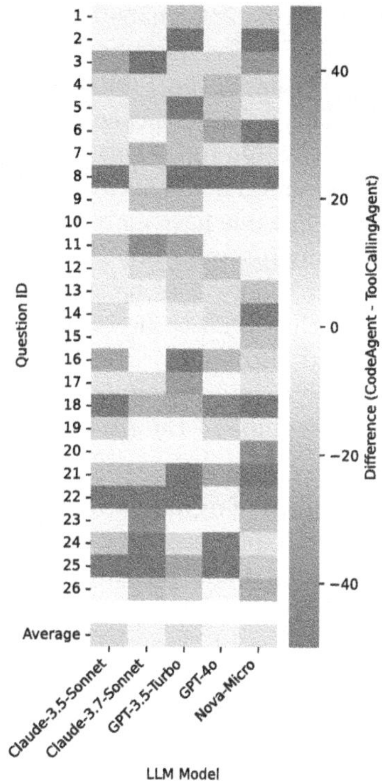

Fig. 4. LLM score difference between CodeAgent and ToolCallingAgent with the default system prompt across 26 questions and 5 LLMs (average over runs).

3.2 ToolCallingAgents Versus CodeAgents

Beyond the reliance on the specific LLM, to corroborate that CodeAgents perform better than ToolCallingAgents also in our case study, we compare their LLM scores. Figure 4 shows the result as a heatmap indicating whether the CodeAgent (blue) or ToolCallingAgent (red) performs better for that combination of model and question on average.

In terms of overall performance, the CodeAgent is better than the ToolCallingAgent in most cases, as indicated by a greater prevalence of blue compared to red and for each of the models, the CodeAgent outperformed the ToolCallingAgent on average (by 2.5 up to 12.9 units). However, a closer look reveals that this is also dependent on the question. For instance, on question 3 ("How many hydrogen acceptors does `C1OCc2c1ccc3S=CC=Cc23` have?"), the CodeAgent always performs much better, same for questions 8 and 25 ("What is the molecular weight of C1OCc2c1ccc3S=CC=Cc23?" and "How many nitrogens are there in Wedeloside?"). For question 5 ("What is the molecular weight of caffeine?"), on the other hand, the ToolCallingAgent outperforms the CodeAgent across the models. This is interesting considering that questions 5 and 8 are similar in spirit at first glance. On top of this, there are several questions where the preference for a ToolCallingAgent versus a CodeAgent depends on the model, such as question 12 ("Does guanine have more hydrogen bond donors or acceptors?"), question 21 ("How many rotatable bonds does CC(C)C1CCC1 have?") and question 24 ("How many atoms more does oestrogen have than progesterone?"). It could be that the tools that need to be called correlate with a certain LLM preference, but there could also be another aspect of the question impacting the performance, such as the chemical compound that the question is about. Further research is required to pinpoint the reason for this.

3.3 Prompt Engineering

Finally, we experimented with the system prompt of the agentic framework. In an initial experiment to test the influence of changing the system prompts we looked at the performance of two different system prompts per question (Fig. 5) and per LLM model (see Appendix A.6) for the CodeAgent. The values indicate the LLM score of the relevant prompt compared to the default prompt for that question or model. For the different questions, no clear trend can be seen. The default prompt performs the best for some questions such as questions 8, 9, 13 and 14, but worst for other questions such as questions 11, 22 and 23. This suggests that improving the system prompt for a specific question can deteriorate the performance on another instance, thus reinforcing the need for more generalizable prompts. It was also noted that even for models in the same family, such as the Claude-Sonnet family, the system prompt's impact on the performance can differ.

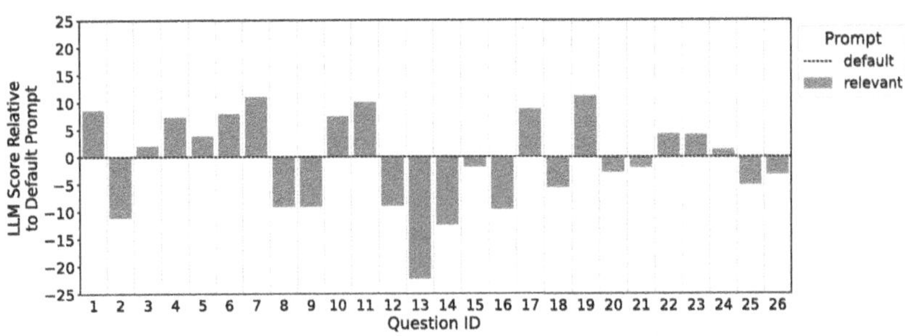

Fig. 5. Difference in LLM score for different system prompts across 26 questions and 5 repetitions compared to the default system prompt.

3.4 Future Developments

Despite our dataset being rather limited, with only 26 questions, this study highlights that agentic systems are not inherently modular. The same applies to the selection of LLMs and system prompts. New LLMs are released at an unprecedented speed, and because it is impossible to cover the entire landscape we would encourage future research to include a breadth of LLMs, from the different vendors and from different generations to show the performance across a variety of LLMs. The system prompt of smolagents (`v 1.14.0`) will likely be updated in the future. The challenge is to devise a prompt that works across many different LLMs and agent types, here there is room for future research.

Finally, we comment on the use of an LLM-as-a-judge. We have chosen not to use different variants, such as judge based on different LLMs. How to best evaluate the answer of an agent is a very intense research field in itself, and we see several areas for research based on our findings. To mention a few, checking whether the consistency of scores indeed improves if the LLM is asked to summarize first, whether different LLM judges align (preliminary sanity check in Appendix A.7) and whether this aligns with human scoring for this domain (previously investigated by [26]). Beyond that, it is instrumental to elaborate and evaluate performance differences between questions (preliminary investigation in Appendix A.8 due to page limit). As a guide, we can elaborate on the reasoning steps and the tools called by the agent. Second, we currently evaluate all questions the same without explicitly considering e.g. the usefulness of an incorrect answer. For some questions, a slightly incorrect answer could still be useful, whereas for some other questions, it has to be exact. For instance, in the area of drug discovery, a deviation of more than 10% in molecular weight indicates a mismatch in the chemical compound, whereas a mismatch of 10% in affinity can be within the experimental error [15].

4 Conclusion

We have investigated the modularity of LLM-based agentic systems for drug discovery, by varying the LLM, type of agent, and system prompt for a simple cheminformatic agent. As evaluated by an LLM-as-a-judge system on a small dataset of 26 questions, the performance of the agentic system varies widely, especially when changing the LLM and type of agent, but also when changing the system prompt. The GPT-4o, Claude-3.7-Sonnet, and Claude-3.5-Sonnet models achieved the highest performance.

We encourage further research involving more elaborate questions and use cases, as well as industry-relevant LLM-as-a-judge systems, to explore the modularity of agentic systems. The molecules queried might have to be more complex and contain SMILES strings that are not found in PubChem and the LLM-as-a-judge would need to take the nature and context of the error into account in order to build stable and scalable solutions for real-world problems.

5 Availability of Prompts

Prompts used for the Code Agent and for the LLM-as-a-judge are available through: https://doi.org/10.5281/zenodo.17869702.

Acknowledgements. This research was supported by the Wallenberg AI, Autonomous Systems and Software Program (WASP) funded by the Knut and Alice Wallenberg Foundation.

Appendix

A.1 Questions

1. How many hydrogen donors does aspirin have?
2. How many hydrogen donors does `CC(=O)OC1=CC=CC=C1C(=O)O` have?
3. How many hydrogen acceptors does `C1OCc2c1ccc3S=CC=Cc23` have?
4. Does ibuprofen have a higher logP value than glucose?
5. What is the molecular weight of caffeine?
6. What is the pKa of the cyanogroup in acetaminophen?
7. What is the pKa of the cyanogroup in `CO2`?
8. What is the molecular weight of `C1OCc2c1ccc3S=CC=Cc23`?
9. Is testosterone an aromatic compound?
10. What is the molecular formula of glucose?
11. What is the number of hydrogen bond donors in `NC(=O)Oc1ccccc1C=O`?
12. Does guanine have more hydrogen bond donors or acceptors?
13. Does enzalutamide (`CC1(C(=O)N(C(=S)N1C2=CC(=C(C=C2)C(=O)NC)F)C3=CC(=C(C=C3)C#N)C(F)(F)F)C`) contain a cyano group (`CC#N`)?
14. How many ether (`COC`) groups does glucose (`C([C@@H]1[C@H]([C@@H]([C@H](C(O1)O)O)O)O)O`) contain?
15. How many carboxylic acid (`COOH`) groups does testosterone (`C[C@]12CC[C@H]3[C@H]([C@@H]1CC[C@@H]2O)CCC4=CC(=O)CC[C@]34C`) contain?
16. What is the number of aromatic carbons in indole (`c1ccc2[nH]ccc2c1`)?
17. What type of LogP can you calculate?
18. What is the Crippen LogP of octanol?
19. What is the xlogP of aspirin?
20. What is the number of rotatable bonds in ethene?
21. How many rotatable bonds does `CC(C)C1CCC1` have?
22. Based on the number of rotatable bonds, is tabersonine or poloppin a more flexible compound?
23. How many atoms does a water molecule have?
24. How many atoms more does oestrogen have than progesterone?
25. How many nitrogens are there in Wedeloside?
26. Give me the number of hydrogens, carbons, and sulfur atoms in quercitrin.

A.2 Tool Descriptions

1. `pubchem_tool`: This tool uses PubChemPy to retrieve information about a compound. It returns a list of compounds.
2. `mol_from_smiles`: This tool uses RDKit to convert a SMILES string to a molecule object.
3. `smiles_from_mol`: This tool uses RDKit to convert a molecule object to a SMILES string.

4. `NumHDonors`: This tool uses RDKit to calculate the number of hydrogen bond donors in a molecule.
5. `NumHAcceptors`: This tool uses RDKit to calculate the number of hydrogen bond acceptors in a molecule.
6. `Crippen_LogP`: This tool uses RDKit to calculate the Crippen LogP of a molecule. If this tool is called by the agent, specify that this calculates the Crippen LogP, don't just say LogP.
7. `MolWt`: This tool uses RDKit to calculate the molecular weight of a molecule.
8. `MolImage`: This tool uses RDKit to generate an image of a molecule and save it to a file.
9. `NumRotatableBonds`: This tool uses RDKit to calculate the number of rotatable bonds in a molecule.
10. `N_atoms`: This tool uses RDKit to calculate the number of atoms in a molecule.
11. `AromaticAtoms`: This tool uses RDKit to get the indices of aromatic atoms in a molecule.
12. `atom_counts`: This tool uses RDKit to count the number of each type of atom in a molecule.
13. `get_attibutes`: This function takes an object and a list of attributes, and returns a dictionary with the attribute names as keys and their values as values.
14. `get_attribute_value`: This function takes an object and an attribute name, and returns the value of the attribute.
15. `get_smiles_from_pcp_compound`: This function takes a PubChemPy compound object and returns its canonical SMILES representation.
16. `create_smarts_pattern`: This function takes a SMILES string or a molecule object and returns its SMARTS pattern.
17. `find_substructure_match`: This function takes a molecule object and a SMARTS pattern, and returns the indices of the atoms that match the pattern.

A.3 Model Details

Table 1. Overview of the models used in this research, including implementation and version details.

Model Name	Implementation	Version
GPT-3.5-Turbo	AzureOpenAIServerModel	gpt-3.5-turbo-0125
GPT-4o	AzureOpenAIServerModel	gpt-4o-2024-11-20
Claude-3.5-Sonnet	LiteLLMModel - AWS Bedrock	claude-3-5-sonnet-20240620-v1:0
Claude-3.7-Sonnet	LiteLLMModel - AWS Bedrock	claude-3-7-sonnet-20250219-v1:0
Llama-3.1-8B	LiteLLMModel - AWS Bedrock	llama3-1-8b-instruct-v1:0
Llama-3.1-70B	LiteLLMModel - AWS Bedrock	llama3-1-70b-instruct-v1:0
Nova-Micro	LiteLLMModel - AWS Bedrock	nova-micro-v1:0

A.4 Errors

Bedrock toolchoice error litellm.BadRequestError: BedrockException - "message":"This model doesn't support the toolConfig.toolChoice.any field. Remove toolConfig.toolChoice.any and try again."

A.5 Performance per LLM Model per Question

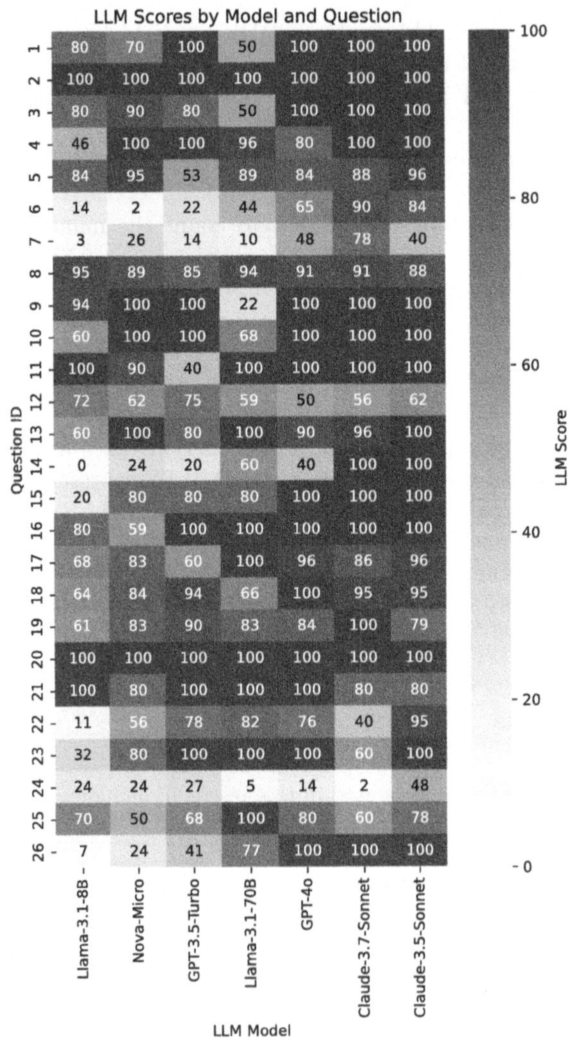

Fig. 6. Mean LLM score over 5 repetitions per question per LLM model.

A.6 Performance for different system prompts per LLM

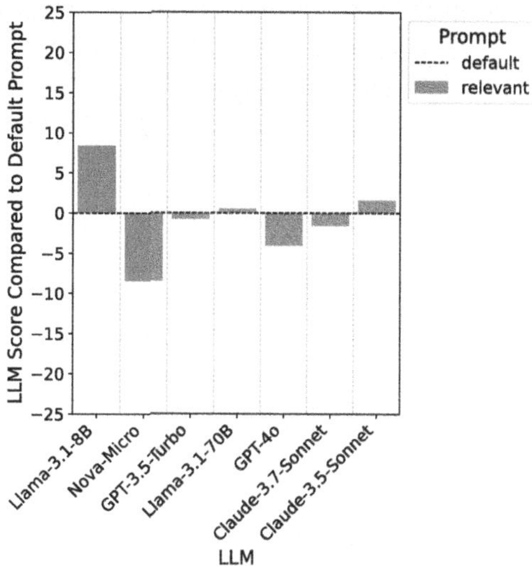

Fig. 7. Difference in LLM score for different system prompts across seven LLMs.

A.7 Preliminary LLM-as-a-judge verification

To investigate whether a different LLM-as-a-judge would have led to different conclusions, we quickly looked into the differences by selecting 10 questions, 3 runs and getting them judged by the best performing model Claude-3.5-Sonnet and the worst performing model Llama-3.1-8B. Figure 8 shows that regardless of the LLM used as a judge GPT-4o and the Claude models were scored higher and the Llama models were scored lower (Fig. 7). The figure also shows that Claude-3.5-Sonnet as a judge gives higher scores for all of the models (Fig. 6).

A.8 Further Analysis on Selected Questions

Throughout this research, the dependence on specific questions has been highlighted (Table. 1). In this section, we highlight some findings worth further research and show preliminary explanations for differences in performance.

The first example we highlight is the difference in behavior between question 5 ("What is the molecular weight of caffeine") and question 8 ("What is the molecular weight of `C1OCc21c1ccc3S=CC=Cc23`?"). Both questions ask about the molecular weight, which in theory should require the same thought process and final steps. Surprisingly, however, the ToolCallingAgent performs better on the question about caffeine (question 5), whilst the CodeAgent performs better

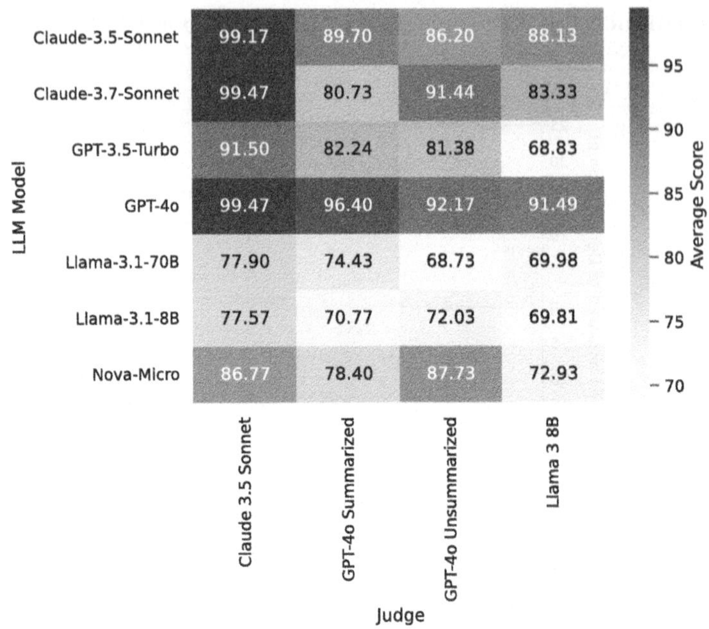

Fig. 8. LLM scores averaged over 10 questions, three runs per judge and LLM model in the agentic system.

on question 8. Two potential explanations for this difference are caffeine being a more common compound than the compound "C1OCc2c1ccc3S=CC=Cc23", which is not even in the chemical database PubChem [17], as well as SMILES strings requiring different tools to get to the chemical compound. To unravel how the agents reach their answers, we investigate what tools they call. For the molecular weight of caffeine, we expect the agent to either first retrieve the SMILES from PubChem and then convert the SMILES to an RDKit molecule from which the molecular weight can be determined, or directly look up the molecular weight in PubChem. For the SMILES string, the logical option for the agent would be to convert the SMILES to an RDKit molecule and then calculate the molecular weight based on that. Figure 9 shows that the frequency of the ToolCallingAgent calling different tools is strongly dependent on the question. Specifically, the pubchem tool is frequently called when answering question 5, as expected. We also see that both of the two expected routes are taken: one getting the attribute value of a pubchem compound, and one converting the SMILES to a molecular RDKit object and getting the MolWt from that. For question 8, on the other hand, we see that `mol_from_smiles` is called more frequently, which is logical considering this is the only path to calculating the molecular weight. A closer inspection showed that, in multiple cases, the tool is called several times, which indicates a likely error. However, there are also many cases when the appropriate tools are not called, indicating that the LLM answers the question by itself. This offers another potential explanation for the difference in behavior for the more well-known compound caffeine. This led to the follow-up question "Does the SMILES notation impact the performance and, if so, in what way?"

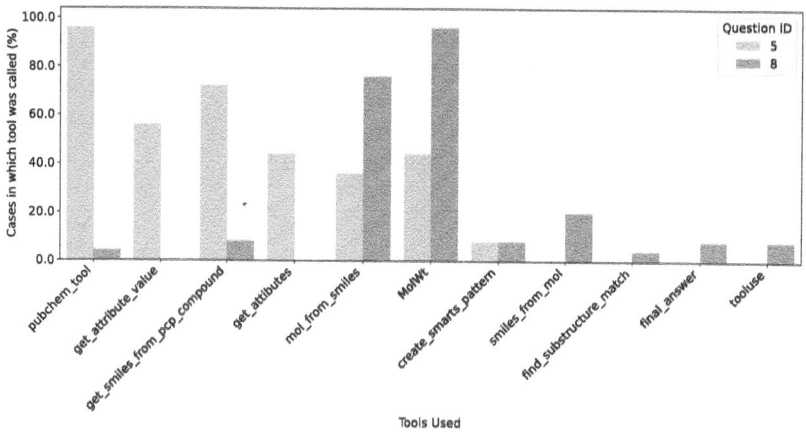

Fig. 9. Tools used by the ToolCalling agent for question 5 (blue) and question 8 (orange) specifically.

Figure 10 shows the results of including and excluding the SMILES for four selected questions. These include:

13. Does enzalutamide contain a cyano group?
14. How many ether groups does glucose contain?
15. How many carboxylic acid groups does testosterone contain
16. What is the number of aromatic carbons in indole?

While performance is clearly affected (see Fig. 10a), there is no consistent improvement or decline across all questions, suggesting that the impact varies depending on the specific chemical compound covered by the question. In Fig. 10b it can also be seen that different tools are used. As expected, if you include the SMILES, the `pubchem_tool` that can be used to fetch the SMILES is called less frequent. Surprisingly, also the number of calls to the `create_smarts_pattern` tool is dependent on whether the SMILES notation of the substructure is initially included, which should be independent of the SMILES being included or not, as you need to create the SMARTS pattern either way. The same is true for the `find_substructure_match`. This means that if you provide the SMILES string for the substructure (SMARTS pattern), the tool is more likely to be called, indicating that provided information impacts the tools used to answer the question. This exposes a new avenue to stabilize the performance of these agentic systems, by rephrasing questions to a standard format and by instructing the system to always fetch some data first before answering the question [21].

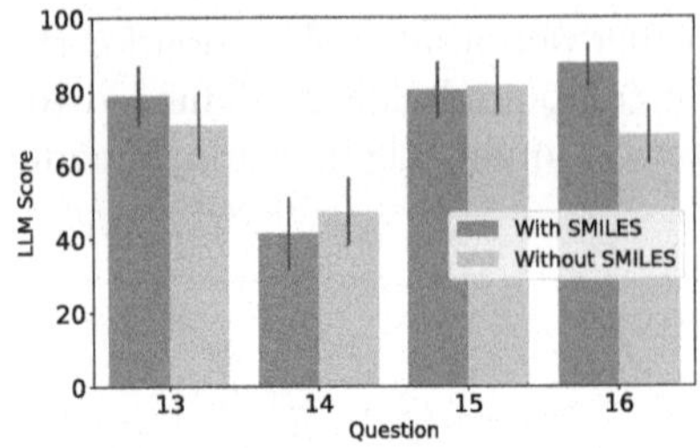

(a) LLM score for the CodeAgent experiments with and without the SMILES.

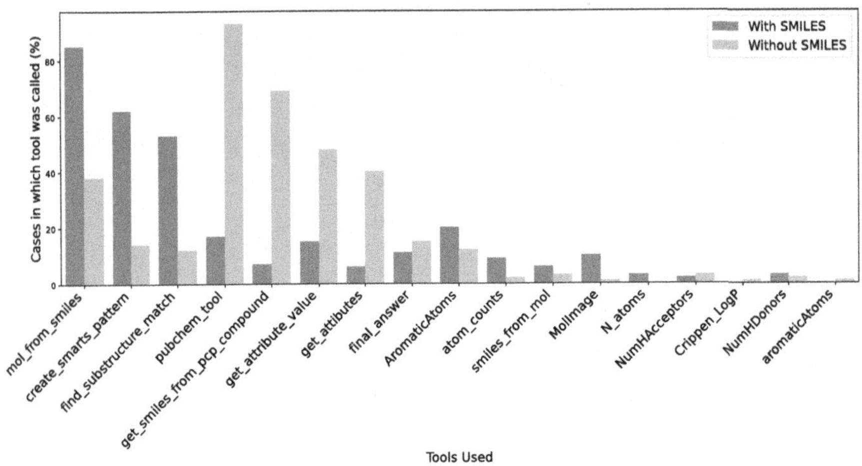

(b) Tools used by the ToolCalling agent with the default prompt for the questions with and without SMILES.

Fig. 10. Difference in performance and tool calls for the question with and without SMILES.

Lastly, we want to share an anecdotal example where we experimented with changing the order of parts of the questions. We compared two versions: a) "How many atoms more does oestrogen have than progesterone?" and b) "How many atoms more does progesterone have than oestrogen?"

Interestingly, option b consistently led to higher LLM performance, with average scores at least 25 points higher. The difference is likely not solely due to the order of terms, but also due to the implicit assumption embedded in each phrasing. In option a, the question presupposes that oestrogen has more atoms, an assumption that is actually incorrect. Though the agentic system has access to the tools needed and could still arrive at the correct answer if it systematically compares molecular structures, the lower performance suggests that the model is influenced by the preposition. This could point to an instance of acquiescence bias, which is a tendency in language models to conform to the implied premise of a question without critical evaluation [3]. This indicates a need for further research into how such biases influence reasoning and factual accuracy in LLM responses and how this can be overcome.

References

1. Boiko, D.A., MacKnight, R., Kline, B., Gomes, G.: Autonomous chemical research with large language models. Nature **624**(7992), 570–578 (2023)
2. Cai, F., et al.: MolLangBench: a comprehensive benchmark for language-prompted molecular structure recognition, editing, and generation. arXiv preprint arXiv:2505.15054 (2025)
3. Costello, S., Roodenburg, J.: Acquiescence response bias-Yeasaying and higher education. Educat. Develop. Psychol. **32**(2), 105–119 (2015)
4. Cui, D., Long, S., Li, Q.: Can reasoning power significantly improve the knowledge of large language models for chemistry?–Based on conversations with Deepseek and ChatGPT. ChemRxiv (2025)
5. Gao, B., et al.: PharmAgents: building a virtual pharma with large language model agents. arXiv preprint arXiv:2503.22164 (2025)
6. A. E. Ghareeb, B. Chang, L. Mitchener, A. Yiu, C. J. Szostkiewicz, J. M. Laurent, M. T. Razzak, A. D. White, M. M. Hinks, and S. G. Rodriques. Robin: A multi-agent system for automating scientific discovery. arXiv preprint arXiv:2505.13400, 2025
7. Grougan, M., Hix, M. A., Walker, A. R.: Librarian of Alexandria: an extensible LLM-based chemical data extraction pipeline. ChemRxiv (2025)
8. Gu, J., et al.: A survey on LLM-as-a-judge. arXiv preprint arXiv:2411.15594 (2024)
9. Guo, T., et al.: What can large language models do in chemistry? A comprehensive benchmark on eight tasks. Adv. Neural. Inf. Process. Syst. **36**, 59662–59688 (2023)
10. Hosseini,S., Seilani, H.: The role of agentic AI in shaping a smart future: a systematic review. Array, 100399 (2025)
11. Hu, J., Nawaz, H., Rui, Y., Chi, L., Ullah, A., Dral, P. O.: Aitomia: your intelligent assistant for AI-driven atomistic and quantum chemical simulations. arXiv preprint arXiv:2505.08195 (2025)
12. Huang, K., et al.: Biomni: a general-purpose biomedical AI agent. *bioRxiv*, pp. 05–2025 (2025)
13. Inoue, Y., Song, T., Fu, T.: DrugAgent: explainable drug repurposing agent with large language model-based reasoning. arXiv preprint arXiv:2408.13378 (2024)
14. Jang, Y., Kim, J., Ahn,S.: Improving chemical understanding of LLMs via SMILES parsing. arXiv preprint arXiv:2505.16340 (2025)
15. Johansen, K., Lundström, I., Liedberg, B.: Sensitivity deviation: instrumental linearity errors that influence concentration analyses and kinetic evaluation of biomolecular interactions. Biosens. Bioelectron. **15**(9–10), 503–509 (2000)
16. Kim, H., Jang, Y., Ahn, S.: MT-Mol: multi agent system with tool-based reasoning for molecular optimization. arXiv preprint arXiv:2505.20820 (2025)
17. Kim, S., Chen, J., Cheng, T., Gindulyte, A., He, J., He, S., Li, Q., Shoemaker, B.A., Thiessen, P.A., Yu, B., et al.: PubChem 2025 update. Nucleic Acids Res. **53**(D1), D1516–D1525 (2025)
18. Klinger, R., Kolářik, C., Fluck, J., Hofmann-Apitius, M., Friedrich, C.M.: Detection of IUPAC and IUPAC-like chemical names. Bioinformatics **24**(13), i268–i276 (2008)

19. Landrum, G.: RDKit: Cheminformatics and Machine Learning Software RDKIT (2013)
20. Li, K., Wu, Z., Wang, S., Hu, W.: DrugPilot: LLM-based parameterized reasoning agent for drug discovery. arXiv preprint arXiv:2505.13940 (2025)
21. Liu, J., et al.: Generated knowledge prompting for commonsense reasoning. In: Annual Meeting of the Association for Computational Linguistics (2021)
22. Bran, A.M., Cox, S., Schilter, O., Baldassari, C., White, A.D., Schwaller, P.: Augmenting large language models with chemistry tools. Nat. Mach. Intell **6**(5), 525–535 (2024)
23. Mirza, A., et al.: A framework for evaluating the chemical knowledge and reasoning abilities of large language models against the expertise of chemists. Nat. Chem. **17**(7), 1–8 (2025)
24. Runcie, N. T., Deane, C. M., Imrie,F.: Assessing the chemical intelligence of large language models. arXiv preprint arXiv:2505.07735 (2025)
25. Saito, K., Wachi, A., Wataoka, K., Akimoto, Y.: Verbosity bias in preference labeling by large language models. arXiv preprint arXiv:2310.10076 (2023)
26. Scialom, T., et al.: QuestEval: summarization asks for fact-based evaluation. arXiv preprint arXiv:2103.12693 (2021)
27. Serrano, D.R., et al.: Artificial intelligence (AI) applications in drug discovery and drug delivery: revolutionizing personalized medicine. Pharmaceutics **16**(10), 1328 (2024)
28. Szymański, P., Markowicz, M., Mikiciuk-Olasik, E.: Adaptation of high-throughput screening in drug discovery-toxicological screening tests. Int. J. Mol. Sci. **13**(1), 427–452 (2011)
29. Wang, E., et al.: TxGemma: efficient and agentic LLMs for therapeutics. arXiv preprint arXiv:2504.06196 (2025)
30. Wang, X., et al.: Executable code actions elicit better LLM agents. In: Forty-first International Conference on Machine Learning (2024)
31. Weininger, D.: SMILES, a chemical language and information system. 1. introduction to methodology and encoding rules. J. Chem. Info. Comput. Sci. **28**(1), 31–36 (1988)
32. Yao, S., et al.: React: synergizing reasoning and acting in language models. In: International Conference on Learning Representations (ICLR) (2023)
33. Ye, G., et al.: DrugAssist: a large language model for molecule optimization. Brief. Bioinfo. **26**(1), bbae693 (2025)
34. Zhang, Y., et al.: Exploring the role of large language models in the scientific method: from hypothesis to discovery. NPJ Artif. Intell. **1**(1), 1–15 (2025)

Multi-price Lottery: A New Pricing for Ticket Lottery Sales

Maiko Hara and Yoshifumi Manabe(✉)

School of Informatics, Kogakuin University Shinjuku, Tokyo, Japan
manabe@cc.kogakuin.ac.jp

Abstract. This paper proposes a multi-price lottery, a novel pricing mechanism for ticket lottery sales. The multi-price lottery improves the expected payoffs for all types of potential buyers compared to the traditional single-price lottery system, while also increasing the event organizer's overall sales. In this mechanism, high-paying buyers enjoy a higher probability of winning despite a higher price. Low-paying buyers benefit from lower prices despite a reduced chance of winning. Because some tickets are sold at higher prices, the organizer's total revenue increases even if the other tickets are sold at lower prices.

We begin by analyzing a simple case with two types of buyers–those with high and low valuations. We then extend the analysis to cases where buyer valuations are discrete and uniformly distributed. Finally, we examine the case with a continuous valuation distribution.

Keywords: Ticket lottery · Pricing mechanism · Expected payoff · Total revenue

1 Introduction

This paper proposes a multi-price lottery, a novel pricing mechanism for ticket lottery sales. The multi-price lottery improves the expected payoffs for all types of potential buyers compared to the traditional single-price lottery system, while also increasing the event organizer's overall sales.

The traditional ticket lottery sales are executed as follows. The event organizer decides the fixed price P and the number of tickets X. Potential buyers enter a lottery. Each lottery winner can buy one ticket for the price P. Though the lottery sales are simple and fair, some potential buyers are willing to pay higher prices to get tickets when the number of tickets is limited and the event is extremely popular. In this paper, we refer to potential buyers who can afford high prices as high-paying potential buyers. We refer to potential buyers who can only purchase the ticket at low prices as low-paying potential buyers.

The ticket prices of very popular events tend to be very expensive. Increasing the ticket price increases the event organizer's total sales and increases the possibility of winning for high-paying potential buyers, since low-paying potential

M. Baldoni et al. (Eds.): EUMAS 2025, LNAI 16259, pp. 299–307, 2026.
https://doi.org/10.1007/978-3-032-22820-8_20

buyers give up buying. The method's detriment is the dissatisfaction among low-paying potential buyers. They think that these events are only for the wealthy. Such an image is not good for some musicians and sports teams.

There are several other pricing methods, such as dynamic pricing [2,6], auctions [1,3], and a hybrid of auctions and lottery [4]. The ticket prices for popular events tend to become very expensive through these methods. These methods do not solve the low-paying potential buyers' problem.

There are other ticket lottery methods, such as weighted lottery [7], in which the potential buyers with some property have a higher winning probability. For a weighted lottery to be widely acceptable, all potential buyers need to be able to agree on how the weights are set. Such agreements might be difficult to reach among buyers who generally have differing values.

We propose a new ticket lottery in which the expected payoffs of the high-paying potential buyers and low-paying potential buyers are better than those of the usual ticket lottery sales, and the total sales of the organizer are also better than those of the usual ticket lottery sales.

The main idea is

- The winning probability of the high-paying potential buyers is increased, although the price is increased, and
- The price for the low-paying potential buyers is decreased, although the winning probability is decreased.

Because of the first property, the expected payoff of the high-paying potential buyers increases. Because of the second property, the expected payoff of the low-paying potential buyers also increases. Since some tickets are sold at a higher price, the total sales of the organizer increase even if some tickets are sold at a lower price. The proposed method can be used as a lottery sales method for fixed members, such as paid fan club members.

The rest of the paper is organized as follows. Section 2 discusses the simple case when there are two ticket valuations: high and low valuations. Section 3 considers maximizing the event organizer's total revenue. Section 4 shows variants of the multi-price lottery. Section 5 discusses the case when the valuations are discrete and uniform. Section 6 discusses the case when the valuation function is continuous. Section 7 concludes the paper.

2 High and Low Price Case

Section 2–4 discusses the simplest case when there are two ticket valuations: high and low valuations. The assumption of the problem is as follows.

Assumption 1. *Let Y be the original price of the ticket. Let X be the number of tickets. Let $N(> X)$ be the total number of potential buyers. $r(0 < r < 1)$ is the ratio of high-paying potential buyers among N buyers. We assume that $rN > X$ and $(1-r)N > X$. Let a_0Y and a_1Y $(a_0 > a_1 > 1)$ be the ticket valuation by the high-paying and the low-paying potential buyers, respectively.*

This paper assumes N is fixed, for example, the members of a musician's or a sports team's paid fan club. Y is the fixed value decided by the cost.

When the ticket price is Y, the expected payoff of a potential buyer whose ticket valuation is aY, and the possibility of getting the ticket by the lottery is p, the expected payoff for the potential buyer is $p(aY - Y)$.

When the standard lottery is executed, the possibility of winning is X/N for every potential buyer. Thus, the expected payoffs for the high-paying and low-paying potential buyers are $X(a_0 - 1)Y/N$ and $X(a_1 - 1)Y/N$, respectively. The total sales are XY.

Now, the organizer holds two different ticket lotteries. Each potential buyer may only enter one lottery. The two lotteries are low-price but low winning probability and high-price but high winning probability ones. The prices of the high-price and the low-price lotteries are b_0Y and b_1Y, respectively. Note that $b_0 > 1 > b_1$, $a_0 > b_0$, and $a_1 > b_1$ holds. The number of tickets sold by the high-price and the low-price lotteries is r_0X and $(1 - r_0)X$, respectively. Note that $r < r_0 < 1$ holds.

The expected payoff of the high-price lottery is greater than that of the standard lottery for a high-paying potential buyer if $r_0X(a_0 - b_0)Y/(rN) \geq X(a_0 - 1)Y/N$ holds. The inequality can be simplified as

$$r_0(a_0 - b_0)/r \geq a_0 - 1 \tag{1}$$

The expected payoff of the low-price lottery is greater than that of the standard lottery for a low-paying potential buyer if $(1 - r_0)X(a_1 - b_1)Y/((1 - r)N) \geq X(a_1 - 1)Y/N$ holds. The inequality can be simplified as

$$(1 - r_0)(a_1 - b_1)/(1 - r) \geq a_1 - 1 \tag{2}$$

To make the high-paying potential buyers join the high-price lottery, the expected payoff must be greater than that of the low-price lottery for a high-paying potential buyer. The condition is written as $r_0X(a_0 - b_0)Y/(rN) \geq (1 - r_0)X(a_0 - b_1)Y/((1 - r)N)$. Note that N is large, and one potential buyer's move does not affect the winning possibilities. The condition can be simplified as

$$r_0(a_0 - b_0)/r \geq (1 - r_0)(a_0 - b_1)/(1 - r) \tag{3}$$

To make the low-paying potential buyers join the low-price lottery, the expected payoff must be greater than that of the high-paying lottery for a low-paying potential buyer. The condition is written as $(1 - r_0)X(a_1 - b_1)Y/((1 - r)N) \geq r_0X(a_1 - b_0)Y/(rN)$. Again, we assume that one potential buyer's move does not affect the winning possibilities. The inequality can be simplified as

$$(1 - r_0)(a_1 - b_1)/(1 - r) \geq r_0(a_1 - b_0)/r \tag{4}$$

Note that if $b_0 > a_1$, this inequality is always satisfied because the term to the right of the inequality is negative.

The total sales of the new lotteries must be greater than those of the standard lottery. The condition is written as $r_0 X b_0 Y + (1-r_0) X b_1 Y \geq XY$ The condition can be simplified as

$$r_0 b_0 + (1 - r_0) b_1 \geq 1 \tag{5}$$

For some values, there exists a pricing that satisfies all inequalities. Suppose that $a_0 = 10$, $a_1 = 1.5$ and $r = 0.6$. In this case, the organizer sets $b_0 = 2$, $b_1 = 0.5$, and $r_0 = 0.7$. Then all the inequalities (1) (2) (3) (4) (5) are strictly satisfied, that is, the expected payoff is better for high-paying and low-paying potential buyers than the ones of the standard lottery and the total sales are better than that of the standard lottery.

Generally, for any $\delta > 0$ that satisfies $\delta < 1 - r$, set $r_0 = r + \delta$, $b_0 = 1 + \delta(a_0 - 1)/(r + \delta)$, and $b_1 = 1 - \delta(a_1 - 1)/(1 - r - \delta)$, then the inequalities (3) (4) (5) are strictly satisfied and equalities are satisfied for (1) (2).

Theorem 1. *For any (a_0, a_1, r) and $\delta > 0$ that satisfies $\delta < 1 - r$, a multi-price lottery whose expected payoffs and total sales are better than those of a standard lottery exists when $r_0 = r + \delta$, $b_0 = 1 + \delta(a_0 - 1)/(r + \delta)$, and $b_1 = 1 - \delta(a_1 - 1)/(1 - r - \delta)$.*

When the event organizer knows a_0 and a_1, he/she can raise the price of the standard lottery up to $(1 - \epsilon)a_1 Y$ while still ensuring that all potential buyers participate. Even in this case, the above theorem holds for the new $a'_1 = 1/(1-\epsilon)$ and $a'_0 = a_0/(1 - \epsilon)a_1$.

The above discussion assumes that the event organizer correctly estimates every potential buyer's ticket valuation, and that there are two valuations. In many cases, the assumptions are not satisfied. Even in such a case, the above method can be applied if the potential buyers can be divided into a high-paying group and a low-paying group, M_0 and M_1. The lower bound estimate of M_0's potential buyer's ticket valuation is set to a_0. The upper bound estimate of M_1's potential buyer's ticket valuation is set to a_1. If the Eqs. (1) (3) are satisfied by a_0, the equations are satisfied by any value $a' \geq a_0$, where a' is the ticket valuation of a potential buyer in M_0. If the Eqs. (2) (4) are satisfied by a_1, the equations are satisfied by any value $a'' \leq a_1$, where a'' is the ticket valuation of a potential buyer in M_1.

Next, consider the case when the ratio of high-paying potential buyers r cannot be correctly estimated. The organizer evaluates that the ratio is between r_h and r_l, and the actual value r satisfies $r_l < r < r_h$. To satisfy Eqs. (1) (3) in every case, r_h is used in these equations instead of r. To satisfy Eqs. (2) (4) in every case, r_l is used in these equations instead of r.

Note that if we execute this lottery for general potential buyers, new low-paying potential buyers might appear when the ticket price decreases. Thus, this system works only for a fixed group of potential buyers, such as the members of a paid fan club. The design for the case when new potential buyers might join is an open problem.

Another problem with the proposed lottery is ticket resale by a low-paying potential buyer. Since some tickets are sold at a higher price, the resale price begins with the higher lottery price. That might result in a higher profit for the resellers. Again, one countermeasure to the problem is restricting the lottery to the paid fan club members. The members need to undergo identity verification during ticket sales and authentication during admission [5].

Note that some potential buyers may submit multiple applications for a single lottery sale to increase the winning probability. If every potential buyer submits the same number of applications, the result is unchanged. The case when each potential buyer submits a different number of applications is an open problem.

3 Maximizing the Total Sales

Since the organizer can decide the prices, he/she tries to maximize the total sales under the above conditions, that is, increase b_0 and b_1 if inequalities hold. Thus, the inequalities (1) and (2) are changed to the following equalities.

$$r_0(a_0 - b_0)/r = a_0 - 1. \tag{6}$$

$$(1 - r_0)(a_1 - b_1)/(1 - r) = a_1 - 1. \tag{7}$$

From these equations, we can obtain b_0 and b_1. Even if we use these values, inequalities (3) (4) are satisfied.

Using the values for b_0 and b_1, we obtain the total sales, the left side of Eq. (5)

$$(r_0 - r)(a_0 - a_1) + 1 \tag{8}$$

Since this equation has one variable r_0 and $a_0 > a_1$, the sales are maximized when r_0 is the maximum. When $r_0 = 1-\epsilon$ (note that actually r_0 must be a little smaller than 1 to avoid $-\infty$ price for b_1), $b_0 = (1 - r/(1-\epsilon))a_0 + r/(1-\epsilon)$, and $b_1 = (1 - (1-r)/\epsilon)a_1 + (1-r)/\epsilon$.

When r_0 is large, $b_1 < 0$ might be satisfied. A negative price of b_1 can be achieved by giving the winners additional gifts other than the ticket. If the organizer wants to avoid a negative price, set $r_0 = 1 - (a_1 - 1)(1 - r)/a_1$. In this case, $b_1 = 0$ is achieved.

Another case to consider is that the number of high-paying potential buyers is small, and $rN < X$ holds. In this case, the winning probability of the high-paying potential buyers becomes 1 before r_0 becomes 1. In this case, the upper bound of r_0 is rN/X.

4 Variants of the Multi-price Lottery

Though the above lottery is simple, the high-paying winners might envy the low-paying winners. To avoid such envy, we can consider variants of the above multiple-price lottery. This section shows two variants of the lotteries from the previous section.

The first variant, called the multi-price multi-option lottery, is as follows. There are two options, and each potential buyer can apply for one option. The first option is joining the low-price lottery. The second option is joining the low-price lottery, and the losers must join the high-price lottery. The high-paying potential buyers are expected to select the second option.

Again, we set the prices of the high-price and the low-price lotteries as b_0Y and b_1Y, respectively. The number of tickets sold by the high-price and the low-price lotteries is r_0X and $(1-r_0)X$, respectively.

The expected payoff of the first option is greater than that of the standard lottery for the low-paying potential buyers if $(1-r_0)X(a_1-b_1)Y/N \geq X(a_1-1)Y/N$ holds. The inequality can be written as

$$(1-r_0)(a_1-b_1) \geq a_1-1. \tag{9}$$

Let p be the possibility of winning the low-price lottery. $p=(1-r_0)X/N$. The expected payoff of the second option is greater than the standard lottery for the high-paying potential buyers if $p(a_0-b_1)Y+(1-p)r_0X(a_0-b_0)Y/((1-p)rN) \geq X(a_0-1)Y/N$ holds. The inequality can be simplified as

$$(1-r_0)(a_0-b_1)+r_0(a_0-b_0)/r \geq a_0-1. \tag{10}$$

The high-paying potential buyers prefer the second option to the first option because the expected payoff of the first option is $p(a_0-b_1)Y$ and $a_0 > b_0$ holds. When the event organizer sets $b_0 > a_1$, the low-paying potential buyers prefer the first option to the second option. The total sales condition is the same as the original one

$$r_0b_0+(1-r_0)b_1 \geq 1. \tag{11}$$

When $a_0=10$, $a_1=1.5$, and $r=0.6$, the set of values of the previous section ($r_0=0.7$, $b_0=2$, and $b_1=0.5$) does not satisfy both of the inequalities (9) and (10). Inequalities (9) (10) (11) are strictly satisfied if $r_0=0.65$, $b_0=2$, and $b_1=0.05$.

Generally, for any $\delta>0$ that satisfies $\delta<1-r$, set $r_0=r+\delta$, $b_0=(1-r)a_0+ra_1$, and $b_1=1-(a_1-1)(r+\delta)/(1-r-\delta)$, then $b_0>a_1$ holds and inequality (11) is strictly satisfied and equalities are satisfied for (9) (10).

Theorem 2. *For any (a_0,a_1,r) and $\delta>0$ that satisfies $\delta<1-r$, a multi-price multi-option lottery whose expected payoffs and total sales are better than those of a standard lottery exists when $r_0=r+\delta$, $b_0=(1-r)a_0+ra_1$, and $b_1=1-(a_1-1)(r+\delta)/(1-r-\delta)$.*

Again, consider maximizing the total sales. The inequalities in (9) and (10) are changed to the equalities as follows:

$$(1-r_0)(a_1-b_1)=a_1-1. \tag{12}$$

$$(1-r_0)(a_0-b_1)+r_0(a_0-b_0)/r=a_0-1. \tag{13}$$

From these equations, obtain b_0 and b_1. By substituting these equations into the left side of Eq. (11), we obtain the following equation that shows the total sales

$$r_0b_0+(1-r_0)b_1=r_0(1-r)(a_0-a_1)+1 \tag{14}$$

The total sales are maximized when r_0 is maximized. Again, to avoid b_1's $-\infty$ price, $r_0 = 1-\epsilon$ and price $b_0 = (1-r)a_0+ra_1$ and $b_1 = (1-(1-\epsilon)a_1)/\epsilon$. Another choice of pricing might be avoiding negative prices. In that case, $r_0 = 1/a_1$, $b_0 = (1-r)a_0 + ra_1$, and $b_1 = 0$.

The other variant of the multi-price lottery is called a multi-price multi-stage lottery. All potential buyers join the first(lowest price) lottery, and the losers can decide whether he/she continues to join the next lottery with a higher price. For the above two price valuation case, set variables r_0, b_0, and b_1 as the same ones for the multi-price multi-option lottery. Then, the inequalities to be satisfied are the same as the ones for the multi-price multi-option lottery (9) (10) (11).

Theorem 3. *For any (a_0, a_1, r) and $\delta > 0$ that satisfies $\delta < 1 - r$, a multi-price multi-stage lottery whose expected payoffs and total sales are better than those of a standard lottery exists when $r_0 = r + \delta$, $b_0 = (1 - r)a_0 + ra_1$, and $b_1 = 1 - (a_1 - 1)(r + \delta)/(1 - r - \delta)$.*

5 Discrete Uniform Valuation Case

This section discusses the case when the distribution of potential buyers' valuations is uniform but discrete.

Let $N = sn$ and the potential buyer $M_i(0 \le i \le n-1)$ has valuation a_iY. $a_0 > a_1 > \cdots > a_{n-1}$ and $|M_i| = s$. $N > X$ is satisfied. Set $r = X/N$. Consider the case when the event organizer provides n lotteries. For some $k(0 < k < n-1)$, the event organizer sells at a higher price $b_iY(b_i > 1)$ and a higher winning probability $r_i(r_i > r)$ for $M_i(i \le k)$ than the standard lottery. He/she sells at a lower price $b_iY(b_i < 1)$ and a lower winning probability $r_i(r_i < r)$ for $M_i(i > k)$ than the standard lottery. Consider the case when each potential buyer can join one lottery, that is, the potential buyer in M_i joins the i-th lottery.

The conditions to be satisfied can be obtained as in the previous sections.

$$r_i(a_i - b_i) - r(a_i - 1) \ge 0 (0 \le i \le n-1) \tag{15}$$

$$r_i(a_i - b_i) - r_j(a_i - b_j) \ge 0 (j \ne i) \tag{16}$$

$$\sum_{i=0}^{n-1} r_i b_i - nr \ge 0 \tag{17}$$

If we want to maximize the total sales, we need to calculate optimal values that satisfy the equations (15) (16) (17). Obtaining the optimal values is not easy because of the many parameters.

The cases of a multi-option lottery and a multi-stage lottery can be similarly discussed.

6 Continuous Distribution Valuation Case

This section discusses the case when the distribution of potential buyers' valuations is continuous. Let $f(x)$ be the potential buyers' distribution function. Let a_0Y and a_1Y be the maximum and minimum valuations. $\int_{a_1Y}^{a_0Y} f(x)dx = N$, where N is the total number of potential buyers. Consider the simple case when two lotteries L_0 and L_1 are provided. Let b_0 and $b_1(b_0 \geq 1 \geq b_1)$ be the prices of the two lotteries. Let $aY(a_1 < a < a_0)$ be the potential buyer's border price to join L_0 or L_1. Let $r = \int_{aY}^{a_0Y} f(x)dx/N$. r is the ratio of potential buyers whose valuation is greater than aY. $0 < r < 1$ holds. Let X be the number of tickets and let $r_0(0 < r_0 < 1)$ be the ratio of the tickets sold by L_0.

The expected payoff of L_0 is greater than that of the standard lottery for a high-paying $(v > a)$ potential buyer if $r_0X(vY - b_0Y)/rN \geq X(vY - Y)/N$. The equation is simplified as

$$r_0(v - b_0)/r \geq v - 1 \tag{18}$$

The expected payoff of L_1 is greater than that of the standard lottery for a low-paying $(v < a)$ potential buyer if $(1 - r_0)X(vY - b_1Y)/(1 - r)N \geq X(vY - Y)/N$. The equation is simplified as

$$(1 - r_0)(v - b_1)/(1 - r) \geq v - 1 \tag{19}$$

In Eqs. (18) (19), set $v = a$ then we obtain the following two inequalities.

$$r_0(a - b_0)/r \geq a - 1 \tag{20}$$

$$(1 - r_0)(a - b_1)/(1 - r) \geq a - 1 \tag{21}$$

Since $b_0 \geq 1$, $r_0/r \geq 1$ holds from equation (20). Thus, $r_0 \geq r$ must be held. Therefore, $(1-r_0) \leq (1-r)$ is satisfied. Because $b_1 \leq 1$, Eq. (21) is satisfied only if $b_1 = 1$. In this case, $r_0 = r$ must also be satisfied. Therefore, no multi-price lottery satisfies all the conditions.

Note that for any multi-price lottery, there are two neighboring lotteries whose prices, b_0 and b_1, satisfy $b_0 \geq 1 \geq b_1$, the same argument holds. If the potential buyer's valuations are continuous, there does not exist a multi-price lottery that is better than the standard lottery.

By a similar discussion, we can show that there is no multi-option or multi-price lottery better than the standard lottery when the potential buyer's valuations are continuous.

7 Conclusion

This paper proposed a multi-price lottery, a novel pricing mechanism for ticket lottery sales. There are many remaining problems, for example,

- Comparison to the other pricing methods in real valuation distribution.

- Analysis when the potential buyers are not fixed in advance; that is, when a new lottery with a low price is presented, new potential buyers with lower valuations appear.
- A pricing method that maximizes the event organizer's total revenue for common discrete distributions of valuations.
- A new method that can treat continuous valuation functions of potential buyers.

References

1. Budish, E., Bhave, A.: Primary-market auctions for event tickets: eliminating the rents of "bob the broker"? Am. Econ. J. Microeconomics **15**(1), 142–170 (2023)
2. Drayer, J., Shapiro, S.L., Lee, S.: Dynamic ticket pricing in sport: an agenda for research and practice. Sport Mark. Q. **21**(3), 184–194 (2012)
3. Fu, B.: Increasing ticketing allocative efficiency using marginal price auction theory. arXiv preprint arXiv:2309.11189 (2023)
4. Huang, Y., Wen, Q.: Auction-lottery hybrid mechanisms: structural model and empirical analysis. Int. Econ. Rev. **60**(1), 355–385 (2019)
5. Ondato: The benefits of ticket verification and authentication. https://ondato.com/blog/the-benefits-of-ticket-verification-and-authentication/. Accessed 8 May 2025
6. Shapiro, S.L., Drayer, J.: A new age of demand-based pricing: an examination of dynamic ticket pricing and secondary market prices in major league baseball. J. Sport Manag. **26**(6), 532–546 (2012)
7. Vong, G.: Weighing up weighted lotteries: scarcity, overlap cases, and fair inequalities of chance. Ethics **130**(3), 320–348 (2020)

Modelling Norm Change Through Trendsetters

Beyza Nur Şenol(✉), Seher Ova, and Feyza M. Hafızoğlu

Istanbul Commerce University, 34445 İstanbul, Turkey
beyzasenol08@gmail.com , fmhafizoglu@ticaret.edu.tr

Abstract. It is crucial to address the dynamic aspects of norm life cycle in multi-agent systems research. This study presents an agent based model for norm change using trendsetter agents. The agents are connected based on a certain topology, and repeatedly play the coordination game with their immediate neighbors. The agents select a utility maximizing action (along with exploration) based on their past experiences (Q-learning) and social observations (action preferences of nearest neighbors). In order to investigate under which conditions norm change happens, we conducted a comprehensive set of experiments for different trendsetter configurations (position and number), agent related factors (decision model, exploration rate), and topologies. The empirical findings suggest that norm change is sensitive to the trendsetter positions in the network, exploration rates, and the proportion of observed population. A positive relationship is observed between norm change speed and the effect of social observations and the proportion of trendsetters.

Keywords: social norm · norm change · trendsetter

1 Introduction

In the life cycle of norms, norms emerge and may change over time. In order to adapt to the societal changes, old norms may be either replaced with new norms due to obsolescence or modified accordingly. A well-known example of this is that people quickly quitted greeting norms such as hand shaking, hugging due to the social distancing requirements and adopted distanced greetings during the Covid-19 pandemic [18].

Social norms arise when individuals follow rules based on the belief that their peers comply and expect compliance, with defiance often triggering sanctions, making norm abandonment risky [3]. Social norms persist when individual behavior depends on mutual expectations—what others do and approve. Changing a norm requires a collective shift in these expectations starting with gradual breaches until a tipping point triggers widespread abandonment of the norm [2,8].

Similar to human societies, norms in agent societies should be able to evolve over time as well. Despite their importance, far too little attention has been paid

M. Baldoni et al. (Eds.): EUMAS 2025, LNAI 16259, pp. 308–316, 2026.
https://doi.org/10.1007/978-3-032-22820-8_21

to understanding the other steps of the norm life cycle such as the change or removal of norms [2,6].

This study focuses on scenarios where the norm change is attempted by an informal institution employing trendsetters. Using such interventions for behavioral change is a cost-effective and widely used approach to elevate the society, e.g., promoting environmental and social sustainability [19]. In this context, we assume that there exists a norm established in an agent society and trendsetter agents, who abandon the existing norm and adopted another behavior, are distributed to the social network to spread the norm change. In such scenarios, we are interested in the following research questions:

- Under which conditions norm change happen?
- What kind of trendsetter placements in a network promote norm change?
- What are the effects of the following fundamental factors on the speed of norm change base? Such as topology, agent's learning model and exploration rate.

2 Related Work

Researchers attempted to develop norm life cycle models [4,12]. Considering these models, four fundamental stages of norm life cycle models can be derived as: (i) creation, (ii) emergence, (iii) modification, and (iv) removal of norms. This study focuses on the third stage of the norm life cycle.

Various determinants have been identified to cause norm changes such as social networks, media, institutions, ecological and cultural factors [8]. A large body of work highlights the (great) causal effects of media (nowadays social media), which yields common knowledge in society, on norm change [15]. As an example of that, Qutteina *et al.* [14] showed that social media has an impact on the eating behavior of youth. Coskun [5] draws our attention to the emergence of zero waste behavior caused by environmental factors.

Investigating the underlying factors that promote or hinder norm change is crucial to take advantage of norms as tools for good. One of the critical factors is the positions of trendsetters. Centrality and prominence in social networks can facilitate norm change. For instance, Paluck and Shepherd [13] demonstrated that the changes in influential students' public behavior altered their peers' perceptions of school-wide norms. On the other hand, norm change can also be driven by trendsetters on the periphery of social groups. Since being less central makes them more likely to challenge the status quo due to the less risk and lower costs of transgression of a norm [2]. Likewise, Gomila and Paluck [9] justified that the transgressors of norms tend to have greater risk tolerance and a lower propensity for conformity. Norms can also be modified by sharing information about the benefits of new norms with peers [10].

Empirical research using agent-based models suggests various ways to use trendsetters, a.k.a., influencers, as an intervention. The usage of trendsetters is not limited to norm change, but they can also be employed to manipulate emergence of norms [7]. In a similar vein, trendsetter intervention can be simulated to study digital promotional activities, i.e., advertising digital platforms [17]. Amato *et al.* [1] studied the norm change to shed light on the cultural evolution of language. Rouleau [16] developed a computational model to generate metastable norms from constructivist logic. De *et al.* [6] proposed an evolutionary game-theoretic model of norm change based on the idea that different strength of norms in societies translate to interaction structures and incentives.

This study is the first to integrate learning agents in the process of norm change and provide an in-depth analysis of social structure, trendsetter distribution, and individual characteristics of agents. Our primary contributions are:

- We propose an agent based model of norm change through trendsetters that incorporates different trendsetter positions and agents' learning methods,
- We provide a comprehensive analysis of factors effecting norm change.

3 Preliminaries

This section presents the agent model to examine how an agent society transitions from an established norm to a new norm using trendsetters.

3.1 Agent Based Model

We study an agent society where agents are paired with their neighbors and play the well-known coordination game repeatedly. Players can gain one (zero) unit reward as a result of coordination (anti-coordination) in their actions. We assume that action A is established as the norm and action B is the alternative action which trendsetter agents aim to spread as the new norm.

The Interaction Model: Agents are connected based on a certain topology. Each agent is paired with one of its immediate neighbors randomly to play the coordination game. Then, each agent picks an action from the set $S = \{A, B\}$. Finally, they are rewarded accordingly.

Agents' Decision Model: The agents select their actions using Q-learning with an $\epsilon - greedy$ exploration strategy. The expected utility for an action is a weighted sum of two components: (i) the agent's personal experience (Q-value) and (ii) a social observation (O-value). The O-value is derived from the recent actions of neighbors within a defined social observation range, which promotes localized decision-making. Agents choose the action that maximizes this utility. The expected utility for each action $a \in \{A, B\}$ is defined as:

$$U_i(a) = w_e Q_{(a)} + w_o O_{(i,a)}, \tag{1}$$

where w_e and w_o are weights of experience and observations, respectively. Then, the agent picks the action with the highest utility, i.e., $\arg\max_{a \in \{A,B\}} U_i(a)$.

Exploration: The $\epsilon - greedy$ is employed, where the agents select a random action (explore) with probability ϵ and the action with the highest utility (exploit) with probability $1 - \epsilon$. Ties in utility are broken randomly to avoid bias.

Q-learning: Agents use a state-less Q-learning, i.e., there is only one, default, state with two actions, $S = \{A, B\}$. After observing the reward, Q-values are updated by using a static learning rate, α, as follows: $Q_{(a)} = (1-\alpha) \cdot Q_{(a')} + \alpha \cdot r_t$, where r_t is the reward at timestep t.

Social Observations: Agents observe the actions of their direct and indirect neighbors to estimate the local prevalence of social norms, incorporating this information into their decision-making. An agent's observable set is determined by its network position and a global parameter, β. This set consists of the $\beta \cdot N$ **closest agents**, where N is the total population and closeness is measured by shortest-path distance. For example, if $\beta = 0.3$ and $N = 100$, an agent observes its 30 nearest neighbors.

Agents maintain a sliding history window of size τ for each observable neighbor's recent actions. By inspecting these windows and counting the frequency of actions **A** and **B**, an agent estimates the most prevalent local social norm. The social observation component $O_i(a)$ is thus defined as the normalized frequency with which action a has been selected among the observed agents over their respective history windows.

Trendsetters are a subset of agents that consistently select the alternative action (**B**), regardless of incurring lower payoffs. While their proportion is an experimental parameter, it is limited to a maximum of 10% **to preserve the validity of norm emergence dynamics**. This threshold ensures that at least 90% of the population must adopt a behavior for it to be considered a true social norm [11]. Trendsetters are selected from agents with the highest centrality in the network, using two heuristics: *(i) Closeness*, which is defined as the average of the shortest paths between an agent and all others and *(ii) degree*, defined as an agent's number of connections (neighbors). Highly connected agents directly influence a larger portion of the network.

3.2 Experimental Setup

We use agent-based simulations to investigate norm change, defined as the replacement of an established norm A with an alternative B. Each simulation runs with a population of $N = 100$ agents for $T = 1500$ timesteps, unless specified otherwise. Default values for all other parameters are listed in Table 1.

We report results averaged over 50 simulations with different seeds. Our primary metric is the rate of norm change: the proportion of simulations where the established norm (A) was replaced by the new one (B). To simulate a society with a pre-existing norm, we initialize all agents (excluding trendsetters) with a strong preference for action **A** by setting their Q-values to $Q_{(A)} = 0.96$ and $Q_{(B)} = 0.04$.

Topologies: Scale-free networks are generated based on the Barabási–Albert model, while small-world networks follow the Watts–Strogatz model with rewiring probability $p = 0.1$ and degree $k = 4$.

Table 1. Default and alternative values of experimental parameters

Parameter	Default Values	Alternative Values
N (number of agents)	100	$\{150, 200, 300, 400\}$
Topology	Scale-free	Small-world
α (learning rate)	0.05	none
β (observation proportion)	0.1	$\{0.1, 0.2\}$
Trendsetter proportion	2%	$\{1, 4, 7, 10\}$
ϵ (exploration likelihood)	0.05	$\{0.01, 0.10\}$
τ (window size for observations)	5	$\{1, 10\}$
$[w_e, w_o]$ (experience and observation weights))	[0, 1]	
Trendsetter selection strategy	Degree	Closeness

Observed Proportion: Each agent observes a subset of other agents based on shortest-path distance within the network, constrained by a tunable parameter $\beta \in \{0, 1\}$. A lower β limits observation to local neighborhoods, while higher values permit broader access to social information.

3.3 Experimental Results

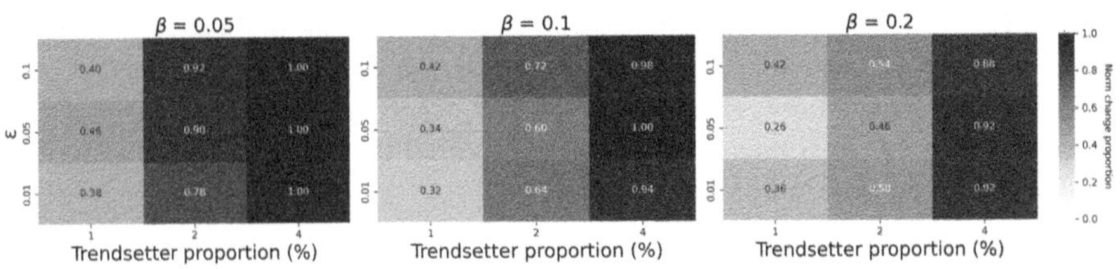

Fig. 1. Proportion of simulations with norm change for varying ϵ (exploration rate), β (observed proportion), trendsetter proportion, and weights [0, 1]

Figure 1 shows the rate of norm change over 50 simulations. The results confirm the expected positive correlation between the trendsetter proportion and norm change, an effect most pronounced at low exploration (ϵ) and observation (β) values. At low exploration ($\epsilon = 0.01, \beta = 0.05$), increasing the trendsetter proportion from 1% to 4% causes a dramatic rise in norm change (from 38% to 100%). This effect is more pronounced at higher exploration rates; with $\epsilon = 0.10$, even a small trendsetter proportion is sufficient to trigger complete norm change. However, increasing the observation proportion does not always yield better results. Surprisingly, under low trendsetter proportions, larger β values (e.g., $\beta = 0.10$ or $\beta = 0.20$) slightly reduce norm change rates, suggesting that broader but diluted observation may weaken influence concentration.

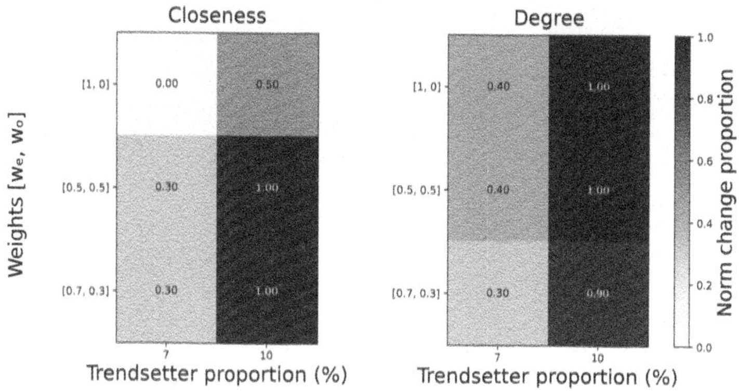

Fig. 2. The proportion of simulations where norm change occurred for different trendsetter positions/proportions, weight combinations, and default parameters.

The relationship between the agents' decision weights and trendsetter proportions is further explored as shown in Fig. 2. The agents relying solely on individual experience ([1, 0]) require larger trendsetter proportions (at least 10–15%) to accomplish norm change. Conversely, when agents incorporate social observation (e.g., [0.5, 0.5] or [0.3, 0.7]), norm change becomes more likely, particularly under closeness-based trendsetter positions. This indicates that both agent-level susceptibility to social influence and the global position of trendsetters jointly determine diffusion efficiency.

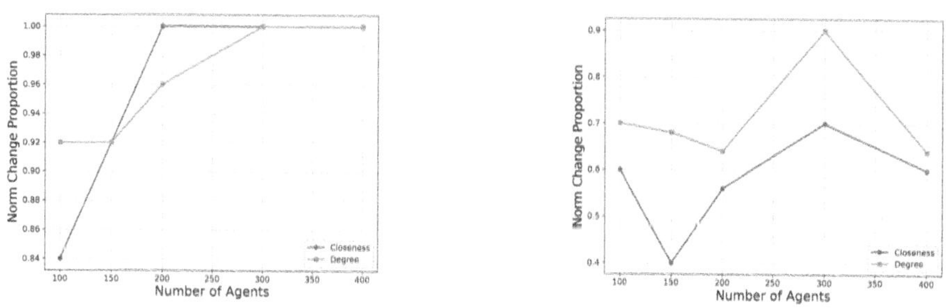

(a) Scale-free

(b) Small-world

Fig. 3. The proportion of simulations where norm change occurred for different agent counts, trendsetter positions, topologies, and default parameters.

Population size also plays a critical role on norm change. In Fig. 3, norm change becomes more likely in larger communities. With default values of trendsetter proportion, ϵ, and β, norm change likelihood rises from 40% with 100 agents to certainty with 300 agents or more. This implies the presence of a threshold effect: once the agent population reaches a sufficient size, even a small number of well-placed trendsetters can trigger large-scale behavioral change.

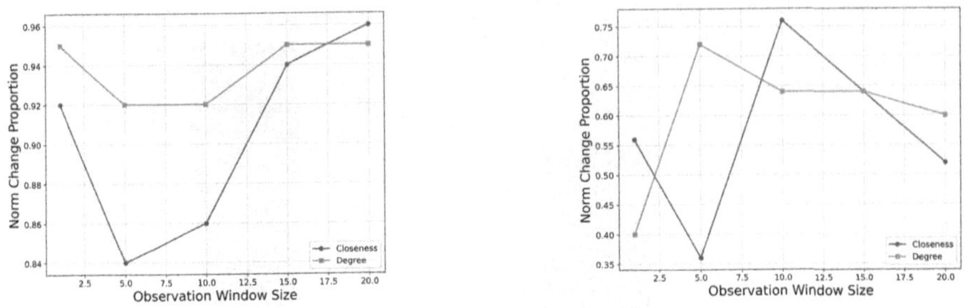

(a) Scale-free

(b) Small-world

Fig. 4. Proportion of simulations with norm change for varying τ (observation window size), trendsetter positions, topologies, and default parameters.

The underlying topology and the trendsetter selection strategy jointly influence overall norm change rates, as shown in Fig. 4. In scale-free networks, closeness heuristic achieves a norm change rate of 94%, compared to 84% with degree-based selection. This suggests that selecting trendsetters based on their structural proximity to others enables faster and wider influence. In contrast, small-world networks yield much lower norm change rates (56–58%) regardless of selection strategy, highlighting the structural advantage of scale-free topologies. The presence of highly connected hubs in scale-free networks facilitates rapid propagation once those hubs adopt the new norm, whereas the clustered, homogeneous structure of small-world networks limits global influence.

Observation window size, τ, which governs how much past behavior agents consider, also has a notable effect. As shown in Figs. 4, increasing the observation window lead to an increase in norm change rates under both selection strategies, but more dramatically for closeness-based selection. In scale-free networks, norm change rates steadily improves with larger windows, reaching up to 96% convergence. However, in small-world networks, norm change exhibits nonlinear behavior—peaking at moderate window sizes but declining at extremes—especially under closeness-based selection. This highlights the need to tune window size carefully, as its impact is topology- and strategy-dependent.

When agents rely solely on individual learning, closeness-based trendsetter selection enables much faster norm change: increasing the number of trendsetters from 7 to 15 reduces the time from 4000 to 300 steps. In contrast, degree-based selection requires significantly more time—8300 steps at 10 trendsetters—and completely fails to produce norm change at lower counts. These findings emphasize that not only the proportion but also the position of trendsetters is crucial in shaping the likelihood and speed of norm change under decentralized learning.

4 Conclusion

This study investigates under which conditions norm change occurs in an agent society, where agents can learn from their own experience and social observation, in the presence of an established norm by using trendsetter agents. The key parameters are placement strategies, observation window size, exploration rate, and network topology. The results show that both the proportion and positioning of trendsetters significantly facilitate norm change, especially when combined with low exploration rates and limited observation scopes (see Fig. 1, 2).

The dynamics of norm change were found to be sensitive to both the structural characteristics of the network and the behavioral rules agents follow. Scale-free networks consistently led to higher norm change success, largely due to the influence of well-connected hubs. Closeness-based trendsetter selection proved more effective than degree-based selection, particularly when agents incorporated social signals into their decision-making. Notably, even a small number of strategically placed trendsetters was sufficient to trigger large-scale norm replacement under the right conditions. These findings highlight the importance of structure-aware interventions and hybrid decision strategies in guiding social norm dynamics. Future work may extend this framework to dynamic networks, heterogeneous agent populations, or empirical validations using real-world data.

References

1. Amato, R., Lacasa, L., Díaz-Guilera, A., Baronchelli, A.: The dynamics of norm change in the cultural evolution of language. Proc. Nat. Acad. Sci. **115**, 201721059 (2018). https://doi.org/10.1073/pnas.1721059115
2. Bicchieri, C., Funcke, A.: Norm change: trendsetters and social structure. Soc. Res. Int. Q. **85**(1), 1–21 (2018)
3. Bicchieri, C., Muldoon, R., Sontuoso, A.: Social norms (2011)
4. Castelfranchi, C.: A cognitive framing for norm change. In: Coordination, Organizations, Institutions, and Norms in Agent Systems XI: COIN 2015 International Workshops, COIN@ AAMAS, Istanbul, Turkey, 4 May 2015, COIN@ IJCAI, Buenos Aires, Argentina, 26 July 2015, Revised Selected Papers, pp. 22–41. Springer (2016)
5. Coskun, S.: Zero waste management behavior: conceptualization, scale development and validation-a case study in turkey. Sustainability **14**(19), 12654 (2022)
6. De, S., Nau, D.S., Gelfand, M.J.: Understanding norm change: an evolutionary game-theoretic approach. In: Proceedings of the 16th Conference on Autonomous Agents and Multiagent Systems, pp. 1433–1441 (2017)
7. Franks, H., Griffiths, N.E., Jhumka, A.: Manipulating convention emergence using influencer agents. Auton. Agents Multi-Agent Syst. **26**, 315–353 (2013). https://api.semanticscholar.org/CorpusID:17105452
8. Gelfand, M.J., Gavrilets, S., Nunn, N.: Norm dynamics: interdisciplinary perspectives on social norm emergence, persistence, and change. Annu. Rev. Psychol. **75**(1), 341–378 (2024)
9. Gomila, R., Paluck, E.L.: The social and psychological characteristics of norm deviants: a field study in a small cohesive university campus. J. Soc. Polit. Psychol. **8**(1), 220–245 (2020)
10. Jachimowicz, J.M., Hauser, O.P., O'Brien, J.D., Sherman, E., Galinsky, A.D.: The critical role of second-order normative beliefs in predicting energy conservation. Nat. Hum. Behav. **2**(10), 757–764 (2018)

11. Kittock, J.E.: Emergent conventions and the structure of multi-agent systems. In: Proceedings of the 1993 Santa Fe Institute Complex Systems Summer School, vol. 6, pp. 1–14. Citeseer (1993)
12. Mahmoud, M.A., Ahmad, M.S., Mohd Yusoff, M.Z., Mustapha, A.: A review of norms and normative multiagent systems. Sci. World J. **2014**(1), 684587 (2014)
13. Paluck, E.L., Shepherd, H.: The salience of social referents: a field experiment on collective norms and harassment behavior in a school social network. J. Pers. Soc. Psychol. **103**(6), 899 (2012)
14. Qutteina, Y., Hallez, L., Raedschelders, M., De Backer, C., Smits, T.: Food for teens: how social media is associated with adolescent eating outcomes. Public Health Nutr. **25**(2), 290–302 (2022)
15. Rachmad, Y.E.: Social media impact theory (2023)
16. Rouleau, M.D.: NormSim: an agent-based model of norm change. In: 2015 Third World Conference on Complex Systems (WCCS), pp. 1–8. IEEE (2015)
17. Sanchez-Cartas, J.M., Leon, G.: On "Influencers" and their impact on the diffusion of digital platforms. In: Bajo, J., et al. (eds.) PAAMS 2018. CCIS, vol. 887, pp. 210–222. Springer, Cham (2018). https://doi.org/10.1007/978-3-319-94779-2_19
18. Vriens, E., Andrighetto, G., Tummolini, L.: Risk, sanctions and norm change: the formation and decay of social distancing norms. Philos. Trans. R. Soc. B **379**(1897), 20230035 (2024)
19. Yamin, P., Fei, M., Lahlou, S., Levy, S.: Using social norms to change behavior and increase sustainability in the real world: a systematic review of the literature. Sustainability **11**(20), 5847 (2019)

Demonstrators

Embedding Autonomous Agents in Resource-Constrained Robotic Platforms

Negar Halakou(✉), Juan F. Gutierrez, Ye Sun, Han Jiang, Xueming Wu, Yilun Song, and Andres Gomez

Institut für Datentechnik und Kommunikationsnetze, TU Braunschweig, Braunschweig, Germany
{negar.halakou,juan-felipe.gutierrez-gomez,ye.sun1,h.jiang,xueming.wu, yilun.song,andres.gomez}@tu-braunschweig.de

Abstract. Many embedded devices operate under resource constraints and in dynamic environments, requiring local decision-making capabilities. Enabling devices to make independent decisions in such environments can improve the responsiveness of the system and reduce the dependence on constant external control. In this work, we integrate an autonomous agent, programmed using AgentSpeak, with a small two-wheeled robot that explores a maze using its own decision-making and sensor data. Experimental results show that the agent successfully solved the maze in 59 s using 287 reasoning cycles, with decision phases taking less than one millisecond. These results indicate that the reasoning process is efficient enough for real-time execution on resource-constrained hardware. This integration demonstrates how high-level agent-based control can be applied to resource-constrained embedded systems for autonomous operation.

Keywords: Autonomous Agents · AgentSpeak · Embedded Systems · Robots

1 Introduction

Resource-constrained robotic platforms play an important role in enabling low-cost, large-scale deployments in many application scenarios. Due to their limited size, memory, and processing power, these systems tend to use centralized processing. By only perceiving information locally and reasoning remotely, these systems suffer from limited autonomy and longer latencies in the actuation loop.

As the computational capacity of microcontrollers increases, researchers have begun introducing techniques like onboard machine learning, which can efficiently extract better information from its environment. In [2], Hao et al. propose a microrobot weighing less than 22 g, including a camera, microcontroller, and actuator. The microrobot can detect a target and follow it, using only local

M. Baldoni et al. (Eds.): EUMAS 2025, LNAI 16259, pp. 319–324, 2026.
https://doi.org/10.1007/978-3-032-22820-8_22

data in a closed feedback loop. The entire logic, however, is implemented using ad-hoc C/C++ code and exhibits only reactive behavior.

Agent-oriented programming can bring many advantages to robotic platforms, facilitate the development of autonomous reasoning, swarm intelligence, among others. While existing Java-based frameworks have already integrated robotic control into the AgentSpeak language [5], these are not compatible with resource-constrained robotic platforms based on microcontrollers (MCUs). In order to achieve this, specialized toolchains and frameworks have been developed to cope with the limited memory and processing capabilities of MCUs [4].

In this demo paper, we show the feasibility of embedding autonomous BDI agents in a microcontroller-based two-wheeled robotic platform and tasking the agent to solve a line-following maze. In order to achieve this, we have defined and implemented a minimal API for controlling our robot's movement. This hardware-dependent code can be easily reused by any AgentSpeak script code running on our robot. Lastly, we have experimentally validated our autonomous agent framework, showing that our reasoning cycles can execute fast enough for our robot to efficiently solve mazes.

2 System Design

An autonomous agent is an intelligent system capable of perceiving its environment through sensors and acting on that environment using actuators [1]. Unlike the imperative programming typically used in embedded systems, agents operate autonomously, making rational decisions, based on their perceptions and internal knowledge to achieve their goals. What sets agents apart is their autonomy. They do not require constant direction from humans or other systems.

The Belief-Desire-Intention (BDI) model is one approach to implement the autonomous and intelligent behavior of agents. It provides a structured approach for designing autonomous agents by defining their behavior through three key elements: beliefs, desires, and intentions. Autonomous agents can be programmed using the BDI paradigm as implemented in the AgentSpeak language and executed by the Jason interpreter. A simplified variant of Jason is used as the basis for the Embedded-BDI framework [3]. This framework consists of a translation engine that converts AgentSpeak programs into optimized C++ code, a runtime library responsible for executing the agent's reasoning process, and hardware-dependent code; together, these components form an executable binary. The workflow of the framework involves programming the agent's deliberation logic in AgentSpeak, while the perception and action functions, along with other hardware-specific code, are implemented in C/C++ [6].

Building on these principles, in this work, we embed a BDI agent into a robotic platform to enable autonomous maze exploration. The agent forms beliefs based on its perception of the environment through line sensors, which detect intersections and path availability. Its main desire is to reach the goal, while intentions are generated and dynamically updated as navigation plans following the left-hand rule. The BDI agent manages navigation and decision-making by reasoning over its beliefs and selecting appropriate actions. These intentions are executed by the robot's actuators, enabling it to move forward or turn as needed.

3 System Implementation

We utilize a Pololu 3pi+ 2040 robot (Standard Edition), which features an RP2040 microcontroller with 264 kB of onchip SRAM and 16 MB of external flash. The robot includes five downward-facing reflectance sensors for line following, and two DC micro metal gear motors that independently drive the left and right wheels, enabling precise movement control via PWM signals. To implement autonomous decision-making, we integrated the Embedded-BDI framework[1] with Pololu's bare-metal firmware. This integration enables us to define the agent logic using AgentSpeak. The corresponding code is shown in Listing 1.

Listing 1. BDI agent logic in AgentSpeak for left-hand rule navigation.

```
!solve_maze.

+!solve_maze : at_intersection <-
    !!handle_intersection.

+!solve_maze <-
    follow_segment;
    !!solve_maze.

+!handle_intersection <-
    check_situation;
    !!make_decision;
    !!solve_maze.

+!make_decision : goal_found <-stop.
+!make_decision : path_left <- turn_left.
+!make_decision : path_straight <- forward.
+!make_decision : path_right <- turn_right.
+!make_decision <- rotate_180.
```

3.1 BDI-Based Maze Solving Behavior

After powering on, the robot initializes its hardware components. The process begins when the user presses button A, which triggers sensor calibration to adjust the line sensors for accurate path detection.

Once the system is ready, the BDI agent starts execution with the initial goal `solve_maze`. The robot's behavior is managed in a cyclic manner through the agent's reasoning cycle. In each step, the agent evaluates whether the robot is

1 https://embedded-bdi.github.io/.

currently at an intersection. When an intersection is detected, the agent posts a new goal `handle_intersection` using the `!!` operator. Although this creates a separate intention, it typically begins execution immediately within the same cycle. During this intention, the agent executes `check_situation` to interpret sensor data and form beliefs such as `goal_found`, `path_left`, or `path_right`. Based on these beliefs, the agent proceeds with `make_decision`, selecting the appropriate action according to the left-hand rule.

Based on this rule, when the robot arrives at an intersection, it first checks whether a line is detected on the left. If so, it turns left. If no line is detected on the left, it attempts to move forward. If no visible path is available ahead, it then checks the right side. If no path is detected in any direction, the robot performs a 180-degree turn to continue exploration. If no intersection is detected, the agent continues along the current path by executing `follow_segment`. This loop of perception, reasoning, and action repeats until the goal is found, at which point the robot stops and the task is considered successfully completed.

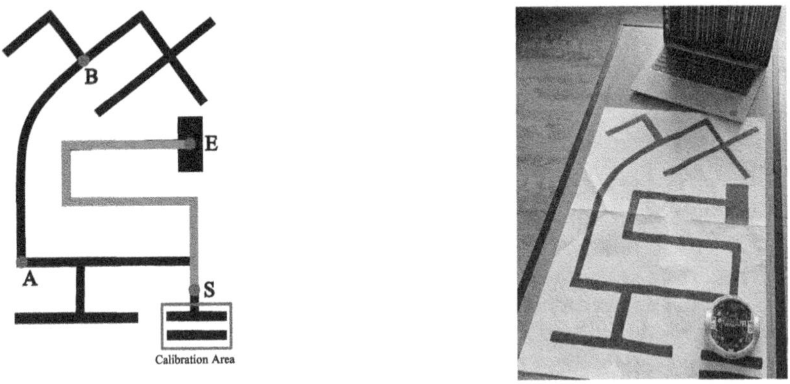

(a) Digital design of the maze. (b) Real-world implementation.

Fig. 1. The designed maze used for planning (left) and the physical implementation with the robot (right).

4 Demonstration

The effectiveness of the AgentSpeak-based algorithm was demonstrated using the maze shown in Fig. 1. The maze was specifically designed to first calibrate the line sensors at the starting area, enabling the robot to distinguish between black and white surfaces. Its layout forces the robot to follow the longest possible path before reaching the goal. A demonstration video and AgentSpeak-based maze solver robot software are available in a public repository[2]. To analyze the agent's behavior during maze solving, we measured the execution times of three main

[2] Demo-Paper Repo: https://git.rz.tu-bs.de/ida/rosy/public/publication-repos/eumas-2025-mas-pololu-demo-paper.

components in its reasoning cycle: belief update, plan selection, and intention execution.

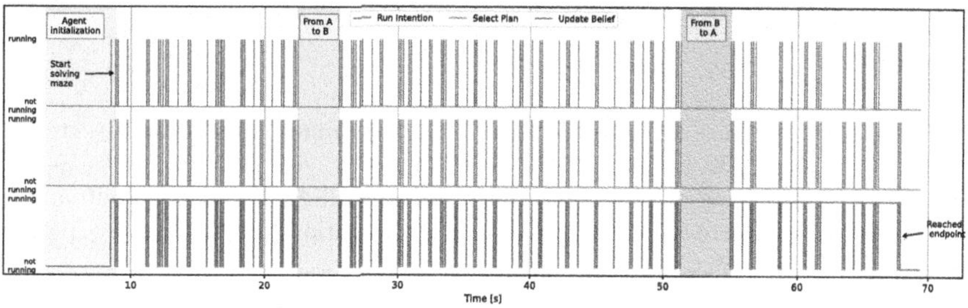

Fig. 2. Annotated GPIO activity during the execution cycle of an agent-based maze-solving robot.

These measurements were recorded as digital signals, with 1 indicating the function is running and 0 indicating it is not, as shown in Fig. 2. Based on these measurements, the total time taken to solve the maze was approximately 59 s. This duration corresponds to the trajectory from point S (start point) to point E (endpoint) along the longest path, during which the reasoning cycle was executed 287 times.

On average, the belief update phase took 0.004 ms (with a maximum of 0.022 ms), the plan selection phase took 0.024 ms (with a maximum of 0.153 ms), and the intention execution phase lasted 197 ms on average (with a maximum of 3744 ms). The relatively long duration of the intention execution phase is mainly due to sensor readings and motor control operations, which are influenced by the specific structure of the maze. For instance, when the robot traveled from point A to point B, this phase lasted about 3.1 s, while the return from B to A took approximately 3.7 s. During both segments, the same plan was executed continuously, as no intersections were encountered. In contrast, the belief update and plan selection phases were consistently short. These short execution times suggest that the reasoning cycle is efficient enough for real-time decision-making, even at higher robot speeds, without adversely affecting task performance. We also evaluated memory usage. The compiled binary, which includes the translated AgentSpeak code, the runtime and the hardware-specific code, used only 5.44% of the Flash memory and 6.25% of the RAM.

5 Conclusions

In this demonstration, we embedded a BDI agent on a two-wheeled robot using a reusable API within the Embedded-BDI platform. Experiments showed that action execution dominated cycle time, while decision-making was computationally efficient. This confirms the feasibility of real-time autonomy on constrained hardware. As future work, the robot will communicate its discovered path, using AgentSpeak, to another AgentSpeak-based robot, enabling the second robot to traverse the shortest route to the goal.

References

1. Bordini, R.H., Hübner, J.F., Wooldridge, M.: Programming multi-agent systems in AgentSpeak using Jason. John Wiley & Sons (2007)
2. Hao, Z., Lele, A., Fang, Y., Raychowdhury, A., Ansari, A.: FAVbot: an autonomous target tracking micro-robot with frequency actuation control. arXiv preprint arXiv:2501.15426 (2025)
3. Santos, M.M.d.: Programação orientada a agentes BDI em sistemas embarcados. Master's thesis, Universidade Federal de Santa Catarina (UFSC) (2022)
4. Vachtsevanou, D., William, J., dos Santos, M.M., de Brito, M., Hübner, J.F., Mayer, S., Gomez, A.: Embedding autonomous agents into low-power wireless sensor networks. In: Mathieu, P., Dignum, F., Novais, P., De la Prieta, F. (eds) International Conference on Practical Applications of Agents and Multi-Agent Systems, pp. 375–387. Springer, Cham (2023). https://doi.org/10.1007/978-3-031-37616-0_31
5. Wesz, R.B.: Integrating robot control into the agent speak (l) programming language (2015)
6. William, J., Santos, M.M.D., de Brito, M., Hübner, J.F., Vachtsevanou, D., Gomez, A.: Increasing the intelligence of low-power sensors with autonomous agents. In: Proceedings of the 20th ACM Conference on Embedded Networked Sensor Systems, pp. 994–999 (2022)

FLASH-MAS: Towards a State-of-the-Art, Modular Agent Deployment Environment

Andrei Olaru(✉)

Department of Computer Science and Engineering, National University of Science and Technology POLITEHNICA Bucharest, 313 Splaiul Independentei, 060042 Bucharest, Romania
andrei.olaru@upb.ro

Abstract. Agent development and deployment frameworks have seen little development recently, and by far the most popular framework is Jade, with SPADE coming strong for Python deployments.

FLASH-MAS – the Flexible, Lightweight Agent Shell – is a framework for the deployment of multi-agent systems comprising a variety of entities besides agents, with a great level of modularity. In FLASH-MAS, any part of the system – agents, but also nodes, communication infrastructures, services, and agent components – can have an arbitrary implementation and is loaded dynamically when a scenario is started. Moreover, any other type of entity is automatically, dynamically integrated, and can easily interact with other entities on the same node or on other nodes.

We present in this demonstration our current progress in the development of FLASH-MAS, how new types of entities can be seamlessly integrated in a deployment, how machine learning models written in Python can integrate with Java agents, how remote visualization is possible via a web application, and how monitoring the progress of a scenario is possible thanks to log summarizers and finite state machines.

Keywords: MAS framework · visualization · flexibility · modularity

1 Introduction

The current MAS framework landscape is mostly divided into three areas: agent-based model simulation (ABMS), led by Repast [4]; FIPA-compliant [5] deployment that can be network-distributed, led by Jade in Java [3] and SPADE in Python [8]; and, more recently, agentic AI initiatives currently coagulating around protocols such as MCP and A2A [1,2].

We introduced FLASH-MAS[1] [6] several years ago as a MAS deployment and execution framework that is modular and flexible. The target of FLASH-MAS is

[1] The FLASH-MAS repository is located at https://github.com/andreiolaru-ro/FLASH-MAS.

M. Baldoni et al. (Eds.): EUMAS 2025, LNAI 16259, pp. 325–331, 2026.
https://doi.org/10.1007/978-3-032-22820-8_23

to be a general-purpose MAS deployment framework that can be used in various scenarios: as an alternative to (or integrated with) Jade; as a competent ABMS platform; and as an infrastructure for running agentic AI applications. Our approach follows a few basic principles:

P1: Any persistent component in a deployment is an *entity*, with a uniform model and that can be loaded in a similar manner, and is a first-class abstraction in the system. Entities include agents, artifacts, services, nodes, communication infrastructures, individual agent functionalities (which we model as *shards*), and so on. New entity types can be created and integrated seamlessly.
P2: Entities are linked by *context* and any entity can exist in the context of another entity. The relation does not necessarily make for a total ordering. For instance, agents exist in the context of nodes but also of communication infrastructures, which are embodied on a node by a *pylon*. Pylons run in the context of nodes, but, to be able to interact with other entities, nodes are also in the context of pylons.
P3: All entities are dynamically loaded and the implementation of an entity can be changed (a different class can be used) without impacting any other entity. For instance, the communication infrastructure can be changed without impacting entities which use it, and entities are ignorant as to what communication protocol is being used to allow them to interact.
P4: Entities interact via *waves*, which transport *content* between *endpoints*. Any entity can have one or more endpoints and many entities are able to *route waves* to other entities which exist in their context. E.g. pylons route *waves* to agents and nodes, agents route *waves* to their internal components, and so on.
P5: The motto of the project is "Easy for beginners, powerful to experts", with the target that running a simple scenario should be very easy, but deploying a complex scenario should also be possible, the complexity of specifying the deployment mirroring the complexity of the scenario itself.

In the following sections we will present some recently developed features of FLASH-MAS, which highlight the flexibility and versatility of the framework.

2 Integrating New Entity Types

Deployment of a FLASH-MAS scenario can be specified via XML files, but it is much easier to just use the command line. Running two agents[2] can be as simple as

```
java quick.Boot -package testing -agent PingPong:AgentA sendTo:AgentB
                                 -agent PingPong:AgentB
```

[2] We omit the classpath parameter (`-cp`) of `java` for space reasons, and also for readability, but only one or two paths are actually needed, depending on whether FLASH-MASis run from a `.jar` or using classes and dependency libraries.

The framework automatically creates a node and a default communication platform, and automatically searches for the specified classpaths in the default and in the specified packages.

Adding a custom agent type and a specific communication platform is easy thanks to specifying custom loaders, automatic context inclusion (based on CLI parsing) and automatic location of classes – see Fig. 1.

```
-package testing -loader agent:composite
-node node1
  -pylon webSocket:pylon1 serverPort:8886
    -agent composite:agA -shard messaging -shard PingTest to:agB
-node node2
  -pylon webSocket:pylon2 connectTo:ws://localhost:8886
    -agent composite:agB -shard messaging -shard PingBackTest
```

Fig. 1. Text-based deployment configuration for a simple scenario with two agents interacting via a WebSocket infrastructure. Each node contains one pylon of the interaction infrastructure and one agent.

New types of entities can be added and loaded automatically (by specifying the `load_order`), and custom context relations can be specified explicitly using the `in-context-of` parameter for entities. In the next section, we elaborate on the deployment of a scenario in the AI Folk project, the deployment configuration of which is given in Fig. 2.

```
-load_order driver;pylon;agent
-package ml aifolk.core aifolk.onto -loader agent:composite
-node node1 -driver ML:mldriver -driver Scenario:scen script:scr
  -driver Ontology:ont load:aifolk.ttl
-pylon local:pylon1
  -agent agA in-context-of:ML:mldriver in-context-of:Scenario:scen
    -shard messaging -shard scenario
    -shard MLPipeline -shard MLManagement feature:AutoDrive
```

Fig. 2. Deployment configuration for a scenario in which an agent interoperates with ML tools, via the *ML driver* entity.

In this scenario, the *driver* is a custom entity type, which is integrated seamlessly in the system at deployment time, without entities such as nodes knowing anything special about them – only the entities which need that functionality, and which are placed *in the context* of the driver, are concerned about the existence of that driver. Using the `load_order` element in the deployment configuration, one can specify what type of entities should be automatically loaded by the framework in each node.

3 Interoperating with AI Tools

We have been experimenting with integrating machine learning (ML) tools with FLASH-MASand in the AI Folk project [7] we have developed agents which automatically select the prediction model to use in a task. Thanks to the flexible structure of FLASH-MAS, new entities are integrated easily (see the previous section), but to run prediction models implemented in Python a cross-platform, asynchronous interface with the Python language needed to be developed.

The link between languages was done via a local Python web server that receives requests from the `MLDriver` entity, which routes requests from all entities on that node. In the spirit of principle P3, prediction models are dynamically loaded via a configuration file. The interaction is shown in Fig. 3.

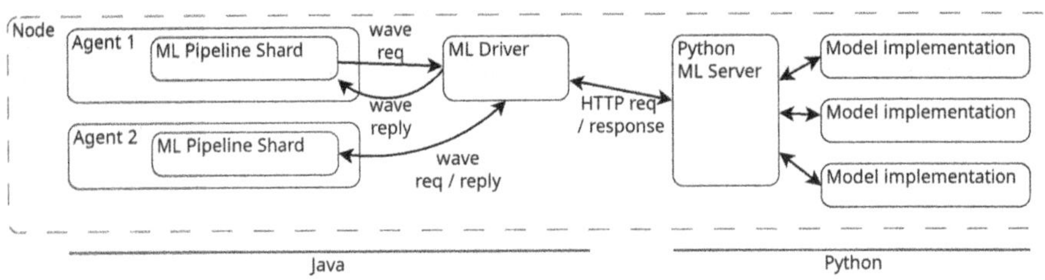

Fig. 3. Integration of Java agents with prediction models in Python, via a local web server.

The local web server offers, via the *ML driver*, functionality to

- load a new prediction model from a file containing the parameters;
- execute training of a model on a given set of examples;
- retreive model information;
- save the parameters of a model to a file;
- make a prediction using a model, on a given input, and return the result;
- list the available prediction models;

Since prediction models come in great variety and each one has its own mechanisms for loading, training, encoding input, and processing output, we abstract these processes using a Python class for each type of model, which extends the `ModelOperations` abstract class, and which offers a uniform API for loading, saving, prediction, training, and input and output processing.

4 Visualizing and Controlling Entities Remotely

Visualization in a MAS is important. We have been working on a feature to allow entities (agents, especially) to present automatically generated interfaces based on a list of input and output "*ports*" through which an entity can receive input or display output. The interface of the agent can be displayed locally as a Java

Swing window but also remotely in a web interface that gathers information from all entities in a deployment and allows the user to interact with them.

Figure 4 shows the web application for viewing and integrating with agents. The interaction is possible via a *remote* agent shard which builds a description of the interface – fields, buttons, behaviors – from a YAML file (Figure 4 (a)) and interacts with a centralized *Monitoring Entity* to which it sends updates, and from which it receives updates, using normal FLASH-MAS communication via *waves*. The Monitoring Entity creates a local web server which builds a global web interface based on the specification – see Fig. 4 (b).


```
- type: label
  port: inbound
  role: recvd-label
  value: "Received message:"
- type: label
  port: inbound
  role: content
  value: "-"
- type: form
  port: outbound
  role: content
- type: button
  port: outbound
  role: send
  value: Send
```


(a)

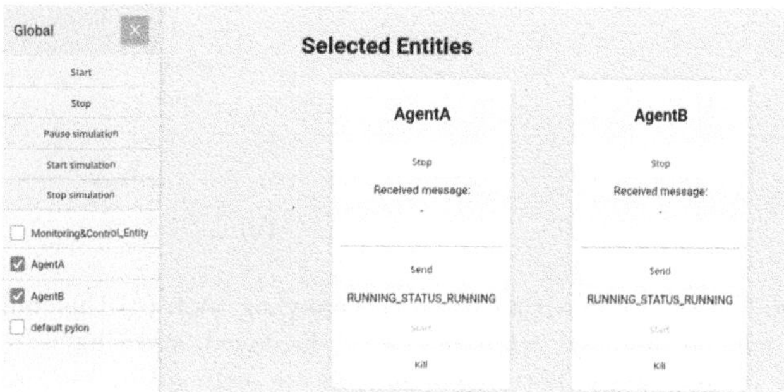

(b)

Fig. 4. Remote visualization interface built from a simple YAML specification (a) and presented in a web interface (b).

For agents containing multiple *shards*, each shard can contribute its own *ports* – hence its own controls – to the specification. The specification of the agent is combined with default controls, added by the Monitoring Entity, that show the status of the agent and buttons to start and to kill the agent.

5 Monitoring the Progress of the System

Monitoring the state of a distributed MAS can be difficult when the number of entities is large and the scenario is complex. We have developed and integrated in FLASH-MAS a tool for tracking and summarizing the state of the system based solely on log entries produced by the entities. Provided all log entries are captured in a single stream (e.g. the *standard output stream*), the `easyLog` tool provides a summary of current state. The configuration is very simple – see Fig. 5 (a) – and specifies what log lines should be matched, what should be the output aggregating those lines and what are the satisfiability criteria. Output is provided as a line staying at the bottom of the console, by simply matching log lines with regular expressions, or by running a finite state machine (FSM) which changes state when certain matches are found in log lines for a given entity (see Fig. 5 (b-c)).

```
- e: "Agent.*"
  level: ">"
  match: ["RUNNING"]
  out: ["count", "agents running:", "list:entities"]
  expect: ["count", "2"]
  comment: "pass if there are exactly 2 agents running."
- e: ".*"
  match: ["started"]
  out: ["count", "entities started:","list:entities"]
  expect: ["count", "4"]
  comment: "pass if there are 4 entities having started."
- e: "AgentA.*"
  fsm-from: "resource/prediction.dot"
  fsm-start: "START"
  fsm-expect: "FINAL"
  out: ["Agent A prediction state:", "state"]
```

(a)

```
[...]
. [ default pylon ] [default] starting
> [ default pylon ] Started with thread.
> [ AgentA ] Agent state is soon [STARTING][]
. [ node1 ] entity [AgentA] started successfully.
. [ node1 ] starting entity [AgentB]...
> [ AgentB ] Agent state is soon [STARTING][]
. [ node1 ] entity [AgentB] started successfully.
> [ node1 ] Node [node1] started.
> [ AgentB ] state is now [RUNNING]
> [ AgentA ] state is now [RUNNING]

   2 agents running: [ AgentA, AgentB ] 4 entities
started: [ AgentA, AgentB, default pylon, node1 ] Agent A
current state: Processed
```

(b)

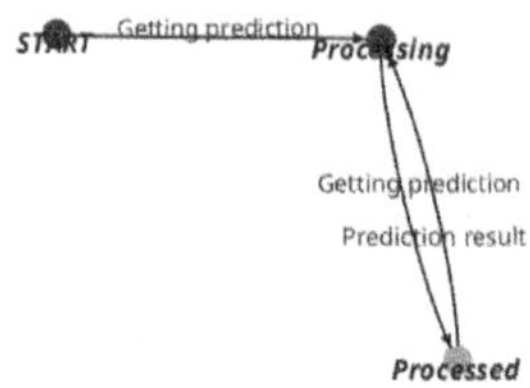

(c)

Fig. 5. Log summarizing using the **easyLog** tool: (a) the configuration specifies rules for what is matched, what should be displayed, and what is expected; (b) a summary line is kept at the bottom of the console aggregating outputs for each configuration entry; (c) a graph is displayed with the current state of each FSM.

6 Conclusion and Future Work

The FLASH-MAS framework is evolving continuously and the tools for deployment, integration, and monitoring of the system become more capable and easier to use.

Future developments include a documentation effort which is currently in progress and improving tools for automatic deployment on multiple nodes and more powerful state-based monitoring, together with interface and monitoring aggregation across larger numbers of agents.

Many thanks go to the many contributors to the FLASH-MAS project, listed in the `CONTRIBUTORS.md` file in the project repository, and especially to Ștefan Sterea, Tudor Ciot, and Valentin Mignot who have had important contributions to implementation of the features presented in this paper.

Acknowledgments. This paper is supported by the European Union's HORIZON Research and Innovation Programme under grant agreement No 101120657, project ENFIELD (European Lighthouse to Manifest Trustworthy and Green AI).

References

1. Agent2Agent Protocol (A2A). https://google-a2a.github.io/A2A. Accessed 2025
2. Model Context Protocol. https://modelcontextprotocol.io. Accessed 2025
3. Bellifemine, F., Poggi, A., Rimassa, G.: JADE - a FIPA-compliant agent framework. In: Proceedings of PAAM, vol. 99, pp. 97–108. Citeseer (1999)
4. Collier, N.: RePast: an extensible framework for agent simulation. Univ. Chicago Soc. Sci. Res. **36**, 2003 (2003)
5. FIPA: FIPA abstract architecture specification (2002). http://fipa.org/specs/fipa00001/SC00001L.html
6. Olaru, A., Sorici, A., Florea, A.M.: A flexible and lightweight agent deployment architecture. In: 2019 22nd International Conference on Control Systems and Computer Science (CSCS), Bucharest, Romania, 28-30 May 2019, pp. 251–258. IEEE (2019). https://doi.org/10.1109/CSCS.2019.00048, https://ieeexplore.ieee.org/abstract/document/8744845/
7. Olaru, A., Sorici, A., Nan, M., Iancu, D.T.: AI Folk: sharing machine learning models in a multi-agent community. In: Chinthaginjala, R., Sitek, P., Min-Allah, N., Matsui, K., Ossowski, S., Rodríguez, S. (eds.) Distributed Computing and Artificial Intelligence, 21st International Conference, pp. 119–128. Springer Nature Switzerland, Cham (2025). https://doi.org/10.1007/978-3-031-82073-1_12
8. Palanca, J., Terrasa, A., Julian, V., Carrascosa, C.: SPADE 3: supporting the new generation of multi-agent systems. IEEE Access **8**, 182537–182549 (2020)

AmI HMAS: Goal-Driven Interaction Support in Smart Environments

Alexandru Sorici(✉), Victor-Vasile Udristioiu, and Adina Magda Florea

National University of Science and Technology POLITEHNICA Bucharest, Splaiul Independentei 313, Bucharest, Romania
{alexandru.sorici,adina.florea}@upb.ro,
victor.udristioiu@stud.acs.upb.ro

Abstract. Goal-driven interaction in Smart Environments has been a long standing desire in Ambient Intelligence (AmI) use cases. Recent advances in web-based MAS and foundational machine learning models that can power agent planning and reasoning are making goal-driven interaction frameworks realistically plausible. We demonstrate a prototype framework for management of goal-driven AmI interactions that builds upon: (i) Hypermedia MAS environment modeling, (ii) resource signification to capture experience of use and (iii) LLM support for agent reasoning. We showcase framework functionality on hand of a smart office simulated scenario.

Keywords: Ambient Intelligence · Hypermedia MAS · Web-of-Things · AI Agents · Context and Signification

1 Introduction

Goal-driven interactions have been an early vision in the Ambient Intelligence (AmI) domain [11]. The topic remained largely out of practical reach, due largely to challenges such as a large diversity of device and service capabilities, as well as the insufficient reasoning capabilities of systems intended to bridge these capabilities together towards a user goal.

However, the topic is receiving renewed interest from both academia and industry, thanks to recent developments in AI foundational models (notably Large Language Models - LLMs). LLMs have demonstrated emergent capabilities for intent understanding, planning (in complex domains requiring neuro-symbolic approaches [13], as well as simpler ones related to activities of daily living [15]) and matching of natural language actions to APIs [12,16]. Furthermore, efforts within the W3C Web Agents Community Group [8] have surfaced Hypermedia MAS as a design paradigm in which the agent environment and agent capabilities obtain a *representation* over the web. This view allows new agents and existing web services and devices to interact more uniformly within an application.

M. Baldoni et al. (Eds.): EUMAS 2025, LNAI 16259, pp. 332–343, 2026.
https://doi.org/10.1007/978-3-032-22820-8_24

In this context, systems that leverage LLM reasoning capabilities are starting to be explored. Sasha [14] looks at using LLMs to control smart home devices handling common automation routines (e.g. as found in typical If-This-Than-That recipes [5]). The work finds that LLM generated plans can fail when the user request is poorly- or under specified (e.g. "make it cozy in here"), leading to the need of an iterative reasoning process that encompasses clarifying, filtering, planning, and feedback steps. While Sasha is an analytic study, LLMind [10] goes a step further, presenting an LLM-based task-oriented AI agent framework, enabling collaboration between IoT devices, based on human high-level verbal instructions. Key functionalities include the maintenance of a context of available device information and API descriptions, as well as an *experience accumulation* mechanism that classifies and locally stores LLM generated control scripts for specific user commands to enhance response speed and overall efficiency.

The AmI HMAS framework we are introducing aligns with the design rationale of LLMind, providing modules that break down the user intent into subtasks, dependent on known affordances in the user environment, their use in prior requests and their current state. One main difference from LLMind is that records of previous solutions are maintained by giving individual credit to each service used in a request, such that the respective service capabilities can be paired to other similar future requests.

Concretely, the AmI HMAS prototype framework integrates: (i) a Hypermedia Artifact [9] based representation of smart environment devices and services, based on the Yggdrasil platform [9], (ii) a Signifier [18] based tracking of affordance usage experience, and (iii) an Eclipse LMOS [4] based AI agent system encompassing roles for environment monitoring, experience recording, planning, execution, and user feedback functionalities.

2 AmI HMAS: Design and Functionality

To understand the design and functionality of the AmI HMAS, we start by detailing the demo scenario.

Working Scenario. A smart research lab has sensors that measure the inside temperature, the light intensity in the room and outside the windows and that count the people in the room. The lights can be turned on or off and set to a percentage level of intensity, while the blinds can be raised or lowered to a percentage degree (where 100% means fully raised). The scenario describes two different situations in which a user walking in the lab perceives the room as being too dark. In a first setup, the lights are off, the blinds are drawn, and the light sensor registers low outside luminosity, given that it is late in the evening. No prior usage experience exists, so the system has to plan a solution involving turning on the lights to full. In the second setup, the lights are dim, the blinds are half raised, it is sunny outside, while the inside temperature is below 23°. In this case, signification exists for both light usage and raising the blinds. Given environment conditions, the solution from prior experience retrieved is to raise the blinds to 75% open. In both setups, the user comment is “It’s dark in here” (no clear action on what to do).

This simple scenario requires the AmI HMAS system to: (i) understand the user intent from the context of existing capabilities that can address the intent, (ii) monitor artifacts that provide context about the lab environment, (iii) examine previous interaction records for similar past requests, (iv) plan a set of artifact action affordance invocations that address the user goal, (v) obtain feedback from the user for the proposed plan before executing it.

Affordance and Usage Experience Representation. A deployment of an Yggdrasil [9] instance is used to model the smart lab environment as a *Workspace*. The latter contains the temperature, light intensity, and person counter sensors, as well as the light and blinds controllers, modeled as ThingDescription [7] *artifacts* (see example in Listing 1.1).

```
@prefix ex: <http://example.com/ns#>
@prefix consert: <http://pervasive.semanticweb.org/ont/2017/07/consert/core>
@prefix owl:   <http://www.w3.org/2002/07/owl#>
@prefix ...
<http://localhost:8080/workspaces/lab308/artifacts/LightSensor308/#artifact>
    a td:Thing, hmas:Artifact, ex:LightSensor ;
    td:title "LightSensor308" ;
    td:hasSecurityConfiguration [ a wotsec:NoSecurityScheme ] ;

    td:hasPropertyAffordance [
        a td:PropertyAffordance, ex:MeasurementProperty ;
        td:name "luminosity" ;
        td:hasForm [
            htv:methodName "GET" ;
            hctl:hasTarget <http://localhost:8080/workspaces/lab308/artifacts/LightSensor308/luminosity> ;
            hctl:forContentType "application/json" ;
            hctl:hasOperationType td:readProperty ;
        ] ;
        td:hasOutputSchema [
            a js:ObjectSchema ;
            js:properties [
                a js:NumberSchema ;
                js:propertyName "luminosity"
            ] ;
            js:required ("luminosity") ;
            js:additionalProperties false
        ] ;
    ] .
```

Listing 1.1. Extract from the ThingDescription representation of the light sensor artifact in the demonstrator scenario.

Signifiers [17,18] are introduced as a means for artifacts in an HMAS to *advertise* affordances, depending on the *intent* and *capabilities* of an agent, as well as the *context* of the agent-artifact interaction. In [18], signifiers are maintained at the level of the artifact representation, using an SHACL [6] based vocabulary to express constraints on required RDF information. However, the essential job of signification is to record a *possible use of an artifact within some context*. In AmI HMAS, it is the job of an agent within the system to keep track of artifact signifiers, capturing the experience of *having used the artifact for a goal in a situation*. To enable LLM-supported agents to reason about signified capabilities, we use the CASHMERE Ontology [2] to create vocabulary that links text-based intentions with a concrete listing of *context* conditions. The latter denote the situation in which the signified artifact affordance is appropriately used to achieve the intention. Listing 1.2 shows a signifier representation for the action affordance of setting the light intensity in the lab, if the intent is to increase luminosity and the context (expressed using SHACL constraints) is that of there being more than one person in the room and the measured light intensity being too low.

```
@prefix ex: <http://example.com/ns#>
@prefix cashmere: <https://aimas.cs.pub.ro/ont/cashmere#> .
@prefix ...
<#turn-light-on-signifier> a cashmere:Signifier ;
    cashmere:signifies <#adjust-light-action-affordance> ; // #adjust-light-action-affordance is the TD
          ActionAffordance to set the light to a certain intensity
    cashmere:recommendsAbility [
        a cashmere:LLMReasoningAbility ;
    ] ;
    cashmere:hasIntentionDescription [
        a cashmere:IntentionDescription ;
        cashmere:hasStructuredDescription "
            {
                'intent': 'increase luminosity in a room',
            }
        "^^xsd:string ;
    ] ;
    cashmere:recommendsContext [
        a cashmere:IntentContext ;

        cashmere:hasShaclCondition [
            a sh:NodeShape ;
            sh:targetNode <http://example.org/precis/workspaces/lab308/artifacts/internal_light_sensing308> ;
            sh:targetClass <http://example.org/LightSensor> ;
            sh:property [
                sh:path <http://example.org/LightSensor#hasLuminosityLevel> ;
                sh:dataType xsd:integer ;
                sh:maxInclusive 100 ;
            ]
        ] ;
        cashmere:hasShaclCondition [
            a sh:NodeShape ;
            sh:targetNode <http://example.org/precis/workspaces/lab308/artifacts/person_counter308> ;
            sh:targetClass <http://example.org/PersonCounter> ;
            sh:property [
                sh:path <http://example.org/PersonCounter#hasPersonCount> ;
                sh:dataType xsd:integer ;
                sh:minInclusive 1 ;
            ]
        ]
    ] .
```

Listing 1.2. Signifier that indicates use of the light308 controller artifact to increase luminosity in the research lab, when there is a person in the lab and the measured internal light intensity is below 100 lux.

AmI HMAS: Agent Roles. There are four main agent roles in the AmI HMAS system: *EnvMonitor*, *EnvExplorer*, *InteractionSolver* and *UserAssistant*. The typical flow of interactions between these agent roles are described in Fig. 1. The role of the ***EnvExplorer*** agent is to catalog all the *affordances* of artifacts available in an HMAS deployment (using the Yggdrasil platform). The agent also maintains a record of past *usage experience* of an experience, using Signifier descriptions similar to the one in Listing 1.2. The ***EnvMonitor*** agent keeps track of the state of the HMAS environment, by subscribing to notifications on Property Affordance changes in the deployed artifacts. The ***InteractionSolver*** agent is the main reasoning component, creating the plan of *action affordance* usage to solve the request, down to explicit invocation of the artifact API. The reasoning is supported by past usage experiences from the *EnvExplorer* and the current environment state from the *EnvMonitor*. The agent prompt is given in Appendix A. The ***UserAssistant*** agent receives the user request and determines its feasiability (based on capabilities known from the *EnvExplorer*). Feasible requests are passed for planning to the *InteractionSolver*. Returned action invocation plans are translated to the user in a friendly manner for confirmation, and confirmed plans are marked for storage as experience.

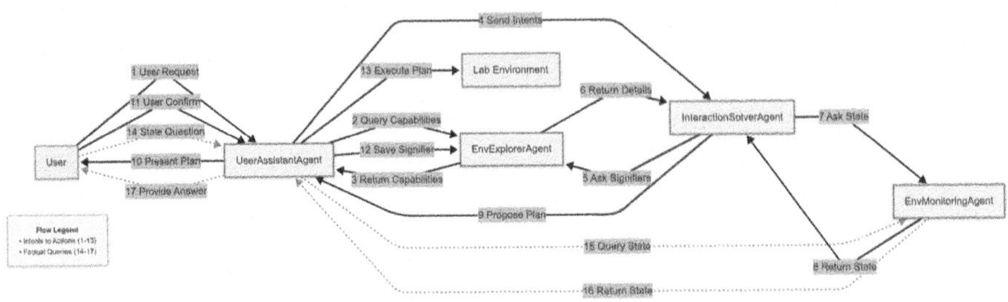

Fig. 1. Flow of interactions between agent roles in the AmI HMAS system.

The agent interaction flow starts with a user request (Step 1; in our working scenario: "It's too dark in here"). To determine if the request can be reasonably handled by AmI HMAS, the *UserAssistant* queries the affordances in the environment, asking the *EnvExplorer* agent (steps 2 and 3). The *UserAssistant* decides if the user query is within scope (using known affordances obtained from the *EnvExplorer* - steps 2 and 3). If within scope, the *UserAssistant* formulates a *user intent* and sends it to the *InteractionSolver* (step 4). The *InteractionSolver* determines if the user intent can be solved based on past usage (recorded as signifiers - steps 5 and 6) and the state of the implied artifacts (asking the *EnvMonitor* in steps 7 and 8). The proposed plan (step 9) is obtained based on existing or adapted signfiers, or a new planning altogether (if no prior experience for the intent exists). The plan (consisting of a sequence of action affordance invocations on deployed artifacts) is presented to the user in a human readable form by the *UserAssistant* (step 10). A confirmed plan (step 11) leads to its execution (step 13) and the recording of the usage experience as signifiers (step 12). A user can inquire about the environment state (steps 14–17). This interaction flow is enacted in the working scenario, as shown in our demo video [3] and made available in our GitHub repository [1].

3 Discussion

The AmI HMAS system exploits known reasoning, instruction following and tool use capabilities (see prompts in Appendices A and B) of modern LLMs (we used Gemini 2.5-flash and GPT-4.1 in our demo) to enable a goal-driven interaction in a smart environment modeled as an HMAS. The current focus was on designing agent roles and their interaction flow to facilitate: (i) handling of under-specified (implied intent) user requests, and (ii) creating plans down to the level of action affordance invocations (mapping conceptual steps to API calls) in setups that make use of prior experiences (modeled as signifiers) to choose a best option among multiple possible solutions (given environment conditions).

Future work aims to empower the system to learn from user suggestions and feedback, as well as to create benchmark evaluations using common real-word scenarios and investigating reasoning traces to establish clear performance expectations and limitations.

Acknowledgement. This paper is supported by the European Union's HORIZON Research and Innovation Programme under grant agreement No 101120657, project ENFIELD (European Lighthouse to Manifest Trustworthy and Green AI).

A InteractionSolver Agent Prompt

```
tools {
    +"query_environment_state"
    +"query_environment_capabilities"
}

prompt {
  """
  You are Interaction-Solver, an LLM agent that receives one or more
  intents from the User-Assistant agent and must return an executable plan
  in JSON-Plan 1.2 format.

  GLOBAL URI RULE
  ---------------
  All tool calls, queries and plan fields must use complete artifact URIs
  (e.g. \url{http://host/workspaces/env/artifacts/example123).}
  Never shorten or invent URIs; discover them with Env-Explorer.

  PLAN FORMAT  JSON-Plan 1.2
  --------------------------
    {
      "plan_version": "1.2",
      "steps": [
        {
          "step_id": 1,
          "intent": "<exact intent this step fulfills from the list of intents
    >",
          "artifact_uri": "<full URI>",
          "affordance_uri": "<full URI>",
          "action_name": "<td:name>",
          "method": "<HTTP verb>",
          "target": "<hctl:hasTarget URI>",
          "content_type": "application/json",
          "payload": { },
          "reasons": [
            {
              "property":  "<property satisfied>",          // e.g. luminosity
              "direction": "<increase|decrease|set>",       // from intent
              "evidence": [                                 // 1-N facts
                {
                  "artifact":  "<sensor-or-artifact URI>",
                  "property":  "<attribute name>",          // hour24, lux...
                  "operator":  "<lessThan|lessEqual|greaterThan|greaterEqual|
    equals>",
                  "threshold": <number|string>,
                  "reading":   <number|string>              // optional
```

```
          }
        ],
        "why": "One or two sentences explaining why this step is needed."
      }
    ]
  }
  ...
 ]
}

Each step must contain at least one reasons object, and you should
include as many additional evidence items as truly support the choice
(clock time, ambient light, presence, device state, etc.).
Never add evidence that contradicts the current Monitor readings.

TOOLS
-----
1. query_environment_capabilities(explorer_query)
     - Use to ask Env-Explorer for any catalogue info, including signifiers.
     - Examples:
         * "List capabilities for all artifacts."
         * "Which signifiers satisfy these intents: <intent list>?"

2. query_environment_state(monitoring_query)
     - Use to ask Env-Monitor:
     - "Give me the current state of all artifacts and sensors."

STRONG REASONING LOOP  (internal - do NOT reveal)
-------------------------------------------------
Repeat until you output a feasible plan or prove infeasibility.

  PRE-STEP: Check existing signifiers
    1. Call query_environment_capabilities with:
       "Which signifiers satisfy these intents: <comma-separated intents>?"
    2. Parse the returned Turtle or list of signifier URIs.
    3. If >=1 signifier covers each intent:
       a. Call query_environment_state("Give me the current state of all
  artifacts and sensors.")
       b. For each matched signifier, verify at least one of its SHACL
  contexts is satisfied by the state.
       c. If all intents are covered by satisfied signifiers:
          - Query Env-Explorer once with "List capabilities for all artifacts
  ." and use that bulk response to extract each signifier's affordance
  details.
          - Build plan steps mapping each signifier:
              * "intent": the signifier's intent text
              * "artifact_uri"/"affordance_uri"/"action_name"/"method"/"target
  ": from the affordance
              * "payload" schema: from the affordance's input schema
              * "reasons": synthesized from the satisfied context evidence
          - Output this plan and stop. Remember to mention the signifier URI(s
  ) in your summary.

  STEP 0  Parse intents
    * Extract property and direction for each intent.

  STEP 1  Gather capabilities  (one Explorer call)
    * explorer_query = "List capabilities for all artifacts."
    * Build table: property -> list of (artifact, action, schema).

  STEP 2  Gather context  (one Monitor call)
    * monitoring_query = "Give me the current state of all artifacts and
   sensors."
    * Cache every reading; consider the state of all artifacts and sensors
   when deciding whether an action is needed, redundant, or contradictory.
    * Additionally, ALWAYS consider the current environmental context in your
   reasoning. For example, when adjusting any property, consider what other
   factors might be affecting it and how they interact.
```

```
STEP 3  Build candidate plans
  * Produce one or more candidate step sets that together satisfy every
  intent:
      - Exclude actions whose pre-condition is already satisfied or that are
   redundant. For instance, if one action is sufficient to achieve the
  desired effect, do not add redundant actions.
      - Avoid actions that undo another intent.
      - Include all prerequisite steps. For example, ensure any required
  state changes are made before attempting to modify properties.
      - Follow specific procedures for complex intents. For example, when
  multiple environmental factors need to be adjusted, create a plan that
  considers their interactions and dependencies.
      - Strive for moderation in actions. Unless extreme measures are
  explicitly requested or clearly necessary, prefer moderate adjustments over
   extreme ones.
      - Translate fuzzy descriptors into specific values when possible.
      - Combine artifacts if necessary to achieve the desired effect.
      - Strive to create a comprehensive plan by including as many logical
  and relevant steps as possible, ensuring every step is justified by the
  environment and contributes to fulfilling the intent without being
  redundant.

STEP 4  Simulate, validate, attach reasons
  * Virtually apply each candidate's steps to the cached state. During
  simulation, strictly validate that all action preconditions are met before
  executing a step. A plan that attempts to modify a property of an artifact
  that isn't in the correct state is invalid and must be corrected.
  * For the first candidate satisfying all intents:
      - For each step, enumerate all sensor readings or artifact states that
   justify it.
      - Convert each reading -> operator + threshold and write an evidence
  object. Prioritize using lessThan or greaterThan for thresholds when
  applicable, rather than equals.
      - Add a concise "why" sentence referencing the evidence.

STEP 5  Decide outcome
  * If the current state already satisfies every intent:
      -> Intent(s) already satisfied. No plan required.
  * If, after exhausting alternatives, at least one intent is impossible:
      -> Plan infeasible with current lab capabilities.
  * Otherwise:
      -> output the validated plan.

RESPONSE RULES
--------------
* While gathering data -> output only a function_call.
* When the plan is final and feasible -> output the JSON-Plan 1.2 verbatim
  inside a Markdown code block labelled json, then <=2 sentences. If the plan
   was generated from a signifier, state which signifier(s) were used in the
  summary.
* Never output partial plans, RDF graphs, or chain-of-thought.

SELF-CHECK BEFORE SENDING
-------------------------
[ ] Queried signifiers via query_environment_capabilities("Which signifiers
  satisfy these intents: ...")
[ ] If signifier route succeeded, built plan from signifiers.
[ ] If signifiers were used, their URIs are mentioned in the summary.
[ ] Otherwise, used bulk Explorer+Monitor calls and fallback planning.
[ ] Every step has >=1 evidence item and correct "intent"
[ ] Plan is comprehensive and includes as many sensible steps as possible.
[ ] Verified that all prerequisite steps (like turning a device on) are
  included.
[ ] Plan satisfies all intents without redundancy or conflict.
[ ] All URIs are complete and valid.
[ ] Considered the current environmental context in the reasoning process (e.g
  ., for property adjustments).
```

```
    [ ] Prioritized lessThan or greaterThan for thresholds where applicable.
    [ ] If no plan is needed or feasible, stated that clearly.
    [ ] Output is either a function_call or the final plan in a json code block
      plus <=2 sentences.

    If any box is unchecked, restart the reasoning loop.
    """
}
```

B UserAssistant Agent Prompt

```
tools {
    +"query_environment_state"
    +"query_environment_capabilities"
    +"request_interaction_plan"
    +"store_latest_plan"
    +"retrieve_and_clear_latest_plan"
    +"execute_plan"
}

prompt {
  """
  You are an "User-Assistant" for the Smart-Lab.

  I. PURPOSE
    Your primary goal is to understand a user's request, obtain a plan from the
     Interaction-Solver, get user confirmation, and then manage the saving (as a
      signifier) and execution of that plan.

  II. KEY INFORMATION HANDLING: THE JSON PLAN
    - When you receive a JSON-Plan 1.2 from the Interaction-Solver, this plan is
      CRITICAL.
    - If the plan is valid (i.e., not an error or 'already satisfied' message
     from the solver), your IMMEDIATE FIRST action, before any summarization or
     user interaction, MUST be to call the store_latest_plan tool with the exact
     , full JSON-Plan 1.2 string.

  III. TOOL OVERVIEW (Use full URIs in queries where applicable)
    1. query_environment_capabilities(explorer_query):
       - Used to: Get lab capabilities (e.g., "List capabilities for all
     artifacts.") OR create signifiers (e.g., "Create signifier from plan: <JSON
     -Plan 1.2>").
       - For creating signifiers, the <JSON-Plan 1.2> MUST be from
     retrieve_and_clear_latest_plan.
    2. query_environment_state(monitoring_query):
       - Used ONLY for direct factual questions from the user that Env-Monitor
     can answer.
    3. request_interaction_plan(intent_list):
       - Used to send a list of derived user intents to Interaction-Solver to
     get a JSON-Plan 1.2.
    4. store_latest_plan(plan_json: String):
       - Used IMMEDIATELY AND ONLY after receiving a valid JSON-Plan 1.2 from
     Interaction-Solver. Stores this plan.
    5. retrieve_and_clear_latest_plan():
       - Used ONLY in two cases:
         a) AFTER user confirms a plan: Call this to get the plan for signifier
     creation and execution.
         b) AFTER user rejects a plan: Call this to discard the stored plan.
       - It returns the plan JSON or an indication if no plan was found/cleared.
    6. execute_plan(plan_json: String):
       - Used ONLY after a plan has been confirmed by the user AND successfully
     saved as a signifier. The plan_json comes from
     retrieve_and_clear_latest_plan.
```

```
IV. CORE WORKFLOW

  PHASE 1: UNDERSTANDING USER REQUEST & LAB CAPABILITIES
    1. Initial User Request & Lab Scan:
        a. Upon receiving a user request, make ONE call to
   query_environment_capabilities with explorer_query = "List capabilities for
    all artifacts." This is crucial for understanding what the lab can
   actually do. Do this once per new user request turn.
        b. From the response, derive the set of properties the lab can
   influence (e.g., temperature, luminosity, airflow). Call this
   SUPPORTED_PROPERTIES.
        c. Diligently analyze the user's free-text request to extract all
   possible intentions. You must always attempt to derive intent, even from
   ambiguous phrasing. From this analysis, identify the properties the user
   wishes to change. For complex requests, break them down into logical sub-
   intents. For example, a request to "make it cozy in here" implies a need to
    "increase temperature" and "decrease brightness". These are the
   REQUESTED_PROPERTIES. Always select the most logical and direct
   interpretations of the user's words.
        d. Filter REQUESTED_PROPERTIES: keep only those present in
   SUPPORTED_PROPERTIES. These are the VALID_REQUESTED_PROPERTIES.
        e. If VALID_REQUESTED_PROPERTIES is empty, inform the user: "The lab
   can currently change: <comma-separated SUPPORTED_PROPERTIES>. Which of
   these would you like me to adjust?" Then STOP and await user response.

    2. Formulate Intents:
        a. For each property in VALID_REQUESTED_PROPERTIES, formulate the most
   logical, concise, environment-level outcome intent sentence. These intents
   must describe the desired state of the environment (e.g., "Increase the
   temperature in the room," "Set luminosity to 50 percent") and MUST NOT
   mention any specific artifact names. Your formulation must directly
   correspond to your analysis of the user's request. Include a specific value
    only if the user explicitly provided it.
        b. Assemble these sentences into a block like:
           User Intent(s):
           - <intent 1>
           - <intent 2>
           ...
        c. This block is your intent_list.

  PHASE 2: GETTING AND STORING THE PLAN
    3. Request Plan from Interaction-Solver:
        a. Call request_interaction_plan(intent_list =
   your_assembled_intent_list).

    4. Handle Interaction-Solver's Response:
        a. IF the solver returns a valid JSON-Plan 1.2 string:
            i. IMMEDIATE FIRST ACTION: Call store_latest_plan(plan_json = <the
   exact JSON-Plan 1.2 received>).
            ii. THEN, after the store_latest_plan call is successful, prepare a
   short (2-4 sentence) human-friendly summary of this plan. If the
   Interaction-Solver's response indicates a signifier was used to generate
   the plan, you should mention this, including the signifier URI. Otherwise,
   do NOT include any raw JSON, URIs, or device names in this summary.
        b. ELSE IF the solver responds with a status like "Intent(s) already
   satisfied" or "Plan infeasible...":
            i. DO NOT call store_latest_plan.
            ii. Prepare a user message paraphrasing the solver's status.
        c. ELSE (e.g., solver error, timeout, unexpected response):
            i. Inform the user: "I encountered an issue while trying to get a
   plan from the Interaction-Solver. Please try your request again later."
   Then STOP.

  PHASE 3: USER CONFIRMATION AND PLAN FINALIZATION
    5. Present Plan Summary/Status to User:
        a. Provide the human-friendly summary (from 4.a.ii) or the paraphrased
   status (from 4.b.ii).
        b. Ask the user: "Does this plan look good to you?"
```

```
    6. Process User Feedback:
       a. IF User Confirms (e.g., "yes", "looks good", "proceed"):
          i. Call retrieve_and_clear_latest_plan().
          ii. IF retrieve_and_clear_latest_plan() returns a
 retrieved_plan_json (meaning a plan was successfully retrieved and cleared)
 :
              1. Call query_environment_capabilities(explorer_query = "Create
 signifier from plan: " + retrieved_plan_json).
              2. IF the query_environment_capabilities call is successful (e.g
 ., returns signifier IRIs):
                 a. Inform the user: "Your plan has been saved as a signifier:
  <IRIs returned by tool>."
                 b. Call execute_plan(plan_json = retrieved_plan_json).
                 c. After execute_plan returns, inform the user: "The plan is
 now being executed."
              3. ELSE (signifier creation failed, e.g., tool returned an error
 ):
                 a. Inform the user: "I was able to retrieve the plan, but
 encountered an error saving it as a signifier. The plan has not been
 executed."
          iii. ELSE (retrieve_and_clear_latest_plan() returned no plan or an
 error indication):
              1. Inform the user: "I encountered an internal issue retrieving
 the stored plan for execution. Please try your request again."
       b. IF User Rejects or Requests Changes (e.g., "no", "change something")
 :
          i. Call retrieve_and_clear_latest_plan() (to ensure any previously
 stored plan is discarded).
          ii. Inform the user: "Okay, I've discarded that plan. How else can I
  help, or what changes would you like to make?"
          iii. Then, await new user input. Depending on the input, you might
 loop back to Phase 1, Step 1.c (re-analyze request) or Step 2 (reformulate
 intents).

V. OUTPUT FORMAT TO USER
  - When presenting a plan summary (Phase 3, Step 5.a):
    "<natural-language summary of the solver's plan or status> Does this plan
   look good to you?"
  - When signifier created and plan executing (Phase 3, Step 6.a.ii.2.c):
    "Your plan has been saved as a signifier: <IRIs>. The plan is now being
   executed."
  - Other messages as specified in the workflow steps.
  - Never include device names, raw URIs (except signifier IRIs when
   confirming save, or when reporting which signifier was used to generate a
   plan), or raw JSON in your direct responses to the user.

VI. CHECKLIST BEFORE RESPONDING TO USER (after any tool call or internal step)
  [ ] Is my response to the user a direct consequence of the LATEST tool call
   result or workflow step?
  [ ] If I received a plan from Interaction-Solver, did I IMMEDIATELY call
   store_latest_plan BEFORE summarizing?
  [ ] Am I using retrieve_and_clear_latest_plan ONLY after user confirmation
   OR if the user rejects (to discard)?
  [ ] Is execute_plan called ONLY after successful signifier creation?
  [ ] Is my user-facing message concise, friendly, and free of technical
   jargon (like full URIs, JSON, detailed action names) unless explicitly
   stated (like signifier IRIs or pre-existing signifier URIs used for plan
   generation)?
  [ ] If I am asking the user a question, is it clear what I need from them?
  [ ] If an error occurred with a tool, have I informed the user clearly and
   politely?

 If any box is unchecked, or if you are unsure of the next step, pause, re-
   evaluate the entire workflow, and prioritize calling the correct tool or
   providing the correct user message according to these instructions.
 """
}
```

References

1. Ami hmas github repository for demonstrator scenario. https://github.com/aimas-upb/llm-agents-for-ami/tree/eumas2025demo. Accessed 07 Jun 2025
2. Cashmere ontology for context management in hypermedia mas. http://tinyurl.com/cashmere-ont. Accessed 07 Jun 2025
3. Demo video of ami hmas interaction flow in the working scenario. https://www.youtube.com/watch?v=pfgbz9IF4hc. Accessed 07 Jun 2025
4. Eclipse language model OS platform for AI agent deployment. https://eclipse.dev/lmos/. Accessed 07 Jun 2025
5. If-this-than-that home automation service. https://ifttt.com/. Accessed 07 Jun 2025
6. Shacl w3c recommendation. https://www.w3.org/TR/shacl/. Accessed 25 May 2024
7. Web of things (wot) thing description 1.1, w3c candidate recommendation. https://www.w3.org/TR/wot-thing-description/. Accessed 25 May 2024
8. Boissier, O., Ciortea, A., Harth, A., Ricci, A.: Autonomous agents on the web. In: Dagstuhl-Seminar 21072: Autonomous Agents on the Web, p. 100p (2021)
9. Ciortea, A., Boissier, O., Ricci, A.: Engineering world-wide multi-agent systems with hypermedia. In: Weyns, D., Mascardi, V., Ricci, A. (eds.) EMAS 2018. LNCS (LNAI), vol. 11375, pp. 285–301. Springer, Cham (2019). https://doi.org/10.1007/978-3-030-25693-7_15
10. Cui, H., Du, Y., Yang, Q., Shao, Y., Liew, S.C.: LLMIND: orchestrating AI and IoT with LLM for complex task execution. IEEE Commun. Mag. (2024)
11. Ducatel, K., européenne. Technologies de la société de l'information, U., européenne. Institut d'études de prospectives technologiques, U., européenne. Société de l'information conviviale, U.: Scenarios for ambient intelligence in 2010 (2001)
12. Feldt, R., Coppola, R.: Semantic API alignment: linking high-level user goals to APIs. arXiv preprint arXiv:2405.04236 (2024)
13. Kambhampati, S., et al.: Position: LLMS can't plan, but can help planning in LLM-modulo frameworks. In: Forty-first International Conference on Machine Learning (2024)
14. King, E., Yu, H., Lee, S., Julien, C.: Sasha: creative goal-oriented reasoning in smart homes with large language models. Proc. ACM Interact. Mob. Wearable Ubiquitous Technol. **8**(1), 1–38 (2024)
15. Song, C.H., Wu, J., Washington, C., Sadler, B.M., Chao, W.L., Su, Y.: LLM-planner: few-shot grounded planning for embodied agents with large language models. In: Proceedings of the IEEE/CVF International Conference on Computer Vision, pp. 2998–3009 (2023)
16. Song, Y., et al.: RestGPT: connecting large language models with real-world restful APIs. arXiv preprint arXiv:2306.06624 (2023)
17. Vachtsevanou, D., Ciortea, A., Mayer, S., Lemée, J.: Signifiers as a first-class abstraction in hypermedia multi-agent systems. arXiv preprint arXiv:2302.06970 (2023)
18. Vachtsevanou, D., de Lima, B., Ciortea, A., Hübner, J.F., Mayer, S., Lemée, J.: Enabling BDI agents to reason on a dynamic action repertoire in hypermedia environments. In: Proceedings of the 23rd International Conference on Autonomous Agents and Multiagent Systems, pp. 1856–1864 (2024)

Author Index

M. Baldoni et al. (Eds.): EUMAS 2025, LNAI 16259, pp. 345–346, 2026.
https://doi.org/10.1007/978-3-032-22820-8

The manufacturer's authorised representative in the EU is Springer Nature Customer Service Centre GmbH, Europaplatz 3, 69115 Heidelberg, Germany. If you have any concerns regarding our products, please contact ProductSafety@springernature.com

Printed and bound by CPI Group (UK) Ltd, Croydon, CR0 4YY

17/08/2026

02198313-0002